The Irish in America

The Irish in America

By CARL WITTKE

LOUISIANA STATE UNIVERSITY PRESS

Baton Rouge

OTHER BOOKS BY CARL WITTKE

Refugees of Revolution, The German Forty-eighters in America (Philadelphia, 1952)
The Utopian Communist, A Biography of Wilhelm Weitling, Nineteenth-Century Reformer
  (Baton Rouge, 1950)
Against the Current: The Life of Karl Heinzen (Chicago, 1945)
We Who Built America: The Saga of the Immigrant (New York, 1939)
German-Americans and the World War (Columbus, 1936)
George Washington und Seine Zeit (Bremen, 1933)
Tambo and Bones, A History of the American Minstrel Stage (Durham, 1930)
A History of Canada (New York, 1928; revised 1933, 1941)

Preface

I<small>N THE</small> mountains of Kentucky and Tennessee, they still sing an old immigrant song about "O'Reilly's on the rolling sea bound for Amerikee"—a song which dates back to the earliest days of Irish immigration to this continent. Between 1820 and 1920, over four and a half million O'Reillys and their kinfolk left the Emerald Isle for the United States. Along with millions from other lands, they and their descendants played their part, for good or ill, in the building of America. By 1900, the number of Americans of Irish parentage totaled about 10 per cent of the foreign-born population of the United States.

In the light of these figures, and in view of the importance of the Irish element in the history of the United States, it is a striking fact that the story of Irish immigration remains largely to be written. With such notable exceptions as William Forbes Adams' *Ireland and Irish Emigration to the New World from 1815 to the Famine* (1932), and Oscar Handlin's *Boston's Immigrants, 1790–1865, A Study in Acculturation* (1941), which cover only parts of the subject, much that has been written about the Irish in America falls far short of proper standards of historical objectivity, and much of it is mere antiquarianism. A number of Irish-American historians, incensed by Scotch-Irish writers who claim all Irishmen who attained any degree of success for their own, or resentful of inadequate or prejudiced comments of earlier Anglo-Saxon historians, have reciprocated with filiopietistic books and articles which also claim too much and go to the opposite extremes. Like all foreign-born groups, the Irish have their champions in the arena of historiography. Furthermore, because of the predominant role of the Irish in the Catholic Church in the United States and the influence of the Church upon its immigrant constituencies, much of the history of Irish immigration is overcharged with the high voltage of religious controversy and gives undue attention to what is but one chapter, however important, in the story of the Irish in America.

This volume is an attempt to deal with the major aspects of Irish immigration to the United States and with the repercussions from America upon Ireland in the long struggle for Irish independence from England. This book cannot be regarded as a definitive study, but it will help fill a gap in the literature of the history of immigration, and it is an honest attempt to deal objectively, yet sympathetically, with a group whose history is both a colorful and controversial chapter in the total story of American immigration.

Because the Irish population in the colonial period was small, and the number of Irish Catholics even smaller, the narrative begins with the national period and deals with the nineteenth and twentieth centuries, through the postwar years of World War I, which mark the final phase of the struggle of the "sea-divided Gael" for Irish nationhood. This study is not concerned, save only incidentally, with the Scotch-Irish, nor with the many controversies in historiography and theology between Irish and Scotch-Irish.

The literature on the Scotch-Irish element in the United States is extensive, and the published proceedings of Scotch-Irish congresses and societies in the United States are as ardently filiopietistic and uncritically laudatory as the Irish-American publications which they criticize. As the late Professor Frederick L. Paxson observed in an article in the *American Historical Review,* "The Scotch-Irishman has shown as much ability to survive in the world of historiography as he showed in the eighteenth century while pushing the farmer's frontier up the interior valleys, through the gaps to the West, and down the river courses toward the Mississippi."

As a matter of fact, the term "Irishman" was used for a long time to describe Ulster Protestants as well as Catholic Irish, and the label "Scotch-Irish" was not known in North Ireland. By 1815, the so-called Scotch-Irish already were a mixed race; many had intermarried with native Irish women, and their children grew up in Ulster as "Irish." Religion, though important, was not of itself enough to make a nationality. In the colonial period of American history, the distinction between Irish and Scotch-Irish could be made, if at all, only on religious grounds. Moreover, Catholics sometimes became Protestants in the colonies for economic or social reasons, because of intermarriage, or because there were no priests to keep their faith alive. As far as national grievances were concerned, the Irish of North Ireland also resented the Church of England, had their economic life strangled by the same British commercial system which crippled the rest of Ireland, and complained about the same injustices in the system of landholding.

The sharp distinction between Irish and Scotch-Irish developed in the

United States in the last half of the nineteenth century for reasons that were primarily American. After the great influx of Irish immigrants and the problems created by this sudden boiling over of the melting pot, the Scotch-Irish insisted upon differentiating between the descendants of earlier immigrants from Ireland and more recent arrivals. Irish-American writers, on the other hand, retorted that the whole idea was "a new fangled notion, first promulgated in America," and "born of sheer ignorance and pharisaical, Calvinistic pride."

References to a distinction between Protestant and Catholic Irishmen in the colonial period are rare. To be sure, the Scotch-Irish of Londonderry, New Hampshire, "were surprised" in 1720 to hear themselves "termed Irish people, when we so frequently ventured our all for the British Crown and Liberties against the Irish Papists." But such protests were exceptional. Immigrants from Ireland in colonial times were simply labeled "Irish." Massachusetts Puritans were opposed to all "Irish immigrants," and Cotton Mather, in a sermon in 1700, denounced proposals to bring "Irish" to the colony as "formidable attempts of Satan and his Sons to Unsettle us." There are many references to "Irish" redemptioners; a tract in Maryland in 1680 was known as "New Ireland"; and Moravian missionaries in 1749 recorded in their diaries that they had "passed confidently and safely through the Irish settlement," when they obviously referred to the Scotch-Irish frontier area of Augusta County, Virginia. Theophile Cazenove, in a journal which described his trip through New Jersey and Pennsylvania in 1794, spoke of an area around Bethlehem as "the Irish settlement, where the Irish came in 1740." The Charitable Irish Society of Boston, organized in 1737, consisted originally of Protestants who described themselves not as Scotch-Irish, but simply as "of the Irish Nation," and in its earlier days, the organization had both Protestant and Catholic presidents. The same was true in Philadelphia, where the first president of the Friendly Sons of St. Patrick was General Stephen Moylan, whose brother was a Catholic bishop, and the next was a Protestant of North Ireland.

There was little difference in social habits among the Irish of North and South Ireland in the colonial period. "Wakes," for example, were as common among the Irish from North Ireland as among the immigrants from other parts of the island. The colonial Irish had a reputation for contentiousness, turbulence, and pugnacity; whiskey was an essential of their social life—at baptisms, weddings, and funerals—and they were frequently charged with intemperance. Secretary Logan of Pennsylvania observed in 1729 that five Scotch-Irish families caused more trouble than fifty of any other nationality. Arthur Lee, in 1784, in a description of early Pittsburgh, referred to "Scots and Irish" living in "paltry log houses," "as dirty as in the north of Ireland, or even Scotland."

The Protestant Irish championed the stern, aggressive, unbending creed of dogmatic Presbyterianism and defended their views as militantly as any Irish Catholic bishop who considered his own Church the sole instrument of truth and salvation. The Irish of colonial days, the majority of whom were Protestant, revealed a native capacity for politics comparable to that of later arrivals from Ireland, and they were cordially hated by more conservative elements in the colonies for a leveling, frontier type of democracy which easily degenerated into lawlessness. Many of the derogatory comments about the Irish during the latter half of the nineteenth century were hurled at the "Irish," as a nationality group, in the eighteenth century.

The colonial "Irish" played an important role in the American Revolution, whether they were Protestants or Catholics. They were the cutting edge of the frontier, and the zeal for education on the part of Irish Presbyterian and Catholic schoolmasters added to the intellectual progress of early America. Without accepting the philosophy of racial superiority or the extravagant claims of John Fiske, the elder Henry Cabot Lodge, Theodore Roosevelt, and others who have written about the "Scotch-Irish" of colonial times, the conclusion is inescapable that they made a notable and lasting contribution to the history of this nation; but with that element in the immigration from Ireland, this study is not concerned.

In gathering material for this volume, I received aid and suggestions from many sources. First of all, I must mention a generous grant from the American Philosophical Society which made it possible to have microfilmed a number of Irish-American newspapers that were in the library of the American Irish Historical Society and the State Historical Society of Wisconsin. The list includes *The Shamrock* (1810–16); *The Citizen* (1854–55); *The Irish News* (1856–60); the *Illustrated Celtic Monthly* (1879–80); *The Irish World and American Industrial Vindicator* (1877–79, 1892, 1895–96, 1898, 1900, 1904); and *The Gaelic-American* (1914–22). Dr. Russell Anderson, former director of the Western Reserve Historical Society, Dr. Lyon N. Richardson, director of the Western Reserve University Libraries, and Dr. James H. Rodabaugh, of the Ohio Historical Society, extended unusual privileges for the use of important sources. Miss Kathleen Cohalan of the American Irish Historical Society in New York made Irish-American newspaper materials available for microfilming. I must also acknowledge my indebtedness to the Cleveland Public Library, the State Historical Society of Wisconsin, and the interlibrary loan department of the Western Reserve University Library. The Reverend Henry J. Browne, archivist of the Catholic University of America, called my attention to graduate theses at that institution which otherwise would have been overlooked. I have also benefited greatly from the work of the late Richard J. Purcell, an able scholar in the field of Irish immigration, and from the theses of several of his graduate students.

CARL WITTKE

Table of Contents

The Irish in America

CHAPTER I

"The Loved Island of Sorrow"

IRISH orators were wont to refer to their native island as the Niobe of nations—the unhappy mother condemned to see herself bereft by a brutal fate of all she loved best. In proportion to its total population, no other country has lost so many of its people by emigration, and through the dreary centuries, the harp of Erin has given off many a melancholy strain. A large number of Ireland's sons and daughters left their green isle because they were enterprising and adventurous enough to seek larger opportunities elsewhere, but many had no choice, except the choice between starvation and emigration. They fled from famine and pestilence and arrived penniless and destitute in their new destination. "The perennial desolation of a lovely and fertile island" drove Irishmen to Canada, Australia, Latin America, and other lands, and more especially across the sea to the great republic where

> Erin's harp shall wake again
> In rapture from its slumbers.

Ireland once had a unique culture. In the sixth century, learning flourished and scholars and missionaries crossed over to the Continent, carrying the torch of learning and the Christian religion. Later, as W. F. Adams has written, Ireland became "a mere eddy" on the outer shores of Europe, and before long, the Irish people found themselves "forever separated from, yet circumscribed by" their Anglo-Saxon neighbors on two continents. For centuries, Ireland was forced to endure alien rule. As a result, every Irish grievance, and every movement for progress and reform, was overshadowed by a bitter struggle to recapture Ireland's independence and to regain for her people the control of their own destinies. The language of Ireland was proscribed and largely forgotten; the cultivation of Irish history was frowned upon; and the economic development of the island was blighted by a commercial policy designed to advance the fortunes of her conquerors. Deprived of many normal activities in the fields of politics and economics, the unquenchable spirit of Irish nationhood sought expression in other ways.

3

It would be difficult to find a country where the causes for large-scale emigration were as compelling as in the Ireland of the eighteenth and nineteenth centuries. Ireland was conquered territory. Her people hated the foreign church which their conquerors forced upon them, and they suffered under a system of landholding and trade restrictions which ruined their economy and robbed them of their incentives. Economists are agreed that Ireland experienced a progressive deterioration of her farming population from 1815 until well past the middle of the nineteenth century.

A series of fruitless rebellions, ruthlessly suppressed; a succession of famines in a land where the masses lived perilously near the margin of subsistence even in good times; restrictive legislation which handcuffed economic progress; the abuses of absentee landlordism; unemployment, low wages, high rents, periodic disease, intermittent civil war, and perennial agrarian, political, and religious quarrels—all these constitute such an indictment of Irish affairs that little more need be said to explain the tide of emigration to that

> Fair smiling land of Liberty and Peace,
> Where Plenty gaily treads the flow'ry fields.[1]

It was not surprising that the British government looked with sympathetic eyes upon an emigration that might help relieve the pressures of what seemed an insoluble situation.

John Mitchel, one of the Irish rebels of 1848, insisted that for Irishmen, land was life. Certainly agriculture, and a very primitive kind at that, was the dominant occupation of the great majority of the Irish people. In 1790, the population of Ireland was approximately four and a half million. Twenty-five years later, it stood at about six million. In 1780, colonial and foreign markets had been thrown open to Ireland, and the Act of Union of 1800 opened Great Britain to Irish products. But neither belated concessions such as these, nor the temporary, artificial boom in agriculture resulting from the Napoleonic Wars, could do much to alleviate a situation that was basically unsound.

The soil of Ireland was owned by a landed aristocracy, some of whom lived in the island, but many of whom were absentees in Great Britain who left the administration of their estates to overseers and managers. The land was leased and rented to farmers and agricultural laborers. The latter were a pitiful group who tried to supplement their meager earnings by cultivating a few potatoes on a small plot for which they generally paid the rent in labor. Under the circumstances, it is not difficult to

---

[1] "Lines addressed to America," *The Shamrock* (New York), July 20, 1811.

understand why the landlord who drained Ireland dry for gains which he did not reinvest in the island but spent abroad, while his agents ground down his tenants, and finally evicted them in the most heartless fashion, became the devil in the play.

The average wage of the agricultural laborer in the early part of the nineteenth century was nine pence a day, with about two hundred working days in the year. Sometimes the Irish laborer augmented his income by migrating to England for the harvest season; often he resorted to begging. By 1815, Ireland had from two to three million cotters, living dangerously near the margin of subsistence. They lived in cabins and hovels; they slept on straw or on the ground; and they subsisted on potatoes, milk, and herring. Their potato diet they washed down with whiskey, if they could afford it, or with tea, which was cheaper. But many sowed their potato crops too late in the spring and reaped too late in the fall, and the crop of the lazy and indifferent often was scarcely worth harvesting, or was still ungathered in January. Since there was no poor law at the time for Ireland's landless poor, they had the choice of stealing, begging, or going hungry.

Though much of Irish soil was better than that of England, lack of capital and backward methods of farming reduced its yield. As population expanded (family limitation was neither sanctioned nor practiced in Ireland), competition for land became fiercer and individual leaseholds smaller. One farm in county Clare which had one tenant in 1793 had ninety-six in 1847. The size of these plots shrank as the children married and needed a holding of their own. The reconversion of land from tillage to pasture after the collapse of the agricultural boom of the Napoleonic period led to many evictions, and rents remained high because of the pressure for land. Since all improvements by the tenant reverted in the end to the owner, there was little incentive to fertilize, build fences, or drain the fields. Because the lessee felt insecure, he became lazy and an improvident idler. As John Stuart Mill put it, "The inducements of free human beings are taken away and those of the slave not substituted."

Despite their unenviable place in Irish legend, song, and story, not all landlords were absentees or cruel. There is no doubt about their reputation as a class among the Irish masses; yet they had their problems too. But many of the stories about them were false or overdramatized. Some were themselves poor; their rents were almost always long in arrears; and some were never paid. Many Irish simply squatted on the land and dared anyone to put them off. If evictions were frequent, in a sense they were "the price of agricultural efficiency." Landlords were blamed for problems and difficulties which really stemmed from the prevailing British policy of mercantilism, which all nations followed at the time and which limited Ireland to agricultural production.

Under the circumstances, it is not surprising that Irish peasants were described as ignorant, poor, unorganized, intemperate, improvident, and often brutal. Many never tasted meat. Their huts had no windows and frequently no chimney. The pig shared the wet, cold room with the family, and wet peat proved to be poor fuel. Dirt and disease were the inevitable concomitants of such a standard of living, and the rate of illiteracy was high. In 1831, nearly half the Ulster Protestants could not write their names. For the cotters, there were practically no educational opportunities, and the instruction given to those slightly more fortunate by priests in Roman Catholic "hedge schools" was very elementary and practically limited to religion and Irish folklore. The peasants had no vote and no stake in the government. When they were evicted, they sought revenge by force and through secret societies and gangs, which the government found practically impossible to suppress. Local courts were powerless before what amounted to organized and publicly condoned crime. Interlopers were warned to leave or have their place set on fire. The Irish were known for their love of fighting, in the old country as well as in the new, and brawling at fairs and on various social occasions was all too common. Drunkenness was a serious vice among already destitute laborers and peasants, and illegally distilled poteen was cheap and easy to get.

People of the lowest economic level usually were too poor to emigrate and did not leave until they were faced with the inexorable choice between flight and death. The Irish emigration before 1830 came largely from the farming class that stood between the gentry and the lowest type of peasant laborer. Although they usually had a lease of around thirty acres, for twenty-one years or longer, even this group, though somewhat higher in the social scale, suffered from the disastrous system of subletting and had no real inducement to improve their holdings. In some counties, the average size of farms was ten acres or less, and many were under five. A man with thirty acres was a "large farmer," though he too lived in a hovel, subsisted from his potato crop, and frequently had to do outside work to meet his rent. Well after 1865, the Irish farmer still lived in one-story cabins with mud floors and walls and grateless hearths.[2]

[2] For this discussion, I have borrowed heavily from John E. Pomfret, *The Struggle for Land in Ireland, 1800–1923;* W. F. Adams, *Ireland and Irish Emigration to the New World from 1815 to the Famine;* and Frances Morehouse, "The Irish Migration of the 'Forties,'" *American Historical Review,* XXXIII (1927–28), No. 3, pp. 579–92.

Conditions in the larger cities of Ireland such as Dublin and Cork also help explain the Irish emigration. Dublin, with a population of about 175,000 in 1830, had its slums. It was dirty, unlighted, unpaved, and without adequate police protection, sewage system, or water supply. Special tolls hampered its trade, and its government was in the hands of a corporation whose special privileges went back to the days of the Stuarts. The most enterprising shopkeepers, artisans, and professional men cast longing looks across the Atlantic, whence came glowing accounts of opportunities for men of ability and experience.

The industrial revolution had little impact upon Ireland, except in Ulster, where the linen industry was important. Many farmers also were master weavers, and their women did the spinning. But Ireland lacked capital, good coal and iron, and water power, and her domestic industry could not compete with English factories. With the introduction of machine production, the Ulster linen industry had to meet the rivalry of other countries in the manufacture of flax and yarn, and, after 1815, competition became difficult. Though the cotton industry in Belfast was still relatively prosperous, general conditions were such that artisans with enterprise and enough money for the trip were ready to try their luck in the United States. Irish affairs reached a crisis during the "Great Famine" of the late 1840's, but the experiences of those critical years merely reemphasize the basic defects in the whole Irish economic pattern. |

| It is hard to believe that so appalling and frightful a disaster as the potato famine of the late 1840's could be overdramatized. Yet it must be pointed out that there had been at least five potato famines of considerable magnitude from 1817 to 1848. In the accounts of these catastrophes, one finds the same lurid tales of death and disease, further subdivision of the land, and heartless evictions. The tide of Irish emigration already was running strong by 1840, and the immediate effect of the potato crisis of the closing years of that decade may have been exaggerated. Nevertheless, the destruction of human life was appalling, and about a fourth of Ireland's population of 8,000,000 died of fever and famine. In 1847, the Irish emigration to the United States exceeded 105,000, as compared with 44,821 in 1845; and it reached nearly 113,000 in 1848.

There was a potato blight in North America in 1844, and one in Europe in 1845. In Ireland, it lasted five years and was a turning point in Irish history. Disraeli spoke of "a single root changing the history of the world." [3] We read of walking skeletons, dying children, and women too weak to stand. Neither the English nor the Irish had a specific solution

[3] Quoted in Arnold Whitridge, *Men in Crisis*, 294.

for the disaster, and many simply surrendered fatalistically to "a visitation of Providence," while the clergy preached Christian fortitude and resignation and suffered and died with their people.

Ever after, the Irish believed that their lives had been sacrificed in the famine for the British merchant class, and that the British government, beholden to this class for their political support, was afraid to take effective steps to deal with the disaster and, therefore, callously allowed Irishmen to die. Actually, the British government made some genuine efforts to deal with the emergency. It is also true, though, that other Irish food crops, wheat and oats in particular, grown largely to pay the rent on farm plots, continued to be exported in the famine years to England, where Irish food was needed to feed British troops and England's industrial population. The British government made appropriations for public works, and Irishmen were employed on unproductive and noncompetitive projects. Both Sir Robert Peel and Lord John Russell were fearful, however, that too much government aid might undermine free enterprise, and thought it wise to stimulate private charity as much as possible. An appropriation of £100,000 was made for the purchase of Indian corn and rice, which "the benevolent" were expected to buy at a low price and make available to the hungry, though there were insufficient mills to grind the grain when it arrived. Indian corn meal from the United States was boiled and dished out as corn-meal mush in hastily improvised soup kitchens, and at Cork great kettles were kept boiling with mush to feed the starving poor. The British government and private individuals spent millions of pounds for relief, and there were kind as well as hard-hearted landlords. The latter took advantage of the crisis to force further evictions, but others chartered ships to help their tenants leave, paid their passage and provided food for the journey, and were themselves impoverished by a genuine desire to help their people.

But it was the Americans who received the credit for relief during the "Great Starvation." Help came from fellow countrymen already settled in the United States, and the Irish did not forget the American relief ships which brought cargoes of corn and clothing. They remembered the large sums raised in the leading cities of the United States by many societies and organizations for the victims of the Irish famine. In the nation's capital, the vice-president and members of Congress attended a public meeting for relief for Ireland; two American men-of-war set sail with supplies, and railroad and canal companies carried packages marked "Ireland" without charge. Horace Greeley made a personal contribution and appealed for funds in his *Tribune;* temporary buildings were erected on Ward's Island in New York to hospitalize the victims of starvation when they arrived afflicted with "ship fever"; and Mayor Josiah Quincy collected $50,000 in Boston for the famine-stricken. The New York Relief Committee raised $102,000 in May, 1847; Philadelphia, $55,000; New Orleans, $50,000. In February, 1847, eleven ships sailed from New York in one day laden with food for Ireland. Four left the next day from Philadelphia, and six from Baltimore in April. By July, 1847, the Relief Committee of Dublin had received money and food from the United States valued at over a half million dollars.[4] The late 1840's set a pattern for later occasions when Ireland needed help to weather her chronic economic crises, and the memories of the disaster years were kept alive both in Ireland and among the Irish in America. The generous response from the United States to Ireland's cry for help played no small part in convincing Irishmen that the American Republic had both a great heart and a full larder.

In addition to the economic factors which were basic to the Irish exodus to the United States, it must be remembered that ever since the union of Ireland and Great Britain in 1800, which deprived the former of her own parliament, another objective of Irish policy had been to regain national independence—a cause for which Irishmen fought with both constitutional and violent revolutionary methods. Daniel O'Connell wanted repeal of the Union, but by constitutional and political means. He dreaded a revolution to separate Ireland from the British Isles; he opposed the violence of secret societies; and he denounced both Orangemen and Ribbonmen. In the closing years of his career, he was denounced by "Young Irelanders," who once worshipped him, because he refused to substitute force and rebellion for parliamentary methods.

The political situation in Ireland deteriorated rapidly in the early nineteenth century, and, to quote W. F. Adams, "the twenty-nine years from the Union to Catholic Emancipation are almost unrelieved by any wise or generous act toward Ireland." The average Englishman knew little about the Irish, but he remembered that in 1798 and 1803, when the Celts rose in rebellion during the Napoleonic Wars, Ireland had stuck "the Irish knife in the back of England while she was fighting for her life."[5] Peel regarded the Irish as barbarians, hated their church and "papal superstition," and fought for a Protestant ascendancy in Ireland. London newspapers welcomed the emigration of Irishmen, whom they described as "scum" and "demons of assassination," "occupied in shooting Protestants from behind a hedge."

Irish politics were never tranquil, and mobs and riots were fairly

[4] J. B. McMaster, *History of the People of the United States*, VII, 223–25.
[5] Adams, *Ireland and Irish Emigration*, 242.

common on election days. Every local issue was colored by the conditions of alien rule and the burning desire of Irish leaders to regain home rule or independence for their country. Incessant political agitation and sporadic rebellions played a part in Irish emigration. Some of the most distinguished Irish-Americans of the last century were refugees from abortive rebellions and risings who came to the United States as exiles. Their number was relatively small, but, like the "Forty-eighters" of the German immigration, they provided a certain intellectual and political leadership for their Irish countrymen in America, and labored in this country for a revival of Irish nationalism. The innate conservatism of the majority of Irish immigrants and the opposition of their Church to the more radical political refugees made their role a difficult one.

Religion was a minor cause of Irish emigration, but in America the Irishman's Catholicism assumed major importance in his relations with his fellow Americans. His hostility to the Church of England, the church of the alien conqueror, was deep-seated, and even dissenting ministers in Ireland were often as ardently nationalistic and anti-British as the Roman Catholic priests who represented over four-fifths of the population.

In 1829, Peel and Wellington chose Catholic emancipation rather than rebellion and war with the Irish. The Catholic Emancipation Act admitted Roman Catholics to Parliament and opened many high offices to them. At the same time, however, the voting qualifications for Irish freeholders, who had been the backbone of the fight for Catholic rights, were raised, and the franchise was taken away from large elements in the population. The election of members to Parliament was made dependent on the middle class. These efforts to conciliate the Church, and at the same time to detach the upper classes from the Irish masses, illustrate the close relationship between religious and political affairs in Ireland. After 1829, the agitation in Ireland became a national rather than a purely Catholic issue; yet the two were inextricably intertwined. Tithes for the Church of England continued to be collected after 1829, and the poor still paid the bulk of them, to support a church which they abhorred and which, in many places, had almost no parishioners. When it became difficult to enforce the tithe, the British government converted it into additional rent to be paid by the landlord and passed on to the tenant in the form of higher rates. The average Irishman hated Protestantism as one of the causes of his country's misery.

One other consideration must be mentioned in this brief summary of conditions which account for Irish emigration, and that is the encouragement which prospective emigrants received from those already in the United States. "America letters" have been important in the history of every emigration. Reports from the United States seemed to agree that "if a man likes work, he need not want for victuals," and that "there is a great many ill conveniences here, but no empty bellies." A little brochure entitled "Hints to Irishmen Who Intend with their Families to Make a Permanent Residence in America" was published in 1816 by leading Irish refugees of the uprising of 1798. It described the scale of wages in America, the good treatment accorded foreigners, the demand for laborers in the cities and on the Erie Canal, and stressed the need for farmers and artisans.[6] The pamphlet was reissued in Dublin, Belfast, and other Irish cities. *The American Daily Advertiser* of July 26, 1817, listed cheap land, high wages, plenty of food, and freedom from military service, rather than its unique form of government, as the chief attractions of the United States.[7] John Doyle wrote home from New York to his wife in Ireland to point out that America was free from "visits from tax gatherers, constables or soldiers," and that "every one [is] at liberty to act and speak as he likes . . . to slander and damn government, abuse public men in their office to their faces, wear your hat in court and smoke a cigar while speaking to a judge." [8]

Irishmen also wrote home to say that board was as good every day in the United States as it was on Christmas day in Ireland. There were exaggerated reports of a country where there were no taxes on the necessaries of life and no rents for land. Others stressed the opportunities for free public education, the advantages of a free press, and the absence of a "sedition" law. One writer referred to the land where "ideas fly into every garret and cellar and cottage, like the light of the gorgeous sun, and spread their generating impulses through the minds of all." [9] Still another emphasized the absence of artificial distinctions and penal colonies in America, and the rights which women enjoyed. Newspapers and letters reported the wages for various kinds of service. An old Irish lady of Philadelphia was moved to recommend the United States for its fine almshouses,[10] and a popular emigrant song included the lines,

> They say there's bread and work for all,
> And the sun shines always there.[11]

Such communications from America, reinforced by remittances which

---

[6] Alexander Flick (ed.), *History of the State of New York,* VIII, 23.

[7] Cited in McMaster, *History of the People of the United States,* IV, 391.

[8] "Letter of John Doyle," *Journal of the American Irish Historical Society,* XII (1912-13), 197-204.

[9] Thomas Mooney, *Nine Years in America,* 7-11.

[10] Carl Russell Fish, *The Rise of the Common Man,* 260.

[11] Franklin E. Fitzpatrick, "Irish Immigration into New York from 1865 to 1880" (Master's thesis, Catholic University of America, 1948), 19.

gave more tangible proof of its prosperity, circulated widely in Ireland. They were supplemented by the advertisements of ship companies in search of human cargo. Placards appeared in the remotest villages and frequently were posted near the chapel gates. Railroad and canal companies advertised for workmen at intriguingly high rates of pay. For many Irishmen, the United States began to be the Promised Land.

Chapter II

Farewell to Erin

IT IS a serious moment in any man's life when he says farewell to his native land forever and watches its coastline sink beneath the horizon for the last time as he sets out on a perilous voyage to a new home which he has never seen. Immigrants, to be successful, need stout hearts as well as healthy frames.

The departure usually was celebrated by a typical Irish leave-taking, for the Irish are a warmhearted and sociable people. After a night of jollification, which ended only with the sunrise, a procession of relatives and neighbors escorted the departing down the road, sometimes to the accompaniment of the village bells. The priest bestowed a special blessing before his parishioners left their homes. In many cases, the furniture already had been sold to raise money for the journey. In others, relatives in Canada or the United States helped pay for the passage and the food needed for the ocean voyage. On occasion, a kindly landlord contributed to his tenant's emigration fund; perhaps more often the prospective immigrant went to the pawnbrokers for money. The emigrant's baggage was hauled in an Irish cart to the port town and here the owner waited for his sailing, and perhaps recalled a favorite emigrant song about the "heart that now bleeds for thy sorrows, and will waste on a far distant shore." [1]

Accounts of the emigrant trade, the hazards of the ocean voyage, and life in the crowded ports at both ends of the journey are available by the score. They tell more or less the same sad story of fraud, exploitation, hardships, privations, disease, suffering, and death. Undoubtedly some were written by those who had safely passed the ordeal and wanted to adorn a tale. But after due allowance for overdramatization, for which the Irish had special gifts, the fact remains that immigration, during most of the last century, was rugged business.

[1] From "The Emigrant's Farewell," *The Pilot* (Boston), August 16, 1862; quoted in Oscar Handlin, *Boston's Immigrants, 1790–1865—A Study in Acculturation*, 129–30. See also Marcus L. Hansen, *The Immigrant in American History*, 31; and the same author's *The Atlantic Migration, 1607–1860*.

The routes across the Atlantic and the ports of embarkation and arrival were largely determined by the necessity of making commerce a two-way trade, even if the profits in one direction came from human cargo. The competition of shipping lines and shipping houses was unusually keen by the 1850's. As Marcus L. Hansen observed, it was the Canadian timber trade that "made New England overwhelmingly Irish." [2] Rhode Island and Connecticut merchants trading with the southern ports of Ireland probably were the first to bring Irishmen as ballast on their westward sailings. Ireland had to import timber to build houses, and she needed barrel wood for the export of her eggs, pork, and butter to England. By 1830, there was an active cooperage industry in every port which received lumber from America. Much lumber also came from the Maritime Provinces of British North America, and Irishmen found it possible to get cheaper rates to Canada than to New York; the run was shorter, and fewer potatoes and salt herring were needed during the voyage.

From New Brunswick and elsewhere in the Maritimes, thousands of Irish set out on foot or in coastwise vessels for the south. Many walked along the coast to Maine and thence into other parts of New England, working for farmers and at odd jobs along the way, or living on the kindness of New Englanders who fed them and gave them a place to sleep. Their route still is marked by a string of little Catholic churches in Maine and elsewhere. Others came by way of coastwise vessels from Nova Scotia to Boston or Providence. Thus, from 1817 to 1842, New England's Irish immigration was closely allied to the early timber trade. As late as 1848, an Irishman could go to Newfoundland for five dollars if he were willing to sleep on the deck of a small fishing boat and subsist on salt cod. In much the same fashion, Irish immigration to the Middle Atlantic States also was connected with the export of lumber and other American products from New York, Philadelphia, and Baltimore. From these seacoast towns, flax seed, pot and pearl ashes, tobacco, flour, cotton, and naval stores were carried to leading Irish ports, and Irishmen came to America as ballast on the return voyage. When the center of cotton production shifted from the older areas of the South to the new Gulf States, the immigrant trade shifted with it from Charleston to New Orleans, and before the end of the 1830's, the latter city had a sizable Irish element in its cosmopolitan population.

The immigrant traffic was a highly competitive business. Both England and the United States tried to mitigate its hardships by various passenger acts, but for a long time they proved ineffective against the evils of over-

[2] Hansen, *The Immigrant in American History*, 160; and the same author's "The Second Colonization of New England," *The New England Quarterly*, II (1929), 539–60.

crowding. The immigrant frequently was the victim of fraud and false promises from the time he reached his port of departure to the time when he disembarked in the United States. There was collusion between immigrant-boardinghouse keepers and passenger brokers in Liverpool, from where so many Irish set sail, as there was in New York; and in both cities, immigrants were overcharged for food, lodging, and baggage. The same abuses existed at Irish ports after direct connections between Ireland and America had been provided.

At every port in the United Kingdom, ships competed for passengers when the immigrant tide was at full flood, but as early as the 1820's, Americans had 75 per cent of the business. Frequently, American shipping interests were associated with Irish merchants and importers who chartered an entire vessel, advertised for passengers, and sold them passage on "beautiful ships" said to "sail remarkably fast" and abundantly provided with food, water and fire, and a ship's doctor. Many Irish preferred to bring their own food supply because it was cheaper. Newspapers, special offices, and handbills advertised for human cargo, and frequently such announcements were grossly misleading, for many ships were old, undermanned, and, in some cases, hardly seaworthy.

Before 1845, the voyage across the Atlantic might take anywhere from four to ten weeks, or longer, depending on the prevailing winds. In 1849, the average time from Liverpool to New York was thirty-five days. All shipping companies advertised quick trips. As late as 1856, only 5 per cent of the immigrants came in steam vessels. Emigrant ships in the 1840's were equipped with wooden bunks and straw-stuffed sacks for mattresses. The walls were usually whitewashed. As a rule, single women were quartered at one end of the steerage, the men at the other, and married couples in between. Passengers not only slept in their berths, but frequently ate there. Most Irishmen in the early, heavy immigration brought their own food. In 1850, they were advised to provide themselves, if they could afford it, with oatmeal, rice, flour, bacon, ham, fish, butter, milk, and eggs. The latter were to be rubbed with suet and bedded "on their ends in salt and oatmeal" to keep them edible during the voyage. Immigrants also were urged to bring a little salts, senna, or castor oil, and to take "one or two doses . . . during the voyage, and especially one on arrival in America," to ward off fever caused by the change in climate.[3] Actually, Irish steerage passengers lived largely on oatmeal porridge, which they sweetened with molasses whenever they could afford it, and their main meal consisted of herring and potatoes. The supply of fresh water generally did not last out the voyage, and

[3] Mooney, *Nine Years in America,* 45–46.

there was no water for washing. The crowded quarters were fumigated with vinegar. Irish immigrant ships from Liverpool were in specially bad repute for filth and a high death rate.[4]

In the overcrowded steerage, there was little space for ventilation or movement among the passengers. The decks were often dirty and unscrubbed. Many passengers, rather than cook their own food, ate it raw. Ham and butter spoiled quickly. On one-deck ships, passengers slept on top of cargo; otherwise they were crowded between decks, with a five-foot clearance stipulated by law. British passenger acts and customs officials tried to check overcrowding, and a United States statute of 1848 required fourteen square feet of deck space for each traveler, except for infants less than a year old, and prescribed the amount of water and food to be issued each passenger per week. But the enforcement of such meager regulations left much to be desired, and wind and weather were more decisive factors in the health of the passengers than government regulations. By 1850, the English inspected all departing ships and sought to eliminate fraud by a system of licensing "passenger brokers." Complaints about rough treatment of immigrants by officers and crews were frequent, and women and girls were likely to find themselves in special jeopardy.

In 1816, it cost £7 to go from Belfast to Baltimore; in 1850, the rate from Liverpool to Boston, New York, or Philadelphia was about £4, with lower fares for children. The immigrant tide responded quickly to fluctuations in economic conditions here and abroad. Emigration before the Great Famine years consisted largely of small farmers, weavers, shopkeepers, and artisans, who were able to pay the passage for themselves and their families. Moreover, during the first two decades of the nineteenth century, most of the Irish came from Belfast, Dublin, and districts where economic conditions were somewhat better than in Ireland as a whole.

During the famine years, conditions on shipboard approached the unbearable, and there were many references to Irish "fever" and "coffin ships." Some voyages lasted as long as 160 days. Long before the ships reached America, the food and water supply had run out. There was much dysentery and "ship fever"—a kind of typhus. Many passengers were indifferent to, and untrained in, the simplest rules of sanitation. Moreover, the lack of toilet facilities was appalling. Lice and the "itch" were common afflictions, indicating how few of the travelers were able

---

[4] Gilbert Tucker, "The Famine Immigration to Canada, 1847," *American Historical Review*, XXXVI (1930–31), No. 3, pp. 533–49.

or cared to keep clean.[5] The sick were without medical help; there was no privacy during the voyage, even for the change of undergarments; and the stench when the hatches were opened at the port of arrival was incredibly bad.[6] The noise of the steerage must have been almost unbearable, with the retching of the sick, the rattle of tin dishes and utensils at mealtime, the crying of children, and the sounds coming from the violent motion of the ship.

Despite such horrible conditions, probably both the abuses of the immigrant trade and the number who became ill and died en route have been exaggerated. There is no doubt that the mortality rate among children was frightfully high. Nevertheless, in 1854, for example, the *Cultivator* from Liverpool, with 945 passengers aboard, had but one death, whereas another vessel sailing from Rotterdam reported seven from a total passenger list of 265. In April of the next year, among 9,271 passengers who arrived in New York on twenty-one ships, there were seven deaths among the adults and eight among infants.[7] The statistics compiled by New York newspapers in the 1850's and 1860's show that the number of deaths was considerably larger.[8] Obviously, some packet lines were better and safer than others. One of the best seems to have been the American firm of Enoch Train and Company. In 1849, Bishop John B. Fitzpatrick of Boston wrote an endorsement "from personal knowledge," which the company featured in its advertising with a similar recommendation from the Reverend Theobald Mathew, famed temperance crusader from Cork. Statistics for this company on the immigrant trade from Liverpool to Boston in 1853 show that of 13,506 who embarked, only thirty-eight were lost on the voyage.[9]

Despite the grim accounts of the immigrant traffic, there were some diversions on shipboard which made the hazardous journey at least a little more palatable. There were dancing and jigging on deck to the tunes of an Irish fiddler. The immigrants played games and cards and sometimes gambled away what they could little afford, and they sang the old familiar songs. The women spent many hours sewing and knitting. "Bowling at sea" was a popular deck game, and then there was

[5] Edwin C. Guillet, *The Great Migration*, 71; also Chapters VIII to X.

[6] See Thomas Addis Emmet, *Incidents of My Life*, 138–42. Dr. Emmet worked in the fever wards and was resident physician at the Emigrant Refugee Hospital on Ward's Island. See also a letter by William D. Lynahan to his wife in 1855, in Robert F. McNamara, *A Century of Grace, History of St. Mary's Parish, Corning, New York*, 29–30.

[7] *The Citizen* (New York), July 8, 1854; May 26, 1855.

[8] See Carl Wittke, *We Who Built America, the Saga of the Immigrant*, 116.

[9] I am indebted for this item to Dr. Ray Ginger.

always the sheer fascination and beauty of the sea itself. The conduct of officers and men was not always bad, and, as early as 1811, the Irish passengers on the *Perseverance,* from Belfast to New York, inserted a card of thanks in the New York *Shamrock* expressing their appreciation for the "humane and gentleman-like conduct" of the captain and recommending him and his ship to their Irish countrymen.[10] By the 1860's, the Cunard, Inman, Guion, and National lines called with steamers at Queenstown, Ireland, and the Allan Company's steamers put in at Greencastle. They made the ocean voyage in about two weeks, and it was no longer necessary for Irishmen to cross over to Liverpool to embark. Yet charges of overcrowding persisted in the 1870's, despite more stringent regulations.[11]

When New York harbor at last came in sight, and the Irish immigrant cast his first look upon the promised land, the still heavily wooded Staten Island may well have reminded him of his native, green island home. But he must have been quite bewildered when he landed at the wharf and took his first walk through the teeming streets of the American metropolis. In the middle of the last century, the harbor was still full of sails; there were as yet no hooting tugboats; and there was no Statue of Liberty "to lift her lamp beside the golden door." Staten Island still was an area of farms and wooded hills. New York's brick or wooden houses were hardly over three stories high, and church spires, rather than skyscrapers, peeked out above their roof tops.

One can readily imagine the eagerness of the newly arrived immigrants to set foot on American soil as they thronged on the deck with their baggage and caught their first glimpse of what they expected to be a paradise. There were wild welcomes and shouts of "Glory be to God" and "The Saints be with us." Yet, to use a phrase of Philip Bagenal, the Irish alighted "like tired migratory birds on the eastern shores of the shelter continent" to find the perils of the port city as great as those on shipboard. Immigrant runners, recruited from the lowest of the city proletariat, rushed to the gangplank to fight with other bullies for the immigrant's luggage and to carry him off to the immigrant hotel or boardinghouse by which they were employed. New York Irishmen were among the worst of these "shoulder hitters" and human vultures who preyed upon their unsuspecting and helpless countrymen.

Irish immigrants had been warned early in the century against runners and boardinghouse keepers, "a nest of vipers who would be urging you to go to tippling-houses with them, to drink whiskey, and talk about Ire-

[10] *The Shamrock* (New York), April 13, 1811.
[11] Fitzpatrick, "Irish Immigration into New York," 23–28.

land." [12] Irish-American papers like the New York *Citizen* and *The Irish News* carried many articles describing how immigrants were abused and fleeced in American ports. /The hangouts of the worst runners were in the notorious Five Points section of New York, the Hook, and lower Cherry Street—areas noted for rioting, lawlessness, and crime, and where the police were more or less helpless.

Thus the newly arrived immigrant was likely to fall victim to a combination of exploiters—runners, boardinghouse keepers who overcharged him and held his baggage for payment, commission agents and brokers who sold him bogus tickets if he wanted to proceed to the interior, dishonest forwarders of his baggage, and just plain thugs and thieves. To identify themselves as friends from Ireland, the male runners wore green neckties; the female, green ribbons. Irish boardinghouses in New York, Boston, and elsewhere had rather unsavory reputations, and frequently were combined with grog shops located on the first floor. A saucer of free tobacco on the counter was standard equipment; runners crowded around the bar; the immigrant's baggage was piled in the cellar; and the upstairs rooms were dirty and overcrowded.

The newspapers carried accounts of outrages on unprotected and inexperienced Irish immigrant girls who were seduced on shipboard by the crew or others on promise of marriage upon arrival in the United States. By the late 1850's, a Women's Protective Emigration Society was operating in New York for the protection of Irish girls—to find them jobs or to send them under surveillance into the interior, where they could be under the watchful care of the Church. [13]

Many Irish were fleeced shortly after their arrival of their few remaining dollars or were robbed of their baggage, making it doubly necessary for them to remain where they had landed and take any kind of available employment. In 1847, a Board of Commissioners of Emigration was finally created for New York, partly through the efforts of Thurlow Weed and Bishop Hughes, to supervise the inspection of ships, to aid the immigrant in any way possible, and to look after the destitute. One of the ten members of the board was the president of a German organization for the aid of immigrants; another was Andrew Corrigan, president of the Irish Emigrant Society. The board was frequently criticized for inefficiency and neglect, particularly by papers like the *Irish-American,* which, on January 27, 1850, referred to "hundreds . . . cast on shore from

[12] Quoted from John Melish, *Travels,* in Edith Abbott, *Historical Aspects of the Immigration Problem,* 228.

[13] See *The Irish News* (New York), March 21, September 5, 1857; February 20, March 13, 1858.

emigrant ships . . . [who] parade, daily, the streets of New York, as *howling beggars* . . . sleep in droves . . . in the station houses," and to "women left to shiver on benches." [14]

In 1855, Castle Garden, a large structure which had housed circuses and menageries and in which Jenny Lind had given her concerts, was opened as a compulsory landing place for immigrants in New York. Here they could get sound and official advice instead of turning to sharks and runners, buy railroad tickets, exchange their money for American dollars, have their baggage transported, and get help in writing letters and seeking jobs. The runners went to court to protest against this illegal interference with their vested rights, held indignation meetings, and fired rockets over Castle Garden in their rage against this invasion by government of the sacred precincts of free enterprise.[15] Fortunately, they lost their case, and Castle Garden remained New York's great port of entry until 1892, when the service was transferred to Ellis Island. Hundreds of thousands of Americans entered the United States via Castle Garden. Here thousands of Irish had their first contacts with American officialdom. Health inspection remained perfunctory, however, and for many years was hardly more than a simple count of the number of passengers. The seriously ill and diseased, and especially those suffering from contagious maladies, were sent to immigrant hospitals on Ward Island in New York and to similar facilities in other Atlantic ports of entry.

If Irish immigrants had enough initiative and money left to proceed inland, they frequently were overcharged both for fare and baggage or were sold "through" tickets which turned out to be good for only part of the journey. Railroad and canal companies competed eagerly for their business and employed their own set of agents to direct traffic to their lines. Immigrants who came up the Mississippi from New Orleans found the river boats as crowded and as dangerous as the ocean craft, and many an Irish immigrant who died on the way up the river was buried at the first landing place.[16] In 1855, the *Citizen* of New York recommended the Michigan Central Railroad to Chicago over the Michigan Southern because of better treatment and better accommodations for immigrants.[17]

[14] Quoted in Robert Ernst, *Immigrant Life in New York City, 1825–1863*, 30.

[15] See the *Metropolitan Record and Vindicator* (New York), April 28, 1860; November 30, 1867; also Richard J. Purcell, "The New York Commissioners of Immigration and Irish Immigrants," *Studies—An Irish Quarterly Review of Letters, Philosophy and Science*, XXXVII (1948), 29–41. This work hereafter cited as *Studies*.

[16] See "A Friendly Mission—John Candler's Letters from America, 1853–1854," *Indiana Historical Society Publications*, XVI (1951), No. 1, p. 73.

[17] *The Citizen* (New York), October 27, 1855. See also Wittke, *We Who Built America*, Chapter VII.

To somewhat offset these depressing accounts of the exploitation and mistreatment of immigrants, often by their own countrymen, it may be pointed out that long before Castle Garden was opened, Irishmen in the United States organized societies to help their fellow countrymen make an easier transition from their old to their new home. The activities of such Irish societies not only testify to the traditional warmheartedness of the Irish people, but also to the fact that there was already a responsible, thrifty, and rising group of Irish-Americans in this country who were both interested in the problems of immigration and able to give substantial help.

The Hibernian Society of Philadelphia for the Relief of Emigrants from Ireland (1790) was an outgrowth of the Hibernian Club and the Friendly Sons of St. Patrick of that city. The Shamrock Society published advice to Irish immigrants in 1817.[18] There was an Irish Emigrant Association in Baltimore before 1818. The Irish Emigrant Society of New York was founded by Dr. Robert Hogan, president of the Friendly Sons of St. Patrick, in 1814. He had the aid of Dr. William J. Macneven, a political refugee of the Irish rising of 1798; the support of papers like *The Shamrock* and the *Truth Teller;* and the blessing of Bishop Hughes. The society was incorporated in 1844 under New York law. Prominent Protestant and Catholic Irishmen and Irish fraternal associations supported its work, which included distributing literature at the Battery in New York and directing immigrants to the society's office. Here they were given help in finding good boardinghouses and jobs. The society reported cases where immigrants were unfairly or cruelly treated on shipboard and exposed swindlers, dishonest hotel and boardinghouse keepers, and brokers who cheated customers in sending remittances to the old country. In 1843, the society published an address to the people of Ireland which was full of valuable suggestions for prospective emigrants. On one occasion, the society rescued twenty-eight boarders from Bernard Duffy's boardinghouse, where they were being held against their will on the claim that they had not paid their bills. In 1847, the organization urged Congress and the New York legislature to take steps to protect the health of immigrants, and its agitation was in part responsible for the creation of the New York Commission of Immigration. In addition, it was this group which developed New York's well-known Emigrant Industrial Savings Bank, established in 1850.

Similar programs were carried out in Philadelphia, New Orleans, and elsewhere with the hearty support of the clergy, who acted as a clearing-

---

[18] See Erna Risch, "Immigrant Aid Societies before 1820," *Pennsylvania Magazine of History and Biography*, LX (1936), 15–33.

house for Irish immigrants. The New York *Shamrock,* one of the earliest Irish papers in this country, acted as a free employment agency; Irish societies helped immigrants remit funds to Ireland or forward money to the interior. A Hibernian Benevolent Society was at work in Chicago in 1848. In Boston, the office of the Irish Emigrant Society was near the Commons. In 1850, it found jobs for Irish girls at the rate of a hundred a day and counted among its contributors a number of middle-class Irish of fairly comfortable means. Religious orders like the Sisters of Mercy, whom Bishop Hughes brought over from Dublin, sheltered over 2,300 girls from 1849 to 1854 and found employment for over five thousand in the same period.[19]

[19] See Richard J. Purcell, "The Irish Emigrant Society of New York," *Studies,* XXVII (1938), 583–98; Mooney, *Nine Years in America,* 118–19; Aaron I. Abell, "The Catholic Factor in Urban Welfare: The Early Period, 1850–1880," *The Review of Politics,* XIV (July, 1952), 312; and *The Citizen* (New York), September 22, October 13, 1855.

Chapter III

City Pioneers

THE immigrant tide from Ireland already was running strong before the Great Famine. In the 1830's, about 650,000 Irish came to America, though not all came to the United States. During the pre-famine years, the majority of the newcomers were Catholics, but there were also many Protestant Irish among them. About two-thirds of the immigrants then were laborers. The proportion of women was about 30 per cent in 1827 and rose to 48 per cent in 1835. The earlier immigration of the 1830's included small farmers and artisans, who were poor but independent, enterprising, and with enough resources to guarantee a fair start in the United States. In later years, the majority of immigrants were the poorest laborers, among whom illiteracy was high and industriousness and an independent tradition of self-help often lacking.

The failure of the potato crop in 1845 and 1846 completely transformed the character of Irish immigration as Irishmen fled from hunger, disease, and death. After 1840, the number who came directly to the United States was greater than the totals for British North America, and, by 1845, fully two-thirds came directly to the "land of promise." [1] The vast majority went into personal and domestic service, or did common, unskilled labor, and there was no large decrease in these catagories until the first American-born generation of Irish. By 1890, 15.5 per cent of the Irish in America were engaged in agriculture, fishing, and mining; 1.6 per cent in the professions; 15 per cent in trade and transportation; 25 per cent in manufacturing; and 42 per cent still were listed as working in personal and domestic services.

From 1820 to 1910, the total Irish immigration to the United States was 4,212,169, of whom 58 per cent lived in the four states of Massachusetts, New York, Pennsylvania, and Illinois. If the Irish of Connecticut, New Jersey, Ohio, and California are added, the total would account for 75 per cent of the American Irish. Moreover, in every census of the present century, the Irish-American population, if native Irish and those with

---

[1] For excellent statistics covering the years before 1848, see Adams, *Ireland and Irish Emigration*, Appendix.

one or both parents from Ireland are included, exceeded the entire population of their island home.

In 1850, the Irish constituted 42.8 per cent of the foreign-born population of the United States; in 1860, nearly 40 per cent; in 1890, 20.2 per cent; and in 1900, 15.6 per cent. In 1910, 81.3 per cent of the American Irish lived in urban communities of 2,500 or more. New York, Philadelphia, Chicago, Boston, San Francisco, and St. Louis were strongholds of the Irish. About one-fourth of the total immigration, by the turn of the century, was distributed over twelve North Central States—Ohio, Indiana, Illinois, Michigan, Wisconsin, Missouri, Iowa, Minnesota, Kansas, Nebraska, and the Dakotas. In the farm belt, about one-third of the Irish were engaged in agriculture.[2] The number of Irish in the South always was relatively small, though there were important Irish colonies in New Orleans, Vicksburg, Memphis, and several other southern cities. From 1841 to 1855, over 1,600,000 left Ireland for the United States. For the thirty years after 1865, the immigration averaged about 50,000 a year. It fell off thereafter—except for the 1880's, when Ireland experienced another famine and land war—but the annual figure never dropped below 25,000 before World War I. After the war, 78,411 came during the seven years from 1927 to 1934, though the number dropped to 256 in 1932, and many returned during the decade of depression to their native island.

The Irish helped make New York the largest American city: first by settling there, and second, by building the Erie Canal. For a long time, New York City has harbored more Irishmen than Dublin. The Greenwich Village section was inhabited largely by poor Irish laborers. By 1830, the New York Irish had their own newspapers and societies, and were able to point to some professional men, merchants, and active politicians in their group. Brooklyn had an Erin Fraternal Association in 1826. In the late 1840's, the Irish swarmed into the neglected tenements and boardinghouses, built their shanties, and took over the old houses in the notorious Five Points district of New York. The Old Brewery, for example, dating from 1792, was converted into a human rookery for several hundred men, women, and children. Irish and Negroes shared its ramshackle facilities, and the neighborhood was noted for lawlessness and crime. In later years, Irishmen were joined in these crowded quarters by other nationality groups. The New York Irish fanned out along Water, Cherry, and Monroe streets and occupied the wards along the East River. Although they settled in other parts of Manhattan, they preferred the East Side. It is significant to note that there was also a

---

[2] H. J. Desmond, "A Century of Irish Immigration," *The American Catholic Quarterly Review*, XXV (1900), 518-30.

"Dutch Hill" in New York in the 1860's. Here poor German squatters settled, paid neither rent nor taxes, did the lowest kind of work—such as peddling and picking rags—and, like the Irish, kept pigs, cows, and chickens.[3]

Occupations engaged in by the Irish were varied. Irish immigrant women went into the garment trades after 1840 to operate the newly invented sewing machines and to make pants and vests. The Irish male tailors usually made the coats. The majority of the carters, cabmen, and carmen in New York were Irish. Many Irishmen, with their innate love for animals, went to work in livery stables. It was not an uncommon experience for the immigrant to begin by cleaning horses and washing carriages in livery stables, then become a driver, fitting up "shanty stables" on vacant lots, and finally managing his own cabs and wagons. They hauled freight from the wharves and depots or drove patrons to the theater in Dublin "covered cars."[4] Many Irish who began as stable boys eventually owned their own omnibus and livery stable.

By the middle of the nineteenth century, New York already had a number of successful Irish mercantile firms and small businesses, among which the number of dispensaries of liquor remained out of all proportion. For the most part, the Irish did the heavy, hard, dirty work of the city. Although among the first generation there were masons, bricklayers, plasterers, carpenters, and tailors who worked in sweatshops, there were more helpers and hodmen, porters, street cleaners, waiters, hostlers, bartenders, boatmen, stevedores and longshoremen, and unskilled, brawny laborers who did the digging, blasting, and laying of pipes for the city. Others worked in warehouses, quarries, and shipyards. In 1880, the two largest categories among the Irish of New York City still were domestic servants and laborers.[5] A number of Irish hotels advertised "superior bar rooms" where most of the employees were Irish. By 1855, Irishmen were also active in the fish and oyster business and produce markets, while Irish women worked as laundresses, charwomen, waitresses, and chambermaids. Eighty-seven per cent of the foreign-born laborers in the city at this time were Irish. Irishmen also accounted for four-fifths of the teamsters and carters and for a large percentage of those engaged in the building trades.[6]

By 1860, nearly half of New York State's million foreign-born were

---

[3] Ernst, *Immigrant Life*, 39–40, 67, 69, 89.

[4] Mooney, *Nine Years in America*, 152–54.

[5] For figures on various occupations, see Fitzpatrick, "Irish Immigration into New York," 53–54.

[6] See Thomas L. Nichols, *Forty Years of American Life*, II, 72.

Irish.[7] The Irish scattered widely as they dug canals across the state, and though, in Thomas D'Arcy McGee's oratorical language, "their shanties spring up like mushrooms in the night and often vanish like mists in the morning," many developed into permanent settlements and parishes. By 1832, the Irish were numerous enough in Buffalo to be assigned a special section in the potter's field. In 1853, McGee published his *Celt and Catholic Citizen* for a short time in Buffalo.[8] Irishmen settled around the salt works of early Syracuse, near the quarries of Onondaga County, and engaged in the lumber and cooperage business in Oswego County. Rochester, like Buffalo, largely a product of the Erie Canal, had a Hibernian Benefit Society in the 1830's; and Albany, with easy boat connections with New York City, became an Irish center early in the nineteenth century, many Irish names appearing in its city directory as early as 1813.

Irish immigrants settled in New England also. In 1832, the villagers of Pittsfield, Massachusetts, were thrown into great excitement because "two wild Irishmen" were seen sitting in a park beneath its Old Elm.[9] In 1849, "seeing an Irishman" in South Boston and an Irishman with a pig and chickens on Brookline Street was still something of a sensation.[10] By 1850, however, the six New England States, with a little over one-tenth of the population of the United States, had one-fifth of its Irish, and, by the 1870's, the Boston Irish were electing their people to the legislature and filling city jobs. By 1885, the children of Irish parents in Boston outnumbered the children of the older stock, and Boston no longer was "the Boston of the Endicotts and the Winthrops, but the Boston of the Collinses and the O'Briens." [11]

As suggested earlier, many of the early Irish came to New England via British North America. The Great Famine opened the floodgates to this area, and because the Irish provided much-needed labor for the region's industrial revolution, they were tolerated by Boston Brahmins. By 1850, about 65 per cent of Boston's Irish working population were engaged in public works, as stevedores at the wharves, or as house and yard servants. Most of them had arrived penniless and had been "immobi-

---

[7] For the distribution of the Irish in New York State before the Civil War, especially as marked by new Roman Catholic parishes, see Richard J. Purcell, "Immigration from the Canal Era to the Civil War," Chapter II in *History of the State of New York* (ed. by Alexander Flick), VII.

[8] Flick (ed.), *History of New York*, VII, 35.

[9] Note in *The Catholic Historical Review*, I (1916), 484.

[10] Robert A. Woods (ed.), *The City Wilderness, a Settlement Study*, 53–54.

[11] *Donahoe's Magazine*, quoted in Arthur M. Schlesinger, *Political and Social Growth of the American People, 1865–1940*, 254.

lized" in the port where they landed. Irish girls solved the domestic-help problem for New England families, and, it was generally agreed, gave loyal and often jovial service for low pay. Many Boston Irish worked with horses, but relatively few of the first generation followed a trade or were in business, except for saloons and boardinghouses. In the expanding textile industry, the Irish worked for less pay than the girls from native New England families and helped convert Boston and other cities into manufacturing centers.[12]

Within the limits of Old Boston, the Irish at first were sharply segregated. Because they had to live near their jobs and get cheap rent, they congregated in the North End and the Fort Hill areas—around the docks, markets, stores and shops, and in the garment district. With the coming of the horsecar, they spread into West and South Boston and into Charlestown, where old houses and warehouses were transformed into immigrant tenements. In South Boston, the Irish slums were buildings from three to six stories high, where whole families lived in a single room without sunlight or ventilation. Even the cellars were inhabited, and such quarters, rented at a dollar and a half a week per room, were not regarded as too objectionable by Irish who had come from hovels without floors and had walked and slept on dirty straw. One need not dwell on the lack of sewage and sanitation facilities, the filth and disease, the lack of privacy, and the one privy which had to serve the whole house. Tenants hardly could be expected to be clean under such conditions, and slovenliness, disorder, indifference, intemperance, and immorality were perhaps inevitable results. The majority of Boston's groggeries were operated by Irish. The rate of pauperism was high and traceable, in large measure, to the drink-evil. Small wonder that every Irishman was a "shanty Irishman," and that old New Englanders were disturbed because the Irish were increasing far more rapidly than the older strains.[13]

Canal building and road construction helped distribute Irish laborers throughout New England. In the early 1820's and 1830's, contractors brought in hundreds of Irish pick-and-shovel workers. In 1827, approximately 400 were working on the Enfield Canal near Hartford, Connecticut, and 170 came to New Haven to help build the Farmington Canal.[14] The building of the Blackstone Canal led to the development of Woon-

12 See Handlin, *Boston's Immigrants*, Chapters III and IV; also Barbara Miller Solomon, "Background of Immigration Restriction," *The New England Quarterly*, XXV (March, 1952), 45–59.

13 See Robert H. Lord, John E. Sexton, and Edward T. Harrington, *History of the Archdiocese of Boston, 1604 to 1943*, II, 345, 453–57, for Irish efforts to ameliorate these conditions. See also Mooney, *Nine Years in America*, 118.

14 Lord, Sexton, and Harrington, *History of the Archdiocese of Boston*, II, 91–92.

socket, Rhode Island. Other Irish shanty towns developed in Pawtucket, Rhode Island, Lowell, Massachusetts, and elsewhere.[15]

Many Irish worked for a time for New England farmers, who continued to employ them though they complained of their clumsiness and laziness in the fields. Although there was a difference between the earlier immigrants and those who came during and immediately after the Great Famine, all Irishmen got the reputation of being lazy, dirty, stupid, unreliable, unstable, and turbulent. Progress upward began when the Irish entered the New England mills. By 1860, they were the dominant labor element in the industrial areas and were rising steadily in the economic scale.

Many Americans in the New England textile areas learned their trade from Irish weavers who came to the United States before 1848. The percentage of Irish employed in typical New England mills rose steadily from 1830 to 1860. By 1873, the labor force in both cotton and woolen manufacturing in New England was predominantly Irish. Wages were low, and the working day extended from sunrise to sunset; but for Irish laborers, such conditions were a vast improvement over what they had known in Ireland.[16] Lowell, "the city of spindles," had its "New Dublin" and Irish "Acre" as early as 1833, with about five hundred Irish living in a hundred cabins near the canal.[17] Fall River employed about three thousand Irish in factories and foundries by 1850.

In New Hampshire, the Irish were attracted to the quarries and foundries, as well as to mill and construction jobs.[18] Here, as elsewhere, Irish canal, road, and railroad builders stayed on to supplant native workers in the mills. Dover, New Hampshire, was the first sizable Irish Catholic settlement in the state. It developed around the town's cotton mills. In Rhode Island, the overflow of Irish from Boston furnished the labor for its textile mills.[19] The many "little Dublins" in the Middle Atlantic States testify to the number of Irish labor gangs who stayed on to work in factories whose millraces they had built.

In the Brooklyn Navy Yard, the Irish earned $1.12 a day, but many lost their jobs during the panic of 1857. The Philadelphia Navy Yard

---

[15] Ibid., II, 89.

[16] For details, see Arthur H. Cole, The American Wool Manufacture, I, 240, 368–73.

[17] See George F. Kenngott, The Record of a City, 29; for typical family budgets, as late as 1910, see 127, 133–36; also William Cardinal O'Connell, Recollections of Seventy Years, 12 et seq., 23 et seq.

[18] See Richard J. Purcell, "Schools and Early Irish Teachers in New Hampshire," The Catholic Educational Review, XXXII (1943), 618; and Robert D. Quirk, "The Irish Element in New Hampshire to 1865" (Master's thesis, Catholic University of America, 1936).

[19] Sister Mary E. Walsh, "The Irish in Rhode Island from 1800 to 1865" (Master's thesis, Catholic University of America, 1937).

employed many Irish workers who lived around the wharves and docks, an area infested with sailors' boardinghouses of a low order. Philadelphia had its quota of Irish clubs and fire companies and a short-lived Hibernian Society for the Relief of Emigrants from Ireland, organized by Protestant and Catholic Irish before the end of the eighteenth century.[20]

It is unnecessary to follow the course of Irish immigration to all the city centers of the United States, for much of the story would be repetitious. There were thirty-four Murphys in the Cleveland directory in 1857. By the 1870's, Cleveland had an "Irishtown," as well as areas known as "Shanty Town," "Vinegar Hill," "The Triangle," the "Flats," and "Whiskey Island"—some of which were in bad repute with the police. The Irish who worked in the early rolling mills of the Cleveland area in the 1860's lived in Newburgh, a section of grimy houses with a railroad running through the heart of the village. They were paid $1.65 a day.[21]

In 1850, there were 51,562 Irish in Ohio. Nearly 14,000 lived in the lowlands along the river in Cincinnati, and, by 1870, that city had 18,624 of the state's approximately 83,000 Irish. The first meeting of the Friendly Sons of St. Patrick was held in Toledo in 1859. By 1870, the Irish population of this city, recruited largely from the residue of canal and railroad builders, passed the 3,000 mark. One of the early colonies here was known as "The Hill." By 1944, the Toledo city directory had nine columns of names beginning with "O'" and many other typically Irish names.[22] The Irish came to Akron and Youngstown with the canal and the railroad, as they did in many other cities.

There was an "Irish Settlement" in Kane County, Illinois, in the late 1830's,[23] and the Irish were pioneers in the lead mines that produced the town of Galena. Elgin had its "Irish Grove" in the 1840's; there was a politically active group of Irish in Joliet; and there was a Hibernian Benevolent Emigrant Society in Chicago in 1848.[24] The state of Illinois counted 87,573 Irish in 1860, with the largest concentration in Chicago. Here they constituted the first proletariat of the rising western metropolis.[25]

[20] See John H. Campbell, *History of the Friendly Sons of St. Patrick and of the Hibernian Society for the Relief of Emigrants from Ireland.*

[21] William G. Rose, *Cleveland, the Making of a City,* 322.

[22] Stephen J. Bartha, "A History of Immigrant Groups in Toledo" (Master's thesis, Ohio State University, 1945).

[23] Cornelius J. Kirkfleet, *The History of the Parishes of the Diocese of Rockford, Illinois,* 231.

[24] Arthur C. Cole, *The Era of the Civil War, 1848–70,* 21.

[25] Bessie L. Pierce, "The Fabric of Chicago's Early Society," in *Essays in Honor of William E. Dodd,* 109. See also Gilbert J. Garraghan, *The Catholic Church in Chicago, 1673–1871.*

There were seven Irish-born members in Wisconsin's first constitutional convention. Most of the early Irish in this state came as laborers for the lead mines. After the lead-mining boom passed its peak, Irish workmen scattered over the state. From 1850 to 1870, the Irish element ranked second only to the German among the foreign-born. In Milwaukee, 15 per cent of the population was Irish and lived in the "Bloody Third" ward. Milwaukee had its Emmet Guards, a Catholic Total Abstinence Society, and other Irish organizations.[26]

The St. Louis Irish published the *Pilot* in 1839. The city's Hibernian Benevolent Society was incorporated in 1843, the United Sons of Erin and the Roman Catholic Total Abstinence Society two years later, and an Irish militia company in 1846.[27]

Of nearly 65,000 immigrants who arrived in New Orleans in 1860, nearly 25,000 were Irish. They developed the river-front sections of the town, to which they gave the name "Irish Channel"—long notorious as one of the tougher parts of the city. Most of the New Orleans Irish, even by the time of the Civil War, were unskilled laborers, carters, coachmen, porters, and railroad workers. In the hotels of this city, as in some of the best hotels throughout the South, Irish waiters had driven out the Negro.

The Irish population in southern cities always was relatively small as compared with that of the metropolitan centers of the East, but it was significant in a number of the towns below Mason and Dixon's line. As early as 1837, a roving reporter wrote about the Irish of Louisville. In this city, "Irish porters were cracking their whips and roaring alternative staves of blasphemy and song."[28] Charleston's Hibernian Society, a nonpolitical and nonsectarian organization of South Carolina, dated from 1799. Its badge was a silver harp, and one of its main objectives the relief of distressed immigrants from Ireland.[29] Georgia's relatively small number of Irishmen were part of the state's 11,000 white "laborers" in 1850. They were especially numerous in Savannah.[30] The Irish population of Memphis was about 4,000 in 1860; Mobile had a substantial number of Irish laborers; and there were several Irish colonies in Texas

[26] Bayrd Still, *Milwaukee, the History of a City;* also Humphrey J. Desmond, "Early Irish Settlers in Milwaukee," *Journal of the American Irish Historical Society,* XXIX (1930–31), 107–108; James S. Buck, *Pioneer History of Milwaukee;* and H. J. Desmond, "Early Irish Settlers in Milwaukee," *The Wisconsin Magazine of History,* XIII (1929–30), 365–75.

[27] John D. Crimmins, *Irish-American Historical Miscellany,* 288–89.

[28] Warren S. Tryon, *A Mirror for Americans,* III, 564.

[29] John I. Cosgrove, "The Hibernian Society of Charleston, South Carolina," *Journal of the American Irish Historical Society,* XXV (1926), 150–58.

[30] Richard H. Shryock, *Georgia and the Union in 1850,* 175.

besides the sizable settlement in Galveston.[31] In the Far West, San Francisco had the largest foreign-born population, of which the Irish constituted 10 per cent in 1880.[32]

The ubiquitous Irishman turned up in every state of the Union, though the great majority always resided in the East. Whenever they settled in the interior, they usually made their first contacts with the region as laborers on internal improvement projects. Laborers with strong backs and a willingness to work were in demand for tasks which native Americans no longer wished to perform. The Irishman with his pick and shovel was largely responsible for the speedy completion of the network of communications which welded the scattered settlements of the United States into a national unit.

[31] John C. Linehan, "The Irish Pioneers of Texas," *Journal of the American Irish Historical Society,* II (1899), 124–26.
[32] See Hugh Quigley, *The Irish Race in California.*

Chapter IV

"Drill, My Paddies, Drill"

In his flowery manner, Thomas D'Arcy McGee spoke of Ireland as supplying "the hands which led Lake Erie downwards to the sea, and wedded the strong Chesapeake to the Gentle Delaware, and carried the roads of the East out to the farthest outpost of the West." [1] In more prosaic language, many internal improvement projects would have been long delayed had there not been thousands of Irish available, at the right time, for the heavy, hazardous work which native Americans refused to undertake. If the Irish immigration to the eastern cities displaced native workers and depressed wages, the Irish had the field largely to themselves when it came to building roads, canals, railroads, and other public works. Americans talked jokingly about the wheelbarrow as one of the greatest inventions of all time because it taught Irishmen to walk on their hind legs. But the fact remains that America in the nineteenth century needed men of muscle, brawn, and strong backs to take great physical risks and work long hours at back-breaking jobs. Irish laborers filled this need. Eventually, many were able to rise in the economic and social scale, turn their wheelbarrows, picks, and shovels over to later arrivals from Europe, and become bosses and contractors, employing men as unskilled as they once had been. Until well along in the latter half of the nineteenth century, however, the Irishman was the chief source for cheap, unskilled labor.

From the beginning of the last century, Irishmen were employed in road-building gangs, whose construction camps of shacks and tents resounded with Irish brogue. The building of the National Road was but one project, though one of the most important, on which Irishmen were employed in large numbers. A farmer, watching the progress of the National Road between Braddock's Grove and Uniontown, Pennsylvania, was fascinated by "that great contractor, Mordecai Cochran," and "with his immortal Irish brigade, a thousand strong, with their carts, wheelbarrows, picks, shovels and blasting tools, grading the commons, and

[1] Isabel Skelton, *The Life of Thomas D'Arcy McGee*, 244.

climbing the mountainside . . . and leaving behind them a roadway good enough for an emperor to travel over."[2] Laborers were plentiful at six dollars a month, and more Irishmen applied than could be employed. Even at that low rate, there were Americans who believed that six dollars was "unfortunately high, and rye whiskey, still more unfortunately cheap."[3] Among the contractors who built the National Road were such typical Irishmen as Philip McGinnis, Tully Gallager, and Thomas Monaghan. As the National Road progressed through Ohio, local farmers joined in the work with pick and shovel, sometimes for a week or a month during the slack season, hauled dirt and stone, or did grading with their teams, but they by no means displaced the Irish. In 1839, a Catholic priest celebrated Mass and baptized the children in an Irish labor camp in northwestern Ohio, where Irish laborers were pushing a road through the "Black Swamp" from Fremont to Perrysburg, on the Maumee River. Irish settlements in Perry County developed from gangs who worked on the National Road. Through the efforts of a priest who accompanied them, land was bought and a village and church erected.

In the canal-building era, Irish were imported in droves by contractors who supplemented the already available supply of workers by advertising in the Catholic press and in the Irish papers of Cork, Dublin, and Belfast—sometimes deliberately calling for more men than needed in order to keep wages down. Many Irish subcontractors had few scruples about exploiting their own kind. In the first stages of canal- and road-building projects, Irish "board and turf huts" and shanties, constructed out of anything available, marked the route of these internal improvement projects. Wages before 1830 ranged between seventy-five cents and a dollar and a half a day, and, as the labor supply increased, were even lower, from fifty cents to a dollar a day. Yet there were hundreds eager to work for that amount. The wage rate on the canals was somewhat higher in the summer months than in the winter. Rations of whiskey were part of the contract in the construction camps, and heavy drinking and brawling, especially after payday, were the unhappy consequences which helped give the Irish a reputation for fighting and rioting. Some of the battles along the canal routes were fought between rival gangs whose hostility dated back to their troubles in the old country. "Corkonians" and "Far Downers" and "Connaught Men" nursed their local grudges in America, and Irish laborers terrorized their competitors in the labor market as they had learned to do at home. Much of the turmoil

2 Quoted in Philip D. Jordan, *The National Road*, 86–87.
3 W. J. Howlett, *Life of Rt. Rev. Joseph P. Machebeuf*, 53–58.

was directly traceable to miserable working and living conditions and to a demand for better wages and better treatment.

There were unscrupulous contractors who stirred up fights to avoid paying their men their wages and who exploited them in company stores. When it rained, workers lost their pay, but the charge for board and lodging in the bunks of their crude shanties continued. The diggers often stood knee-deep in water, and cholera epidemics and dysentery killed many of them. They had to cut out trees through the width of the canal area, and they toiled through hot summer days infested with swarms of mosquitoes carrying malaria. Work usually was not suspended until winter actually set in. Deaths from "canal fever" were numerous. In 1826, digging was stopped on the canal out of Cleveland for several months in the summer when health conditions became too bad even for the calloused standards of that day. Accidents, injuries, tuberculosis, cave-ins, and deaths were numerous along the canals. Many an unmarked grave along the route was the last resting place of an Irish pick-and-shovel worker killed in the line of duty and unceremoniously buried to make room for the next hand. No matter how lonely or unhappy the men might be, how poor and monotonous their diet, how boring and exhausting the daily toil in the "ditch," from sunrise to sunset, there were always more willing to come from the eastern proletariat or from among recent arrivals on immigrant ships. The Boston *Pilot* and other Irish-American papers repeatedly warned the Irish to avoid canal and railroad jobs, for they were "the ruin of thousands of our poor people" who were treated "like slaves." [4]

The Irish canal worker was practically without recourse. If he was cheated of his wages by the contractor, or forced to pay high prices for supplies at the contractor's store, he had no remedy — save to form a secret society as he had done in Ireland. Violence and gang warfare resulted. Yet these societies had some of the objectives of labor organizations and fought with crude weapons for better terms of employment and to keep competitors out of the field. It was during these years that the term "Irish nigger" came into common use to describe the lowliest of the Irish laboring class.

The building of the canals is a story of turbulence, violence, brawling, and factional fights among the Irish—some of which was perhaps "a normal part of social life," and the result of too much liquor, by men without church or family ties to restrain them. There were also Irishmen who behaved well and who were ambitious to get ahead, but,

[4] *The Pilot* (Boston), July 31, 1852.

unfortunately, they were characterized with the rest as "wild Irish." Missionary priests celebrated Mass whenever they could in the miserable Irish shanties along the canal, and men walked for miles to attend, contributing from their meager earnings to the building of rude little churches whose first priests were arbiters and social workers as well as shepherds of the souls of their flock.

As early as 1818, there were three thousand Irishmen working on the Erie Canal. By 1840, New York State had thirteen canals, completed or under way, for a total of 944 miles. On all of them, the Irish were the professional canal builders.[5] The Black River Canal brought the Irish to Jefferson County, New York, early in the century; they came to Saratoga County with the Champlain Canal (1818) and, in 1831, helped build the Schenectady-Saratoga Railroad.[6] Corning, New York, was once a busy canal port. The Chemung Feeder Canal ran from Elmira to Seneca Lake and connected the Susquehanna River system with the Erie Canal. Irishmen started digging the feeder canal in 1830 and finished it three years later. In 1849, the town's first Catholic church was built, and the parish received new additions when Irish railroad workers settled along the Erie tracks, in districts known as "Irish Hill" or "Catholic Hill," "Dublin," "Corktown," and "Windy Row."[7] The Erie Canal helped make Rochester a metropolis. Its early Roman Catholic population was largely recruited from Irish canal builders, who lived in a section of the city known for years as "Paddy's Land."[8]

The building of the Chesapeake and Ohio Canal provides another illustration of how "Yankee ingenuity and Hibernian brawn" burrowed across Pennsylvania. Labor was recruited in 1829 by advertisements in the press of Ireland which stressed that laborers could count on "meat three times a day, plenty of bread and vegetables, with a reasonable allowance of liquor, and eight, ten or twelve dollars a month for wages."[9] Workmen, brought over at the expense of the company, signed contracts before leaving Europe which reduced them to a status approximating that of indentured servants. It is not surprising, therefore, that there were

[5] For the evolution of a rather typical canal worker in Syracuse into a successful salt manufacturer and merchant worth $200,000, and for similar cases, see Theresa Bannan, *Pioneer Irish of Onondaga*, 24 *et seq.*

[6] Flick (ed.), *History of New York*, VII, 38.

[7] McNamara, *A Century of Grace*, 30.

[8] Frederick J. Zwierlein, "Catholic Beginnings in the Diocese of Rochester," *The Catholic Historical Review*, I (1916), 282-98; also the *Metropolitan Record* (New York), October 27, 1860.

[9] George W. Ward, *The Early Development of the Chesapeake and Ohio Canal Project* (Johns Hopkins Studies in History and Political Science, XVII, Nos. 9-11), 90.

much disorder and insubordination in the Chesapeake and Ohio Canal camps, and that many workers ran away from contracts.[10] Mrs. Frances Trollope commented on the "miserable lodging" of these Irish laborers and on the "large allowance of whiskey" used to stimulate them to harder, longer tasks and to enable them "to stand the boiling heat." [11] On one occasion, laborers from county Cork fought off their competitors from county Langford as vigorously as they drove off Yankee and Teuton rivals. President Jackson called out federal troops for the first time in a labor dispute because of a gang war among the builders of the Chesapeake and Ohio. Wages were ten to fifteen dollars a month, only five dollars in winter months, and no allowance was made for days lost because of illness. Under the circumstances, one may assume that many so-called Irish "riots" were in reality unorganized and ineffectual strikes. Ralph Waldo Emerson was outraged, as he indicated in his *Journal*, to find Irishmen in Massachusetts working a fifteen-hour day for fifty cents.[12]

Much of the history of the Ohio canals can be culled from the records of that state's Board of Public Works. They contain letters of application for jobs as contractors and subcontractors from Irishmen with several years' experience in canal building in New York and Pennsylvania. These letters throw light on the functions and responsibilities of the superintendents, whose pay was only fifteen dollars a week on some sections of the canals in 1829, and who, with their labor gangs, not only dug the ditches, but kept them in repair, raised their banks, repaired the slips and locks along the route, and inspected the canal for safety. The payrolls and timekeepers' accounts are full of Irish names, although more Irish were employed in some areas than in others, and more after 1848 than before.

Wages for canal laborers in Ohio ranged from ten to thirteen dollars a month. During the early years of the canal-building era, laborers received thirty cents a day, plain board, and the customary "jiggerful" of whiskey for a day's work from sunrise to sundown. An account book for crews on the Miami Canal from 1840 to 1843 not only records wages as low as seventy-five cents a day, but also the supplies furnished workmen on account. The latter included shoes at $1.75 a pair, socks, and pantaloons. Laborers were charged for pots, "wash," coffee and coffee mills, flour, and pork. "Three bed ticks" cost $2.25; potatoes were

---

[10] Walter S. Sanderlin, *The Great National Project, a History of the Chesapeake and Ohio Canal* (Johns Hopkins Studies in History and Political Science, LXIV, No. 1), 1–331.

[11] Frances Trollope, *Domestic Manners of the Americans* (ed. Donald Smalley), 290–91.

[12] See John R. Commons, *et al.*, *History of Labour in the United States*, I, 415; and Arthur B. Darling, *Political Changes in Massachusetts, 1824–1848*, 309.

twelve and a half cents a bushel; butter, five and nine cents a pound; eggs, five cents a dozen; and whiskey, twelve and a half cents a quart. Patrick Gorman paid a dollar for a shirt; Barney Sholts, $1.40 for five yards of "driling"; and James Flin, $1.25 for "knifes and forks." Page after page listed the Irishmen who came daily for their whiskey. One day Patrick Cody took beer, but never deviated again from the standard Irish stimulant.[13]

Such details are typical for other states as well, for life among the "canalers" was much the same—whether in New York, Indiana, Ohio, or Iowa. Whiskey dens dotted the route, and fights enlivened the battle with nature and the elements. The "Irish of the canal zone" helped create a stereotyped picture in the American mind which took years to erase. Most Americans would have accepted at face value Mrs. Anne Royal's description of the "Teagues," a name derived from the Irish caricature in Hugh H. Brackenridge's *Modern Chivalry*. She reported that Irishmen lived only about eighteen months after coming to the United States, being killed off during that time by drink and work on the canals, and that they were "thrown into the ground from four to six together, without coffins." She described the newcomers as drunken, dirty, poorly clothed, and less respectful, less moral, sober, and industrious than the freed Negro.[14]

Overlapping and following the canal era was the period of railroad building. The popular saying that there was "an Irishman buried under every tie" is evidence of the role played by Irish laborers in the construction program. Building through new country was hard, rough, and perilous work, and Irish newspapers in the 1850's contained many accounts of Irish laborers crushed by falling embankments which had not been properly braced, or buried under cave-ins, or maimed or killed by blasts of powder that went off too soon. Cheap immigrant labor built the railroads as it had dug the canals. The Irish railroad worker toiled for low wages, lived in dirt and disorder, and courted physical injury, disease, and death. Many Irishmen left their families in the tenements of the East to go out West with labor gangs that became, in Oscar Handlin's phrase, "the guano of the American communication system." They frequently lived in boardinghouses operated by railroad contractors, ate a monotonous diet, and climbed up outside ladders to crowded rooms to sleep.

The Erie Railroad, through its contractors, hired thousands of Irish

13 The Ohio Canal Papers are in the archives of the Ohio Historical Society in Columbus.

14 See Tryon, *A Mirror for Americans*, I, 74.

who built the section of the road which went through the mountainous regions around Port Jervis, New York. Their experiences were typical of railroad building in difficult terrain. Irish drilling crews were lowered from high ledges in big wicker baskets to dig holes in the rock, set the powder charge, light the fuse, and be pulled up hastily by ropes before the explosion occurred. Contractors were slave drivers and accidents numerous. Fights broke out between Irish railroad gangs and nearby canal workers. Occasionally, someone was killed. On Sundays, idle workers sought a little variation from the week's hard routine, roamed the countryside, raided orchards and potato fields, stole chickens, and stripped an occasional clothesline. In 1847, a battle broke out west of Port Jervis, on the Erie line, between Corkonian and Far Downer railroad workers. The Far Downers routed the Corkonians out of their camp and demanded that they be discharged, which indicates that labor troubles were at least partly responsible for the violence. The Corkonians lost their jobs and were beaten by fellow Irishmen in another engagement, whereupon the Far Downers, seeking new adventures, threw down the gauge of battle to a German crew which was working under an armed guard. The sheriff's deputies could not cope with the rioting, and peace was restored only by moving in a company of state militia, which remained on duty in the area for a month.[15]

In Pennsylvania, the Irish built the railroads which hauled coal from the mines in which many of their countrymen were employed. A fellow Irishman, touring the country to sell his "epic poem" on the history of Ireland, found they preferred "a quart of good Monongahela whiskey to all Homer's poetical inventions." [16] In 1839, a dollar a day was normal pay in Pennsylvania, and when railroad workers struck for an additional twelve and a half cents, many contractors simply increased the whiskey ration, which already was one and a half pints daily, distributed in nine installments. On the Connecticut Railroad, Irish laborers were paid seventy cents a day in 1848, and went on strike for an increase of fifteen cents.[17]

When the Illinois Central and other middle western railroads were built, contractors opened employment agencies in New York and offered high wages and free transportation to the job. Hundreds of posters were displayed in public places offering wages of $1.25 a day and promising good board for two dollars a week. The majority of the early labor gangs

---

[15] Stewart H. Holbrook, *The Story of American Railroads*, 56–59.

[16] Jeremiah O'Donovan, *A Brief Account of the Author's Interview with His Countrymen*, 87–88.

[17] Norman Ware, *The Industrial Worker, 1840–1860*, 68–70.

that built the Illinois Central Railroad were Irish, though in due time this company, like the Erie and the New York Central, preferred Germans, with whom the Irish were bitter competitors. Irish laborers were transported from New York to Chicago for $4.75. Life in the labor gangs was rough and turbulent; groggeries followed the Illinois Central to dispense cheap whiskey, which many Irishmen drank to make them immune to cholera. There was so much rioting on the Illinois Central that people spoke of "a murder a mile." The turnover in the labor force was rapid; farmers in the neighborhood complained about hard-drinking, brawling Irish railroad workers, and the company tried to bring in family men who were likely to be more stable and orderly and stay longer on the job. Many workers who laid the ties eventually took up railroad lands and settled down as successful farmers.[18]

In Iowa, Irishmen hauled freight between Iowa City and Des Moines before the railroad came and then helped build the road. An Irishman from county Clare had the contract to cut through the streets of Keokuk and build the yards for the Wabash Railroad.[19] The Chicago and North-western brought the Irish to Lisbon and Cedar Rapids, and in Davenport and Scott County, Irishmen built the railroad and many of the bridges.

In Wisconsin, Irish railroad laborers frequently worked in winter in the pineries and rafted lumber down the rivers. In Georgia, the Irish built the Western and Atlantic Railroad from Atlanta to Chattanooga, settled up and down the line, and helped operate and maintain the road. In the 1850's, young, physically fit Irishmen were recruited at Ward's Island to build a railroad across the Isthmus of Panama.[20]

The Union Pacific was built by Mexicans, Chinese, and Germans as well as Irish, but many miles of the road were laid down by Irish veterans of the Civil War, who worked with gun in hand to repel Indian attacks. It was the Irish on the Union Pacific who inspired one of America's folk songs—"Poor Paddy, He Works on the Railroad"— and provided the well-known stanza,

> Then drill, my Paddies, drill—
> Drill, my heroes, drill,
> Drill all day, no sugar in your tay
> Workin' on the U. P. railway.

[18] Paul W. Gates, *The Illinois Central Railroad and Its Colonization Work;* and Holbrook, *American Railroads,* 102–103.

[19] Sister Mary Helen Carey, "The Irish Element in Iowa up to 1865" (Master's thesis, Catholic University of America, 1944), 67–68.

[20] Thomas A. Emmet, *Incidents of My Life,* 145.

CHAPTER V

As Others Saw Them

THE testimony concerning the first-generation Irish, crowded into city tenements and slums during the last century, when the United States was experiencing its first major crisis in assimilation and acculturation, is confusing and contradictory, though clearly weighted toward the unfavorable. Most derogatory comment about the later, "new" immigration from southern and eastern Europe was made about the Irish a century ago. Obviously, there are Irish today who have not risen from the slums or shaken off the bad habits of a lifetime. There are thousands of others, the children and grandchildren of poor immigrant Irish, who took full advantage of every opportunity to rise to positions of influence, responsibility, and importance. Today the Irish are regarded among the most American of Americans, and some Irish-Americans, forgetful of the antagonisms with which their forefathers were confronted a century ago, now look with contempt upon later immigrants.

It is important, therefore, to describe life among first-generation Irish immigrants, in terms of how others saw them, in order to understand the difficulties they encountered upon their arrival in this country.

The very appearance of these Irish, as they were disgorged from immigrant ships in the eastern seaports, attracted the attention and the ridicule of native Americans. Many an Irishman stepped off the boat in a cape, high-waisted coat, knee breeches, wool stockings protruding from a rusty pair of shoes, and a brimless caubeen on his head.[1] Their brogue called attention to their speech, which, however vivid, was frequently the language of an illiterate. Many Irishmen were unduly noisy and bad-mannered. Instead of searching for a job immediately, they often waited too long for something to turn up, and thus depleted their meager reserves. Fastidious, sharp-tongued Brahmins like George Templeton Strong concluded: "Our Celtic fellow citizens are almost as remote from us in temperament and constitution as the Chinese."[2]

---

[1] Thomas B. Gunn, *The Physiology of New York Boarding Houses*, 263–69.
[2] Allan Nevins and Milton H. Thomas (eds.), *The Diary of George Templeton Strong*, II, 348. Hereafter cited as *Strong's Diary*.

There is abundant evidence that the majority of the Irish immigrants were ignorant and uneducated and poor managers, but even their severest critics admitted that these characteristics did not prove innate inferiority. Indeed, many testified to their sprightly talk, their unusually good natures, and their ability to learn. In comparing the Irish with the Germans, some observers found the former more excitable and less frugal and cautious, but equally industrious, and more witty, generous, and grateful. Theodore Parker, New England Unitarian Brahmin, believed that the Irish were "the worst people in Europe to make colonists of," but by 1880, the Boston *Transcript,* aware of their great contribution to New England's industrial transformation, invited more of them to come. Though the Irish lacked technical skill, they were not afraid to use their strong bodies in hard work which others shunned.

Irishmen were unusually gregarious and seemed to prefer contentiousness to loneliness. In the United States, they perpetuated the local loyalties of the old country in political and social clubs and Irish saloons. The family was the keystone of their life in America, and even in their worst moments, Irishmen showed great love for their homes and children. In contrast with the "cold, shrewd, frugal, correct, meeting-going Yankee," the Irishman was a "jolly, reckless, good-natured, passionate" Paddy. In the eyes of Yankee critics, he also was "priest-ridden, whiskey-loving and thriftless." [3] The Irishman, notoriously short on formal education and book learning, hated New England's Puritan "culture"; Puritanism was completely foreign to his nature.[4] McGee wrote slashing editorials about the "grotesque theology," "the narrowness of soul," and the gloominess of the New England Puritan, contrasting the Irish Saturday-night dances with the dreary, joyless Sundays of the sober, long-faced Yankees.[5]

The Boston *Pilot* and Brownson's *Review* castigated the Irish for their lack of cleanliness, and particularly for their disgraceful conduct at "Paddy funerals" and "Irish wakes." [6] There was always food, tobacco, and liquid refreshment in abundance on such occasions, and a solemn evening frequently ended with boisterous laughter, raucous jokes, and even fistic encounters. "Dry" wakes were unusually rare.

McGee, writing in the New York *Nation,* admitted that his countrymen had not been taught "fundamental cleanliness, sobriety, caution, perseverance, or the other minor details," and he thought them sadly

[3] See a journalist's comment of 1860 in Maurice R. Davie, *World Immigration,* 66.

[4] See *The Catholic Historical Review,* XII (1928), 360–61, for a quotation from the *New York Times* on this point.

[5] *Manchester Daily Mirror,* April 6, 1857, reported the arrest of two Irishmen for dancing on Sunday. See also Quirk, "The Irish Element in New Hampshire to 1865," 42.

[6] See *The Pilot* (Boston), May 6, July 1, August 26, 1854.

deficient in self-respect, steadfastness, discretion, and moral courage—and inferior in all these respects to Americans. He was particularly disturbed because the immigrants' children, taunted as "Paddies" in the public schools, were therefore eager to make the gulf between them and their parents as wide as possible.[7]

Many Irish were not suited by previous experience for city life, and it proved corrupting to their morals and their sense of independence. None spoke more devastatingly of the poverty and filth in which their fellow Catholics lived—in the damp, oozing cellars and unventilated garrets—than McGee, or Brownson, or the editors of Irish Catholic papers. Bishop John Hughes described the utter destitution of the Irish who arrived in New York in 1847 and 1848, the high rate of disease, the "awful mortality" among the adults, and "the consequent dereliction of their numerous offspring." He referred to "the dangerous and bad class" among them, "the scattered debris of the Irish nation," and favored stopping all immigration for at least a decade.[8] Bishop John Lancaster Spalding, who had been a priest in New York before going to Illinois, stated that "the descriptions by the sanitary inspectors of these habitations [slums] would soil a page intended for all eyes." He concluded that apparently people must drink in such an atmosphere, for "the perfectly sober would die from mere loathing of life."[9]

Such comments could hardly have been exaggerated when one realizes that there was no proper sewage or garbage disposal in the city slums at the time; that offal was simply dumped into the streets where it was left uncollected; that existing privies were old and decayed; and that there was no effective system of building inspection. Accidents and fires were numerous, and the stench from the kerosene stove—which was used almost continuously for cooking, heating, and ironing—grew almost unbearable as the oxygen was burned out of the air in the dark, overcrowded rooms. "Cat Alley" in New York housed the substratum of "Irish, of volcanic properties,"[10] and Five Points, with its delapidated old frame houses, teemed with "wild Irish" said to be "worse than savages" and "too mean to swab hell's kitchen."[11] On moving day, the inhabitants dumped the straw out of their beds into the street and burned it.

George Templeton Strong's descriptions of Irish shanties of "rotten

[7] Skelton, *The Life of Thomas D'Arcy McGee*, 170, 229–30.
[8] Henry J. Browne (ed.), "A Memoir of Archbishop Hughes, 1838–1858," United States Catholic Historical Society *Historical Records and Studies*, XXXIX–XL (1952), 164–68.
[9] Quoted in Theodore Maynard, *The Story of American Catholicism*, 452.
[10] Jacob A. Riis, *The Battle with the Slum*, Chapter XII.
[11] Tryon, *A Mirror for Americans*, I, 135–36.

boards and a piece of stove-pipe for chimney" sticking out like smallpox pustules in parts of New York, and of the dastardly activities of the "Dead Rabbit Club," the Bowery Boys, and the gun-fighting Irish "Five Pointers" were substantiated from sources far more friendly to the Irish than this crusty and snobbish New Yorker.[12] At the height of the Know-Nothing crusade, when the Irish were on the defensive everywhere, the New York Irish weekly *Citizen* referred to the "noisy, turbulent intolerant class" among the Irish, "who did no credit to the character of their native country, and were of little benefit to the land of their adoption."[13] McGee, who wrote a *History of Irish Settlers in North America* in 1855, frankly admitted that crossing the Atlantic worked no miracle upon the Irish, and that they remained the creatures of their own antecedents, "untrained to freedom," and "a poor figure, at first, as freemen." But he insisted they were very teachable if properly handled.[14]

It is well to recall James Bryce's comment that "New York was not an Eden before the Irish came; and would not become an Eden were they all to move on to San Francisco." The Britisher Philip H. Bagenal observed that the Irish were by no means the worst who lived in the human rookeries of the slums,[15] and as their places were taken eventually by Italians, Poles, and Jews, the results seem to have been equally bad.[16]

The reports about the female of the Irish immigration concern mostly servant girls, employed in domestic service by the thousands, and they are as contradictory as other appraisals of the Irish of a century ago. In 1850, in New York, girls received from four to seven dollars a month, plus board, for work as domestics. The top figure of seven dollars usually was paid only to those who were good cooks or laundresses. Girls "fresh out of the bogs" of Ireland, speaking only "Irish," and brought up in floorless mud cabins, without shoes and stockings even to go to Mass, had much to learn. The Wehle family in 1851 employed an Irish servant girl for $1.50 a week and claimed that she came downstairs backward because she always used a ladder in the old country.[17]

---

[12] Nevins and Thomas (eds.), *Strong's Diary*, II, 347–51; IV, 155.

[13] For similar comments about other cities whose Irish neighborhoods were described as "a perfect hive of human beings . . . huddled together like brutes, without regard to sex, or age, or sense of decency," see Abbott, *Historical Aspects*, 593–95.

[14] See also the *Boston Reporter*, quoted in Sister Mary Cecilia Paluszak, "The Opinion of the *Catholic Telegraph* on Contemporary Affairs and Politics" (Master's thesis, Catholic University of America, 1940), 18; and Mathew E. Hickey, "Irish Catholics in Washington up to 1860" (Master's thesis, Catholic University of America, 1933).

[15] See Abbott, *Historical Aspects*, 533.

[16] See also Oscar Handlin, *This Was America*, 210, 404.

[17] Josephine Goldmark, *Pilgrims of '48*, 232–33.

But even in this instance, the family testified that the girl was excellent in cleaning and scrubbing, though not as good in cooking or laundering. Harriet Martineau sympathized with American housewives who had to employ "low Irish" as servants.[18] More convincing, because they were the comments of an observer in excellent repute with the Church and a frequent contributor to Irish-American papers, were the observations of Dr. D. W. Cahill published in a letter in the *Metropolitan Record* of February 11, 1860. "Being the daughters of laborers, or needy tradesmen, or persecuted, rack-rented cotters," he pointed out, "they are ignorant of the common duties of servants in respectable positions. They can neither wash nor iron clothes. They don't understand the cleaning of glass or silver plate. They cannot make fires expeditiously, or dust carpets, or polish the furniture. Many of them never saw a leg of mutton boiled or roasted. Several of them cannot even prepare for their own dinner bacon or pork . . . ."

Advertisements in the city papers specifically asked for "Protestant girls" to do housework and, throughout the 1850's, there were many "Help Wanted" columns which carried the statement, "No Irish need apply." It is clear from such announcements that the prospective employer imposed no restrictions of either nativity or color—except on the Irish.

However, many Irish girls became permanent fixtures in good households, where they enjoyed a reputation for dependability, honest and faithful service, and an instinctive "Irish" good nature. Their ability to save was truly impressive, as measured by the generosity of their contributions to their Church, Irish relief, and their families in Ireland, and belied the common notion that all Irish were wasteful and unthrifty.

The health of the immigrant was another concern of many Americans. It was discouraging to discover that the health of the Irish did not conspicuously improve because they had moved to a more prosperous country. The rate of tuberculosis was much higher in the United States than in Ireland; the death rate from all causes was double that of Ireland and higher than for most immigrant groups. The statistics for immigrants hospitalized at Ward's Island showed a disproportionally high figure for the Irish until the close of the century. The rate of insanity was higher among the Irish than among most foreign-born, especially among young women; the high mortality rate among adults meant a disproportionate number of widows and orphans to be supported; and infant mortality was unusually high.

[18] Harriet Martineau, *Society in America*, II, 249.

Many factors contributed to this discouraging situation. First of all, many Irish immigrants arrived in a debilitated state, and, like the first generation of any immigrant group, generally received poor medical care. There were few Irish physicians, and newcomers were inclined to rely on home remedies, some of which were based on superstitions common to most folk medicine. Other factors were the bad air of the tenements, the change to bad eating habits, too heavy drinking, self-neglect, and poor nursing care in time of illness. In 1846, Theodore Parker spoke of "the perishing classes in Boston" and reported that he seldom saw a "gray-haired Irishman," inferring that they all died young.[19] The highest death rates generally appeared in those wards where housing conditions were the worst.

Equally disturbing was the disproportionate number of Irish in the almshouses, for this meant higher taxes for the property holder and heavy burdens on private charity. Even before 1845, of the 40,000 foreign-born paupers in New York, from one- to two-thirds were Irish. Many of the first generation were a financial liability in that they paid little or no taxes and made heavy demands on charity and public dispensaries. In the 1850's, the number of destitute Irish in the almshouses of New York City was out of all proportion. Half the needy in 1852 were German and Irish immigrants, with the Irish far in the lead.[20] From 1849 to 1891, the proportion of native Irish in the New York City Alms House was as high as 60 per cent, and dropped below that figure only twice during the period.[21] As late as 1906, the Irish had more paupers, beggars, and inmates of almshouses than the Italians.[22]

Statistics from 1834 to 1845 for the Irish in Boston's "House of Industry" show that the percentage of inmates born in Ireland rose from 28 per cent to 37 per cent during that period. On the other hand, although immigration was rising, the number of Irish inmates did not show a comparable increase. However, the Irish ratio always was well above that of the native-born.[23] A survey of 1,349 tramps interviewed in 1893 showed that among the foreign-born "knights of the road," the Irish led with 20 per cent.[24] As late as the turn of the last century, 60

[19] Henry R. Warfel, Ralph H. Gabriel, and Stanley T. Williams (eds.), *The American Mind*, 410.

[20] Ernst, *Immigrant Life*, 56.

[21] Florence E. Gibson, *The Attitudes of the New York Irish Toward State and National Affairs, 1848–1892*, 16–18.

[22] Philip Davis (ed.), *Immigration and Americanization*, 147.

[23] Darling, *Political Changes in Massachusetts*, 163–64.

[24] Arthur M. Schlesinger, *The Rise of the City, 1878–1898*, 118.

per cent of those who received poor relief or were admitted to the poor-house from the North End of Boston were immigrant or second-generation Irish.[25]

The Chicago *Post* of September 9, 1898, made the caustic observation, "Scratch a convict or a pauper, and the chances are that you tickle the skin of an Irish Catholic." [26] Nearly a dozen years earlier, the Chicago *Tribune* had made derisive references to "Erin, the soft, green isle of the ocean," which furnished so many Irish names for the police records of the city. According to the *Tribune,* Irish lawbreakers averaged twice the number of those from "almost any other inhabitable land on earth" and furnished the ringleaders of riots in nine cases out of ten.[27] In 1859, in New York, 55 per cent of all arrests made were Irish, as compared with 23 per cent for native Americans, 10 per cent for Germans, and 7 per cent for English and Scotch. In number of actual convictions in court, the Irish rated over five times as many as native Americans.[28]

Such figures were alarming to Americans who regarded Irish immigration with grave misgivings. The notion was widely held that the Irish were congenital criminals, and it became a habit to look for an Irishman in every case which involved a disturbance of the peace. Nevertheless, it is important to remember that criminal statistics for immigrants, and especially for the Irish, included many arrests for drunkenness, petty thievery, and disorderly conduct, or the involuntary violation of city ordinances, rather than more serious offenses. The crime rate for serious offenses among the city Irish was relatively low, and sex crimes were almost unknown.

The Irish also had a bad reputation for rioting, which gave rise to several popular sayings such as "The Irish are never at peace but when they're fighting," and "We boys is sociable with pavin' stones." Nearly every sizable American city in the 1840's and 1850's experienced a period of mob violence when enraged crowds mobbed theaters and actors whom they did not like, attacked newspaper offices, or demonstrated against Negroes, landlords, or Catholics. Rioting was not limited to the Irish. At election time, the anti-Irish rioted quite as easily as the Irish. A century ago, the police force of many cities was poor and not uniformed, and gangs infested many city streets. Membership was

[25] Robert A. Woods (ed.), *Americans in Process, a Settlement Survey North and West Ends, Boston,* 332–33.
[26] Quoted in Charles H. Coleman, *The Election of 1868,* 302.
[27] *Chicago Tribune,* December 23, 1853.
[28] Ernst, *Immigrant Life,* 58.

largely, but by no means wholly, Irish; not all gangs were equally vicious; and some were relatively harmless social clubs.[29]

Almost anything could set off a first-class riot. In 1806, for example, there was a bloody fight in New York when non-Catholics turned out to interrupt a Catholic Christmas service.[30] Twenty years later, Yankee cooper apprentices and Irish workmen rioted in Boston over a labor dispute.[31] The Irish played a prominent part in the famous Astor Place riots of 1849, resulting from the rivalry between the two actors Edwin Forrest and William Macready. Election-day riots occurred frequently in many cities. In these disturbances the Irish were victims as well as instigators. George Templeton Strong described one of these riots, in 1851, as "a battle of the peoples, like Leipzig," between "German loaferism" and "the gutterhorn soaplocks and shortboys of the wharves and their Irish allies." [32]

Many riots were traceable to religious causes. Finding an effigy of their patron saint on St. Patrick's day, hanging on a lamppost with a shamrock in his hat, a shillelagh in one hand, and a bottle in the other, had the expected effect.[33] When Orangemen paraded on the anniversary of the Battle of the Boyne, the result was the same. The majority of anti-Catholic riots before 1850 were not under Orange leadership, however, and Irish attacked the parades of Orangemen as readily as anti-Catholics struck at Irish "Papists." [34]

In 1853, the eviction of an Irishman from a circus tent in Somerset, Ohio, for refusing to put out his pipe led to a riot by Irish railroad laborers which had to be put down by the militia. In New York, in 1853, a stage driver drove through a gap in a Hibernian parade, probably because his horses were frightened by firecrackers, and a good-sized riot resulted. Strong was provoked by similar incidents, as late as 1870, to denounce the "execrable Catholic canaille," and to comment that "the

---

29 See Herbert Asbury, *The Gangs of New York,* 28–29.

30 Louis D. Scisco, *Political Nativism in New York State* (The Columbia University Studies, XIII, No. 2), 18.

31 Lord, Sexton, and Harrington, *History of the Archdiocese of Boston,* II, 202.

32 Nevins and Thomas (eds.), *Strong's Diary,* II, 48; I, 177–78. For other examples, see *The Citizen* (New York), November 18, 1854; New York *Tribune,* June 15, 1854; McMaster, *History of the People of the United States,* VIII, 298–99; Abbott, *Historical Aspects,* 627–28; and W. D. Overdyke, *The Know-Nothing Party in the South,* 25–26.

33 *The Irish News* (New York), April 21, 1860; see also *The Citizen* (New York), September 9, 1854.

34 See, for various incidents, Gibson, *The Attitudes of the New York Irish,* 245–50; John Francis Maguire, *The Irish in America,* 438; Emmet, *Incidents of My Life,* 256–58; and Gustavus Myers, *History of Bigotry in the United States,* 212–13.

gorilla is their superior in muscle and hardly their inferior in moral sense." [35] *The Citizen,* the *Irish-American, The Irish News,* and other papers reported riots and fights in which Irish were involved with sharp references to "semi-barbarians" who were a "disgrace to Ireland" and who brought discredit to the better class of Irishmen in America. *The Citizen* was equally incensed over the inane rivalry of fire companies, many of whose members were Irish, and joined the better Irishmen in rebuking the "noisy, intoxicated rowdies" who brought the whole Irish nation into disrepute.

Many of the Irishman's troubles and much of his unfavorable reputation were directly traceable to too great a devotion to the bottle. Irish leaders have recognized this fact and have been unusually severe in their criticisms of their countrymen. It was this common weakness, perhaps more than any other Irish characteristic, which produced the stereotype of the red-nosed, quarreling Irishman which has not yet been completely erased from the American mind.

The old-fashioned saloon was often referred to as "the poor man's club" and "the Nursery of Democracy." Even Bishop Spalding, who condemned the "whiskey pest" as "endemic," believed that the Irish, a kindhearted people who loved company in the misery of the great cities and factory towns, drank "to dull the sense of pain." [36] Perhaps it was Irish love of sociability that led so many to become saloonkeepers and bartenders. The percentage of Irish liquor dealers was high; the business required relatively little capital; customers were plentiful; and the saloon, in the early days, was an entree to politics. "Bottled goods" were sold in many Irish groceries.

As early as 1817, the Shamrock Society of New York warned Irish immigrants against the "pernicious habit" of drinking liquor and stressed its degrading effects. In the 1830's, Father Bernard O'Reilly was president of a Hibernian Temperance Society in Rochester, and other priests joined in combatting the drink-evil.[37] There was an Irish temperance society in Utica in 1831 and one in Boston in 1835 which appealed to all, regardless of politics or creed, who were ready to "snap the chains of the tyrant." Bishop Hughes supported the movement in New York.

In 1849, Father Theobald Mathew of county Tipperary came to the United States. Among the causes in which he had been interested in Ireland were workhouse reform and boys' and girls' industrial schools,

[35] Nevins and Thomas (eds.), *Strong's Diary,* IV, 295.

[36] J. L. Spalding, *The Religious Mission of the Irish People and Catholic Colonization,* 98.

[37] Frederick J. Zwierlein, *The Life and Letters of Bishop McQuaid,* I, 82; also Zwierlein, "Catholic Beginnings in the Diocese of Rochester," *The Catholic Historical Review,* I (1916), 291.

but he is best known for his fight upon "demon rum." By 1841, he claimed to have administered the pledge of the "teetotaller" to half of Ireland, though he made an exception for liquor used for medicinal purposes. On July 24, 1849, Father Mathew was given a public reception in Boston; he rode through the streets in a handsome barouche, was presented by the governor to a huge crowd on Boston Common, and the next day was officially received at City Hall. He spoke in Faneuil Hall, received high praise from William Ellery Channing, and had dinner with the President in the White House. For a short time, it looked as though Protestants and Catholics could unite in his great moral crusade.

Father Mathew soon encountered the opposition of influential members of the hierarchy, however, when he appeared on the same platform with Protestant ministers and entertained "sentiments too liberal toward Protestants in matters of religion." He was charged with forgetting that there was "but one true Church," and that its prayers and sacraments were more important than social reform.[38] Though Bishop Hughes entertained the crusader in New York, Bishop Francis Patrick Kenrick remained cold to his efforts, and Bishop John B. Fitzpatrick of Boston sharply attacked the Irish reformer for appearing at a meeting with "sectarian fanaticks, Calvinistic preachers and deacons and other such."[39] Bishop Rappé of Cleveland approved of Father Mathew. However, the latter continued to complain that "the Priests have interfered with my Teetotallers" and absolved them from the pledge by substituting something less rigid.[40]

Despite such discouraging experiences, Father Mathew persuaded thousands to sign his pledge. Six thousand responded in New Orleans alone. The temperance crusader probably traveled as much as 37,000 miles in the United States, and may have enlisted as many as a half million in the battle against the drink-evil. While he did not inaugurate the movement, his two-year tour of America gave tremendous impetus to the American Catholic and the American Irish temperance movement.

Father Mathew had to face powerful opposition from both German and Irish Catholics who resented any interference with their personal habits and who championed the Continental Sunday, which allowed open saloons on the Sabbath. Many Catholics questioned the wisdom

38 Sister Joan Bland, *Hibernian Crusade, the Story of the Catholic Total Abstinence Union of America*, 30–31. See also George F. Clark, *History of the Temperance Reform in Massachusetts, 1813–1883.*

39 Sister Bland, *Hibernian Crusade*, 38.

40 See also Hugh J. Nolan, *The Most Reverend Francis Patrick Kendrick, Third Bishop of Philadelphia, 1830–1851*, 411; Theodore Roemer, *The Catholic Church in the United States*, 221; and J. G. Shea, *History of the Catholic Church in the United States*, IV, 187.

of fraternizing with reform groups, some of which had a reputation for radicalism. Nevertheless, many Hibernian temperance societies sprang up in the wake of Father Mathew's tour. They not only were concerned with the drink-evil, but opened reading rooms and libraries, social halls, gymnasiums, game rooms, and bowling alleys, and actively interested themselves in raising the social and cultural level of Irish immigrants. Such temperance societies received high praise from papers like the Philadelphia *Catholic Herald* and the Boston *Pilot,* which expressed the hope that their pleasant reading rooms and coffee bars might eventually displace the tavern. Henry Clay credited Father Mathew with having achieved a social revolution. *The Irish News* praised the Irish crusader for his "gentle, benign, saintly labors" and suggested that Irish-Americans raise a monument to him. In Cleveland, Irish teetotallers sang "Dare to be a Murphy" and the "Murphy Hymn," an appeal to join in the great crusade, which ended with the lines,

> And the Jubilee of Freedom
> To the slaves of Rum proclaim,
> The Murphy Boys are marching on.

The Hibernian crusade against liquor was revived in later years, and the story has been well told, in detail, in Sister Joan Bland's study. In its later manifestations, it was definitely and uncompromisingly Catholic, with emphasis on prayer, sacraments, and supernatural help, and there was to be no fraternization with temperance movements in which Protestants were prominent. It was frankly stated that one reason for reviving the movement was to make Catholics socially more acceptable and to dispel the bad reputation Irish Catholics had for drinking. "We are known as a religion of saloonkeepers," said the bishops of Cleveland and Peoria, "of men who drink and men who provide the means of drinking." [41]

The national convention of the Catholic Total Abstinence Union of America held in Philadelphia in 1872 had a representation from 207 societies. Sentiment was sharply divided about the program to be followed. Some did not believe in moral suasion, but instead wanted political action. Some advocated high license fees or prohibition; others regarded prohibition as sheer fanaticism. The organization published its own papers, songbooks, and propaganda pamphlets, sponsored lectures, and probably reached the floodtide of its effectiveness in 1893 to 1895. It refused to co-operate with the Anti-Saloon League and continued to encounter opposition among Irish and Germans, some of whom regarded

---

[41] Sister Bland, *Hibernian Crusade,* 127.

"the temperance swindle as an outflow of Puritan bigotry." James McMaster's *Freeman's Journal,* an influential New York Catholic paper, opposed all legislation dealing with personal habits. Only a minority of the membership advocated prohibition, but it included such distinguished leaders as Archbishop Ireland. He called upon his Church to speak out against the saloon and to exclude liquor dealers from membership in Catholic societies. In his opinion, a "tidal wave of abstinence" was vital "for the future of Irishmen in America." [42] Cardinal Gibbons agreed with the majority in opposing drastic measures.

The indictment against the Irish for intemperance and close affiliation with the saloon business continued into the present century. Yet parallel to the charges against the Irish for improvidence, self-neglect, and drinking runs an amazing record of thrift, as revealed by the remittances sent each year to Ireland.

The Irish were not "birds of passage," waiting eagerly for the moment when they might return to their native land with their pockets full of American dollars. Instead, they sent money home to bring more of their people to the United States. Remittances to Ireland were £200,000 in 1847, £439,000 in 1853, and £2,000,000 by 1863. An estimate for the period from 1848 to 1864 indicates that the Irish sent home $65,000,000 during those years. Obviously, some were sending more than they could afford.[43]

Meetings for Irish relief produced generous contributions, and remittances to Ireland were especially heavy at Easter and Christmastime. Most of the money came from Irish laborers and servant girls and represented gifts, not loans. In 1851, the Emigrant Industrial Savings Bank of New York was chartered as the result of the efforts of the Irish Emigrant Society, and the accounts of its original 2,300 depositors averaged $238.56.[44] In the next thirty years, this bank alone sent $30,000,000 in remittances to Ireland, and there were other Hibernian banks in New Orleans, Chicago, San Francisco, and elsewhere. The Irish also organized building and loan associations to help them acquire homes, although they were not as active in this field of banking as the Germans. In their charities, they were surpassed only by the Jews, and though their interests were often extremely parochial, their response to appeals for aid was generous. Many an Irish workman or domestic regularly laid fifty cents or a dollar each month "on the altar of their country."

42 John Ireland, "The Catholic Church and the Saloon," *The North American Review,* CLIII (October, 1894), 498–505.

43 See Adams, *Ireland and Irish Emigration,* 392; *Catholic Encyclopedia,* VIII, 144; and Pomfret, *The Struggle for Land in Ireland,* 40–41.

44 Ernst, *Immigrant Life,* 133.

Chapter VI

Militia, Firemen, and Policemen

THERE are special reasons why immigrants join various organizations in a "nation of joiners," for in a strange land where they are as yet unassimilated to the culture pattern of the majority, organizations to promote social intercourse and keep alive the memories of a common fatherland fulfill a deep emotional need. This was one reason why, before the Civil War, practically every immigrant group had its militia companies. Because the foreign-born were not welcome in the military organizations of native Americans, they had no choice but to form their own. The Irish loved uniforms, parades, and ceremonial and convivial occasions. Some of their leaders urged them to revive the military spirit of their ancient fighting ancestors, for they believed the development of militia companies in the United States would go far toward eliminating the factional rivalries that divided the Irish element.

Every foreign-born group of any consequence in America's larger cities had its own militia companies before 1860. In 1853, the Irish militia of New York numbered 2,600 men; the German, 1,700; and in addition, there were smaller units from other nationality groups, including the "Scotch-Irish" Highland Guards, Scottish Guards, and Caledonian Fusileers. Irish units had various names—Jasper Greens, Hibernia Greens, Napper Tandy Light Artillery, Emmet Guards, Irish Rifles, Irish-American Guards, and Mitchel Light Guards. Irishmen had great pride in their outfits and arrayed themselves in brilliant uniforms. The Citizen Guard, devoted to John Mitchel, the Irish exile of 1848, and convinced that its ultimate purpose was the liberation of Ireland, paraded in black frock coats and pantaloons, white belts and continental hats ornamented with a tri-color rosette and plume. New York's Napper Tandy Light Artillery perpetuated the name of James Napper Tandy, the United Irishman and Dublin merchant who became a famous revolutionist in 1798, and whose career has been celebrated ever since in a ballad with the lines, loved by all Irishmen:

O! I met with Napper Tandy
And he took me by the hand.
And he said, "How's poor Ireland,
And how does she stand." [1]

Organized in New York in 1851, the Napper Tandy's roster of officers included such typical Irish names as Fay, Flynn, and Rooney. The company decked itself out in green jackets with yellow braid, light blue pantaloons with scarlet stripes, and blue caps with yellow bands and tassels. In 1854, they transported their cannon to Coney Island for their first annual target excursion. They fired the salutes for John Mitchel and Louis Kossuth when these rebels of 1848 arrived in the United States.

The Montgomery Guards dated from 1836, when the New York Cadets excluded all foreign-born from their ranks and forced the Irish to create their own organization. By the 1850's, they were part of the regular New York militia, but they still wore their distinctive uniforms —light green coats, white shoulder knots with green crescents, dark trousers, and bearskin caps. The Emmet Guards, formed in 1846, preferred blue uniforms and wore brass breastplates with the insignia "Hands of Friendship." [2] The first Irish regiment in the United States seems to have been the Ninth New York State Militia. It was formed in 1850, and included about seven hundred men, the Irish Dragons, Guyon Cadets, Felon Guards, Carroll Light Guard, Erina Guard, Saarsfield Guard, and some other units.[3]

Providence, Rhode Island, had an Irish organization of 179 men in 1855. In Bangor, Maine's Gratton Guards carried a flag with a likeness of George Washington on one side and the harp of Ireland on the other. Other Irish units were scattered throughout New England. One reason for their dissolution during the Know-Nothing excitement of the 1850's, when Governor Gardner of Massachusetts stripped them of their arms, was the fact that they frequently enrolled unnaturalized immigrants. Chicago had its Shield's Guard, in honor of an Irish hero of the Mexican War; Charleston, South Carolina, its Irish Volunteers; and Philadelphia, the Hibernia Greens. In Milwaukee, the Montgomery Guard and the City Guards were Irish units.[4] The most arduous duties

---

[1] See Margaret J. McCormack, "I Met with Napper Tandy," *Journal of the American Irish Historical Society*, XXIX (1930–31), 132–40.

[2] *The Irish News* (New York), April 12, 1856.

[3] Ernst, *Immigrant Life*, 128.

[4] See further, *The Citizen* (New York), July 8, December 9, 1854; August 4, September 15, September 29, 1855; *The Irish News* (New York), January 2, 1858; and William H. Bennett, "Some Pre-Civil War Irish Militiamen of Brooklyn, New York," *Journal of the American Irish Historical Society*, XXI (1922), 172–80.

of these companies seem to have been a drill once or twice a week, under officers whom they themselves elected and who, therefore, could not be too demanding. Other responsibilities included turning out for parades on March 17 or July 4, firing salutes on special occasions, participating in "soirees," attending gaudy military balls, listening to speeches, and going on picnics and excursions.

Militia day in old New England towns was largely an occasion for crowds on the village green to drink sweet cider or rum, for peddlers to hawk their wares, pretty girls to ogle their martial heroes, and officers of the company to indulge in spread-eagle oratory. If this was so in staid New England, one need not be surprised to find that the social program of Irish militia companies generally overshadowed more serious martial business. The ballroom proved more inviting than the drill ground; and at banquets, toasts were drunk by the dozens. When one company visited another in a neighboring city, as was standard procedure, hospitalities were even more lavish, and little serious business interfered with the conviviality of such occasions. In 1855, the Montgomery Guards of New York were seriously embarrassed on a visit to the St. Patrick's Society of Montreal when they found themselves unexpectedly involved in singing "God Save the Queen" and rising to a toast to Her Majesty.[5]

Irish military companies were conspicuous in Fourth of July and St. Patrick's Day parades, but they also marched on other occasions on the slightest provocation. In 1854, there was a big military parade in New York for the funeral of James McGrath, a police-court judge who had been captain of the Emmet Guards. The sociable soldiers marched periodically to target practice and made the occasion a joyful excursion. Soldiering was not too serious a business in peacetime. Still, despite the Irishman's disapproval of the Lincoln administration, when the Civil War came, whole companies of Irish militia enlisted, and some made notable records of courage and heroism on the battlefield.

If it was exciting for an Irishman to be a soldier, to be a "fire laddy" in a volunteer company was the epitome of delight. To this day, Irish make up a large part of America's fire-fighting forces. An instinctive love of excitement and danger, as well as the more prosaic reason of finding quick security in a civil service job, help explain the eagerness with which Irish have enlisted in American fire and police departments.

Even in the largest cities, fire fighting was left to volunteers until the time of the Civil War. Each firehouse had a volunteer company, and

[5] *The Citizen* (New York), September 22, 1855.

rival companies raced each other to the one fireplug in the neighborhood, while the best fighters were sent ahead to seize and hold the hydrant or cistern until their company arrived. While men brawled and fought, sometimes with knives and guns, the building might burn to the ground. "Running with the machine" was a favorite pastime for hoodlums in New York, Philadelphia, and elsewhere, and their presence and brawling at a fire made the work of the firemen still harder. Several cities were the scenes of pitched battles when "runners" and firemen fought with stones and pistols and hammered each other with firemen's trumpets.

The tradition of volunteer fire companies goes back to a period long before the Irish took over. The early fire companies of New York included Roosevelts, Stuyvesants, DePeysters, Beckmans, Irvings, and other representatives of the best families. By 1828, the firemen of New York were incorporated under a board of trustees to distribute relief to widows and orphans of firemen, aid disabled fire fighters to send their children to school, and carry out the functions of a voluntary pension fund which received occasional aid from the Common Council.[6] By the 1840's, the Irish controlled many volunteer companies. They wore brilliant uniforms and carried ponderous equipment. Their engines, or "machines," were beautiful creations with highly polished brass trimmings and painted decorations. Being a fireman combined opportunities for social activity at the station houses with a chance for excitement, fame, and performance of unusual feats. The life of a fireman was a curious combination of the heroic and the ludicrous. Stewards were attached to each volunteer company to ladle out liquor from a barrel hauled to each fire for the revival of exhausted firemen. Hard drinking was part of the fireman's life, although in the 1840's whole companies took the pledge in a temperance crusade in New York and accepted beautiful silk banners as rewards for a totally unexpected, albeit temporary, change in habits. Gambling flourished at some of the firehouses, and each company had its favorite rendezvous in a neighborhood saloon, frequently operated by an Irishman.[7]

Like militiamen, volunteer firemen staged brilliant parades on national holidays and other occasions. In New York, they marched in 1825 to mark the completion of the Erie Canal; in 1842, to celebrate the introduction of Croton water; and in 1858, to mark the laying of the first Atlantic cable. Each company usually had its own band and an animal

6 Augustine E. Costello, Our Firemen: A History of the New York Fire Departments, 88.

7 J. Frank Kernan, Reminiscences of the Old Fire Laddies and Volunteer Fire Departments of New York and Brooklyn, 34.

as a mascot. A dog usually was attached to each station house and ran
with the men to every fire. The engines were decorated with ribbons,
flags, flowers, and streamers, and trumpets and hose reels were gaily
festooned. William H. Philip, a portrait painter who joined the New
York department in 1850, decorated the panels of hose carriages with
such scenes as "The Battle of Bunker Hill" and "Washington at the
Battle of Monmouth." The firemen marched in dark pantaloons, boots,
leather belts, red flannel shirts, and firemen's helmets.

When the alarm sounded, the company set off for the fire at breakneck
speed, with a man with a trumpet leading the way and shouting orders
to his men. Competition began immediately upon arrival at the scene
of conflagration to see which company could throw the highest stream
of water. Pumping the engine was still done by hand, so the rivalry
sometimes reached the point where the hose was burst by pressure or
deliberately cut by rival firemen and their runners. The crowd stood by
and cheered their favorites, while the foreman shouted orders in an effort
to make himself heard above the din. Young men who appeared in fireman's garb, but had no connection with the company, only added to the
confusion. False alarms were turned in just to see the men race through
the streets with their apparatus.

The volunteers specialized in balls and entertainments, usually gala
affairs to raise money for the firemen's benefit fund. In New York, they
were held at Niblo's Garden, the Academy of Music, or the Astor Place
Opera House. Each company usually recruited an outstanding singer to
entertain the men at the station house, direct them in chorus singing, and
perform at famous chowder parties to which politicians were regularly
invited. Among the fire laddies' favorite songs were "Red Robbin" and
"The Angel's Whisper." Another favorite, "The Clasped Hands of the
Fire Brigade," stressed a fireman's devotion to duty:

> They came from the altar to face the flame,
> From prayers to fight the fire;
> And the flame which burns but never binds,
> Was a bond to draw them nigher.[8]

Daniel Collins of New York was famous for his rendition of "The Bells
of Shandon" and "Dear Irish Boy," which he sang at fires and at banquets in the station house. Denis Slattery was called on again and again
to sing his favorite:

> Oh, steer my bark to Erin's Isle,
> For Erin, Erin is my Home.

8 Costello, *Our Firemen,* 173.

Though not all firemen were Irishmen, the Irish volunteer fireman
became a favorite stage character. Any play which featured "Mose the
Fireman" could be counted on to fill any East Side theater in New York.
The leading character was "one of the b'hoys," "fightin' Mose," and he
was made up as a typical Irishman. He chewed and spit tobacco like
a virtuoso, and he was "boilin' over for a rousin' good fight," but he was
a loyal, courageous fire fighter, and a hero who could outrun all others
with the machine. Playwrights produced a whole series of plays, such
as *Mose and Jakey in Philadelphia,* featuring Irish lads of the Bowery
type; and Mose the fireman did not disappear from the stage until the
middle of the 1850's. By that time, the full-blown stage Irishman of the
purely urban type, who was as much a stereotype as Mose had been, was
ready to take his place.

What has been written about New York could be repeated for Baltimore, Philadelphia, Boston, and other cities. Fire fighting remained
under the almost exclusive control of volunteers until the Civil War. It
was a mixture of grim, hazardous business, with much drinking, brawling, and a plethora of social festivities. There was a close link between
fire companies and local politicians, and they generally frequented the
same saloons and clubs. It was to the advantage of aspirants for local
offices to cultivate the fire laddies. Boss Tweed, for example, though not
an Irishman, belonged to several fire companies and used them as step-
pingstones to become the most powerful figure, for a time, in New York
politics. The list of "old fire laddies" before the Civil War not only
abounds in Irish names, but also includes many who rose from fire
fighting to become aldermen, assemblymen, police judges, sheriffs, and
police chiefs, or who held other elective and appointive offices within the
gift of the party organization.

The solution of the fire-fighting problem was the creation of paid,
full-time, professional firemen. Cincinnati led the way in 1853, and, by
the 1860's, Boston, St. Louis, and Baltimore had followed Cincinnati's
lead. In 1865, the New York legislature passed the necessary permissive
legislation to establish a paid department for New York City and to get
rid, to quote one critic, of the four thousand "irresponsible and badly
organized men" who became "the destroyers instead of the savers of
property." A metropolitan fire department was organized in New York
City in 1865 after bitter protests from the volunteer firemen and those
who derived political benefits from the old system. Many members
threatened to resign rather than wear the city's "livery," and signs were
hung on station houses which read "Closed for Repairs" or "Gone to
Meet the Angels." Editorials in Irish papers such as *The Citizen, The*

Irish News, and the *Metropolitan Record and New York Vindicator* argued vigorously for the retention of the volunteer system and stressed its many virtues. They objected to further centralization, believed the new proposal would increase politics in the fire department, and argued that it was gross ingratitude to repay volunteers for their heroic deeds by abolishing the organizations they loved. Some believed the change was un-American and violated the spirit of "American institutions." The Boston *Pilot,* however, predicted that fire fighting and fire prevention ultimately would be paid for by local governments and administered as a branch of the police.

As soon as paid departments superseded the volunteer companies, new regulations were issued which prohibited racing to fires, using indecent and profane language, bringing liquor into the station houses, and visiting saloons while in uniform. The first report of the fire commissioners of New York City after the new department began to function pointed out that "noise and confusion in our streets on the occasions of alarms of fire have ceased; the sick and dying are no longer disturbed by the yelling of 'runners,' the machinery is drawn quietly to the scene of duty . . . racing and fighting between companies is unknown and the city police are relieved." [9] The report added that the effect upon the youth of the city had been most beneficial. In Baltimore, there was a notable decrease in the number of fires after the volunteer system was abolished in 1858.

Thus came to an end one of the most picturesque institutions of nineteenth-century America, an institution in which men who craved excitement found an opportunity for rowdyism and manliness, rioting and self-sacrifice, needless destruction of property and great heroism. If the second-generation Irish are included, any list of firemen, both under the volunteer and the paid system, would contain many Irish names. Other nationality groups were represented in the larger cities, including a few volunteer Negro firemen in New York, but the Irish were sufficiently numerous to impress upon the whole institution, in the popular mind, so-called "Irish" characteristics. The last New York volunteer company, the Hibernians, organized in 1860, consisted of Irish. In San Francisco, in the 1870's, the fire department was nearly nine-tenths Irish.[10] The Irish continue to supply the departments in many cities with both firemen and officers, and their names appear frequently on local honor rolls. In 1911, for example, of the twenty-two medals pre-

[9] *Ibid.,* 834–35.
[10] Quigley, *The Irish Race in California,* 276–77.

sented to members of the New York department for deeds of valor, eighteen went to men of Irish birth or parentage.[11]

The evolution of an adequate, competent, and dependable police force for the American city has been a slow and painful process which has not yet been completed. It involved unfortunate connections with local politics, the boss, the machine, and favored retainers. For a long time, American policemen did not wear distinctive garb which would make their identification easy and running away from a disturbance difficult. City policemen were not forced to get uniforms until the middle of the last century. Many protested the innovation, which they regarded as an insult to their independence and self-respect as good Americans. A policeman's pay remained low, and continues to limit the number of good prospects for this important public service. In the long story of the evolution of the modern police system, the Irishman, for good and ill, has played such an important part that the Irish policeman remains a fixture in theater, radio, and television.

As early as 1815, New York had a marshal of police named John McManus. By 1848, the local police force included many Irish, and the proportions continued to grow. In 1851, the appointment of a Roman Catholic, Bernard McGinniskin, to the Boston force created something of a sensation. Today, many of the officers, as well as the rank and file of Boston's metropolitan police force, are Irish. New York's police captains in 1856 included John D. McKee, Michael Halpin, and Thomas Hannagan. During the draft riots of 1863, John A. Kennedy, first superintendent of Castle Garden, was superintendent of the police force. It was not until 1859 that a literacy test and American citizenship were made requirements for the New York department. In the 1850's, as well as later, applicants for a place on the force were expected to pay police captains for their jobs and to make a substantial contribution to the aldermen who appointed them. In this vicious system, Irishmen frequently functioned both in the giving and receiving of the sums fixed as standard procedure.[12]

By the 1870's, in the larger departments, the Irish still constituted the rank and file, although the higher officers were often selected from the American-born. However, there were notable exceptions in New York and other large cities.[13] Thomas F. Byrnes, a native Irishman of

---

11 "Irish Fire-Fighters Honored," *Journal of the American Irish Historical Society*, X (1910–11), 337–38.

12 Gustavus Myers, *The History of Tammany Hall*, 202.

13 See Augustine E. Costello, *Our Police Protectors, History of the New York Police*.

meager education and a former gas fitter, became nationally known as New York's "Inspector Byrnes." He solved some famous cases and wrote a book entitled *Professional Criminals of America*. Although never convicted of any personal misdemeanor, he was under investigation when he retired as chief of police in 1895.[14] He was succeeded temporarily by Peter Conlin, stepbrother of the well-known Irish character actor, W. J. Florence. St. Clair A. Mulholland, a Roman Catholic, was chief of police of New York in 1868; and Michael Kerwin, a Civil War veteran and Irish Fenian, was police commissioner. Mrs. Ellen A. O'Grady, a native of Ireland residing in Brooklyn, probably was the first woman in the United States to be made a deputy commissioner. She received her appointment from Mayor Hylan of New York in 1918.[15] Police chiefs were generally removed with changes in the city administrations. Because of their long affiliation with the party, Irish chiefs always fared better under the Democrats.

In New Orleans, in the decade preceding the Civil War, Irish policemen far outnumbered all others in a police force which was largely recruited among the foreign-born elements in the city. In San Francisco, about one-third of the policemen in the late 1870's had Irish names. In 1888, while only 16.4 per cent of the population of New York was Irish, that element furnished 28 per cent of the city's policemen.[16] The rolls of honor of our city police always have contained the names of many Irish patrolmen who were cited for acts of courage and heroism. Irish names also have appeared among those who occasionally betrayed the public trust and yielded to the many temptations to which police are exposed.

The New York Police Academy no longer is monopolized by the Irish, and the same is true in Cleveland, Detroit, Chicago, and other cities. Today, police departments and training schools include Italians, Poles, Jews, Swedes, and representatives of other nationalities. Occasionally, there have been nationality clashes in local police departments. A study of the New York department made twenty years ago revealed that of about 20,000 men, 2,309 were foreign-born and 11,014 were of foreign-born parentage, representing forty-two countries in all. The Irish still were far in the lead, with 1,533 native Irishmen on the force, and 5,671 born in the United States of Irish parentage.[17] Two thousand

---

[14] Allen Johnson and Dumas Malone (eds.), *Dictionary of American Biography*. Hereafter referred to as *DAB*.

[15] Mary C. Dolin, "American Irish Women 'Firsts,' " *Journal of American Irish Historical Society*, XXIV (1925), 219.

[16] See Allan Nevins, *Abram S. Hewitt*, 514.

[17] *New York Times*, December 21, 1933.

of New York's Irish policemen belong to the Emerald Society of the department, which was organized for the preservation of "Gaelic culture." It is obvious from the statistics that although the policeman's life may not always be a happy one, for the Irish it continues to hold many attractions.

CHAPTER VII

The Irish as Farmers

THE Irish immigrant was primarily a phenomenon of the development of urban life in the United States. The number who took up farming as a means of livelihood always remained low, probably in the neighborhood of 10 per cent. The proportion is small, particularly when compared with German or Scandinavian immigrants. In the period from 1870 to 1890 in several of the newer states of the upper Mississippi Valley, we find that one out of every four Scandinavians engaged in farming, one out of every six Germans, but only one out of every twelve Irish.

The nineteenth-century Irish immigrant was not a frontiersman by instinct or choice. The Celt loved people; he wanted to be near his Church and enjoy the pleasures of companionship. He hated great distances and was afraid of the lonely prairie, where there were neither neighbors, villages, or churches. An Irish farmer, who had done well in Missouri and was duly appreciative of the democracy of American society, wrote home in 1821 to say how much he yearned for his native Ireland: "I could then go to a fair, or a wake, or a dance . . . I could spend the winter's nights in a neighbor's house cracking jokes by the turf fire. If I had there but a sore head I would have a neighbor within every hundred yards of me that would run to see me. But here everyone can get so much land . . . that they calls them neighbors that live two or three miles off." [1] Many Irishmen, if they thought of the West at all, were likely to think of it in terms of Indians, tomahawks, ague, and fever.

Even the Irish peasant and agricultural laborer knew practically nothing of the farming methods of the United States, for he had never seen many of the agricultural implements in use here. Moreover, the memories of his experiences on his native soil were such that he had no desire to repeat them. Many Irish immigrants were town laborers. They arrived poor or penniless, and although only eight or nine dollars were needed for the journey from New York to Wisconsin in 1850, including food, most Irish were too poor to leave the port where their

[1] Quoted from *Belfast News Letter,* in Adams, *Ireland and Irish Emigration,* 342.

ship landed. They needed jobs that would yield cash immediately, and even low city wages seemed good in comparison with their earnings in Ireland. The Irishman found the city more attractive and secure than the farm. A gregarious, warmhearted individual, he was loath to exchange its sociability for the loneliness of the prairie. Since the high tide of Irish immigration coincided with the peak of the Know-Nothing movement against foreigners in the United States, it undoubtedly united the Irish of the cities even more closely.

The Irish who distributed themselves on farms from coast to coast were a minor element in the total Irish immigration. Some were able to buy land for a dollar an acre or less. Others worked for their neighbors by the day. Some took service for several years with American farmers in order to learn the business and acquire the necessary funds to buy a farm. The Irish farmer had a reputation for being more wasteful, but also more generous, than other foreigners. Since he was eager to be with people, he responded gladly to pleas for help from his neighbors.

Some Irish-American leaders quickly realized that it would be good for their countrymen to leave the crowded cities, but their appeals to go west were only moderately successful. The New York *Shamrock,* on March 16, 1811, offered a free booklet to those who wanted to buy land and announced that its staff would serve without commission in helping prospective Irish farmers take up land in the interior. In 1817, the Irish Emigrant Society of New York petitioned Congress to set aside public lands in Illinois to which the Irish might repair before "the tempter . . . presents to their lips the cup that turns man to brute, and the very energies which would have made the fields to blossom make the city groan." Similar petitions came from Baltimore and Philadelphia, bearing the signatures of eminent Irishmen like Thomas A. Emmet, Mathew Carey, Luke Tiernan, and Dr. William J. Macneven. They asked Congress to sell land, on fourteen years' credit, to deserving Irishmen, who would serve as a frontier guard against wild Indians. After four hours of debate, the House of Representatives, by a vote of eighty-three to seventy-one, turned down the request—probably with serious consequences for the future of the Irish in America. Opposition to the measure came largely from southern members.[2]

In the 1840's, the Irish Emigrant Aid Society of New York indicated that £5 would enable an immigrant to make the journey from a seaport to good farming country. Immigrant guidebooks advised Irishmen to get out of the eastern cities.[3] Societies were organized in New York and

[2] *Niles' National Register,* XIV (May 23, 1818), 211–15.
[3] See Stephan Byrne, *Irish Emigration to the United States.*

Boston in the 1850's to speed the Irish westward, where the poorest immigrant could acquire forty or eighty acres, pay for it in labor, and become independent.[4] Thomas Mooney advised the Irish to set their faces "towards the setting sun" and work their way as they traveled westward.[5] The New York *Citizen* urged that the advantages of homestead legislation not be restricted to citizens of the United States. *The Irish News* advised Irishmen to go west, but cautioned them against Canada, "the American Siberia," where everything was inferior to the United States and the country filled with Orangemen.[6]

The canal- and railroad-building projects already described proved more effective than the printed page in giving thousands of Irish their first glimpse of rural America. Western states eagerly promoted immigration, and railroad and canal companies had cheap lands to sell. A novelist forecast a new Ireland which would "plant all the joys of an old Land amidst the bright scenes of the New."[7] Many of the Middle West's Irish farmers were laborers on canal and railroad gangs who stayed on when their jobs were finished. Illustrative of this fact were the Irish settlements along the Erie and Lackawanna Railroad, the Little Rock and Fort Smith Railroad, the Erie Canal, and the Illinois and Michigan Canal. Along the latter, Irishmen bought land with the script in which they were paid and which they could unload at face value for land.[8]

In New York State, James McBride and Nicholas Devereaux advertised 100,000 acres in the Genessee region, which they hoped to settle with Germans and Irish. Michael Hogan of county Clare bought 10,000 acres in Franklin County to sell to the city Irish of New York.[9] A hundred Irish farming families settled in the Niagara River Valley in the 1860's; and there were small, but successful, Irish colonies in Susquehanna County, Pennsylvania, and in northeastern Pennsylvania before 1850.[10] In eastern Massachusetts, Irish began to take the places of the sons of native farmers who had departed for the West.

In Ohio, although never in a majority, Irish farmers were widely scattered through the rural areas by 1870. In the 1850's, there was a farming area around Detroit, still known as the "Irish Hills," which was

[4] *The Irish News* (New York), July 5, 1856; *The Citizen* (New York), February 18, 1854; February 3, August 4, 1855; *Freeman's Journal* (New York), March 1, 1856.

[5] Mooney, *Nine Years in America*, 39.

[6] *The Irish News* (New York), June 20, 1857.

[7] Dorothy A. Dondore, *The Prairie and the Making of Middle America: Four Centuries of Description*, 248.

[8] See Gates, *The Illinois Central*, 89.

[9] Flick (ed.), *History of New York*, VII, 38–39.

[10] *Studies*, XXVII (1938), 589.

developed by Irishmen direct from Ireland.[11] An immigrant society in Vincennes, Indiana, advertised in the New York *Freeman's Journal* in 1842 urging Irish settlers to come to an area which was predominantly Catholic. In Illinois, every rural county had Irish farmers by 1870. In Henry County, Irish farmers supported three Catholic churches. Vinegar Hill, Illinois, named after a famous site in county Wexford, Ireland, was developed by Irish laborers in the lead mines. The Boston *Pilot* circulated among Irish farmers in Iowa. Irish farmers came regularly to Mass at the Trappist Monastery near Dubuque. Bishop Mathias Loras wrote to Irish and Catholic papers in the East to attract more Irish to Iowa. The town of Garryowen was settled largely by immigrants from Cork and Limerick.[12] Minnesota's little Irish agricultural islands were sandwiched in among the Scandinavians. By 1860, the state had an Irish population of 12,831—evidence that at least some Irishmen did not abhor the frontier.

Irish immigration to Wisconsin began with lead mining in the southwestern portion of the state. By 1829, there was a Dublin in Wisconsin. In 1866, an Irish Emigrant Aid Society was organized in Madison to bring in unemployed laborers of eastern cities and natives from Ireland. This state also advertised in eight foreign newspapers, including the *Tipperary Free Press,* and promised Irishmen "a tranquil and happy home." Place names such as Emmet, Shields, and Erin testify to the importance of the Irish element. Ozaukee County had eight hundred Irish farmers by 1850. Erin, in Washington County, was 83 per cent Irish. Census returns for 1850 listed 4,400 Irish-born farmers in Wisconsin; ten years later, there were nearly 13,000 Irish engaged in agriculture.[13] The Irish in Wisconsin, in contrast with German and Scandinavian farmers in that state, were likely to buy and sell several times before settling down permanently. Moreover, while others preferred wooded areas despite the hardship of clearing the land, the Irish chose sections where the clearing process would be less difficult.

Although the South was relatively unattractive to immigrants, Missouri contained several prosperous Irish farming communities. By 1850, there were about fifty Irish families engaged in agriculture in Taliaferro County, Georgia, and considerably more in several sections of South Carolina. In 1829, Mexico offered inducements to Irish colonists, and

---

[11] George Fare, *The Catholic Church in Detroit, 1701–1888,* 502.

[12] Ella Lonn, *Foreigners in the Union Army and Navy,* 14–17; and Sister Carey, "The Irish Element in Iowa," 44–46.

[13] See Sister M. Justille McDonald, *History of the Irish in Wisconsin in the Nineteenth Century.*

under the sponsorship of promoters and land speculators such as James Power, James Howetson, John McMullen, and James McGloin, Irishmen settled in the Texas country and joined in the fight for Texas' independence. For a fee of one hundred dollars, a colonist could claim 4,428 acres, and promoters received much larger grants. Refugio and San Patricio, on the Gulf Coast between the Nueces and Guadalupe rivers, were the most important early Irish colonies in Texas. Settlers here came from Ireland, New York, Philadelphia, and other American cities. Some prospered sufficiently to own a few slaves.[14] After the Civil War, as part of the program to attract immigration to the southern states, Texas advertised for additional settlers from Ireland.

In 1858, a letter from San Francisco printed in *The Irish News* of New York proposed forming a stock company in the East to purchase one of the states of Mexico and establish a republic where the green flag might fly over an independent Ireland.[15] A letter to Secretary of State Seward, in 1863, recommended building a "New Ireland" somewhere in the western territories, with Thomas Francis Meagher, refugee of 1848 and Civil War soldier, as governor.[16]

There is little detailed evidence concerning how the Irish farmer fared, but the fact that his descendants are still on the land would seem to indicate that the experiment was not a failure. The late Joseph Schafer, an authority on American agricultural history and a careful student of local conditions in Wisconsin, came to the conclusions that the Irish rural stock was fully as good as that of the cities; that it produced as many priests and professional men as other foreign-born groups; and that "while there is a considerable vestige of permanently unprosperous Irish through the countryside, the proportion of successful farmers among them is as high as among the natives and English stock." [17]

In addition to the individual efforts of Irish immigrants to establish themselves on the land, there were a number of attempts to plant entire Irish communities in the West. To get the Irish to settle in compact groups in farming country, where they could have their own schools and churches, and to create a haven for their co-religionists in the days of nativist bigotry were primary objectives for decades of many lay and clerical leaders. Papers like the *Catholic Telegraph* of Cincinnati constantly stressed the paramount importance of settling Irish immigrants on

[14] See Crimmins, *Irish-American Historical Miscellany*, 435, 459; Shea, *History of the Catholic Church in the United States*, III, 717; William H. Oberste, *Texas Irish Empresarios and Their Colonies.*

[15] *The Irish News* (New York), February 27, 1858.

[16] William D. D'Arcy, *The Fenian Movement in the United States, 1858–1886*, 32.

[17] Joseph Schafer, *Social History of American Agriculture*, 212.

the land. Although the hierarchy was badly, and sometimes bitterly, divided on the matter, Bishop John England considered the creation of western colonies as early as 1822. Bishop Fenwick of Boston in 1833 announced plans in the *Jesuit* for getting the poor Irish out of Boston and settling them in the potato country of Aroostook County, Maine. Bishop John Timon of Buffalo advocated colonization in the West in the 1850's. Furthermore, the Boston *Pilot* and the St. Louis *Leader* approved western colonization projects.[18]

The first serious effort to operate a colonization plan on a nationwide scale was made in 1855 and 1856, and it ended in failure. The driving spirit behind the movement was Thomas D'Arcy McGee, brilliant Irish journalist and orator, who, in the words of his recent biographer, "was never naturalized in the American intellectual world of his day." [19] A sensitive, well-educated Irishman, McGee was deeply devoted to his people and profoundly disturbed by what was happening to them in the crowded American cities. McGee witnessed the battles between his Church and the nativists over schools and Bible reading and the rioting in city streets during Know-Nothing days. He was concerned about what might happen to the religion of the Irish in what he considered the dangerous American atmosphere of freethinking, atheism, and radical reform. Though frequently attacked as a radical by some of the hierarchy and by fellow journalists, McGee was really a conservative at heart. He questioned some features of American democracy, including manhood suffrage and the election of judges. He was bitter toward political bosses who snared the support of his people for their demagogic purposes. He favored an educational system closely supervised by the Catholic Church. He also entertained ambitious plans for libraries, debating clubs, and adult education to raise the intellectual and social level of the Irish in America.

McGee wanted to get Irishmen out of the groggeries and their children out of unventilated bedrooms and dilapidated garrets. He wanted to discourage further immigration until those already here could be raised out of their squalid, dirty surroundings and given an education. He saw the children of Irish immigrants "breaking off" from their churches and Irish patriotic societies. He was shocked to find Irish children losing that "abstract Irish reverence for old age" in "the smartness of the streets"

[18] The best general account which I have followed is that of Sister Mary Gilbert Kelly, *Catholic Immigrant Colonization Projects in the United States, 1815–1860;* see also John O'Grady, "Irish Colonization in the United States," *Studies,* XIX (1930), 387–407; and John C. Murphy, *Attitudes of American Catholics Toward the Immigrant and the Negro,* 22.

[19] Skelton, *The Life of Thomas D'Arcy McGee,* 232.

and disrespectfully referring to their fathers as "the governor" or "the old man." He had little patience with sons of immigrants who were "afraid to profess their religion . . . ashamed of their origin." [20]

McGee had lectured in Canada and was so impressed with the potentialities of that country that he continually referred to them in his *American Celt*. But he also recognized the opportunities which the American West had to offer. The Boston *Pilot* characterized any mass emigration to Canada as "a stampede of asses," but, along with other Irish-American papers, spoke favorably of an Irish hegira to the western United States, hailing McGee's colonization scheme as "the first practical movement for the benefit of our race on this side of the Atlantic." In one of his poems, "Rise and Go," McGee had written:

> In the villages of New England
> Are you happy, we would know?
> Are you welcome, are you trusted?
> Are you not? then Rise and Go!

In another, he contrasted the life of the "perverted peasantry" in New York's Fourth Ward with the joys of the farm and rhapsodized about

> The Irish homes of Illinois
> The happy homes of Illinois
> No landlord there
> Can cause despair
> Nor blight our fields in Illinois.

From such pleas arose the call for a convention in Buffalo in 1856 to discuss colonization projects. The Irish Emigrant Aid Convention met on February 12, 1856, with about eighty Catholic Irish delegates—lay and clergy, from Canada and the United States—in attendance. After High Mass in the Buffalo Cathedral, the delegates created two committees, one on land, the other on finance. The convention's proposals, stated in the simplest terms, called for the sale of stock in joint-stock companies to Irish of sufficient means, and for the use of such funds to buy land, which in turn would be sold to actual settlers on the installment plan. The plan promised to take the Irish into the West and give them "the blessings of rural settlement, with church and school." The finance committee estimated that Irish Catholics in the East had about $48,000,000 in bank deposits, and that at least a hundred thousand were in a position to buy stock in a project described by the committee as safer than eastern banks. Land was available at twenty-five cents to $1.25 an acre; and in each township, forty acres were to be reserved for a church, a school, and

[20] Thomas D'Arcy McGee, *A History of Irish Settlers in North America*, 233, 236–37.

a priest's farm. The title, moreover, would remain in the hands of the ecclesiastical authorities. Agencies in the leading cities were to furnish information to interested immigrants.

The convention adjourned confident that it had acted in all matters "with the advice of our reverend clergy, and invoking the blessing of God on our labors." McGee was optimistic about the future, and the editor of the Boston *Pilot* agreed with him. Local societies in Boston, New Haven, Dubuque, and elsewhere approved the colonization project, and Bishop Loras sent $25 from Iowa as a token of his interest and support. When the stock was offered for sale, another western bishop, Michael O'Connor, bought ten shares. In the first three months, $15,000 was subscribed. Bishops in St. Paul, Cleveland, Pittsburgh, Wheeling, and Buffalo were favorably disposed. By August, 1856, the number of shares which had been pledged totaled 345, of which the clergy took 184. The money was on deposit with the Emigrant Savings Bank of New York.

The convention never met again. Opposition rolled up from several directions, but from none more vigorous than that of the eastern hierarchy, spearheaded by Bishop Hughes of New York. McGee's fondness for "Queen Victoria's Canada," coupled with the fact that about twenty members of the Buffalo convention were Canadians, was enough to damn the project in some Irish quarters. The *Freeman's Journal* of New York characterized the movement as "a Knownothingism which calls itself Irish and assumes to be Catholic." [21]

In the mind of Bishop Hughes, the radicalism of "Young Ireland" seemed to be even worse for the Emerald Isle than the potato rot. He regarded McGee as a dangerous radical, and the two men engaged in forensic battles until McGee was forced to surrender. The rebel of 1848 had offended the bishop by charging that a primary cause for the failure of the Irish rising had been the opposition of the clergy. Hughes attacked McGee in the *Freeman's Journal* without signing his name. At a public meeting in New York, he also rose to denounce Father Jeremiah F. Trecy—a priest from the West who was promoting a colonization scheme in Nebraska. Reports concerning Father Trecy's St. Patrick's colony in Nebraska were highly contradictory. Hughes disapproved of the clergy's becoming recruiting sergeants for a colony, pictured the Buffalo convention as primarily concerned with speculating in land for profit, and contended that settlers would be disillusioned and embittered if they actually went west. The bishop pointed out that most Irishmen would not know how to fell a tree and would find the hardships

21 Sister Kelly, *Catholic Immigrant Projects,* 242.

and hazards too great to bear. Drawing a parallel between the Buffalo proposals and similar projects of the Mormons, he made it clear that he opposed all separate and distinct Irish settlements.[22]

In an editorial on April 4, 1857, *The Irish News* approved the bishop's "sound doctrine and wise counsel" and denounced "selfish and conscience-less demagogues" who would brigade Irishmen into separate camps, contrary to "the spirit of the Constitution." The paper opposed all settlements created "on a distinctly religious basis, or on the grounds of any foreign nationality." Bishop Hughes in the 1840's had spoken in favor of the gradual settlement of the Irish on western farms as individuals, but apparently he regarded organized, group migration as utterly impractical. The *Freeman's Journal,* reflecting the bishop's views, denounced the Buffalo plan as Quixotic and contended that despite all their problems, the Irish were better off in the East. As late as 1881, the editor commented sarcastically, "If the Irishmen in New York are agricultural-minded they have plenty of unoccupied land in Long Island." [23]

Bishop Hughes apparently had decided to oppose colonization projects sometime in the 1850's, probably in part because of his personal feelings toward McGee, Father Trecy, and General James Shields. In 1862, however, Hughes made an eloquent speech in Cork recounting what the West had done for the poor Irish. He also urged Seward to advertise the attractions of the United States more extensively in Ireland. To many of the bishop's critics, both among the laity and the clergy, it seemed that the decisive reason for Hughes' opposition to mass colonization in the 1850's was his unwillingness to lose parishioners and revenue to an organized westward movement, when many of the eastern churches and schools still carried heavy debts.

The Buffalo convention probably would have ended in failure in any case, because there was no real body of public sentiment among the American Irish to sustain it. With the decline of the Know-Nothing movement, one of the arguments for colonization lost its appeal. McGee persuaded himself that the movement had aroused sufficient interest to induce 30,000 Irish families to move west, and he thought that the agitation may have improved conditions somewhat in the eastern cities. As for McGee himself, he departed in 1857 for Canada, disillusioned by his experiences in the American democracy. In Canada, he became a dis-

---

[22] For an account of the meeting and the bishop's speech, see *The Irish News* (New York), April 4, 1857; also Henry J. Browne, "Archbishop Hughes and Western Colonization," *The Catholic Historical Review,* XXXVI (1950), 257–87.

[23] Quoted in Sister Mary Augustine Kwitchen, *James Alphonsus McMaster, A Study in American Thought,* 212–13.

tinguished public figure, an opponent of Fenianism, and one of the builders of Canadian Confederation.

General James Shields' plans for the colonization of Irish farmers centered in Minnesota, where, thanks to his efforts, there are still Shieldsville, Erin, Montgomery, and Kilkenny townships. A native of county Tyrone, Shields came to the United States in 1826 at the age of eighteen. He made a distinguished record in the Mexican and Civil War and had the unique honor of representing two states in the United States Senate. In 1855, Shields led a group of Irish Catholics from Illinois to Shieldsville, in Rice County, Minnesota. By 1857, the county contained 682 Irish farmers, craftsmen, and shopkeepers and supported a Catholic church and school. Despite Bishop Hughes' well-known attitude, Shields advertised in the Catholic press of the East and in Ireland for settlers. The colony remained small but fairly prosperous as a farming community. Shields eventually left it to go to California after a quarrel about his alleged failure to furnish proper deeds to the settlers.[24]

General John O'Neil was another Irish-American military man who looked westward after the Civil War. In 1872, O'Neil decided "to build up a young Ireland on the virgin prairies of Nebraska and there rear a monument more lasting than granite or marble to the Irish race in America." [25] His settlements were begun on a very small scale, however, in Holt County, in 1874, and in the beginning consisted largely of males. With the full support of Bishop O'Connor of Nebraska, O'Neil lectured throughout the United States to advertise his colony. In 1882, the town of O'Neil became the county seat. By 1891, it had a population of 2,000. It was never exclusively Catholic, for there were Presbyterian and Methodist churches in the community. In 1877, O'Neil located twenty-five families of Irish miners from Pennsylvania in Greeley County.

No one wrote more eloquently about the miseries of the Irish in the cities than Bishop John Lancaster Spalding of Peoria, and no physiocrat ever explained the importance of agriculture as the material basis for civilization more convincingly. His book on the religious mission of the Irish people was a moving plea to colonize the Irish, with their churches and schools, in the West.[26] The bishop wanted to get them away from "the intoxication of city life," and he openly criticized the attitude of Bishop Hughes and pointed out illogical absurdities in the arguments the latter had advanced in 1852. Far from discouraging colonization,

[24] Sister Kelly, *Catholic Immigrant Projects,* 198–201.
[25] Sister Mary Evangela Henthorne, *The Career of the Right Rev. John Lancaster Spalding, 1879–1892,* 137.
[26] See Spalding, *Religious Mission.*

Spalding maintained that it was the duty of the Church to promote it. He wanted to get wealthy European Catholics to invest their money in the scheme and was ready to extend the benefits of colonization to other Catholic immigrants from Europe.

Bishop John Ireland of St. Paul was equally convinced of the need for Irish farming communities in the West. In 1876, he organized a Catholic Colonization Bureau and promoted the first colony in Swift County, Minnesota. He secured railroad land, built a church, brought in a priest who understood farming, and banished the saloon. He advised prospective settlers what they would need to begin farming and counseled them against bringing discontented wives, who would prove "far worse than the Colorado beetle." Within four years, Bishop Ireland helped develop five colonies on over 300,000 acres of prairie land. Similar projects were sponsored in Kansas by the Irish Catholic Benevolent Association of St. Louis; in Virginia, by a Philadelphia group; and in Chicago and Milwaukee, by other groups.

The colonization movement received new impetus from a national conference held in Chicago, March 17, 1879, called by the St. Patrick's Society of that city, with the approval of a number of prominent bishops. Its major objective was to work out a plan for a nationwide organization. The call was printed in all the Irish Catholic papers and received editorial support from the St. Paul *Northwestern Chronicle,* the Boston *Pilot,* the New York *Irish-American,* and the *Pittsburgh Catholic.* The convention, with William J. Onahan in the chair, was composed of delegates from middle western farming states, and heard Archbishop Ireland recount his experiences with his Minnesota colonists. He argued that he could prove that Irish from the mines, docks, and mills of the East could make farming pay. Thereupon committees were appointed consisting of laymen and priests, and the Irish Catholic Colonization Society was incorporated under Illinois law, with provisions for the sale of $100,000 worth of stock at $100 a share.

The plan was essentially like earlier projects and involved the purchase of large parcels of land and its resale on easy terms. The society, meantime, would build a church and an immigrant house in the proposed settlement, advance funds for the first plowing, and build individual cottages for $150 to $200. Title was retained by the stock company until all payments had been met, and the society expected to pay 6 per cent interest to its investors. Prospective farmers would find a cottage and thirty acres of plowed land on their arrival.

Most of the stock was subscribed in New York, Boston, St. Paul, Chicago, Buffalo, and Baltimore. According to one report, the relatively poor, who could buy only one or two shares, subscribed more than eight times as much as the men of means. The latter seemed apathetic and needed reassurance from their bishops that this was not another land swindle. The *Cincinnati Enquirer* referred to the enterprise as an "awful trap for credulous emigrants," and the *New York Herald,* as well as Bishop McQuaid of Rochester, reacted equally unfavorably.

In 1879, De Graff, in Swift County, about 120 miles from St. Paul, was founded with Archbishop Ireland's special blessing. By 1881, there were eight hundred families in four villages, each with a church, a school, and a grain elevator. The total cost of a 160-acre farm in the Adrian colony of Minnesota, including a house and the plowing of thirty acres, was $1,174. The down payment for this was only $50, and installments were not to begin until after the second harvest. Bishop Spalding favored the development of farmers' co-operatives. He addressed mass meetings in the East to advertise the project. Circulars were distributed around the country; and in 1884, a resident priest was assigned to Castle Garden to direct immigrants westward. By 1884, the company was paying good dividends, and by 1891, all the stock was redeemed and paid off.

One group, three hundred Irish fishermen and peasants from Connemara, who came in 1880, proved particularly disappointing. They were sent over by a priest from Liverpool and supported by Archbishop Ireland. The latter induced the railroad companies to take care of their fares from New York to St. Paul and got contributions for the destitute Connemara peasants from the St. Patrick's Society of Chicago. On their arrival in Minnesota, the immigrants found houses, clothing, and two months' provisions ready for them. Work was obtainable among neighboring farmers who paid from $1.50 to $2.00 a day. The group apparently included a large proportion of grumblers and lazy ex-paupers who made poor American farmers. They froze in the cold winter because they had been too lazy to sod their shanties, and their potatoes spoiled because they failed to dig cellars to store them. The St. Paul *Pioneer Press* called them "born mendicants." Their experience offered proof that men who had already lived and worked in the United States were better risks than immigrants straight from Ireland.

Another interesting colony in Minnesota was that of John Sweetman, a wealthy Irish landowner who wanted to do something for Irish peasants and laborers. He came to St. Paul in 1880, with letters of introduction from the Bishop of Dublin to Archbishop Ireland, to discuss colonization with an expert. After traveling extensively in the Old Northwest, he undertook to interest wealthy Catholics in Ireland in an Irish-American Colonization Company, Ltd., and bought land from the Chicago and

Northwestern and other railroads. He expected his project to pay dividends to the investors, and settlers were charged 6 per cent interest on their land and 8 per cent on supplies. The company financed the passage to America, offered liberal terms, and advanced seed, food, and equipment. A church was provided at Currie, the county seat of Murray County, Minnesota, in 1884, and a priest was brought over from Ireland. Despite aid from the company, the population of the colony remained in constant flux; unmarried women went off to the cities to find work as servants, and 34 per cent of the families left during the first two years. Finally, the company had to sell land to anyone with money to buy, and could no longer restrict holdings to Irish immigrants. By 1905, all the land had been sold, but the venture never yielded the expected financial profit.[27]

Many of these colonization projects were conceived in a spirit of genuine altruism and represented a noble effort to get the Irish out of the cities. Some were successful and profitable; others were failures. Many immigrants were quickly disillusioned, for farming in the hot summers and the cold winters of the Minnesota or Nebraska prairies was not easy, and conditions in America were very different from those in Ireland.

Although the vast majority of American Irish remained in the cities, the Quixotic dream about Irish farming colonies persisted into the present century. In 1904, a Boston Irishman, in a letter to the *Irish World and American Industrial Liberator,* proposed establishing an Irish colony in a sparsely settled part of the West, where Ireland's ancient system of government might be tried out. In 1917, a plan was launched to found an Irish settlement in Arkansas in memory of Sir Roger Casement, the martyr of the Easter Week Rebellion of 1916. *The Gaelic-American* reported twenty-five Irish farmers from Iowa and Nebraska had signified their eagerness to go.[28]

---

[27] See Alice E. Smith, "The Sweetman Irish Colony," *Minnesota History,* IX (1928), 331–46.

[28] *Irish World and American Industrial Liberator* (New York), July 23, 1904; *The Gaelic-American* (New York), February, 1917.

CHAPTER VIII

The Men of '98 and '48

IN EVERY immigrant group there are likely to be a number of political refugees—men who have been involved in fomenting disobedience to established authority in the homeland and have been sentenced to jail or exile. The American Republic, itself the product of revolution, offered a welcome to refugees and did not regard their conviction for political unorthodoxy as a bar to either admittance or naturalization. The majority of the rebels in popular uprisings always have come from the rank and file of the population, but among the leaders there were usually men of high intellectual ability and achievement. In a new land, men of such caliber, after a period of fruitless waiting for new risings abroad, tried to provide intellectual, cultural, and political leadership for their countrymen in the United States. They considered it their duty to act as the leaven to raise the immigrant mass to greater influence and importance in the adopted fatherland.

Every major disturbance in Europe or America had its repercussions in Ireland and revived the hopes of the Irish for independence. During the American Revolution, Continental leaders hoped the Irish would start trouble with England; Benjamin Franklin shipped revolutionary propaganda to Ireland; the Continental Congress created a standing committee "to correspond" with the Irish; and John Adams predicted in 1780 that they would be independent before the United States.[1] The French Revolution raised the hopes of suppressed nationalities everywhere. The fall of the Bastile was celebrated with parades in Belfast, and at Irish banquets Mirabeau was hailed as a champion of universal liberty. Irishmen believed that the French across the channel were fighting Ireland's battle also. They greeted each other as "citizen" in emulation of the French Republicans; Irish volunteers went to the Continent to aid the revolution; and for years, the French army had an "Irish Brigade."[2] A number of Irish nationalists were active in France and took flight only during the Reign of Terror.

[1] John C. Miller, *Triumph of Freedom, 1775–1783*, 412–14.
[2] See Richard Hayes, *Ireland and Irishmen in the French Revolution*.

The contagion of the French Revolution spread to Ireland, where the misery of the people and the desire for more land, even more than a sentimental interest in Irish nationhood, led to an uprising in 1798. It was followed by another in 1803, which was largely a continuation of the first. The appeal to arms in the latter year was planned by a Society of United Irishmen, founded in 1791, in which Presbyterians were as active as Catholics. Irish exiles in Paris and Brussels believed an attack on the castle and barracks in Dublin would be the signal for rebellion throughout the island. The attempt to overthrow British rule made Robert Emmet the martyr and hero of the Irish people, but it accomplished little else. Both risings were promptly suppressed. Instead of hanging all the rebels, the British government wisely decided to deport as many as possible, or allow them to escape. Rufus King, American minister to London, protested that the United States had enough "wild Irish" already, and the policy of wholesale deportations to America, if ever seriously entertained, was never carried out.

Nevertheless, the United States received its first sizable group of Irish political refugees as a result of the rebellion. Others escaped to France or went in fishing vessels to Newfoundland, where their descendants can still be found. One ship put in at Norfolk, Virginia, with over four hundred of these "men of '98," and others scattered through a number of American states.[3] The number of political refugees cannot be accurately determined, but the list includes men of distinction as well as those of humbler careers. The three outstanding ones were Thomas Addis Emmet, William Sampson, and Dr. William J. Macneven. Emmet, brother of the more famous Robert, after his release in 1798 had been transported out of the island and had been active on behalf of Ireland in Holland, Belgium, and France. He was deeply involved in the plot of 1803 and hoped to induce Napoleon to send the troops designated for Santo Domingo to Ireland instead. In 1804, this Protestant Irishman arrived in New York with letters of introduction from several important men. His original plan was to take up farming in Ohio, but he became a distinguished lawyer in New York. He was admitted to the bar by special act, and, in 1812, became attorney general of his state. An ardent Jeffersonian, he was described as an able and attractive Irishman, with "roguish Hibernian eyes," a florid complexion, and a "winning Corkonian brogue."[4] He defended his Irish countrymen in 1824 when they

---

[3] See John Savage, '98 and '48, the Modern Revolutionary History and Literature of Ireland; Henry M. Field, The Irish Confederates and the Rebellion of 1798; Richard R. Madden, The United Irishmen, Their Lives and Times.

[4] Thomas Addis Emmet, Memoir of Thomas Addis and Robert Emmet, I, 404.

became involved in an Orange riot. When he died at the age of sixty-five, New York's leading newspapers wrote editorial tributes, and many public officials attended his funeral. A monument was later erected by popular subscription in St. Paul's churchyard.

William Sampson was a lawyer and belonged to a good Londonderry family. Arrested and charged with holding a commission in the French army, he was deported to Portugal. He reached New York in 1806. He, too, became a distinguished member of the American bar and defended the Irish in several cases of riot. In a case of great significance in the history of American law, Sampson, a Protestant, fought for the right of Catholic priests not to reveal what they were told during confession. A delightful and flamboyant Irishman, he took part in New York City politics and published not only his memoirs, but a two volume history of Ireland.[5]

Dr. William J. Macneven, the son of Catholic parents in county Galway, was a well-known New York physician and an active Irish leader in this country. Trained at Prague and Vienna, and already established in his practice in Dublin, he was uprooted by the rebellion of 1798, arrested, jailed, and exiled in 1802. After a futile attempt to persuade Napoleon to come to the aid of Ireland, Macneven went to New York in 1805. Two years later, he was lecturing on clinical medicine at the College of Physicians and Surgeons, and, during a notable career, held several professorships, including one in obstetrics and another at Rutgers Medical School. He supported Irish organizations for the aid of immigrants; he was president of the "Friends of Ireland" in 1828; and he published *Pieces of Irish History* and several studies in the field of chemistry and atomic theory. An ardent Democrat, in 1834 he broke with Jackson over the removal of the deposits from the Second Bank of the United States, and was denounced for his political apostasy by the rabidly Jacksonian Irish press.[6]

John D. Burk, who left Ireland in 1796 to avoid arrest on charges of sedition, became a leader in the New York lodge of United Irishmen and co-editor of the New York *Time Piece*. During the crisis with France, President Adams tried to expel him from the United States under the Alien Friends Act, but Burk remained in hiding in Virginia until the law expired. Bernard McMahon, another "exile of Erin," came to the United States in 1796 and became a famous horticulturist. His nursery and seed business attracted the attention of eminent botanists. An evergreen, "Mahonia," was named in his honor; the Lewis and Clark expedi-

[5] *DAB.*
[6] Madden, *United Irishmen,* II, 233 *et seq.*

tion sent him sample seeds; and his *American Gardener's Almanac,* issued in 1806, remained standard for fifty years.[7] John Binns, another Protestant Irishman, came to Northumberland, Pennsylvania, in 1801 with a group interested in establishing a communitarian colony, but he turned to politics and journalism instead. In 1840, he published a manual of Pennsylvania law and, in 1854, a volume of *Recollections.* At the age of eighty-one, the rebel of 1798 was still vigorous enough to introduce Thomas F. Meagher, "the Irish rebel of 1848," to a Philadelphia audience.[8]

John Boyle, a Catholic United Irishman, was a teacher in Baltimore; James Doyle, a New York merchant and organizer of a volunteer fire department; and Bernard Dornin, banished after 1798, one of the first publishers of Catholic books in America.[9] David Reidy fought in the War of 1812.[10] Robert Adrian and Charles Sullivan became schoolteachers in the United States; David Bryson, a merchant; John Dalzell, a farmer in Oneida County, New York; William and John O'Brien, New York bankers; and Keating Rawson, an operator of a tannery in Lansingburg, New York.[11] Samuel Neilson had a marker raised over his grave in Poughkeepsie by the Ancient Order of Hibernians.

Thomas Mulledy, a Virginia farmer, was elected to the state legislature, and sent two sons into the priesthood.[12] Several refugee families settled in Augusta, Georgia, and others scattered through other parts of the South. Father James Harold, deported to Australia in 1799, came to Philadelphia in 1810, was warmly welcomed by the Irish, and became the pastor of a local parish. John McElroy, reared in poverty in Ireland and an ardent United Irishman, came to Baltimore in 1803 in a flax ship, joined the Jesuit Order, and was a successful missionary and a chaplain in the Mexican War.[13] Thomas Aloysius Dorwin, commander of the Norfolk Navy Yard in the 1850's, was the son of a refugee of 1798. John Thomas Doyle, son of another refugee, became a well-known lawyer in San Francisco. William D. Gallagher, another second-generation "man of '98," a journalist and a poet, was secretary to Salmon P. Chase when the latter was secretary of the treasury. Theodore O'Hara, son of an Irish

[7] *DAB.*

[8] Michael Cavanagh, *Memoirs of General T. F. Meagher,* 337.

[9] Watson Boyle, "John Boyle, United Irishman and His American Descendants," *Journal of the American Irish Historical Society,* XVIII (1919), 224–27; E. J. McGuire, "John F. Doyle," *Journal of the American Irish Historical Society,* XI (1911–12), 195–97; and *DAB.*

[10] O'Donovan Rossa, *Rossa's Recollections, 1838 to 1898,* 396–97.

[11] Purcell, "Immigration to the Canal Era," Chapter II in *History of New York* (ed. Alexander Flick), VII, 13–17; and Emmet, *Incidents of My Life,* 77–78.

[12] *Metropolitan Record and New York Vindicator,* January 20, 1866.

[13] *DAB.*

conspirator of 1798, edited the Louisville *Times,* was a Confederate officer, and wrote the famous poem, "The Bivouac of the Dead." [14] Charles
B. Rogers, son of a man who always signed himself "Patrick Rogers of
the Irish Nation," made the first geological survey of New England for
the United States Geological Survey and was the first president of the
Massachusetts Institute of Techonology.[15] Thomas O'Conor, who had
taken the oath as a United Irishman from Wolfe Tone himself, hoped
to establish an Irish farming colony in Steuben County, New York. He
founded *The Shamrock,* the first important Irish paper in New York,
became a sachem of Tammany Hall, and hated England to his dying
day. His son Charles was one of the most famous American lawyers of
a century ago.[16]

Refugees of such intellectual caliber might have been expected to ally
themselves with the Federalist party in America, for that party presumably represented intelligence and success. Unfortunately, the Federalists
were "Anglo-men," and that made them anti-Irish and pro-British snobs
in Irish eyes. Moreover, many Federalists were outspoken in their criticism of Irish refugees who sympathized with the French Revolution. To
the more reactionary of the party, such radicals were Jacobins, "wild
Irishmen," "the most God-provoking Democrats this side of hell," "inflammatory agents," and disturbers of the peace. New Englanders like
Harrison Gray Otis wanted "to prevent the indiscriminate admission of
wild Irishmen."

The Alien and Sedition Acts of John Adams' administration and the
new Naturalization Act were to a large measure the result of a crisis in
Franco-American relations and of a desire by extreme Federalists to crush
ultrarepublican opinion and deprive the opposing party of the political
support of immigrants from the Continent and the British Isles. By 1798,
the alliance between the Democratic party and the Irish already was
being cemented, and Federalists sought a means to keep foreigners from
exercising power and influence in the opposition party. They rightly regarded all Irishmen as anti-British, and they suspected many of plotting
rebellion. In the opinion of leading Federalists, they were "seditious
spirits," "panting after" a more perfect society, and "a torment to America." [17] Because of this attitude, even the most intellectual Irish leaders
joined the Jeffersonians, who championed the rights of the common man
and denounced the repressive measures of John Adams' administration.

[14] *Ibid.*

[15] "Addresses of the Thirtieth Annual Dinner of the American Irish Society," *Journal
of the American Irish Historical Society,* XXVII (1928), 392.

[16] *Ibid.,* 307–309; and *The Citizen* (New York), February 17, 1855.

[17] John C. Miller, *Crisis in Freedom, the Alien and Sedition Acts,* 46.

The Irish never forgot Rufus King's comment in 1798 that the United States wanted no more Irish exiles who would "arrange themselves upon the side of the malcontents." In 1816, when the author of that remark ran for governor of New York, Thomas A. Emmet published a letter in *The Shamrock* opposing his election. Some observers attributed King's defeat in large measure to the bitter opposition of the New York Irish.[18]

The "men of '98" were honored as Irish-American heroes until the last survivor died. A popular song, "Who Fears to Speak of '98," was sung regularly at Irish banquets, where the veterans of rebellion occupied places of honor. *The Irish News,* on July 11, 1857, began publishing a serial story, "The Rebel Bivouac—a tale of '98," and carried an advertisement for a saloon on First Avenue known as "The '98 House." Irish-Americans rehearsed the issues and events of 1798 and 1803 at their patriotic meetings for many years.

The revolutions of 1848 began in Paris and swept through most of western Europe. In their antimonarchical and antifeudal aspects, they represented the belated sprouting of seeds sowed by the French Revolution and scattered over Europe by the Napoleonic Wars. As an international movement, the revolutions transcended state boundaries.

Ireland, where rebellion against the British had become chronic, felt the impact of the Continental earthquake immediately. There was a "Young Ireland" in the Emerald Isle comparable to the "Young Italy" and "Young Germany" of the Continent. With incredible optimism, Irish patriots dreamed of recruiting a brigade of Irish-Americans to come across the ocean to help them fight for freedom. When news of the French Revolution reached Ireland, "Young Irelanders" staged demonstrations in several cities, and John Mitchel's *United Irishman* advocated an appeal to arms to establish a republic. The youth of Dublin marched and sang the "Marseillaise," bonfires blazed from the Irish hills, and the tricolor appeared in the windows of Irish patriots. Collisions between Irish patriots, troops, and police were numerous.

The revolt itself was poorly organized and had little chance of success. Enthusiasm was no substitute for arms and a carefully worked out plan. Only the most haphazard preparations had been made, and men had to fight with pikes under leaders who, though patriotic enough, operated as individuals with a fatal lack of decision. In British history, the uprising was contemptuously known as the rebellion of the widow McCormack's cabbage patch. The advice of the clergy for the people to refrain from violence was probably wise, but it made the priests extremely unpopular with radical revolutionaries. The revolt was suppressed by the familiar

18 *The Shamrock* (New York), February 24, April 13, 1816.

methods, and once again a number of political refugees looked to the United States, where fellow Polish, Italian, Hungarian, and German refugees of the same revolution had found a haven. In New York and other eastern centers, Irish rebels joined this international brotherhood and waited hopefully for a day when they might fight again for republican liberty with American aid.[19]

The Irish "Forty-eighters" also included able and well-educated Irishmen who became men of importance and influence in the United States. But they had relatively little influence upon their Irish-American countrymen. Those who advocated an international republicanism, in the spirit of European rationalism and enlightenment, encountered the active hostility of the Church hierarchy. Among the hundreds of Irish refugees of 1848, men like Thomas D'Arcy McGee, John Mitchel, and Thomas F. Meagher were clearly outstanding and became well-known figures in American life. Many others, without public fanfare, carved out for themselves successful and satisfying careers in their new home.

Of this distinguished trio, McGee was the most intellectually gifted. He was a poet, a journalist, and an orator; he dabbled in history; and in Canada, he developed into a major statesman. Perhaps more than any of his fellow exiles, he never quite conquered his homesickness for Ireland. It remained his "land of dreams," to which "the ship of night" carried him "o'er alien streams homeward through the enchanted air." McGee caught his first glimpse of America as a lad of seventeen when he crossed the Atlantic in 1842 on a sailing ship engaged in the lumber trade. He found a job in Boston on the *Pilot.* In 1845, he returned to Ireland to engage in journalistic activities, particularly for the Dublin *Nation,* the organ of "Young Ireland," which was dedicated to the repeal of the Union. In 1848, McGee tried to stir North Ireland to rebellion and to enlist the aid of the Scots. After the collapse of the rebellion, he left Londonderry for Philadelphia in clerical disguise.

Like refugees of other nationalities, McGee found it relatively easy to start a paper in America. The *Nation* in New York was his organ of personal journalism. The prospectus described the new weekly as a "newspaper devoted to Ireland and her immigrants and the European democracies." McGee advocated American aid for the liberation of Europe and eagerly scanned the political horizon for signs of another revolution. He denounced England, censured the clergy for their opposition to the Irish rebellion, and, at this point in his career, advised the separation of church and state. His views brought on a conflict with

[19] Denis Gwynn, "The Rising of 1848," *Studies,* XXXVII (1948), 7–17; 149–160; see also Carl Wittke, *Refugees of Revolution, the German Forty-eighters in America.*

Bishop Hughes, who attacked him as a bad Catholic, frowned upon organizational support for "Young Ireland," and regarded McGee's proposals for adult education for immigrants with suspicion. Apparently the bishop believed classes for the education of Irish newcomers might turn into political clubs or even secret societies, and he made it clear that he was opposed to all agitations which were likely to separate the Irish as a group from other Americans. The eager young journalist and his clerical adversary carried on their feud via the *Nation* and the New York *Freeman's Journal*. In a sermon, Bishop Hughes accused McGee of stupidly imitating Paine and Voltaire and referred derisively to "political confectioners who seal up the poison of their infidelity in sugar plums of flattery to popular prejudices." [20] There can be little doubt that the bishop's attitude hastened the failure of the *Nation* in 1850.

Thereupon McGee, following the pattern of other refugee intellectuals, tried to sustain himself and his family by lecturing, principally to Canadian and New England Irish audiences. In Boston, he launched the *American Celt,* and here he encountered no clerical opposition, for McGee was neither a rationalist nor a revolutionary. Instead, he was more conservative and deeply religious than some of his fellow exiles and definitely rejected the agnosticism of the liberals. The bigotry of Know-Nothingism drove him to make his peace with the Church and to become its enthusiastic champion.

McGee's activities need not be chronicled in detail. He had to move his paper several times to keep it alive, and he supplemented his earnings by lecturing. He remained an outspoken but sympathetic critic of the failings of his own countrymen and worked hard to raise the social and intellectual level of Irish-Americans. After his failure to get them out of the cities and on the land, he departed in 1857 for Canada. Like other refugees, he was disillusioned by a land of the free which justified Negro slavery and condoned anti-Irish and anti-Catholic bigotry. When he left, a considerable portion of the Irish-American press branded him a traitor to his people, and in the vile, unbridled journalism of that day, called him a liar, a viper, and a slanderer.

Thomas Francis Meagher, son of a well-to-do Irish merchant, well educated, and trained for the law, as a young man fell under the spell of revolutionaries like Charles Gavan Duffy, John Mitchel, and Thomas Davis. In 1848, he was arrested, convicted, and exiled to Van Diemen's Land. In 1852, while still in his twenties, Meagher arrived in New York. Here he was greeted by enthusiastic Irish-Americans, who honored him

---

[20] Skelton, *The Life of Thomas D'Arcy McGee,* 166. See also Josephine Phelan, *The Ardent Exile, the Life and Times of D'Arcy McGee.*

with a parade and a grand reception in Brooklyn. Fellow Irish Forty-eighters, Richard O'Gorman, John Dillon, Michael Doheny, John Savage, Thomas Devin Reilly, and others were on hand to greet him. He reviewed Irish military units; Fordham gave him a degree *in absentia;* and someone composed the "Meagher Polka" and dedicated it to him at Niblo's Garden. The Meagher Club of New York gave him beautifully bound copies of Spark's *Life of Washington* and Bancroft's *History of the United States.* For several months Meagher was busy attending receptions and dinners in his honor, and the papers compared him with Louis Kossuth, the Hungarian liberator. Meagher lectured in many cities on the Irish situation of 1848; and crowds, as long as the novelty lasted, came to listen to his flowery oratory.

Meagher, at this point in his colorful career, was a typical international revolutionist. He identified himself with Kossuth's efforts to liberate Hungary and with Mazzini's to free Italy. Like McGee, he encountered the opposition of some of the hierarchy. He founded *The Irish News* in 1856, practiced law, and married, as his second wife, the daughter of a wealthy Fifth Avenue merchant. He served with distinction in the Civil War, had a difficult time in the postwar years, and ended his days in the West as territorial secretary of Montana. This state erected an equestrian statue, "Meagher of the Sword," at the capitol in Helena.[21]

The third member of this distinguished triumvirate was John Mitchel, who arrived in New York in 1853. The son of a Protestant minister from North Ireland, a graduate of Trinity College, Dublin, and trained for the bar, Mitchel had been chief editorial writer for the Dublin *Nation* and an ardent champion of revolution. He was sentenced to fourteen years' banishment in 1848, and, like Meagher, came to the United States by way of Van Diemen's Land. Like McGee, he never overcame his passionate love for "the fair hills of holy Ireland." Able, well-educated, with a good command of French, Mitchel launched *The Citizen* in New York, published his *Jail Journal,* and promptly became embroiled in a controversy with Bishop Hughes concerning the right of revolution against the Pope as a temporal ruler. He accused the clergy of betraying the Catholic revolutionaries of Ireland, and he urged the Irish "to cut themselves off, not from Religion, but from that political corporation which you call the Church of God." [22] After a year, Mitchel retired to a farm in Tennessee. He was a typical "Latin Farmer" who knew little about agriculture but had a romantic interest in the simple life of the tiller of the soil. Shortly

21 Robert G. Ahearn, *Thomas Francis Meagher, An Irish Revolutionary in America,* passim.

22 See D'Arcy, *The Fenian Movement,* 4.

thereafter, he returned to journalism with his *Southern Citizen* and became an ardent champion of the slave system. He lectured extensively, spent four months in jail during the Civil War because of his violent pro-South attitude, and finally became a financial agent for the Fenians in Paris. Toward the close of his restless career, he was elected to Parliament from Tipperary but barred from taking his seat. His grandson, John Purroy Mitchel, became a reform mayor of New York.[23]

Michael Doheny, one of the lesser lights among the Forty-eighters, became a prominent Irish leader in New York. He was a lawyer and once helped edit the *Tipperary Free Press*. While on the staff of the Dublin *Nation,* he had written a history of the American Revolution for "The Library of Ireland," which the editors sponsored to develop an Irish national consciousness. Doheny escaped in disguise after the revolution. He practiced law in New York, published the *Honest Truth* for a short time, and remained active in Irish organizations, including the Fenians. He was colonel of the Sixty-ninth New York Regiment during the Civil War. A brilliant orator, he lectured frequently on such topics as "Ireland's Past, Present and Future." [24]

Thomas Devin Reilly, a native of Ulster and another contributor to the Dublin *Nation,* worked for Irish independence with his pen rather than with the sword. Nevertheless, he was arrested and outlawed in 1848 for his activity in revolutionary societies. He arrived in New York, penniless and ill, and was sheltered by the Emmet family until he found a job on the short-lived Irish paper, the *People*. In 1850, he went to Boston to write for a labor paper and the co-operative movement, but a year later he returned to New York to cover foreign affairs for the *American Review*. With George N. Sanders and others of the "Young America" group, he published the *Democratic Review,* which advocated a vigorous policy of American intervention in the trouble spots of Europe, including Ireland.[25]

Richard D'Alton Williams, a prominent member of the Irish Protestant Repeal Association who was acquitted for his part in the rising of 1848, taught school in Alabama, practiced medicine in New Orleans, and died of tuberculosis at the age of forty.[26] Dr. Thomas Antisell, a chemist and geologist, continued his scientific work in the United States. Richard O'Gorman, who escaped from Ireland in disguise in 1848 and spent some time on the Continent, became one of New York's leading lawyers and

[23] Louis J. Walsh, *John Mitchel, passim.*

[24] *The Citizen* (New York), November 10, 1855; and Cavanagh, *Memoirs of General Meagher,* 234–35.

[25] Savage, *'98 and '48,* 359–84.

[26] Cavanagh, *Memoirs of General Meagher,* 221–22.

a judge of the Superior Court. A polished and popular orator, one of his specialties was an oration on Tom Moore. John O'Mahony and Terence Bellew McManus became leading American Fenians. Joseph W. Burke, John Kavanagh, William H. Hogan, and James E. McGee were officers in the Union army. Michael Flood Nagle was a filibusterer in Nicaragua in 1856.[27] John Savage wrote for Meagher's *Irish News* and the New Orleans *Times*. Joseph Brenan was an editorial writer for the *Delta* in the same city. Phelim Lynch and B. S. Treanor were leaders among the Boston Irish. William McGarran, who had sheltered McGee in 1848, became a successful merchant in California. Edward Keating was a skilled silversmith and engraver; John Moriarity, a farmer in Michigan; Michael Curran, a humble workman for whose destitute family Meagher gave a benefit lecture in 1855. Some of the refugees never took root in America; others died young. A few, like John Blake Dillon, John Martin, and P. J. Smythe, returned to Ireland after four or five years in the United States.

Although neither as numerous nor as influential as their German counterparts, the careers of some of these Irish refugees of revolution are comparable in many respects to those of the better-known German group. A number in both groups started newspapers and sharply criticized some of the institutions they found in the land of Jefferson and Jackson. They were certain at the beginning of their exile that their sojourn in the United States would be temporary, and they remained poised for the signal which would call them home for a new rising. They were convinced that the United States had a mission to make the western world safe for republicanism. They denounced American neutrality laws, advocated intervention in Europe, and welcomed the Crimean War as an opportunity to put their ideas into practice. Many were republicans in the Continental tradition and dreamed of an international brotherhood of free men. They embraced Kossuth and Mazzini, despite their anticlerical views, as fellow crusaders in a common cause. A few were specifically critical of their Church and of the Pope as a temporal ruler. They attended meetings to celebrate the revolution and to pledge their support for further efforts at liberation. Irish speakers appeared on such occasions on the same platform with German, Italian, Polish, and Hungarian orators.

Perhaps the most interesting aspect of the history of the Irish Forty-eighters was the conflict between a small, radical minority and the Roman Catholic hierarchy. Meagher, for example, who considered him-

---

[27] See Lonn, *Foreigners in the Union Army and Navy*, 224–25; and D. P. Conyngham, *The Irish Brigade, and Its Campaigns*, 548.

self a liberal Catholic and approved of a nonsectarian educational system, was denounced as a "red republican." Furthermore, a large section of the American Catholic press disapproved of his sympathy for Kossuth and Mazzini. Meagher replied with a bitter reference to "the brainless ridiculous donkeys who bray and kick up the dust when poked with a crozier." [28]

Under a barrage of attacks from the Church and the Catholic press, the newcomers either had to capitulate or remain silent. In the opinion of the Boston *Pilot,* Meagher and his kind were "anti-Papal" and "anti-sacerdotal." The same paper derisively referred to Mitchel as "Moses Mitchel." The attack upon Meagher by McMaster, the editor of the *Freeman's Journal,* reached a climax in a disgraceful cowhiding and shooting between the two men. Bishop Hughes branded the radical revolutionists as irreligious, "apostates from the honored creed of their country," and atheists, vigorously defending the Pope's claims to temporal sovereignty. The bishop tried to draw a distinction between American and European liberty, relating the latter to "the genius of destruction and bloodshed." On one occasion, however, he doubted even the founding fathers of the American Republic, who were "deeply tinged with the indifference, not to say the infidelity of those who figured at the head of the first French Revolution." [29]

The clergy so denounced "red republicanism" that the Irish refused to take part in a public reception held in Boston for Louis Kossuth. The *Catholic Telegraph* of Cincinnati branded Kossuth an enemy of the Roman Catholic Church; the *Freeman's Journal* repeatedly discoursed on Mazzini's "foul Republicanism"; and *The Citizen* criticized Kossuth for his arrogance, his praise of England, and his flirtation with American abolitionists. [30]

Charles Gaffan Duffy once wrote from Ireland, "It seems the eternal fate of unsuccessful revolutionists to fly at each other's throats." The experiences of German, Irish, and other Forty-eighters in the United States bear out the charge. It was disastrous for Irish radicals to become involved in a controversy with their Church, to which the bulk of the conservative Irish-American population was deeply devoted. As a result, they lost whatever influence they might have exerted as an intellectual and cultural leaven among their countrymen. Their liberal republicanism

28 Ahearn, *T. F. Meagher,* 35.

29 Browne (ed.), "A Memoir of Archbishop Hughes," *Historical Records and Studies,* XXXIX–XL (1952), 168–74. See also Lawrence Kahoe, *The Complete Works of the Most Reverend John Hughes,* II, 22–24; 790–93.

30 *The Citizen* (New York), July 21, 1855.

was branded as irreligious, atheistic, and destructive of property, law, and order. The fact that international republicans attacked the Pope as a temporal sovereign as eagerly as they denounced the crowned heads of Europe was a major consideration in the conflict between radical Forty-eighters and the hierarchy.

Chapter IX

The Irish and the Catholic Church

T<small>HE</small> flood of immigrants from Ireland in the late 1840's and early 1850's constituted a serious challenge to the Catholic Church in America and caught it largely unprepared for its new responsibilities. From a relatively small membership at the end of the eighteenth century, the Catholic Church mushroomed in the nineteenth into one of the largest religious organizations in the United States. The American hierarchy lacked both funds and personnel to meet the needs of thousands of new parishioners. They had shown little interest in the problem of immigration up to that time, for they had regarded other matters such as building churches, hospitals, almshouses, orphanages, and schools as of greater immediate importance.

Despite the lack of preparation, the Catholic Church made strong efforts to come to the aid of the immigrants when they arrived. Catholic priests bolstered the morale of the bewildered Irish newcomers, gave them spiritual sustenance in their first years of trial and adversity, and helped them make the transition to American ways more easily. As shepherds of their flocks, they exerted a powerful disciplinary influence upon men and women who had been suddenly detached from their familiar moorings. They helped safeguard the integrity of family life and curb the mercurial temperament of the Irish. They worked hard to prevent the moral chaos which might result from such a mass migration and lessened the social dangers inherent in it. If priests also undertook to provide leadership in matters not strictly religious, it must be remembered that as yet there were few laymen among the American Irish with sufficient education and experience to perform that function. McGee regarded the Catholic Church as not only the most important social institution in America, but as a "mistress of philosophy," "a bulwark of order," and "a stay of law." [1]

The challenge that immigration presented to the Catholic Church was magnified by the fact that many priests were foreign-born and involved in the same Americanization process as their parishioners. In the 1840's

---

[1] Skelton, *The Life of Thomas D'Arcy McGee*, 247.

and 1850's, when popular hostility to Roman Catholics found violent expression in nativist mobs and political parties, the task of the clergy was far more difficult than under more normal circumstances. At the same time, nativism produced greater cohesion among the Catholic masses, and the essential characteristics of American Catholic life were hammered out on "the anvil of nativism" and largely determined by the immigration from 1830 to 1860.[2]

In due time, the Catholic Church was faced with the problem of reducing existing racial and national antagonisms between French, German, and Irish Catholics. It became necessary to develop schools and seminaries to provide more native Americans for the priesthood, for recruits from Europe were under serious language handicaps. The problem of Americanizing the Catholic Church, while keeping it within the administrative framework and doctrinal limits of a universal Church, was one of the major challenges to Catholicism in the United States. It provoked controversy well into the present century.

According to Catholic sources, there were 663,000 Roman Catholics in the United States in 1840 and 1,606,000 a decade later. The hierarchy at that time consisted of five archbishops, twenty-four bishops, and nearly two thousand priests. About 700,000 of this sudden expansion in the membership of the Church was due to immigration, of which over 500,-000 came from Ireland. Bishop Francis Patrick Kendrick estimated the number of Irish Catholics in the United States in 1850 at one million and concluded that native Roman Catholics constituted but one-fifth of the entire membership. In the decade between 1850 and 1860, another 602,000 Irish were added.[3]

The Church had earned its place in the affections of the Irish people. In times that were dark, priests and laymen had shared the miseries of their unhappy island. Ireland—the land of legends, saints, holy wells, primitive baptismal fonts, and crosses which were the emblems of eternity —had been a bulwark of Christianity in the early centuries when most of the Continent was wrapped in intellectual and spiritual darkness. The attachment of the Irish people to their persecuted Church was never shaken. In the eighteenth century, when it went into virtual outlawry, its hunted priests remained the leaders of their people.

In the opinion of several American bishops, Irish immigrants had a special spiritual mission in the United States. They were the instruments

2 Thomas T. McAvoy, "The Formation of the Catholic Minority in the United States, 1820–1860," *The Review of Politics*, X (1948), No. 1, 13–34.

3 Nolan, *Reverend Francis Patrick Kenrick*, 418; and Roemer, *The Catholic Church in the United States*, 211, 226.

of God's providence to bring about a revival of Catholicism. In the words of the first Bishop of Rochester, they were "best fitted to open the way for religion in a new country." The Bishop of Peoria wrote a whole book about the religious mission of the Irish in America. The Irish had demonstrated their bravery and devotion in times of trouble; they were inured to suffering hardships for their Church; and they loved their priests, some of whom manifested a remarkable spirit of camaraderie with their people.

In the United States, the Irish continued to sacrifice for their Church. They were prepared to worship in the poorest chapels, for they had known "thatch-roofed chapels on the bleak moor or barren hillside." No amount of misrepresentation could shake them; they were impervious to ridicule; and the nativist agitation and "the Protestant Crusade" made them more belligerent in defense of their separate religious institutions. Their trust in the priest's authority was unlimited. Finally, the Church not only guaranteed salvation, but it was a part of home, a place where they could "renew the comfort of the familiar." Religion had always been a vital part of Irish nationalism.

New parishes were born not only in the large cities, but along the routes of the internal improvements that carried the Irish laborer into the interior. Everywhere, in New York, Connecticut, Ohio, Indiana, and other states, the building of churches paralleled the construction of early canals. Workers on the Erie Canal started a church at Utica. The church at Windsor Locks, near Hartford, Connecticut, was built by canal diggers, and the one at Norwich by workmen on the Worcester and Norwich road.[4] New England millowners frequently donated the land on which their Irish employees built their church. In Philadelphia, in 1839, Irishmen shipping coal on the Schuylkill bought an old vinegar factory and converted it into a chapel. Cleveland's first Irish Catholic church was known as St. Mary's on the Flats, and its first resident pastor was John Dillon of county Limerick, Ireland. In northern Indiana, the building of the road from Indianapolis to Chicago by way of South Bend was marked by a similar development of Catholic parishes.[5] Irish laborers along the Milwaukee Railroad to La Crosse, Wisconsin, named their new parishes alternately St. Mary's and St. Patrick's.

The problem of finding the proper personnel to staff the rapidly expanding Church was not easily solved and explains why so many priests had to be brought over from Ireland. Occasionally, it was necessary to

---

[4] See also James Fitton, *Sketches of the Establishment of the Church in New England.*
[5] John Hugh O'Donnell, "The Catholic Church in Northern Indiana, 1830–1850," *The Catholic Historical Review*, XXV (1941), 142.

suspend unworthy servants of the Lord whose credentials had misrepresented their character or had not been studied too closely. In 1816, for example, Archbishop Neale suspended a priest in Baltimore for "excesses of Liquor." [6] The *Truth Teller*, in 1831, warned Irish laborers against a priest from Brooklyn who was trying to organize an independent Catholic Church.[7] Bishop John England, in 1833, expressed deep disappointment with several Irish clergymen who had been assigned to the United States. The Bishop of Charleston strongly advocated a native clergy, though quite willing to have them partly trained in Ireland.

The Church also had to contend with numerous quarrels with parishioners over parish policies and with rebellion against unpopular priests. In several cases, the disturbers were threatened with denial of the Sacraments. In Worcester, Massachusetts, in 1847, when Father Gibson threatened the Shamrock Benevolent Society with spiritual penalties, members of the turbulent Irish organization nailed a placard on the church door branding the priest as a "Saxon tyrant." Peace was restored only when the priest appealed to the sheriff for help.[8]

The predominance of the Irish in the American hierarchy was not challenged successfully until the "new immigration" began to send their sons into the Church and to insist upon having priests from their own nationality group. Then serious nationality conflicts developed in some parts of the country because German, Italian, and Polish Catholics protested against an alleged monopoly of the priesthood by American Irish. Years earlier, the Irish had denounced "a system of ecclesiastic tyranny by a cabal of unprincipled French churchmen" [9] quite as vehemently as they were now attacked. The struggle between German and Irish Catholics in the late nineteenth century over "Cahenslyism" proved particularly disturbing. Essentially, it involved the demand for greater ecclesiastical autonomy in the American Church for foreign-language groups.[10]

Despite these occasional controversies, the predominance of the Irish element in the leadership of the Catholic Church in the United States has continued. A study of American bishops of Irish birth or parentage from 1789 to 1935 shows that of 464 bishops appointed, 268 were Irish—

[6] Peter Guilday, *The Life and Times of John England*, I, 10–11, 183.

[7] Quoted in Thomas F. Meehan, "Pioneer Times in Brooklyn," United States Catholic Historical Society *Historical Records and Studies*, II (1901), Part I, 187.

[8] Lord, Sexton, and Harrington, *History of the Archdiocese of Boston*, II, 418–19.

[9] Guilday, *John England*, I, 273.

[10] See John J. Meng, "Cahenslyism: The First Stage, 1883–1891," *The Catholic Historical Review*, XXXI (1946), 389–413; XXXII (1946), 302–40, 389–413; also Thomas O'Gorman, *A History of the Roman Catholic Church in the United States*. The latest treatment of the subject, which corrects earlier misconceptions, is by Colman J. Barry, *The Catholic Church and German Americans*.

a total which probably errs on the side of caution, for it counts only those whose fathers were Irish. Studies of specific dioceses show a similar preponderance of Irish names.[11] As late as 1886, according to John Tracy Ellis, of the sixty-nine bishops in the United States, thirty-five were Irish. The Germans ranked second with only fifteen.[12] There is hardly a diocese or an archdiocese in the United States that has not been governed by prelates of Irish birth or descent. This predominance of the Irish was important in several attempts to "Americanize" the Catholic Church—an issue over which bitter controversies developed among the princes of the Church and which has bearing on the perennial question of the extent to which the immigrant has kept the faith in the United States.[13]

One of the first to raise the issue of "Americanizing" the Church was Orestes A. Brownson, a New England intellectual who was a convert to Catholicism. He looked with grave concern on the Irish invasion of his Church and stated frankly that the Roman Catholic Church could not become properly American until it ceased to be Irish, and that it would not grow as it should until it could be proved that Americanism and Catholicism were compatible. Brownson voiced his respect for the Irish peasantry and sympathized with their suffering, but he did not regard them "as the advance guard of humanity." Such statements provoked a vigorous counterattack by his bishop and by the Boston *Pilot* and other papers. In a letter of 1849, Brownson had the temerity to write, "Nobody can deny that in external decorum and the ordinary moral and social virtues the Irish Catholics are the most deficient class of our community." He warned against the danger to the Church if Catholicity should become identified with "Irish hoodlumism, drunkenness and poverty."[14]

Father Isaac Hecker was another who labored to convince Americans that the Catholic Church was not undemocratic, and he pleaded for a more liberal spirit within the Church itself. On one occasion he wrote, the Church "is not national with us, hence it does not meet our wants, nor does it fully understand or sympathize with the experiences and dispositions of our people. It is principally made up of adopted foreign individ-

---

[11] James D. Hackett, *Bishops of the United States of Irish Birth or Descent;* O. B. Corrigon, "Chronology of the Catholic Hierarchy of the United States," *The Catholic Historical Review,* I (1916), 367–89; II (1917), 131–45, 283–301. See also Michael J. Hynes, *History of the Diocese of Cleveland.*

[12] John Tracy Ellis, *The Life of James Cardinal Gibbons,* I, 334. See also Michael A. Corrigan, "Register of the Clergy Laboring in the Archdiocese of New York from Early Missionary Times to 1855," United States Catholic Historical Society *Historical Records and Studies,* II (1901), Part I, 36–81; Part II, 227–67.

[13] See Gerald Shaughnessy, *Has the Immigrant Kept the Faith?*

[14] Arthur M. Schlesinger, Jr., *Orestes A. Brownson,* 214.

[15] Quoted in Handlin, *Boston's Immigrants,* 153–54. See also Isaac Hecker, *The Church and the Age.*

uals." [15] Prelates like John Ireland, James Gibbons, and John Spalding, and others of Irish stock, shared this attitude to a greater or less degree. They argued that all the national differences among the Catholic membership should be ironed out by emphasizing Americanization, abandoning foreign customs, and co-operating, even with Protestants, in civil and moral reforms for the good of all Americans. Such matters had a way of developing into doctrinal controversy, and, on several occasions, appeals were carried to Rome to quiet the factionalism in the American Church.

In the sharp division between what might be called the more liberal and the more conservative wings, one finds prelates of Irish stock on both sides of the controversy, though the "Americanizers" were in the minority. In the end, the Pope sided with the more conservative majority in his *Testem Benevolentiae,* and only Cardinal Gibbons' unusual skill prevented a blast from the Vatican which would have damned "Americanism" as heresy.[16]

The number of distinguished Irishmen in the American hierarchy is so large that only a few can be singled out for special mention. John England was the son of an Irish refugee hedge schoolmaster and Cork tobacconist. He was prepared for his ministry in Ireland. In the United States, he became the bishop of the new diocese of Charleston. His notable career has been fully described in a biography by the late Peter Guilday. Francis Patrick Kenrick, a native of Dublin, was the bishop of Philadelphia. His brother Peter published the *Catholic Herald* and, in 1847, became the archbishop of St. Louis.

John Hughes was the famous fighting Irish bishop of New York and its first archbishop. Cardinal Gibbons referred to him as "active, bold, vigorous, aggressive . . . another Joshua fighting in the valley." Hughes was a native of county Tyrone. His family came to Pennsylvania, where the future prelate worked as a day laborer and as a gardener at Mount St. Mary's Seminary. Here he was educated for the priesthood. He was an uncompromising champion of Roman Catholicism and a builder and promoter of great success. He fought for the bishop's right to control local church property, and he was ready to battle—with bullets, if necessary—the nativists who attacked his Church and called him "Dagger John." A shrewd and masterful prelate, and a public figure of great influence, he held the Irish of New York in the hollow of his hand. He was involved in many controversies and some inconsistencies on public issues, but never in the matter of his Church, which he served with unwavering devotion.[17]

16 See Peter E. Hogan, "Americanism and the Catholic University of America," *The Catholic Historical Review,* XXXIII (1947), 164, 176, 177.

17 See Kahoe, *Complete Works of Reverend John Hughes.*

Bernard John McQuaid, first bishop of Rochester, was an ultramontane Catholic who fought for the orthodox Catholic position and uncompromisingly resisted his fellow prelates who wavered on such questions as schools and secret societies. He was the son of an Irish immigrant laborer who was killed in a fight with a fellow worker. The orphan found refuge with the Sisters of Charity, and the Church, recognizing his ability, gave him his education. Archbishop Michael Augustine Corrigan was another second-generation Irishman, whose father, a cabinetmaker, emigrated in 1828. Young Corrigan rose rapidly from teacher, to president of a seminary, to bishop of Newark, and to archbishop of New York in 1885. Like McQuaid, Corrigan was ultraconservative. He denounced the organizations of Irish nationalists and joined in the attack on Archbishop John Ireland on the school question.

John Ireland came from county Kilkenny. His family went by covered wagon to Minnesota in the 1850's, where the father became a carpenter and a local Democratic politician. Discovered by Bishop Joseph Cretin, Ireland was well educated by the Church and became a priest in St. Paul in 1861. During the Civil War he served in the Union army as a chaplain, and ever after played a national role in the Grand Army of the Republic. An ardent reformer, a total abstainer, a dynamic public figure, and an aggressive bishop, he was variously known as the "Father Mathew of the West" and "the Consecrated Blizzard" of the Old Northwest. He fought municipal corruption, was friendly to labor, except in the Pullman strike of 1894, opposed free silver, was an ardent Republican and a friend of Theodore Roosevelt, was a shrewd colonizer, and was the champion of a Catholic University of America. His liberal views about Americanizing the Church, his attitude on the school question, and on the role of the Church in civic and political affairs brought him into conflict with his fellow bishops. He never received the red hat of the cardinal, though Theodore Roosevelt and John Hay were eager to get it for him. His "spirit of false liberalism" was denounced occasionally from Catholic pulpits, but there is no reason to question his orthodoxy on fundamentals. He regarded himself as a thoroughly loyal son of the Church.

James Cardinal Gibbons was in many ways the most distinguished and the most universally revered of all the American Irish prelates. His family came from Ireland in 1829, and the father died when the boy was thirteen. Six years later, James resolved to become a priest, and he was ordained in 1861. Seven years later, he was the "boy bishop" of North Carolina. In 1886, he became a cardinal. Able, intelligent, conciliatory, and kindly, Cardinal Gibbons was respected as a great American as well as a powerful prelate. He counted among his friends many public men

of all religions. He threw his influence invariably on the side of concili-
ation and fair compromise, and, on several occasions, was able to avoid
action which would have proved disruptive and unwise. Like Ireland,
he opposed the doctrine of papal infallibility, but accepted the decision
unequivocally.

The list of Irish-American churchmen who came from humble origins
and may be called "self-made men" is long and impressive. It emphasizes
anew the role of the Church as a social-work agency, in that it recognized
ability, granted relief to the deserving, and singled them out for training
at the expense of the Church. John McCloskey, first American cardinal,
lost his father early in life and was sent to school by the priests. Bishop
McCloskey of Louisville was the son of a Brooklyn milkman; William
Cardinal O'Connell, the son of a canal laborer. Dennis Joseph Dougherty,
sixth American cardinal, came from the Pennsylvania coal mines, where
he had worked as a breaker boy.

Mathew Anthony O'Brien, one of thirteen children of an Irish distiller,
worked his way to America on an immigrant ship. Bishop Flaget of
Bardstown, Kentucky, gave him his chance, and he became a successful
missionary priest. James Augustine McFaul, bishop of Trenton in 1894,
was sent to school by the Bendictines. John Joseph Keane, whose parents
were driven to the United States by the Irish famine, was educated by
the Christian Brothers and became the first rector of the Catholic University of America. Charles Hyacinth McKenna, son of a widowed mother
who brought her brood to the United States in 1848, worked as a stonecutter in Iowa for a time, until he was singled out by the Bishop of
Dubuque to become a Catholic missionary. John Cristopher Drumgoole's
story is much the same. Brought to New York by his widowed mother,
he became a cobbler until he attracted the attention of a priest. He devoted his life to poor Negroes, waifs, and newsboys. Dozens of similar
cases might be cited. They all point to the importance of the Church as a
social factor in the lives of immigrants.[18]

In a history of Irish immigration which is concerned only incidentally
with the history of American Catholicism, it is impossible to discuss in
detail the many controversies within the ranks of the Church itself because of the conflicting ambitions of members of the clergy, high and
low, or because of specific questions of theology and church practice.
Nevertheless, brief mention must be made of several questions in which
the Irish were prominently involved.

The battle over "trusteeism" was bitter but relatively short. It concerned the question of whether a local parish should incorporate as a

18 See sketches in *DAB;* and James H. Moynihan, *The Life of Archbishop John Ireland.*

local unit and hold title to its property. Local control was defended as being in harmony with the prevailing democratic spirit of America. In 1854, *The Citizen,* for example, favored trustee control and argued that since churches were built by popular subscription, the people, and not the bishop, should own and administer the property. Inevitably, the question of trustee control over other matters, some of them spiritual, became involved. Tumult and schism were the likely results of conflicts with the bishop, and strong administrators like Hughes concluded that, to avoid rebellion and heresy, they must control the church property also. The issue was acute in New York, Philadelphia, and Baltimore before 1845. In Philadelphia it was complicated by antagonism between French and Irish Catholics and by the belligerence of William Hogan, an Irish priest who was supported by Mathew Carey, a successful Irish publicist. After the bishop withdrew his faculties as a priest, Hogan tried to found an independent Catholic Church. In the end, the controversy died down, for the people bowed to the wishes of their priests and bishops. The actual defection from the Church membership was small.[19]

The Church has consistently opposed secret societies unless the clergy has supervision over them. Bishop Hughes' first sweeping condemnation of secret orders was not directed against Masons or Odd Fellows, but against "Corkonians and Connaught men—far ups and far downs" who marshalled Irish laborers on public works into combinations bound by oaths "administered to them by some of their more depraved and designing countrymen." [20]

The hierarchy in America and Ireland, to the disgust of some ardent Irish nationalists, denounced the Fenian Brotherhood, though some priests were active in it. On January 12, 1870, it was condemned by the Vatican, and its members threatened with excommunication. The action was based not only upon the secret character of the society for the liberation of Ireland, but also because it counselled revolution before exhausting all other methods. American Fenians attributed the decision, so damaging to their cause, to English and "Irish bishops of British proclivities." Several Irish-American papers advised that the action be ignored because the jurisdiction of the Church could not be extended properly to purely temporal questions.

During the labor troubles in Pennsylvania, in which the "Molly Maguires" and Hibernians were violent participants, and during the

---

[19] Shea, *History of the Catholic Church in the United States,* III, Chapter XV; also "Trusteeism in the Atlantic States, 1785–1863," *The Catholic Historical Review,* XXX (1944), 135–54.

[20] Kahoe, *Complete Works of Reverend John Hughes,* I, 34.

ascendancy of the Knights of Labor, in which the Irish were prominent, the same issue of secret orders was raised. A number of priests and bishops condemned oath-bound societies in labor matters, but Cardinal Gibbons prevented action by the Vatican which would have condemned the Knights of Labor in the United States. Archbishop Ireland, while personally opposed to secret societies, thought that, with the exception of the Masons, they should not be condemned because they were not specifically anti-Catholic.

More controversial, and still unsettled in many communities, was the question of Catholic parochial schools and their relation to public tax funds collected from citizens of all religions. The public-school movement in the nineteenth century was greatly stimulated by the problem of immigration, and men like E. L. Godkin of *The Nation* believed the foreign-born presented a new and definite challenge to American education. The rate of illiteracy among whites jumped from 3.77 per cent in 1830 to 5.03 per cent in 1850. Many Americans considered public schools the most effective instruments for the Americanization of recent arrivals from Europe.[21] If the Irish had not come in such numbers just as the public-school system was in a critical, formative stage, the controversy over church and state in the field of education might not have been so acrimonious.

Bishop McQuaid, in 1876, tried to summarize the Catholic position in matters of education. He insisted that only the parent has the right to decide where and how his children were to be educated and that it was unfair to tax Catholics, Jews, or even infidels for the support of schools where the Bible was read and offensive religious exercises held. He maintained that Catholics had no desire "to deprive Protestants of their Bible or their schools." But Catholics wanted their children educated in Catholic schools, supported by their own money, and setting their own standards of instruction. What Catholics did not want, according to the bishop, was "Protestant money, nor any state money that was not taken from our purses." Compulsory public-school laws were denounced by Catholic papers like the *Pilot* as "radically unsound, untrue, atheistical." The editor contended that "education must be the work of the Church, not the state," and that the child belonged to his parents and not the state. He cavalierly disposed of such a champion of public schools as Horace Mann as "a tenth-rate schoolmaster."[22]

The First Provincial Council of Bishops in 1829 advised the establish-

21 Merle Curti, *The Growth of American Thought,* 317, 492.
22 See Handlin, *Boston's Immigrants,* 138–39; and Sherman M. Smith, *The Relations of the State to Religious Education, passim.*

ment of parish parochial schools wherever possible, and the Irish have
been among the most faithful supporters of this injunction ever since. In
Boston, teachers were imported from Ireland for the first Catholic school
in 1820. In Lowell, the first parochial school was housed in a rented room
and had an Irish schoolmaster, the parents paying six cents a week per
child. By 1835, there were enough Irish in Lowell to support two schools
as part of the town's school system. Under this "Lowell plan," the Catholics furnished the building and the teachers. The arrangement, which had
the approval of Bishop Fenwick, collapsed during the nativist agitation
in 1852.[23]

In New York, the school question reached the proportions of a major
battle in the period from 1839 to 1842, with Bishop Hughes as the leading protagonist of the Catholic party. Hughes demanded a share of the
city's funds, administered at the time by a Public School Society, a private
corporation controlled by a Protestant majority. Quarrels over textbooks
and the King James Version aggravated the trouble between Protestants
and Catholics. Governor Seward agreed that the latter had genuine grievances and believed many immigrant children were kept out of school
because of sectarian instruction. He encouraged Catholics to petition for
a share of the public funds for their parochial schools. When the request
was refused, Bishop Hughes sponsored a slate of Catholic candidates in
the local election, but the slate polled only 2,200 votes. The controversy,
which we need not follow in all its ramifications, measurably increased
the hostility of American Protestants and Irish Catholics. In the end,
control of the schools in New York City was vested in an elected board
of education under the supervision of a state superintendent of education.
A new controversy developed when the latter recommended daily Bible
reading. Defeated in his major effort, which some Catholics considered
unwise, Hughes turned his great energies to building parochial schools
and providing proper textbooks for them. Eventually, a law completely
secularized the public schools, forbidding religious instruction of any
kind.

In Ohio, in 1853, Archbishop John B. Purcell objected to the taxation
of Roman Catholics for public schools. When the state legislature, four
years later, considered making school attendance compulsory, the *Catholic Telegraph* commented sarcastically, "Why not appoint a committee to
go to Prussia or Russia and bring us over the entire system of 'paternal
government' in a lump?" [24] In Baltimore, although the Protestant Bible

[23] Richard J. Quinlan, "Growth and Development of Catholic Education in the Archdiocese of Boston," *The Catholic Historical Review*, XXII (1937), 27–41.

[24] Quoted in Sister Paluszek, "The Opinion of the *Catholic Telegraph* on Contemporary
Affairs and Politics," 46.

was read to Protestant children in the schools and the Catholic version to Catholics, there was a violent controversy in 1853 over a bill to allot a portion of the school funds to sectarian and private schools.[25]

Catholic leaders have suggested various compromises. Bishop Richard Gilmour of Cleveland offered to put the city's parochial schools under the control of the local school board during regular school hours when no religious instruction would be given, with the proviso that there be complete freedom to teach religion outside these hours and that the city pay the teachers. The offer was declined, although such a plan seems to have worked successfully in some parts of Ohio in the 1870's and 1880's. The Poughkeepsie plan, approved by Cardinal McCloskey, and continued up to 1898, provided that the local school board lease parochial schools on a yearly basis; keep them in repair and pay the salaries of teachers, who were to meet the certification requirements of the state; and retain certain rights of inspection and control. The teachers were to be nuns, wearing their habits, and the schools were to be open to non-Catholics also. No child was required to attend religious exercises. The so-called Faribault and Stillwater, Minnesota, plans, in Archbishop Ireland's province, resembled the Poughkeepsie plan, but provided for religious instruction after school hours.

Most of these compromises came to an end during the American Protective Association crusade of the 1890's, which was directed largely against Catholics and Catholic schools. As late as 1917, Massachusetts battled over a proposed constitutional amendment to forbid specifically the use of public funds for private schools. The controversy ended with what the Boston *Pilot* considered an "unworthy compromise." [26]

The controversy over Bible reading in the public schools, so acute a century ago, has not entirely died down. There were several authenticated cases in 1859 when children were expelled from Boston schools because their fathers ordered them not to read the Protestant Bible. In 1862, when a compulsory Bible-reading law was repealed in Massachusetts, an ardent orator shouted it could never happen "so long as a piece of Plymouth rock remained big enough to make a gun flint of." [27] As late as April 9, 1904, the *Irish World and American Industrial Liberator*

---

[25] Lawrence F. Schmeckebier, *History of the Know-Nothing Party in Maryland* (Johns Hopkins Studies in History and Political Science, XVII, Nos. 4–5), 15–16.

[26] For details, see Smith, *Relations of the State to Religious Education*, Chapter XI. See also J. A. Burns, *The Growth and Development of the Catholic School System in the United States;* and the recent exchanges between James B. Conant, Archbishop Richard J. Cushing, and Allan V. Heely in *The Saturday Review* (May 3, 1952). For statistics on the continued growth of Catholic schools and colleges, showing an increase of 35 per cent in ten years, see the *New York Times*, March 30, 1952.

[27] Smith, *Relations of the State to Religious Education*, 257.

printed under big headlines a lurid tale about a child of ten, whipped "black and blue" in a Boston school "for refusing to read the King James' Version." A closer reading of the article indicated that the incident had occurred over fifty years before and was copied from Martin I. J. Griffin's *American Catholic Historical Researches.*

Discussions over proper textbooks for the schools have been particularly acrimonious, and they involve both Catholic and non-Catholic groups. In 1855, the New York *Citizen* advertised Shea's *School History of the United States* as specially designed for parochial schools and "free from popular errors and false principles." In the 1880's, *Swinton's History,* a text used in the Boston schools, was attacked because of its allegedly unfair references to indulgences. As late as 1920, Edward F. McSweeney of Boston, speaking for the Friends of Irish Freedom, complained heatedly of the *Century Dictionary's* definition of the word "brutal" in connection with a reference to the Irish. He obtained the promise of Charles S. O'Connor of the Boston school committee that the objectionable handbook would be removed from the schools.[28]

Recent opposition to a federal child-labor amendment, in which Catholic bishops joined with President Lowell of Harvard to oppose the measure; the support of the Church for Franco; a recent tendency to equate communism with liberalism; the controversies over family limitation; the activities of such individuals as Father Coughlin, the Irish radio priest; and the necessity for the Archbishop of Boston to denounce a small, fanatical Catholic group for its anti-Semitism have affected the attitude of some liberal Americans toward the Church. Because of the prominence of the Irish in the organization, the entire Irish element has been somewhat involved. Yet it must be remembered that many Catholic leaders have differed with their fellow religionists on these issues and some have fought vigorously in defense of American civil rights.

A minority of fanatical Protestants still refer to the Roman Catholic Church as "the Scarlet Lady of Babylon" or the "Whore of Rome," and regard the Pope as the archenemy of the American form of government. In a milder aspect, the anti-Catholic point of view is revealed in such derogatory references to the Church as "a Paddy superstition." Priests have denounced such organizations as the Christian Endeavor Society, and Irish papers like *The Irish World,* as late as 1896 and 1900, featured articles which blamed practically all the world's woes on "the appalling harvest of unbelief" stemming from the "irreligion and immorality of Germany" and the "so-called Reformation." The same paper indulged

28 *The Gaelic-American* (New York), July 3, 1920.

in occasional attacks on Methodists and "Christian Science Paganism." [29]
A century ago, Bishop Hughes had lectured on the decline of Protestantism as an institution totally without spirituality, and the Boston *Pilot* had referred to Protestant ministers as "the most venal people in the land," "Simoniacs to a man," and had attacked state education in violent terms.[30] The *Pilot* insisted that co-operation between "true Catholics" and "real Protestants" was utterly impossible.

After the lapse of a century, theological controversy still remains grim business, but the area of co-operation between Protestants and Catholics is expanding.

This chapter may well end by pointing out the unquestioned services of the Irish in the many agencies through which their Church in America has acted to alleviate human misery. Wherever the Church went, it built schools, hospitals, orphanages, almshouses, and correctional institutions. It brought in nuns, sisters, and monks to minister to the needy and the unfortunate. One factor in this development was the distrust of Irish immigrants for public institutions controlled by Protestants and from which Catholic priests were barred. In many cases, Catholic institutions were open to all who needed help without regard for their religion. Native Irish priests, as well as American-born Irish like Thomas Augustine Judge of South Boston, became missionaries to the poor and the downtrodden, including the Negro. Irish Catholic societies by the scores have raised and distributed funds to help destitute children, support orphanages, look after the immigrant, and finance many kinds of benevolences.

Bishop Hughes, in 1849, brought over the Sisters of Mercy from Dublin to work among working girls and help them find jobs. They taught refugees of the Irish famine needlework and sewing, the duties of the kitchen and laundry, and made them into competent domestic servants. In 1854, the order established itself in San Francisco and built a school, hospital, and orphanage. Their House of Mercy in Cincinnati was built largely by the working-class Irish.[31]

In the 1880's, the Mission of Our Lady of the Rosary was founded in New York for the care of Irish immigrant girls, and in ten years it had befriended 50,000 and helped many more to reach their destination.[32] Margaret Gaffney, daughter of poor, illiterate Irish immigrants, estab-

29 *The Irish World* (New York), May 30, 1896; April 14, 1900.
30 *The Pilot* (Boston), April 24, 1852.
31 See Helen M. Sweeney, *The Golden Milestone, 1846–1896.*
32 See Peter Guilday, "The Church in the United States, 1870–1920," *The Catholic Historical Review*, VI (1921), 533–48.

lished three houses for six hundred orphans in New Orleans. Mary Frances Clarke of Dublin organized the Sisters of the Blessed Virgin Mary in Philadelphia and later took them to Iowa in answer to a call from the Bishop of Dubuque. Various orders of sisters have always had a preponderance of Irish.

In the earliest days of the heavy Irish immigration, the Church had to deal with some of the lowest and most uncultivated immigrants, and there was a heavy concentration of poverty and crime in the Catholic sections of the United States. It was therefore imperative to raise the economic level of the Irish, thereby increasing American respect for them, and to assume temporarily the burden of caring for the sick, the destitute, and the wayward. It is a notable fact, however, that within a relatively short time, the Irish were able to give generous support to the institutions which had helped them in their years of need. The number of hospitals and orphanages established by successful Irish immigrants or their children is large. It includes institutions as widely scattered as Cornelius Heeney's Brooklyn Benevolent Society for poor orphans and the nationally-known Judge Myles P. O'Connor orphanage in San Jose, California, originally established by an Irish priest to care for unemployed men.[33]

[33] Abell, "The Catholic Factor in Urban Welfare," *The Review of Politics,* XIV (July, 1952), 289–324; also Michael J. Scanlan, "Catholic Charitable and Social Work in the United States," in *Catholic Builders of the Nation* (ed. C. E. McGuire), II, 229–59.

CHAPTER X

The Lure of Politics

IN 1914, Professor E. A. Ross, with a sociologist's love for generalizations, observed that "for all their fine Celtic traits" Irish immigrants had "neither the temperament nor the training to make a success of popular government" because they were motivated by personalities rather than principle. He added that while "the Hibernian domination has given our cities genial officials, brave policemen, and gallant fire fighters," it also has made them the worst governed.[1] The statement obviously makes no distinction between the first and later generations and does not take into account American conditions which help explain the Irishman's role in politics. There can be little doubt that the record during the high tide of Irish immigration was bad, or that it continues to be bad in some areas to the present day. A sympathetic, filiopietistic writer frankly admitted that "the public record of the Irish in the United States has dark spots which cannot be ignored and which it would be futile to attempt to minimize."[2]

The same genius for organization which made the Irish so successful as leaders in the Church and in the field of labor helps account for their success in politics. To all three fields, warmhearted, sociable Irishmen brought a human touch that proved most important. In Ireland, politics had been a struggle, with not too much concern for the rules of the game, and Irishmen had few, if any, ethical scruples about the machine politics of American cities a century ago. Their wit, their flexibility in dealing with people, and their oratorical gifts made them natural leaders for a turbulent urban democracy which had neither accepted nor mastered the techniques of orderly, honest, and efficient government.

Irishmen felt the lure of American politics much as they were attracted by the sociability of the saloon, and it was no accident that the saloon and the political club were closely allied. Political meetings were held by ward politicians in these poor men's clubs, and here party placards were distributed to the marchers in political demonstrations.

---

[1] Quoted in Davis, *Immigration and Americanization,* 320–31.
[2] Edward F. Roberts, *Ireland in America,* 131.

Irish peasants had been tools of their landlords; it was not very different to become the tools of political bosses, who marched them in groups to the polls and cemented the allegiance with free liquor. The racial and religious cohesion of the Irish could be utilized easily for political purposes. Membership in a Church which was under attack when they arrived tended to separate them from the Protestant majority and to accentuate their clannishness. But the Irish immigrant had a tremendous advantage over other newcomers—he knew the English language and could enter American politics without first hurdling a difficult language barrier.

In the 1840's and 1850's, American urban democracy had much to learn about the processes of honest self-government. In many places, there were no registration of voters, no secret ballot, and naturalization was easy. Before elections, agents of local machines scoured the cities to bring in aliens to get citizenship papers from political judges who asked few or no questions and accepted their sponsors' testimony without challenge. Local ward heelers coached the applicants, if that were necessary; provided the required witnesses, who often had not seen the applicants before they met in court; and paid whatever fee was involved. The solemn ceremony usually was concluded with a round of drinks at a nearby saloon. Youths under age were naturalized; little attention was paid to the period of residence in the United States; citizenship papers were handed out in saloons; and fraudulent signatures were unchallenged. Occasionally, newly arrived immigrants were marched directly from the dock to the voting booth. No Australian ballot insured secrecy; therefore, votes could be bought with reasonable assurance. In many wards, there were more votes cast than there were inhabitants.[3]

As late as 1866, a total of 13,023 immigrants were naturalized in two courts in New York City. In 1868, Tammany Hall's naturalization committee opened an office in a saloon, printed 40,000 tickets with the words "please naturalize the bearer," and had squads of clerks make out the necessary papers. Immigrants were presented in lots of 150 or more to a judge who naturalized them en masse and without examination. It was estimated that there were over 68,000 fraudulent certificates of naturalization in New York State in 1868. By the 1860's, the Irish were themselves deeply involved in operating the careless and fraudulent procedures which they learned from native Americans on their arrival. Trading votes and running away with ballot boxes were not initiated by immigrants, and not all the city gangs were Irish. The politics of the slum

[3] Gibson, *The Attitudes of the New York Irish,* 213–27.

were likely to be dirty like the slum itself. The Irish were bought with
whiskey, the Germans with lager beer.

The role of the boss among the city proletariat has been emphasized
by both historians and sociologists. Many a political boss considered
himself a modern Robin Hood who robbed the rich to help the poor.
Tammany Hall learned quickly that benevolences distributed among
poor Irish immigrants paid dividends at the polls, and to this day bosses
and party machines see to it that no supporter of theirs is evicted for
inability to pay the rent. They provide legal aid to the immigrant if he
is in trouble, settle local quarrels, help promising youngsters get a job
or an education, bail out petty offenders, and, in a dozen other ways,
act the part of the kindly "fixer." The boss sends dinners to the poor on
Christmas, sends coal in the dead of winter, and sends flowers to a
funeral.

Such practices, long a part of American urban politics, worked well
in the case of Irish immigrants. If the political organization was autocratic and corrupt, it also was benign. Some bosses were men of clean
personal habits who counseled thrift and sobriety among their followers
and were eager to help the deserving get ahead. If they demanded un-
questioning allegiance, the recipients of their bounty felt they were entitled to it. The importance of the big city machines in the history of the
Democratic party is well known; for decades, and with few exceptions,
they were dominated by men of Irish stock.

Irish immigration added a picturesque and dramatic quality to American politics. In early days, the shillelagh and whiskey were important
factors in elections. The Irish developed many of the shoulder-hitting
methods of American politics of a century ago, and there were many

> Who thinks that freedom must consist
> In proving points, with sticks and fists.

The loafer and the bully were active in elections in places other than
New York. Nevertheless, the turmoil of city politics of a hundred years
ago was attributable in large measure to Irish immigrants who helped
make municipal government more venal and corrupt. But if the Irish
delayed the progress of orderly democratic methods, they were not the
sole cause of corruption, and there was a disposition, as James Bryce
pointed out, to use the Irish "as the cat is used in the kitchen to account
for broken plates and food which disappears."

Some of the better-class Irish immigrants were soon disillusioned
by the contrast between their dreams and the realities of the American

Republic. Bishop Hughes deplored Tammany's use of the Irish as early as the 1840's, and other Irishmen were shocked by vote buying in the open market; by the spoils system; by the hypocrisy of election campaigns; and by the hoodlums, loafers, and rowdies who acted as the bodyguards of office seekers. The Irish *Citizen* repeatedly urged the Irish to give up their clannishness and their subservience to "Irish grog-sellers" and argued that there could be no justification for an "Irish vote" in the United States, except against abolitionists and Know-Nothings. The editor denounced group voting by "bodies of Irish or of Germans, organized in grogshops, and indoctrinated by priests."[4] An English commentator, on the other hand, concluded that the Irish followed their bishops only in spiritual matters and showed great "jealousy of priestly influence in secular affairs." He observed that the second-generation Irish "are more American than the Americans."[5] Three decades later, Archbishop Ireland and other leaders of the Church were still denouncing Irish clannishness. Ireland was convinced that "the future of the Irish Race" in this country depended largely upon their capability of assuming an independent attitude in American politics.[6]

The vast majority of Irish immigrants became Democrats immediately upon their arrival. The party name appealed to them, for it was democracy that attracted the immigrant to the United States. Federalist "Anglomen" had catered to the property classes and had looked with disfavor on European immigration. Their efforts to curtail the influence of America's adopted citizens in the Alien and Sedition Acts had not been forgotten; neither had the defense of the newcomers by the Jeffersonians. By the 1840's, the Democratic party's reputation as the friend of the common man was firmly established. The party was aware of the importance of votes to be recruited from the immigrant tide; therefore, it insisted upon equal rights for immigrants and flattered them with attention and minor jobs. Despite occasional efforts by the Whig party to subsidize Irish-American papers, the Whigs had little appeal for Irishmen and were tainted with nativism besides.

In New York City, Tammany Hall originally was a society for native-born Americans. Irish and Catholics were excluded. By 1800, the Irish in New York already were strong enough to add excitement to the city's politics, and the battle between the followers of Clinton and those of Tammany was a spirited one. Both needed the immigrant vote. Feder-

[4] *The Citizen* (New York), September 9, October 28, 1854.
[5] Nichols, *Forty Years,* II, 75–79.
[6] *Irish World and American Industrial Liberator* (New York), October 8, 1892.

alists referred contemptuously to the tavern where Tammany braves met as the "Pig Pen" where

> There's a barrel of porter in Tammany Hall
> And the Bucktails are swigging it all the night long.

In 1817, the Irish invaded Tammany Hall because the leaders of the wigwam had refused to support Thomas A. Emmet for Congress or to recognize the political influence of Irish voters. Furthermore, it was rumored that Tammany was about to adopt a new constitution which would exclude the foreign-born from holding office in the society. Two hundred strong, the Irish broke into the wigwam, with the usual results —broken windows and furniture and bloody noses. Tammany reinforcements drove the invaders from the hall, but by 1820 the Irish were admitted. Ever after, the Irish brogue was heard in the wigwam and libations were poured to Ireland's sturdy sons. *The Shamrock,* the first Irish paper of New York, in 1816 described the Tammany Society as a noble, generous, honorable, patriotic, hospitable, republican institution.[7] On the other hand, an Irish historian has admitted that "the history of Tammany Hall can scarcely be regarded as a subject of pride in recalling the achievements of the Irish in America." [8]

It is unnecessary to follow the history of Tammany's relations with the New York Irish, except to say that it was marked by riots, especially in the "bloody ould Sixth," vote-buying, fraudulent ballots and naturalization papers, repeaters at the polls, voting by newly arrived immigrants and inmates of jails and almshouses, free distribution of liquor and money, and graft of a high order.[9] Before the end of the 1850's, the Irish had begun to rise on the political escalator from alderman to state legislators and were receiving political recognition from the national Democratic administrations.[10] In 1857, *The Irish News* hailed Tammany as "the old Citadel of the Constitution and the Popular Will."

In Boston, the Irish vote attracted attention by the end of the 1820's. The influence of Irish Catholics on local politics did not become decisive, however, until the days when Hugh O'Brien and Patrick Andrew Collins became mayor. The latter, brought from Ireland as an infant, worked

---

[7] *The Shamrock* (New York), March 9, 1816. See also Roy V. Peel, *The Political Clubs of New York City.*

[8] Roberts, *Ireland in America,* 88.

[9] See Myers, *History of Tammany Hall;* M. R. Werner, *Tammany Hall;* and John I. Davenport, *The Election Frauds of New York City and Their Prevention.*

[10] For examples, see James K. McGuire (ed.), *The Democratic Party in the State of New York,* II, 434–35; III, 82, 234–36.

in coal mines and machine shops and attended Harvard law school. He had a phenomenal rise in politics—twice serving as mayor of Boston and, in 1888, as chairman of the Democratic National Convention. By the first decade of the present century, the city government of Boston was largely Irish, with many Irish mayors and department heads. New Englanders like Henry Adams felt like "pariahs in their homeland," but Henry Cabot Lodge learned to forget his earlier prejudices and woo the Irish vote.

Other American cities felt the political impact of the Irish. In Philadelphia, John Campbell, son of Irish Catholic parents, led the Catholic Democrats in their fight against the nativists. Many of the city's bosses of both parties were Irish. The same was true in Brooklyn. Jersey City had an "Irish-American ring." In the 1880's, the Irish-American William F. Sheehan was a boss in Buffalo. Many of Chicago's city officials were Irish-born, and among its racketeers were Mike McDonald, "Hinky Dink" Kenna, and "Bathhouse" John Coughlin. Timothy O'Brien, affectionately known as "Father Tim," came to Milwaukee from Limerick in 1842. He made a profession of local politics and held such offices as city marshal, captain of police, coroner, court crier, and alderman. Edward O'Neill served four terms as mayor of the Wisconsin metropolis in the 1860's, and P. J. Somers, a Catholic Irish-American, was elected as chief magistrate in 1892. San Francisco in the 1880's was dominated by Christopher A. Buckley, an Irish saloonkeeper and ward boss who helped "Hibernianize" the police force and other departments of the city government.[11]

The importance of the Irish vote in national campaigns will be discussed more fully in later chapters, but as early as 1844 the Whigs blamed the defeat of Henry Clay on "abolitionists and foreign Catholics" in New York State. The Whig press maintained that 10,000 Irish working on internal improvements in New York had swung the election, and that "the President had been chosen by foreigners naturalized for the occasion." William H. Seward and Horace Greeley, in an unsuccessful effort to wean the Irish from their Democratic allegiance, organized Irish repeal meetings in the late 1840's and publicly demanded the release of Irish exiles from Tasmania.

By 1852, both parties sought the votes of the rapidly growing immigration. The Whig New York *Tribune* argued that Irishmen could not accept a Democratic party which supported the "British policy" of free trade. The Democrats replied by accusing the Whigs and their candidate, General Winfield Scott, of nativist leanings. Scott, eager to atone

11 See John P. Bocock, "The Irish Conquest of Our Cities," *Forum*, XVII (1894), 186–95.

for earlier flirtations with nativism, attended Mass in the morning and Protestant services in the evening. In a most flattering manner, he referred to the many brave Irishmen whom he had led to victory in the Mexican War. "The sweet, soft, mellifluous, musical Irish brogue has caught the fancy of General Scott . . . before the election," commented the *Irish-American*. Other papers reminded their readers that after the election the Irish would become "splay-footed bog trotters" again. Patrick O'Dea was employed by the Whigs in 1852 to publish the *Irishman* in the interest of the party, but his sheet had little effect. The Boston *Pilot* denounced such tactics by "Customs House Catholics" and "small Irish politicians" as insults to the mass of Irishmen.[12] Meantime, the *Irish-American* stressed the theme that "the strongest and best hater of England is sure to prove the best American."[13] Bishop Hughes, who once voted Whig to the consternation of his Irish followers, took no part in the campaign of 1852 and urged Catholics to follow their individual judgment.

There is an Irish-American type which still represents the Irish political boss in the minds of many Americans. The stereotype is traceable to early leaders of the large city organizations who helped degrade municipal government and make it a conspicuous failure of American democracy. One of the earliest and most picturesque of these bosses was "the one and only Mike Walsh," leader of New York gang politics. He was brought to this country as a child from county Cork. Although he became a good journalist, he had little formal schooling. He worked successively as a lithographer's apprentice and a deck hand and fireman on a river boat to New Orleans. In New York he was a volunteer fireman. In 1840, he organized his own political club or gang known as "The Spartan Band." It was recruited almost entirely from Irish Democrats dedicated to the overthrow of Tammany Hall, and proved an innovation in city ward and gang politics, both in its ends and the means used to achieve them. An inveterate foe of special privilege, Walsh was an eloquent champion of the common man. In 1843, with George Wilkes, who later founded the *Police Gazette,* Walsh launched the *Subterranean,* dedicated to the cause of the common people. The next year, his paper was merged with George Henry Evans' *Working Man's Advocate.*

Though he was never naturalized, Walsh served several terms in the state legislature and one in Congress. He also served several sentences for libel. He was a good, though abusive speaker, a natural comedian, and a satirist whose specialty was deflating snobs and pretenders. He

12 September 11, October 16, 1852.
13 Gibson, *The Attitudes of the New York Irish,* 54.

denounced prohibition and Sabbatarianism as the work of "miserable puritannical zealots." In Congress he fought waste of the public funds and opposed the extension of slavery, although he thought abolitionists were "insane, though perhaps not dishonest, fanatics." He pleaded the case of the white wage-slave, whose lot he compared unfavorably with that of the Negro in bondage. Defeated for re-election to Congress in 1854 by "Honest John" Kelly, Walsh went on a continental spree, as far as Constantinople, as the agent for a man who wanted to build ships for the Russian Navy. He came back a physical and financial wreck. In 1859, his body was found by the New York police[14] after he had spent a convivial evening in Broadway saloons.

Another well-known Irish boss was John Morrisey, who came to America as a small child. His father was a day laborer, so the boy had to go to work when he was twelve. He was employed in a wallpaper factory and an iron mill, and he grew up in the tough surroundings of factory workers and river men. At seventeen, he was the bouncer for a saloon in Troy, New York; later, he worked as a deck hand on a Hudson River boat and as an immigrant runner in New York. He bummed his way to California and became a prize fighter. In 1853, in a gruelling thirty-seven-round battle in New York, he defeated Yankee Sullivan for the heavyweight championship. He operated a saloon, a gambling house in Saratoga, and was both a labor leader and a political boss in the brawling days of New York's gang wars. As a Tammany leader, he acquired property, served two terms in Congress, and enjoyed the favor of Boss Tweed. A big-hearted boss, he made and lost several fortunes. When he died in 1878, noted politicians were his pallbearers, and fifteen thousand people followed his coffin to the cemetery.[15]

"Honest John" Kelly, the man who picked up the pieces for Tammany after the defeat of the Tweed Ring in 1871, was the son of poor Irish parents who had come from county Tyrone to Hester Street in New York. The father died when John was eight years old. After three years in a parochial school, the boy went to work as James Gordon Bennett's office boy on the New York *Herald*. He attended night classes and learned the trade of grate setter and soapstone cutter, which enabled him to set up a prosperous business. He belonged to the Emmet Guards and a volunteer fire company. He "enjoyed the rapture of the strife," and was respected both as a pugilist and an amateur actor. By the road which led, in his case, from the saloon through the prize ring and the

---

[14] Robert Ernst, "The One and Only Mike Walsh," *The New York Historical Society Quarterly*, XXXVI (January, 1952), 43–65.

[15] *DAB;* and see Jack Kofoed, *Brandy for Heroes.*

political clubs of the Fourteenth Ward, composed largely of Irish and Germans, Kelly became an active politician. He began by fighting Tammany. In 1853, he was admitted to its inner councils. As a faithful Catholic, he fought the Know-Nothings both at the ballot box and in several physical encounters. He rose from alderman to serve two terms in Congress and to become the sheriff of New York City and the Grand Sachem of the Tammany braves. After a trip to the Holy Land, when he contemplated entering a religious order, he returned in time to join in the fight in 1871 to unseat Tweed as the ruler of Tammany Hall. He is credited with having established the policy of collecting campaign assessments for Tammany from all officeholders and candidates. He probably gained his title of "Honest John" because he kept Tammany free from grosser scandals.[16]

Richard Croker, another boy immigrant from county Cork, succeeded Kelly in Tammany Hall. A product of New York's shantytown, he learned the machinists' trade, became a fireman, a good prize fighter, and the leader of the "Fourth Avenue Tunnel Gang." He worked for Tweed, then joined in the fight to unhorse him. An alderman at twenty-five, Croker was elected coroner in 1873 and collected the huge fees of that office. He was indicted for shooting a man in an election row, but never convicted. By 1886, he was the leader of Tammany and chairman of its finance committee, which kept no books. For sixteen years, this man of silence and self-control virtually ruled New York. Enormously wealthy, he finally retired to Europe to lead the life of an English gentleman, keep a racing stable near Dublin, and win the English Derby. He died at eighty and was buried in a mausoleum on his Irish estate.[17]

Charles Francis Murphy, another Irish Tammany leader, was born on New York's East Side and grew up in the gashouse district. He worked in saloons, shipyards, and factories, played amateur baseball, and at the age of thirty-two, owned four handsome cafes which served as Tammany district headquarters. A taciturn man, Murphy never made speeches, but he was the friend and counselor of hundreds of workers and as charitable to Protestant as to Catholic causes. The only salaried political job he ever held was that of dock commissioner, to which he was appointed in 1898. In 1902, he succeeded Croker as the leader of Tammany, and he filled that powerful post for twenty-two years. Several times he nominated reform mayors. He kept police, schools, and courts out of politics, but he permitted many other forms of "honest

---

[16] *DAB;* and see J. Fairfax McLaughlin, *The Life and Times of John Kelley, Tribune of the People.*

[17] See Lothrop Stoddard, *Master of Manhattan, The Life of Richard Croker.*

graft." There is no specific evidence that he made money directly out of Tammany, though he operated extensively in real estate and acquired expensive and aristocratic tastes.

One of Croker's contemporaries was the picturesque "Big Tim" Sullivan, the son of an Irish laborer in a New York tenement house. Tim began working for Tammany in the Five Points area when he was fifteen years old. In due time, he became the owner of six saloons and the uncrowned king of the lower East Side. He was a member of both the state legislature and Congress. He also was half-owner of Sullivan and Considine's vaudeville circuit and the collector of heavy tribute from gambling and boxing shows. A warmhearted giant, Sullivan collected graft from many sources and distributed food and clothes among the poor. Crooked, loyal, and generous, he typified the old-fashioned Irish boss. "Big Tim" was run over by a train in 1913. Twenty-five thousand people attended his funeral.[18]

Other cities have had lesser counterparts of these amazing New York characters. Chicago's boss of the First Ward, near the end of the last century, was Michael "Hinky Dink" Kenna. "Honey Boy" Fitzgerald was mayor of Boston. His singing of "Sweet Adeline" was a feature of all his campaigns. James Michael Curley, a favorite of Boston's Irish since 1900, served four terms as mayor, two terms in Congress, and one term as governor of Massachusetts. He also served two terms in prison.

David C. Broderick, born of Irish parents in Washington, D. C., was a fighter, fireman, and ward politician for Tammany in New York before he went to California in 1849. There he became the Democratic boss of the state and introduced the methods he had learned in the East. He served in both the constitutional convention and the state legislature, and was killed in a duel with the chief justice of California in 1859. James Smith, Democratic boss of New Jersey and the son of Irish immigrants, started to work in his father's grocery and rose to be a leather manufacturer, bank president, and owner of a newspaper. Beginning as an alderman in 1883, he topped his public career by going to the United States Senate, amidst ugly rumors of improper financial dealings. Persuaded that it would be wise to force his party to nominate Woodrow Wilson for the governorship of New Jersey in 1910, he broke with his candidate immediately after the latter took office. John Farley, described by Frederic C. Howe as "a big, raw-boned, profane Irishman of substantial wealth, who made his money as a contractor," was the Democratic boss of Cleveland in the latter part of the nineteenth century. In

18 *DAB;* and Alvin F. Harlow, *Old Bowery Days,* Chapter XXIV.

John Hay's *The Breadwinners,* the mayor of "Buffland" is portrayed as an uneducated, boorish Irish-American.[19]

Less picturesque and dramatic, but far more admirable, were the men of Irish stock who entered American politics to carve out highly respected and honorable careers. The achievements of these second- and third-generation Irish must not be minimized because of the colorful characters of an earlier era. Mathew O'Rourke and James O'Brien took the first steps to expose Tweed and his crooked Irish collaborators; John Foley got the first injunction against the grafters; and Charles O'Conor helped put them in jail. Patrick A. Collins was a good mayor of Boston in 1902. In 1913, David I. Walsh, son of Irish immigrants and a congenital Anglophobe, was the first Irish Catholic to be chosen governor of Massachusetts. The Irish-Americans Edward F. Dunne and William E. Dever are regarded as reform mayors of Chicago. Thomas J. Walsh, a second-generation Irish Catholic, was a liberal Democrat who favored a federal child-labor amendment. He won lasting fame as the investigator of the Teapot Dome scandal in the Harding administration. Tom Taggart, a native of county Monaghan, was mayor of Indianapolis and a powerful and wholesome influence in Indiana politics for many years. Edward J. Kelly, mayor of Chicago, was the son of a Chicago policeman who came from Ireland during the Civil War. Thomas A. Burke, four-time mayor of Cleveland and United States Senator from Ohio, was especially successful in dealing with the problems of a metropolitan area representing over fifty nationality groups. Alfred E. Smith, "the Happy Warrior" with the brown derby, born within the shadow of Brooklyn Bridge, became the distinguished governor of New York. He challenged American toleration with discouraging results when he was the Democratic candidate for president in 1928. The attack launched against him by the Ku-Klux Klan, the *New Menace,* and other anti-Catholic organs helps explain why the Irish vote has remained so solidly Democratic. Justice Frank Murphy, an Irish Catholic, a distinguished administrator, and a Supreme Court Justice, was one of the most valiant and forthright champions of the Bill of Rights ever to sit upon that high tribunal.

[19] James B. Whipple, "Municipal Government in an Average City, Cleveland, 1876–1900," *The Ohio Archaeological and Historical Quarterly,* LXII (January, 1953), 1–24.

CHAPTER XI

"America for Americans"

ALTHOUGH the doors to America stood open, and, until recently, practically unguarded to all who were dissatisfied at home, there has never been a time in our history when American politics were completely free of nativism. The opponents of the foreign-born have never marshalled more than a minority at the polls, but they have been powerful enough, on occasion, to exercise political influence. At several junctures in American history, the well-drilled, vocal minority has produced political upheavals of considerable magnitude.

Federalists, at the end of the eighteenth century, were alarmed about French revolutionary spies and "hordes of wild Irishmen." In the 1830's, local nativist parties arose on the eastern seaboard over such issues as the use of public funds for Catholic parochial schools. In the 1840's, a convent was burned in Massachusetts, and there were riots between Protestants and Catholics, natives and foreign-born.

In the 1850's, the country experienced its most violent and prolonged period of nativism and religious bigotry. Old parties were breaking down in this decade before the Civil War; the Whigs were dying; the Democrats were about to divide. A new Republican party was being born. Confused voters, troubled by the controversy over abolition and secession which threatened civil war, welcomed new issues and new political affiliations. The extraordinarily heavy European immigration in the 1840's and 1850's; the character of some of the immigrants; the rise of an immigrant vote controlled by local bosses; and the clannishness of the new immigration provided the causes for a secret political party which made the immigrant, and particularly the Irish, the whipping boy for all that was wrong with America. Property holders were sure that the melting pot was boiling over and that their taxes would get steadily higher to support indigent, unhealthy immigrants who were undermining property rights and polluting American elections. The Know-Nothing order, which rose to a sudden climax by 1855, appealed to a nation of joiners who found secrecy and ritual attractive. At the same time, it mystified old-line politicians who could not fathom its clandestine procedures. By 1855, sober political prognosticators were predicting that the party would elect a president the next year.

The Irish were the special target of the nativists, but German immigrants also came in for their share of abuse and denunciation. In fact, several of the worst riots involved nativists and Germans. The specific charges against the Germans arose largely from the activity of the refugees of the revolution of 1848. Uncompromising radicals who wanted to reform many features of American life, their ranks included agnostics, freethinkers, atheists, socialists, and innovators of every kind. As a result of their efforts to raise the intellectual and cultural level of their countrymen, the entire German group won a reputation for arrogance, radicalism, and clannishness. The radicals' attitudes toward religion, Americanization, temperance, and the Puritan Sabbath were particularly offensive to many Americans.[1]

"The Irishmen must be surrounded by Americans," warned Edward Everett Hale in 1852,[2] and he advised that the proper ratio would be eight Irish for every hundred native-born. Hale believed this would speed Americanization, and he thought Irish devotion to the Catholic Church was more a matter of national pride than a question of faith. New England, a section that had been little concerned about Catholics before 1830, changed rapidly in its attitude toward Catholicism as Irish immigration increased. New England Yankees were disturbed by the consolidation of the Irish as an isolated, foreign group in the slums, where they clung to their own institutions, resisted normal assimilation, and preserved their group consciousness. Native Americans came to the conclusion that the Irish would always be different, hostile, and under the domination of a militant church which believed that the Irish immigrants had a divine mission to make the United States a Catholic country.[3]

The action of the Irish in urban politics convinced many Americans that the institutions of the Union were being undermined by thousands of newcomers who voted as a solid phalanx and threatened the whole process of free elections. In 1853, the nativist *Providence Journal* warned that there were now six thousand alien barbarian voters in the city, whereas fifteen years earlier there had been not one.[4] Special handbills summoned Irishmen to their posts in New York's elections. In Boston, men "fresh from the bogs of Ireland," argued the nativists, were "led

[1] See Wittke, *Refugees of Revolution,* Chapter XIII.

[2] See Edward Everett Hale, *Letters on Irish Emigration.*

[3] Handlin, *Boston's Immigrants,* Chapter VII.

[4] Richard J. Purcell, "Rhode Island's Early Schools and Irish Teachers," *The Catholic Educational Review,* XXXII (1934), 413.

up to the desk like dumb brutes, their hands guided to make a straight mark," to vote down intelligent and honest native citizens.[5] The *Cleveland Express* believed Negroes were "much better citizens than the hordes of Catholic Irish who are yearly floating to our shores." [6] In New Orleans, Democrats marched the Irish to the polls in droves, and Irish election officials allowed them to vote, sometimes more than once.[7] In many cities, the Irish already shared the spoils of office, holding petty jobs and exercising an authority which was resented by native Americans. The "Irish party" seemed to be growing faster than the native-born in the 1850's, and many Americans found the phenomenon truly alarming.

[Another cause of nativist opposition was a feeling in many areas that the Irish were blocking reform, especially in such fields as abolitionism, women's rights, free-soilism, and temperance.[Many who criticized German Forty-eighters for being too radical and too hasty in their agitation for reform believed the Irish were too reactionary and too slow. In Massachusetts, for example, reformers held Catholic-Irish voters in Boston responsible for the defeat of a new constitution in 1853, which, though distributing representation unfairly for the cities, contained a number of reforms. Theodore Parker publicly charged the Irish with retarding social progress because of their low standard of living and their hostility to free-soilism and abolitionism. "Not an Irish newspaper," he contended, "is on the side of humanity, freedom, education, progress."

The Boston *Pilot* described free-soilism as nothing but "a recrudescence of Puritanism in its most extreme form." Radical antislavery men came to regard Catholicism as a liability to freedom, and honest Know-Nothings wanted to eliminate Irish influence from politics so that social reform might proceed. In 1855, the Massachusetts legislature, controlled by the Know-Nothings, passed a drastic liquor law and granted additional rights to women.[8] In 1859, still under the influence of nativism, Massachusetts proposed an amendment which would have imposed an additional residence requirement of two years after naturalization for a person to be eligible to vote and hold office in that state. Germans regarded the proposal as a frontal attack upon them, and the incident produced a crisis for the new Republican party, which needed the German vote. Actually, the measure was directed primarily against the Irish.[9]

[5] James B. Cullen, *The Story of the Irish in Boston*, 75.

[6] Quoted in *The Citizen* (New York), November 24, 1855. See also a ballad, "Pat's Return from the Polls," *Cleveland Express*, October 3, 1854.

[7] Overdyke, *The Know-Nothing Party*, 59–60.

[8] William G. Bean, "Puritan Versus Celt, 1850–1860," *The New England Quarterly*, VII (1934), 70–89.

[9] For this incident, see Carl Wittke, *Against the Current, the Life of Karl Heinzen*, 287–92.

Another nativist argument was the contention that the Irish were depressing the American standard of labor. Nativists who sympathized with the workers argued that an inexhaustible labor supply was being used by the "money power" to keep wages down. The same group pointed to heavy remittances to Ireland as proof that still more immigrants were on the way to fill almshouses or houses of correction. Native Americans resented the competition of Irish laborers and accused the British of deliberately dumping "the poor, the vicious and the degraded" upon the United States. Still others believed the Jesuits and the Church were encouraging Catholic paupers to immigrate in order to undermine the economic foundations of the nation.[10]

Another irritant to older, conservative Americans was the brazen demand of political refugees for a new American foreign policy under which the United States would abandon its traditional neutrality and isolation and intervene in Europe for the liberation of suppressed nationalities. German Forty-eighters were the most active along these lines, but Irishmen never forgot that Ireland was still in chains and believed the United States was a favorable base of operations for her liberation.

In 1855, reports of secret conventions of Irishmen in Boston, New York, and Philadelphia disturbed native Americans profoundly, for they seemed to indicate that the Irish were organizing for a return to their native land to fight for Ireland's independence. The American public, still committed to isolation, was unwilling to become embroiled in the turbulent politics of Europe. There was talk, even at this early date, that the Irish planned to attack England by way of Canada. Another rumor circulated among nativists to the effect that a Russian agent was at work among the Irish to create a diversion favorable to Russia during the Crimean War. Irish emigrant aid societies frequently were as concerned with preparations for the redemption of Ireland as with helping the immigrant. The Irish-American press gave wide publicity to such statements as that of the Robert Emmet Club of Cincinnati, in 1855, which told the Irish of Ohio that "the sun of Irish independence, so long obscured by the clouds of adversity, is bursting through the darkness of centuries, and may soon shine over a liberated nation." To many nativists, every Celt was a potential filibuster who should be arrested for his conspiracy against American neutrality.[11] Militia companies of the foreign-born were special targets for nativist propaganda. In Cincinnati, the Irish militia were disarmed by the sheriff in 1855, but had their arms restored to them by the governor. Editors of the Irish press

---

[10] See Samuel B. Smith, *The Flight of Popery from Rome to the West.*
[11] Samuel C. Busey, *Immigration: Its Evils and Consequences,* 34–44.

retaliated by advising their readers to continue their military activities as independent organizations and to buy their own arms.

| More responsible for the violence of the Know-Nothing period than all these causes was the fear of the Catholic Church in the United States. Controversies over education and intemperate attacks upon Protestantism by aggressive leaders like Bishop Hughes did the Church little good. Nativists made the most of such indiscreet statements as the one in the *Shepherd of the Valley* of St. Louis, in 1851, which maintained that "the Church is of necessity intolerant. Heresy she endures when and where she must," but if Catholics ever should gain a large majority, "religious freedom in this country is at an end; so say our enemies—so say we." [12] |

\ A flood of pamphlets and books was released upon the country by anti-Catholic writers and reached new levels of obscenity, bigotry, and pornography. It was natural for Catholics to reply to scurrilous charges against their faith, and the nation became involved in a war of arguments over the fundamental issue—whether Catholicism and Americanism were compatible. The Irish bore the brunt of the attack on this issue. In such a large volume of literature, it is difficult to distinguish what was honest argument, or "honest delusion" by sincere nativists, and what was merely an excuse for obscenity. *Maria Monk's Awful Disclosures,* first published by Harper's in 1836 and used again as late as 1928 in the campaign against Al Smith, was the classic example of this genre of anti-Catholic literature. It was followed by more disclosures, by the same author, which sold 300,000 copies before the Civil War. |

The first book told the familiar stories, with lurid details, of what allegedly went on behind convent walls, where illegitimate babies were born and priestly cunning betrayed the innocent and the faithful. Maria Monk's tale was pure fabrication by a girl of low mentality and weak character who had a ghost writer and who was duped by several ministers who wanted to exploit a good story. Two Protestant clergymen inspected the convent where she supposedly was held against her wishes and reported that the story was wholly false. The author's last book described an island in the St. Lawrence where nuns went to have their babies. Maria Monk died in prison as a convicted pickpocket from New York's notorious slum districts. Incidentally, she was cheated out of most of the royalties for her best sellers.[13]

Responsible organizations were seriously alarmed by what they con-

---

12 Quoted in Overdyke, *The Know-Nothing Party,* 216.

13 See Ray A. Billington, "Maria Monk and Her Influence," *The Catholic Historical Review,* XXII (1936–37), 283–96. For a list of anti-Catholic publications, see the bibliography in Billington's *The Protestant Crusade, 1800–1860.*

sidered the Catholic menace. The General Association of Congregational Churches of Massachusetts urged its pastors to save the United States from Popery, and the Baptist Home Mission and the Western Baptist Educational Association solicited funds to subdue the Pope in the Mississippi Valley and to distribute prophylactic literature among the Irish in the West. Lyman Beecher, preaching at "Brimstone Corner" in Boston at the Park Street Church, stressed the relation between despotism and Roman Catholicism. He referred to the Irish as "a dead mass of ignorance and superstition . . . priestdriven human machines." Samuel F. B. Morse, inventor of the telegraph, saw the issue as one between Popery and Protestantism, or Absolutism and Republicanism.[14] Among the names applied to the Papacy were such choice expressions as the Great Harlot, the Great Red Dragon, Anti-Christ, and the Beast. The *American Protestant Vindicator* contemplated with horror that the Pope some day might move his throne to the United States. Only in southern states like Maryland and Louisiana was the Catholic issue minimized by the Know-Nothings.

Violence was bound to follow the battle of books and pamphlets and the incendiary sermons of some Protestant ministers. As early as 1829, homes of Irish Catholics were stoned in Boston. In Cincinnati, in 1833, Protestants moved out of a neighborhood when the Irish moved in. In 1834, the Ursuline convent in Charlestown, Massachusetts, where some Boston Unitarians sent their daughters to school, was burned. A meeting of Boston's best citizens demanded that the state make full restitution for the outrage, and Bishop Fenwick intervened to keep Irish laborers from marching on Boston. When the bishop bought three acres on Bunker Hill for a cemetery, the whole community was aroused. In 1854, a cross was stolen from the Catholic church in Chelsea. A church was blown up in Dorchester and another in Shelby County, Ohio. Priests were insulted in the streets of Boston, and in Bath, Maine, at the laying of the cornerstone of a Roman Catholic church, a mob pulled down the cross and hoisted an American flag in its place.[15] Philadelphia's bloodiest riot had occurred in 1844, when Bishop Kenrick raised the issue of reading the Protestant Bible in the schools. Nativists replied with inflamatory speeches about God, country, and the Bible, battled with Irish laborers from the Kensington area, burned several Irish houses, and gutted two churches.[16] Although Catholic bishops officially declared in May, 1855, that Catholics owed obedience to the Pope only in spiritual matters and not in civil affairs, nativists remained unconvinced.

14 Edward Lind Morse (ed.), *Samuel F. B. Morse; His Letters and Journals,* II, 36.
15 *The Citizen* (New York), August 18, September 1, November 24, 1855.
16 For this and other incidents, see Billington, *Protestant Crusade,* Chapter IX.

There was a veritable epidemic of rabble-rousing street preachers in the 1850's in the major cities led by Father Gavazzi, an apostate monk. In many places their inflamatory addresses led to violence, especially when they ranted about the Church and the Pope in Irish neighborhoods, which they deliberately sought out in order to assert their right of free speech. Some agitators were sincere; others were adventurers and unfrocked priests. One of the most notorious was J. S. Orr, known as the "Angel Gabriel." He attracted a crowd by blasts on a trumpet and appeared in a "tarpaulin hat" with a band around it on which were inscribed the words, "Rule Britannia—Hail Columbia; but down with the Mother of Abominations." [17]

Probably in no decade in American political history was there as much rioting as in the 1850's. There were pitched battles between Irish and Know-Nothings in Philadelphia, Chelsea and Lawrence, Massachusetts, Newark, Baltimore, Brooklyn, and St. Louis. Baltimore was known as "mob town" for its many election fights. In Cincinnati, the Know-Nothings fought the Germans on election day, and the latter erected barricades to protect their section of the city, "over the Rhine." In Chicago, the *Tribune* exonerated the Irish in the riots in the spring of 1855. Louisville had its "Bloody Monday" in the summer of 1855 when nativists rioted with Germans and Irish, set fires, looted houses, taverns, and stores, and inflicted such damage that many members of both nationality groups left the city.

In view of Know-Nothing attacks on both Germans and Irish, it might have been assumed that the two elements would have united against a common foe. This was true in several instances. On the other hand, even in these troubled times, Catholic priests and the Boston *Pilot* denounced German radicals and "infidels" with as much vehemence as they did the nativists. The *Pilot* regarded the German refugees of the revolution of 1848 as atheists, defamers of the Sabbath, freethinkers, "red" republicans, and socialists. It sympathized with Know-Nothings who opposed such "foreign anarchists" and enemies of law and order. The editor favored restricting immigration to keep such undesirables out of the country. Many Germans had an equally low opinion of their Irish fellow-Americans. Christian Esselen, an able, radical German editor, described them as "the praetorian guard of brutal terrorism" and justified the desire of the Know-Nothings to save America from Catholicism, although deploring the methods they used. Bernard Domschke, another radical German editor, referred to the Irish as "American Croats"—"our natural

[17] *The Citizen* (New York), May 13, June 17, 1854.

enemies, not because they are Irishmen, but because they are the truest guards of the Papacy." Some German Forty-eighters "out-knownothinged" the Know-Nothings in their anticlericalism and in their attacks on priestcraft and the confessional. Their tales of priestly immorality were as sensational as the most extreme charges of the Know-Nothings. T. N. Hasselquist, a Swedish clergyman and journalist, justified the nativist movement not only as a protest against Catholics and "wild Irish," but also against "irreligious Germans." [18]

The accomplishments of the Know-Nothings were not impressive. Their program called for the exclusion of paupers and criminals and the repeal of state laws permitting foreigners to vote or get land before they were naturalized. The order opposed "the aggressive and corrupting tendencies" of the Roman Catholic Church, demanded that officeholding be limited to the native-born, favored a twenty-one-year residence requirement for naturalization, and advocated Bible reading in the schools.

In 1854, the Know-Nothings registered local successes in elections in Pennsylvania, Maryland, and Massachusetts. In New York, they came within 35,000 votes of their major opponents in the race for governor. In 1855, they won further victories in Maryland, Kentucky, Tennessee, and Louisiana. A large number of Know-Nothings, variously estimated at seventy-five or a hundred, went to Congress. In Massachusetts, a Know-Nothing governor and legislature were elected in 1854, 1855, and 1856. In 1855, seven states had governors and legislatures either openly or secretly committed to the principles of the order.

The record of the party in Massachusetts was not inspiring. Militia companies composed of foreign-born were disbanded and some fire companies were reorganized. A proposal was made to make organ grinding a workhouse offense in order to get rid of foreign street musicians. Almshouses and houses of correction were investigated and a "smelling committee" of the legislature made a disgraceful junket of their inspection of nunneries and convents. The *Boston Herald* characterized the legislature as a body with the "minimum amount of brains . . . compatible with the existence of a legislature." [19] The record in other states —Maryland, for example—was equally unimpressive, and nativist activities in the halls of Congress accomplished nothing specific. The whole movement cracked into pieces during the mounting slavery controversy, and, during the Civil War, the doors were opened even wider to immigrants. The immediate effect of Know-Nothingism was to make Irish-

[18] O. F. Ander, *T. N. Hasselquist*, 154.
[19] *Boston Herald*, November 1, 1855.

Americans more clannish, nationalistic, and loyal to the Democratic party. Nativist attacks retarded assimilation and welded the Irish into a solid, unified group.

During this nativist controversy, some Irish leaders seized the opportunity to give good advice to their people. The Boston *Pilot* told the Irish to stay at home, pay no attention to street preachers, keep away from political meetings, and go to the polls quietly and singly.[20] The New York *Citizen* admitted that many Irish were "noisy, turbulent, intolerant," and intemperate. John Mitchel, the editor, deplored the fact that "ultra Catholic journals went far beyond the bounds of prudence in writing on religious subjects," and urged the Irish to prove the superiority of their religion by their conduct toward their neighbors. Mitchel believed that papers like the *Freeman's Journal,* the *Catholic Telegraph* of Cincinnati, the Charleston *Catholic Miscellany,* the Boston *Pilot,* the *Crusader of the Alleghenies,* the St. Louis *Shepherd of the Valley,* and *Brownson's Review* misrepresented and caricatured Ireland and were bringing Irish Catholics into disrepute. *The Citizen* defended the right of street preachers to rant as they pleased and the right of Know-Nothings to escort them through the streets. The paper regarded freedom of speech, religion, and assembly as absolute American rights and contended that a man could be a "heretic, infidel, Catholic, Jew or Mormon, at his good pleasure." [21]

The editor of the *Irish-American* voiced views similar to those of Mitchel. Orestes A. Brownson wrote that foreigners had no natural right "to be placed on an equal footing with natural-born citizens," and was roundly denounced thereafter as a "Catholic Know-Nothing" by some of the clergy. Bishop Hughes did not want the Irish-American press to take up the cudgels against the nativists. The bishop also opposed separate Irish organizations and, during the Civil War, thought it a mistake to organize special brigades of Irishmen or other nationalities. Know-Nothingism took root again after the Civil War. Much of the nativism of later generations has been directed against the "new" immigration, but the Irish continued to be attacked, primarily because of their loyalty to their Church. Lodges like the Junior Order of United American Mechanics survived the Know-Nothing debacle of the 1850's and continued to point with alarm to the dangers of unrestricted immigration. The Catholic policy of "separatism" in regard to schools, fraternal orders, and other institutions helped keep the flame of nativism burning.

---

[20] *The Pilot* (Boston), May 13, June 3, July 8, October 14, 1854.

[21] *The Citizen* (New York), January 21, June 10, 17, 24, 1854; June 30, July 15, August 4, September 1, 1855.

In 1887, the American Protective Association, or A.P.A., was founded in Clinton, Iowa, by Henry F. Bowers, son of a German immigrant. A self-educated man who had experienced hardship, frustration, economic failure, and personal tragedy, Bowers had a special grievance against Catholics, for he thought they had deprived him of his chance to get a public-school education. Alarmed by the progress of the parochial-school movement in Iowa, Bowers decided he had a divine mission to launch the A.P.A.[22] During the early 1890's, the organization grew to a million members and collapsed just as rapidly in 1896 and 1897. In Michigan, Anglo-Canadians joined the new Protestant crusade; in Milwaukee, it enrolled Germans; and in Minneapolis, Scandinavians. The A.P.A. admitted foreign-born provided they agreed to have no dealings with Catholics. The movement was strong in the Middle West, where it stressed the school question and the "Jesuit plot" to destroy public education.

Anti-Catholicism and anti-Irishism provided the main emotional drives for the A.P.A. movement. Proper Bostonians were incensed when Mayor Hugh O'Brien closed the public library on St. Patrick's Day. Thomas Bailey Aldrich, profoundly disturbed by the thousands who were entering the United States through gates that were practically unguarded, commented sarcastically, "Columbus did not discover America; it was St. Patrick! He is in full defiant possession now." In 1895, excitement in Boston reached fever pitch when the A.P.A. wanted to enter a float representing "the Little Red School House," with Uncle Sam standing at the door, in a Fourth of July parade. After violent debate in mass meetings and in the Boston city council, the A.P.A. insisted on parading through the city to prove that good Americans could not be kept off the streets by foreigners. The controversy ended in shooting and rioting, which reflected no credit to either side.[23]

The Protestant ministry as a whole remained silent during the agitation, and some preachers profited by accepting lucrative speaking engagements from the A.P.A. A few, like Washington Gladden, Congregational minister of Columbus, Ohio, had the courage to speak out against the false charges of the A.P.A. against the Catholics, though he deplored the attitude of the hierarchy toward public education and attacked their role in local politics. Gladden exposed an alleged encyclical of Leo XIII which pointed out the "duty of the faithful to exterminate all heretics" as a forgery. Gladden also demonstrated that while

22 John Higham, "The Mind of a Nativist: Henry F. Bowers and the A.P.A.," *American Quarterly*, IV (Spring, 1952), 16–24.

23 Lord, Sexton, and Harrington, *History of the Archdiocese of Boston*, III, 146–56.

the A.P.A. proclaimed tolerance for any man's religion, "as long as he does not attempt to make his religion an element of political power," the order required an oath of its members never to support a Roman Catholic for public office or to employ a Catholic if a Protestant was available.[24]

During the A.P.A. excitement, the old familiar stories were repeated about the drilling and arming of Catholic societies and the storing of guns in church basements, the frightful conduct of cunning priests, the impending massacre of Protestants by Catholics at a pre-arranged signal from the Pope, and the refusal of priests to bury veterans until the Stars and Stripes had been removed from their coffins. Much of this anti-Catholic propaganda came from Protestant pulpits.

The connection between the A.P.A. and the Republican party was close in several states. In Ohio, Gladden lost the presidency of Ohio State University because the legislature, under A.P.A. influence, threatened to reduce the budget of the university if the courageous preacher should be appointed to that office. The A.P.A. was successful in local elections, and claimed to control a hundred members of Congress.

Officially, the A.P.A. died in 1911; for all practical purposes, however, it had been dead ten years earlier. It split into factions, and its membership could not sustain the high emotional level necessary for success. Politicians accepted its support and then refused to carry out their promises. The movement went to pieces in the Populist Revolt and the free silver crusade of 1896, which absorbed the interest of the country.

The "Guardians of Liberty," the American Minute Men, Covenanters, Knights of Luther, and the like; the revival of the Ku Klux Klan in the 1920's; and the large circulation claimed by anti-Catholic papers like the *New Menace* indicate that many of the issues between Protestants and Catholics remain unresolved. There are aggressive militants on both sides who insist on keeping the quarrels alive. Wherever such issues persist, and especially in the controversy over public education and parochial schools, the Irish are likely to be involved, no longer as "undesirable immigrants," but because of their loyalty to their Church.

[24] Washington Gladden, "The Anti-Catholic Crusade," *The Century Magazine*, XLVII (1893–94), 789–95; also *The Irish World* (New York) for 1895 and June 6, 1896.

Chapter XII

The Irish and the Negro

THE dark clouds of the slavery controversy settled rapidly over the land in the 1850's and broke into the violent storm of the Civil War in 1861. During the 1850's, thousands of American voters, including naturalized citizens, exchanged their old political allegiances for new party loyalties, but, with minor exceptions, the Irish remained steadfast in their devotion to the Democratic party. The Irishman's contempt for the Negro, the fear of his competition in the labor market, and the Negro's reciprocal contempt and hatred of the Irish help explain why Irish immigrants had no traffic with either free-soilism or the newly formed Republican party.

As early as May 11, 1850, the New York *Tribune* had commented on the strange phenomenon that the Irish, having escaped so recently themselves "from a galling, degrading bondage," should vote against all proposals to give greater rights to Negroes and should come to the polls on election day shouting, "Down with the Nagurs! Let them go back to Africa, where they belong." On the other hand, Negroes were the first to call the Irish "white niggers" or "white buckra." "My Master is a great tyrant," a Negro slave is supposed to have commented in 1850, "he treats me badly as if I was a common Irishman." [1] In Philadelphia, where antagonism between the two groups was great, "to be called an 'Irishman' had come to be almost as great an insult as to be called a 'nigger.'" [2] Frederick L. Olmsted referred to the contempt with which Negroes regarded Irishmen who carried hod for colored masons in the South. He pointed out that Negroes were considered to be worth more than "Paddies," and therefore needed to be spared from the most unhealthful and dangerous tasks. [3]

Negroes and immigrant Irish feared each other's competition in the field of unskilled labor, and the Irishman was particularly disturbed by

---

[1] *Irish-American* (New York), January 6, 1850, quoted in Gibson, *The Attitudes of the New York Irish*, 15.

[2] Nolan, *Reverend Francis Patrick Kenrick*, 228–29.

[3] Tryon, *Mirror for Americans*, II, 352, 372.

possible inroads upon his labor monopoly by freed Negroes. Although the Irish immigrant vigorously asserted the superiority of his white blood, he had to compete with Negroes for jobs at docks and warehouses and in pick-and-shovel gangs. Among women the same competition existed, though on a lesser scale, between Irish and Negro maids in domestic service. "The foreign-born hack-driver, ditcher or hod-carrier has no desire to compete for his wages against the Negro," exclaimed a former United States senator from Alabama, who also remarked that "even the Irish chambermaid looks with jealousy upon the employment of Negro girls in our hotels." [4] In 1842, Irish laborers in the coal yards along the Schuylkill River attacked a band of colored competitors. In 1861, Negroes and Irish fought in Milwaukee, and, in the summer of 1862, there was a demonstration in Brooklyn against Negroes employed in a tobacco factory located in an Irish district.[5] When a Negro was appointed to a minor job in the New York customhouse, the displacement of a good Irish Democrat led to strong criticism in papers like the New York *Leader* and the *Caucasian*. In Cincinnati, there were demonstrations against Negroes who worked for lower wages on Ohio River boats. There were frequent collisions between Irish and Negro dockworkers in New York, and, in 1863, Negroes were imported to break a strike of Irish longshoremen. Such incidents are fundamental to a proper understanding of the Irish immigrant's attitude toward anti-slavery propaganda.

The Irish had no sympathy for radical abolitionists. As early as 1831, the *United States Catholic Miscellany* of Charleston, South Carolina, argued that slaves received better treatment in the South than freed Negroes and poor whites in the North, and that Negro slaves were the "legitimate property" of their owners.[6] Bishop England, who preached to slaves in South Carolina and opened schools for them, was careful to dissociate himself from abolitionism, and counseled Negroes to await happier days in the next world. John Mitchel, impassioned champion of freedom for Ireland, approved of slavery in the United States as a blessing for white and colored. He considered *Uncle Tom's Cabin* an unfair and "harrowing novel," was fascinated by the mode of life of the southern plantation owner, and advocated the reopening of the slave trade. Joseph Brenan, another Irish revolutionary exile, expressed much the same views in the New Orleans *Delta;* so did Thomas F.

---

[4] Harry J. Carman and Reinhard H. Luthin, "Some Aspects of the Know-Nothing Movement Reconsidered," *The South Atlantic Quarterly*, XXXIX (April, 1940), 224.

[5] Brother Basil Leo Lee, *Discontent in New York City, 1861–1865*, 139–41.

[6] Madelein Hooke Rice, *American Catholic Opinion in the Slavery Controversy*, 72.

Meagher in his *Irish News*.[7] The *Catholic Advocate* of Kentucky carried advertisements offering Negroes for sale and rewards for runaway slaves.

Patrick Donohue, an early editor of the Boston *Pilot,* did not defend the slave system as such. Instead, he favored gradual emancipation and saw some good in certain antislavery societies; nevertheless, he objected strenuously to New England abolitionism. He found the societies of the abolitionists "thronged with bigotted and persecuting religionists . . . who . . . desire the extermination of Catholics by fire and sword." [8]

When Daniel O'Connell, the "Great Liberator" and advocate of the repeal of Irish union with Great Britain, approved of the British antislavery movement, he provoked bitter rejoinders in the Irish-American press. Bishop Hughes joined in the hue and cry. Apparently, he feared O'Connell's statements might have a bad effect upon American nativists with a congenital dislike of England and might be interpreted as "a foreigner's" propaganda directed to the Irish, upon whom O'Connell called "to come out of the councils of the slaveholders" and "join in crushing slavery." [9]

The *Catholic Mirror* of Baltimore argued that "our slaves live in Paradise, if we compare their condition with that of the wretched subjects of Great Britain in India." The *Freeman's Journal* of New York denounced abolitionism as "the American manifestation of the lawless liberalism" of Europe and referred to William Lloyd Garrison and his kind as "skeptics in religion," "Deists, Atheists, Pantheists, anything but Christian." The *Gazette* of Bardstown, Kentucky, boasted that there was not a single Catholic abolitionist, north or south.[10]

When the Irishman Mason Jones, in a lecture in New York in 1862, branded slavery as a blot upon the nation, two hundred of his audience stalked out of the hall.[11] Charles O'Conor, one of the nation's foremost lawyers, in a public address in 1859 defended slavery as a "benign institution," described the Negro as "fitted only for pupilage," and made it clear that insofar as he could fathom the plan of the Almighty, the latter had intended the United States for Caucasians. The *Freeman's Journal* did not favor slavery, but believed the Negro would have to work out his destiny and maintained that there was no constitutional way to interfere with slavery where it existed.

In Boston, the Irish consistently opposed any sectional split over aboli-

---

7 *The Citizen* (New York), January 14, 1853; *The Irish News* (New York), August 5, 8, 1857.

8 Rice, *American Catholic Opinion,* 78–80.

9 *Ibid.,* 80–85.

10 Overdyke, *The Know-Nothing Party,* 217.

11 Brother Lee, *Discontent in New York City,* 155–56.

tionism and seemed content to leave the problem to God. In the famous
Burns case, when a Negro fugitive in Boston was returned to his master
by force, two Irish military companies were selected to protect the Negro
from the indignant New England mob, which wanted to set him free.
In 1859, the Boston *Pilot* warned:

> When the negroes shall be free
> To cut the throats of all they see,
> Then this dear land will come to be
> The den of foul rascality.[12]

Orestes Brownson regarded slavery as an evil and accused the clergy of
extraordinary timidity in dealing with it, but he saw no constitutional
way to interfere in the South until the section actually rebelled. Brownson never advocated equal rights for Negroes, for he regarded them as
members of an inferior race. "One of the oldest established facts of nature," added the *Pilot* in 1863, "is the mental and physical fitness of the
Negro for servility." Two decades earlier, the Cincinnati Irish Repeal
Association had expressed the view that the two races never could exist
together on equal terms and had added gratuitously, "The very odor of
the negro is almost insufferable to the white." [13]

Officially, the Catholic Church took no stand on slavery. It would not
enter the "political arena" lest the unity of the Church be disrupted.
Political controversy could be left "to the ministers of the human sects." [14]
The hierarchy did not want sectional strife. Bishop Hughes, upon his
return from Cuba in 1854, preached a sermon in which he pronounced
slavery an evil, but "not an absolute or unmitigated one." In his earlier
days, he had written a poem, "The Slave," which showed that he personally detested slavery. He opposed the slave trade, but he held that
once slaves were here, there was no obligation to free them, only to treat
them "with all humanity and Christian care and protection." In turn,
it was the slave's duty to accept his lot and be faithful to his master, and
both were enjoined to obey "the Supreme Master" who created them.
On other occasions, Hughes denounced Brownson for his alleged abolitionist views, defended the social philosophy of the planter aristocracy,
and wrote against the hysterical propaganda of the abolitionists in the
Metropolitan Record. The early Church fathers recognized slavery as a
consequence of original sin. Hughes believed that original sin, though

---

[12] See Handlin, *Boston's Immigrants,* 137, 205–206.

[13] See *Daniel O'Connell and the Committee of the Irish Repeal Association of Cincinnati,*
1–8.

[14] See Gibson, *The Attitudes of the New York Irish,* 135; for a general, historical
résumé, see Rice, *American Catholic Opinion.*

"the men who are living now had no part in the commission of it," continued to operate upon the human race "for time and eternity." [15] Several priests and religious orders owned a few slaves.

According to Catholic doctrine, slavery was an evil to be borne, but not extended or expanded; the fugitive-slave law was to be obeyed out of respect for property rights, but the African slave trade was to be condemned and remain closed. Philosophically, the Roman Catholic Church was opposed to violent, revolutionary remedies for social ills. In this it did not stand alone. James G. Birney wrote a book to prove that American churches were the bulwarks of slavery and an obstacle to reform. The Episcopalians, at one of their conventions, unanimously rejected a resolution to condemn the slave trade. Many ministers and rabbis justified slavery on Biblical grounds. There were Jim Crow regulations in the North as well as in the South. The *Catholic Telegraph* of Cincinnati was practically the only paper of that faith which opposed slavery, though it stated its position with care and moderation. When war came, it became an uncompromising antislavery journal, justified the Emancipation Proclamation, and eagerly gave battle to the rest of the Catholic press.[16]

At the root of much of the clerical reaction to abolitionists, and this was especially true of Bishop Hughes, lay the feeling that many were radicals and "infidels and heretics." "As a general thing," wrote the editor of the *Pilot* in 1851, "whenever you find a free-soiler, you find an anti-hanging man, woman's rights man, an infidel frequently, bigoted Protestant always, a socialist, a red republican, a fanatical teetotaller, a believer in mesmerism, Rochester rappings. . . . You get in a rather dirty set, you perceive, when you join their ranks." [17] The *Freeman's Journal*, the *Louisville Guardian*, the Cincinnati *Catholic Telegraph*, and the *Metropolitan Record* of New York agreed that the Protestant clergy was "at the bottom of the abolition faction." [18] Irish papers were particularly resentful when abolitionist doctrine came by way of antislavery groups in England, and vehemently denounced a "British philanthropy" which allowed its own white slaves to starve. Meagher's *The Irish News* charged Garrison with advocating free love and treason to the Republic. Irish Catholics could not forget that Protestant preachers and "Puritanni-

[15] Murphy, *Attitudes of American Catholicism*, 48–49; and *The Citizen* (New York), May 6, 1854.

[16] Sister Paluszak, "The Opinion of the *Catholic Telegraph*," Chapter IV. There were two priests of Negro blood in the diocese of Boston in 1861, both the sons of Irish fathers and mulatto mothers. Lord, Sexton, and Harrington, *History of the Archdiocese of Boston*, II, 709.

[17] Quoted in Rice, *American Catholic Opinion*, 100.

[18] Benjamin J. Blied, *Catholics and the Civil War*, 63, 73–74.

cal fanatics" who spoke so eloquently against slavery had also said many
unkind things about Rome.

In 1856, the Republican party made its first bid for control of the national government. Although it made heavy inroads upon the Germans,
who had been Democrats, it had almost no success among the Irish. They
remained faithful to the Democratic party and accepted James Buchanan
as a true Jacksonian uncontaminated by the sectional controversy over
slavery and "bleeding" Kansas. The Democratic platform specifically
condemned the Know-Nothing crusade.

The New York *Citizen* defended the Kansas-Nebraska Act as a piece
of legislation which did no more than apply the democratic doctrine of
nonintervention to the territories. It prophesied that "in two years from
now, to have voted against the Nebraska bill will be an unpardonable
sin." In 1857, the same paper defended the Dred Scott decision and insisted that the decision of the Supreme Court must be respected. *The
Irish News* blamed the trouble in Kansas on New England Yankees, and
the *Catholic Mirror* of Baltimore pointed with pride to the fact that
among 3,500 signers of a petition against the Kansas-Nebraska bill, there
was not a single priest.[19] To the Boston *Pilot* it was inconceivable that
immigrants could support "Black Republicans" who were "hostile to the
Constitution" and engaged in spreading the flames of discord and war.[20]
The editor of *The Irish News* damned the Republican liason with Know-
Nothings and predicted "the foreign vote . . . will preserve the Union."
The Irish were reminded throughout the campaign of 1856 that it was
the Democrats who had defended them against nativists and protected
them from Negro competition, that Frémont was the "English nominee,"
and that the Republicans were "the Puritannical party."

By 1860, the issues were even more sharply drawn. The Irish were as
dubious about Lincoln's qualifications for the presidency as millions of
other Americans, and the Boston *Pilot* commented sarcastically, "Very
good men have made their marks, Lincoln has made his—with an
axe." [21] Although the Republican party organized and subsidized a few
Irish "Wide Awake" clubs, there were few Irish Republicans. The vast
majority of Irish-Americans cast their ballots for Douglas. *The Irish
News* was certain that Lincoln could be defeated easily and that Seward
would have made a stronger candidate. Irish leaders warned that a Republican victory in 1860 would mean the revival of Puritanism and

[19] Overdyke, *The Know-Nothing Party,* 224; *The Irish News* (New York), February 13,
1858; *The Citizen* (New York), March 4, 1854; March 21, 1857.
[20] *The Irish News* (New York), May 31, 1856.
[21] *The Pilot* (Boston), October 13, 1860.

Know-Nothingism and that the Democratic South was "trying to roll back" abolitionism, "this avalanche of Britishism." [22] Lincoln received inquiries during the campaign about his attitude toward "the people who profess the Roman Catholic Church." [23] The New York *Tribune* warned the foreign-born that while the Republican party welcomed "friendly counsel," it would not accept "dictation." "He who votes in our election as an Irishman or German," Greeley added, "has no moral right to vote at all." [24]

Although the Republicans recognized their obligation to the German voters, who, in 1860, had shifted in sufficient numbers from the Democratic to the Republican party in critical states where the vote of the foreign-born may have been decisive, the party as yet owed little to the Irish. Nevertheless, it was not long before the Irish-American press complained that the Irish element was being ignored by the new administration in matters of commissions in the Union army and patronage.

Irish leaders in the newspaper field opposed secession. Some criticized Buchanan's vacillation; others favored the Crittenden Compromise to preserve peace between the sections. When the southern states seceded and the firing on Fort Sumter began, Irishmen in the North shifted fairly promptly to a pro-war and pro-Union position, though they made it clear that under no circumstances were they supporting a "nigger war." Irishmen, moreover, were not eager to fight for those who had recently mocked them as "Papists" and "Paddies." The editors of the Catholic press, with a few notable exceptions, supported the war for the preservation of the Union. Their sudden shift in editorial position must have left their readers somewhat confused. In general, they argued that while the national government had no right to coerce a state, the South had acted rashly, and that after Fort Sumter the choice had to be made between law and anarchy.

"Stand by the Union; fight for the Union; die for the Union," advised the Boston *Pilot* on January 12, 1861. But on February 2, when the governor of Massachusetts called out the militia, the paper contended that nowhere did authority to coerce a sovereign state exist. Several months later, when the fighting began, the editor admitted that it was imperative to support the Union, but before the end of the summer of 1861, he urged keeping "our hearts open to rational terms of compromise." Bishop Hughes, a staunch supporter of the government during

---

22 Gibson, *The Attitudes of the New York Irish,* 117; see also *The Irish News* (New York), May 26, June 30, 1860.

23 David C. Mearns, *The Lincoln Papers,* I, 270.

24 New York *Tribune,* May 8, 1860.

the "melancholy strife," argued with his fellow bishops in the South against the right to secede, and wrote to the Secretary of War in 1861, "The Catholics . . . whether of native or foreign birth, are willing to fight to the death for the support of the constitution, the Government and the laws of the country. But if it should be understood . . . that they are to fight for the abolition of slavery, then, indeed, they will turn away in disgust from the discharge of what would otherwise be a patriotic duty." [25]

Although Lincoln moved cautiously and much too slowly for many of his party, before long Irishmen had to face the issue of emancipation. *The Pilot* branded Frémont's proclamation of 1861, which freed the slaves in his military district of Missouri, a highhanded violation of the Constitution and a defiance of the national government. The *Metropolitan Record* of New York took a similar position, and when Brownson suggested that emancipation might be the most effective way to end the war, it called the proposal the worst evil which could befall laborers and mechanics, who would thereby be reduced to the level of the "pauperized operatives of Europe." The *Metropolitan Record* preached racism and had nothing but contempt for the "insiduous designs" of Wendell Phillips, William Lloyd Garrison, and the "incendiary proclamations of General Frémont, General Hunter and General Phelps." It was equally opposed to Lincoln's proposal to end slavery in the border states by compensating the owners.[26]

The *Freeman's Journal,* one of the worst Negrophobe papers, was edited by an American convert to Catholicism, but its readers were largely Irish. Lincoln's Emancipation Proclamation was condemned in leading Catholic papers—the *Catholic Telegraph* of Cincinnati stands out as one of the few exceptions. The *Metropolitan Record* argued that Irish volunteers had been cheated by the government, which had asked them to serve as Irishmen, and now "made [them] subservient to the emancipation of the negro." [27] When Governor Andrews of Massachusetts advocated arming Negro troops, the Boston *Pilot* angrily replied that such a policy would lead to murderous slave insurrections.[28]

A number of Irish and Catholic papers now moved rapidly to a position so extreme that it may well be described as "Copperhead." John Mullaly's *Metropolitan Record* hammered away at Lincoln's dictatorship and argued that the press was no longer free and that the Bill of Rights was dead. Throughout 1863, the paper attacked the government for viola-

[25] See Ernst, *Immigrant Life,* 291. For the Catholic press, slavery, and the war, see Blied, *Catholics and the Civil War,* Chapter V.
[26] *Metropolitan Record* (New York), January 18, July 5, 1862.
[27] *Ibid.,* February 14, 1863.
[28] *The Pilot* (Boston), March 28, 1863.

tions of the Constitution, arbitrary arrests, the use of Negro soldiers, emancipation, the needless prolonging of a bloody war, and the blunders of the military. In a parody of a nursery rhyme, it railed against high taxes and the debasing of the American dollar:

> Sing a song of Greenbacks,
> Pockets full of trash,
> Over head and ears in debt,
> And out of ready cash.[29]

Mullaly demanded the impeachment of Lincoln to end the "march of despotism" and argued for an immediate armistice, to be followed by a peace convention which would recognize the sovereignty of the southern states. When Clement L. Vallandigham was a candidate for governor of Ohio in 1863, after his military arrest for subversive speeches, the *Metropolitan Record* gave him its full support, denounced the arrest as an outrage against the Constitution, and referred to Ohio as "a Poland in the United States," "blotted out of the list of sovereign states." Mullaly claimed that his anti-Lincoln policies won him 3,000 new subscribers in two months. He collected his anti-administration editorials into a book, and on November 20, 1863, he printed a parody of Tennyson which began:

> Abraham Lincoln, we bow the knee,
>   Republican King;
> Yankees and Yorkers, and Quakers are we,
> The rightful heirs of the men once free,
> But all of us slaves in our worship of thee,
>   Republican King;

It is not surprising that the *Metropolitan Record* was suppressed in Missouri and Tennessee by military order in 1864. When Mullaly started the *New York Vindicator and People's Advocate,* which opposed the war "as unconstitutional" and "subversive of popular freedom," it too was suppressed by General Rosecrans, a convert to Catholicism, who was in command in St. Louis. The *Freeman's Journal* was denied circulation rights in New Orleans and Nashville, and James A. McMaster, the paper's belligerent editor, served a term in prison. In 1863, McMaster lectured for the Sons of Liberty in the Middle West to oppose the draft and expose the "perilous infraction" of the United States Constitution.[30] In 1865, he admitted he had received all the degrees in the Copperhead American Knights. D. A. Mahony, editor of the Dubuque *Herald,* was charged with discouraging enlistments and sent to jail. Charles O'Conor,

---

[29] *Metropolitan Record* (New York), February 13, 1864.
[30] Sister Kwitchen, *James A. McMaster,* Chapter IV.

who volunteered to defend Jefferson Davis in 1865, frequently was referred to as a Copperhead.

To such critics, the campaign of 1864 promised the opportunity for a reckoning with Lincoln and the Republican party. They hoped the Democratic convention would select a candidate whom they could support with enthusiasm. In the opinion of papers like the *Metropolitan Record and New York Vindicator,* Lincoln was renominated by a "convention of Shoddyites and Loyal Leaguers," "a body of political tools and harpies" presided over by Henry J. Raymond of the New York *Times,* with "ten Niggers" among the delegates. Lincoln was described as the weakest of the weak and "of wicked ones the worst." [31]

McClellan's nomination was a disappointment to extreme Irish anti-administration leaders, and they were incensed when he promised to continue the war and said nothing about opposing conscription, a sore issue with many Irishmen. The New York *Tribune* of November 10, 1864, referred to the solid Irish vote for McClellan, organized in "the grog-shops, wherein hate and scorn of 'the naygurs' is systematically inculcated." A pamphlet favoring miscegenation was published in New York and circulated by the Democrats with good effect among the Irish. Allegedly from the pen of a Republican Negrophile, it maintained that "the fusion . . . will be of infinite service to the Irish . . . a more brutal race and lower in civilization than the negro." [32] Nevertheless, there was considerable division of opinion among the Irish in New York and elsewhere. Meagher, for example, a military hero of the war, and others deeply involved in the Union cause advocated vigorous prosecution of the war and denounced Irishmen who refused to budge from an allegiance to the Democratic party, which had begun "the instant the baggage-smashers and cut throat lodging house keepers lay hands on them." [33] Meagher advocated citizenship for the Negro after the war, to the disgust of many of his fellow immigrants.

When Lincoln's career came to a quick end at the hands of a fanatical assassin, even his most violent critics denounced the cowardly deed. But along with prominent leaders of the Republican party, many Irish welcomed Andrew Johnson's succession to the presidency. Although radical Republicans, soon to angle for Irish votes, thought Johnson would follow a vindictive, punitive policy toward the South, many Irish editors welcomed the new president as a foe of radicals and abolitionists. They believed he would rebuild the South and the nation by restoring the rights of the states and the constitutional guarantees of individual liberty.

[31] *Metropolitan Record and New York Vindicator,* June 18, 1864; September 17, 1864.
[32] Brother Lee, *Discontent in New York City,* 163.
[33] *Metropolitan Record and New York Vindicator,* October 22, 1864.

CHAPTER XIII

The Irish in the Civil War

WHATEVER their attitude toward Negroes, abolitionists, state rights, and secession, and however deep their devotion to the Democratic party, when war came the Irish did their full share. They had a conspicuous role in the Union army, which was "an amalgam of nations," and they also played an important part in the Confederate army. There were German and Irish "Legions" in the Civil War; "Ulster Guards" and "Irish Brigades"; "Chasseurs à Pied"; Garibaldi, Lafayette, Steuben, and Pulaski Guards; Schwarze Jäger; "Enfant Perdus"; and Brooklyn Chasseurs. More than 400,000 foreign-born of various national strains helped save the Union; others fought with equal vigor and conviction to establish the Confederate States of America.

Irishmen had done their bit in earlier wars, in 1812 and 1846, when their number was much smaller than in 1861. Brooklyn and Albany had Irish companies in the War of 1812. More than thirty years later, Mike Walsh referred contemptuously to "the little rootbeer war now fomenting in the Rio Grande," but the Irish volunteered in considerable numbers for the Mexican War. A company of Irish Jasper Greens went from Savannah, the Ottawa Irish Volunteers of Illinois were commanded by Captain James F. Egan, and General Winfield Scott had a corps of two thousand native Irish who made a distinguished record for courage. General James Shields, a native Irishman destined for a distinguished public career in the United States, was one of Scott's brigadiers. Other Irishmen in the Mexican War included General Stephen Kearney, a typical soldier of fortune who made the famous march to the Pacific; Major Theodore O'Hara; Captain Wayne Reid, better known for his boys' stories; and Captain Daniel Conahan of the Sarsfield Guards of Cincinnati.

The number of Irish in the Union army has been estimated from 150,-000 to 170,000, but the report of the United States Sanitary Commission in 1869 placed the figure at 144,221 natives of Ireland, about five thousand more than might have been expected in proportion to the total Irish-

American population. Of this number, 51,206 came from New York, 17,418 from Pennsylvania, 12,041 from Illinois, 10,007 from Massachusetts, 8,129 from Ohio, 3,621 from Wisconsin, and 4,362 from Missouri.

In the excitement after the firing on Fort Sumter, many Irish enlisted. Like numerous others, they believed the war would be of short duration. As the fighting dragged on, "bounties" helped keep the ranks filled, and during the last two years, many Irish were drafted. The government carried on a systematic recruiting program among Irish immigrants. Many were enrolled immediately upon landing at Castle Garden. Within twenty yards of this famous point of entry, there were two large recruiting tents, bedecked with gay banners and stocked with whiskey and food, where recruiting officers offered liberal bounties for volunteers. As William H. Russell aptly put it, many immigrants—Irish, Germans, and others—fought not only *con amore* but also *pro dolore* (i.e., for the dollar). Irishmen were persuaded that the war might give them a chance to strike at England, and a number of Irish outfits in the Civil War carried the green flag of Ireland with the American colors.

Federal agents, openly or secretly, recruited among prospective Irish emigrants in Ireland, or lured Irishmen to the United States with promises of jobs on the railroads when their real purpose was to get them for the army. In Dublin, Irishmen who were eager to enlist appealed to the United States consul for free transportation to America. Irish journals here and abroad denounced the recruiting methods of "Federal agents," and the British government lodged formal protests in Washington. One of the most effective recruiting techniques used in this country was to promise a Catholic priest for every regiment. "You have fought nobly for the Harp and Shamrock," read one advertisement, "fight now for the Stars and Stripes. . . . Your adopted country wants you." [1]

There is ample testimony from officers of every nationality and religious persuasion concerning the bravery and reckless courage of Irish soldiers. The New York *Times,* the New York *Herald,* and the New York *Tribune* carried editorials in praise of their loyalty. The Irish were steady and cool fighters, once the battle had begun, and they loved to fight. They frequently tossed away knapsacks and blankets, as they rushed into the wild and reckless charge fighting "like tigers." They were loyal to their outfits and to their officers, who knew how to handle them and spur them on, with matchless Irish oratory, to deeds of valor. The annals of the Civil War, both North and South, record scores of cases of

[1] *Boston Transcript,* October 3, 1861

personal gallantry. The losses among the Irish always were high, including officers.[2]

The problem of discipline in the Union army was by no means limited to Irish soldiers, but the latter were prominently involved. The monotony of barracks life bored many Irishmen, and, while in camp, they proved hard to discipline. The Irish were better soldiers while fighting in offensive spurts than when forced to a sustained defensive. Irish soldiers, frequently intemperate and impetuous, were inclined to take to brawling when life got too dull. Excitable and often eloquently profane, companies of Irishmen were likely to settle their differences with their fists, especially after too much liquor. Conditions usually were worst right after the men received their pay. The chaplain of New York's Thirty-seventh Regiment recorded in his diary: "'Pay Day,' and of course drinking. Such a picture of hell I had never seen."[3] Efforts were made to build morale by singing, celebrations of special holidays, races, dancing, and athletic contests, but frequently such festive occasions only added to the confusion. Serious trouble arose among recruits "from the roughs of the New York fire companies." Some of these outfits looked upon soldiering as a kind of continuous spree, and their infractions of discipline not only disturbed the army but the countryside where they were encamped. Pugnacious, quarrelsome, and often intemperate, they were also loyal to their own code of honor and, above all, were jovial and buoyant spirits.

Like the Germans, the Irish demanded separate Hibernian units in the Union army and, in addition, requested a whole Irish division. When this was refused, they felt sorely aggrieved, and the Irish press echoed their feelings in vigorous language. Irishmen resented it when James Shields was not made a major general and pointed out that there were only two Irish brigadiers. The Boston *Pilot* criticized Lincoln for failure to appoint Irishmen to important jobs in the government, and Archbishop Hughes, in a letter to Seward in the summer of 1861, urged that Colonel Michael Corcoran of the Irish brigade be made a brigadier, because Hughes had "discovered symptoms of wounded feelings among his countrymen."[4]

According to the New York *Times* and the *Brooklyn Eagle,* the Irish Zouaves, or "Fire Zouaves," of New York were among the most undis-

[2] On the foreign-born in the war, the authoritative works are Ella Lonn, *Foreigners in the Union Army and Navy* and, by the same author, *Foreigners in the Confederacy.* See also Frederick Phisterer's volumes on *New York in the War of the Rebellion, 1861 to 1865.*

[3] Reverend Father Tissot, "A Year with the Army of the Potomac," United States Catholic Historical Society *Historical Records and Studies,* III (1908), Part I, 46.

[4] Blied, *Catholics and the Civil War,* 76–77.

ciplined Irish units in the Union army. They marched off to war in
fezzes, red firemen's shirts, and blue pants, and went into quarters at the
Battery. There was so much trouble and drunkenness that seventy-five
were dismissed from the service. The men climbed the gates at night,
eluded the sentries, and disappeared into the city for a spree. New York
papers charged them with cowardice at Bull Run, where relatively few
soldiers seem to have distinguished themselves for bravery. It must be
pointed out, however, that the Zouaves went to the front 850 strong and
left 200 of their men as casualties on the field. New York firemen gave
them a rousing welcome on their return to the city after the engagement.

At the first battle of Bull Run, the Irish charged the Confederates
twice and then retreated with the rest. The Irish colonel of one regiment
was court-martialed for lack of discipline, and he and his men were
charged with drunkenness and brawling. A reporter from the *London
Times* accused Meagher's men of running away from the battle, but there
is evidence that the Sixty-ninth New York Regiment, described by one
correspondent as "strolling, drunken vagabonds . . . picked up in the
low groggeries of New York," "fought like tigers." No less a person than
General William Tecumseh Sherman testified to their valor. Later, at
Fredericksburg, Irish soldiers under Meagher, wearing green twigs in
their hats, made six of the most heroic charges of the war. One regiment
went in with 700 men and came out with 150. The dogged courage of
the Irish at Antietam matched their reckless valor at Fredericksburg, and
officers on both sides of the line testified to their courage. At Chancellors-
ville, the Irish brigade was virtually shot to pieces, and when Meagher
resigned his command, only about 520 men were left of the five regiments
of the original brigade.[5]

It is not difficult to find evidences of insubordination, lack of discipline,
brawling, and desertion among Irish soldiers alongside equally credible
accounts of unusual devotion, valor, and fighting efficiency. The compo-
sition, organization, and administration of the Union army left much to
be desired. Many officers of volunteer forces had no training and held
their commissions because of political influence. Some were appointed
by the governor of their state; others were elected by their own men. Old
military companies whose objective always had been more social than
military were now transferred *in corpore* into the Union army. The annals of the war contain many cases of incompetence, graft, cruelty, heavy
drinking, rioting in camp, disobedience to discipline, and desertion and
bounty jumping. A recruiting officer, paid so much a head for each man
he enlisted, was not likely to be too discriminating. There can be no ques-

[5] See Ahearn, *T. F. Meagher,* Chapter VIII.

tion that units like the Fire Zouaves and "Billy Wilson's boys" were notorious for rioting and lack of discipline. But trouble in many other units stemmed from poor organization, poor equipment, gouging of the men by sutlers who had the lucrative concessions at army camps, and incompetent and untrained officers.

As the war progressed, the Irish element in the United States had many occasions to honor their heroes. In 1862 and 1863, there were numerous ceremonies for the bestowal of swords, medals, and gifts such as saddles and gold spurs to Irish military leaders. Flags with the harp and shamrock embroidered upon them were presented to various units. In Philadelphia, Captain Thomas Kelly of the second company of Shields Guards was given "a handsome sword, revolver, and a full suit of waterproof clothing," and the sword was "blessed by the Bishop's secretary." [6]

With their innate love of pageantry, the Irish arranged parades to see their soldiers off to the front and to give them a hero's welcome upon their return. When the famous Sixty-ninth New York Regiment departed in the spring of 1861, they were escorted by Hibernian Benevolent and other Irish societies, several fire companies, Irish police, and the "Exile Club," and in the parade there was a wagon decorated with banners and the slogan, "Remember Fontenoy." Colonel Corcoran received a large bunch of shamrocks, and the steamer which carried his troops down the harbor pulled out to the booming of cannon and with the lusty cheers of hundreds of New York Irishmen resounding in their ears. Several weeks later, the New York City County Liquor Dealers Protective Society appealed for funds for the relief of the families of the Sixth-ninth.[7] The following September, there was a festival in Jones' Woods for the widows and orphans. The program included singing and dancing and a concert by Bryant's Minstrels, who appeared in white-face. When their ninety-day enlistment expired, and the Sixty-ninth returned from the battlefront to the Battery, the men were greeted with another demonstration by Irish organizations and marched down Broadway with the bands blaring "St. Patrick's Day in the Morning" and "The Night Before Larry Was Stretched." [8]

During the Peninsular campaign in Virginia, the Sixty-ninth was famous for its festive occasions. On May Day, the men decorated their chapel with flowers and crowded the chaplain's tent for the confessional. There were horse and steeplechase races to break the monotony of camp life. Entry fees were collected from the contestants, and purses were dis-

[6] The Metropolitan Record (New York), June 1, 1861.
[7] Ibid., May 4, 18, 1861.
[8] Harlow, Old Bowery Days, 347.

tributed to the winners. Once there was a mule race, with drummer boys as jockeys. At Christmastime, the huts of the men were decorated with evergreen and harps of green twigs, and St. Patrick's Day always was the occasion for special festivities, races and games, Irish reels, jigs and hornpipes, recitations and amateur theatricals, and the consumption of large quantities of food and drink.[9]

It would be pointless to review the history of all the units in the Union army in which there were large numbers of Irish soldiers. Two Massachusetts regiments, the Ninth Massachusetts Volunteers, known as "the Irish Ninth," and the Twenty-eighth Massachusetts carried green flags beside the Stars and Stripes. The first had a prominent part in the Peninsular campaign; the latter, in the second battle of Bull Run and as part of the Irish Brigade. One of the Ninth's flags, presented by Mrs. Harrison Gray Otis, bore the inscription: "As aliens and strangers thou didst us befriend. As sons and true patriots we do thee defend." The flag of the Twenty-eighth featured a harp and a Gaelic inscription meaning "Clear the Road." [10]

The Fifteenth Maine Regiment was recruited by Colonel John McCuskey largely among Irish-Americans from the northeastern part of the state. The Ninth Connecticut was mainly Irish. The Tenth New Hampshire Infantry, commanded by Colonel Michael Donohue, was about one-fourth Irish. Of the 32,846 Union soldiers from New Hampshire, the Irish furnished 3,067.[11] By the end of the war, the bounties offered by towns in New Hampshire, as well as by the state and federal governments, approximated a thousand dollars, and "bounty jumping" became a real temptation.

New York's Sixty-ninth enrolled 6,500 men in a few days. Most of the men re-enlisted when their initial ninety-day term expired. The "Jackson Guard" was known as the Tammany regiment, and the "Irish Rifles" became the Thirty-seventh New York. The Eighty-eighth was known as "Mrs. Meagher's Own" or "The Connaught Rangers" and included Irish veterans of the British army in India and in the Crimea. Meagher raised the "Irish Brigade." By the end of 1861, it included the Sixty-ninth, Eighty-eighth, and Sixty-third regiments. The Second Battalion of Light Artillery was recruited largely in New York City. Its four companies had Irish captains, and the battalion commander was Major Thomas O'Neill. After Corcoran's return from nearly a year's captivity as a pris-

---

9 See Conyngham, *The Irish Brigade and Its Campaigns.*
10 Lord, Sexton, and Harrington, *History of the Archdiocese of Boston,* II, 713–14.
11 Quirk, "The Irish Element in New Hampshire," 57–58.

oner of war, he organized Corcoran's Brigade or "The Irish Legion," which made a notable combat record.

The Twenty-fourth Infantry of Pennsylvania, largely Irish and re-organized as the Sixty-ninth Pennsylvania, fought well at Gettysburg. The Second Philadelphia Regiment of state militia, which consisted almost entirely of Irish-Americans, became part of the Union army in 1861. The Hundred-and-Sixteenth Pennsylvania, commanded by Colonel Dennis Hannan, included Irishmen from Cork to Donegal who distinguished themselves in a number of bloody battles.

The Tenth Ohio, the Eleventh and Seventeenth Wisconsin Infantry, the Thirty-fifth and Sixty-first Indiana, and the Missouri Seventh Infantry were frequently referred to as Irish units. The Twenty-third Illinois was recruited by Colonel James A. Mulligan, editor of Chicago's first Catholic paper, the *Western Tablet,* and included Irish companies from Springfield, Rockford, and Galena. The Ninetieth Illinois was known as the Irish Legion. It was recruited, in part, by Father Dunne, with encouragement from Bishop Duggan. Father Thomas F. Kelly was its chaplain. The Seventeenth Wisconsin Regiment was an all-Irish outfit commanded by John L. Doran. J. O'Rourke was captain of the Montgomery Guards of Milwaukee. Captain Hugh McDermott led the first company of the Seventeenth Wisconsin to Camp Randall at Madison, Wisconsin. When a number of his men roamed the streets and refused to entrain for St. Louis until they were paid, McDermott summoned aid from Chicago and Milwaukee to quiet the insubordinate volunteers.

The number of Irish officers, high and low, who achieved distinction in the Civil War runs into the hundreds. Among the best known were Michael Corcoran of county Sligo, who had joined the Irish constabulary at nineteen. Corcoran came to the United States in 1849 and was the proprietor of New York's "Hibernian Hall." Enlisting as a private in the Sixty-ninth, he was elected its colonel in 1859. Shortly before the war, he had endeared himself to all Irishmen by refusing to enter his men in a parade honoring the Prince of Wales during the latter's visit to New York, and he was court-martialed for insubordination. For a year, Corcoran was a prisoner of the Confederates. Upon his release, he returned to the front as a brigadier. He died in 1863, after a fall from his horse while riding back to camp after a convivial occasion in honor of Meagher, who had come for a visit at Christmastime.

James Shields, a veteran of the Mexican War and already a prominent public figure, served again in the Civil War. Thomas F. Meagher was a popular commander and a brave soldier, though regarded by regular army men as a "political general." He was convinced that Washington never fully appreciated his talents. Vain, brave, proud, an orator of great eloquence, and something of an intellectual aristocrat, Meagher remained a symbol of the unrequited Irish in the Civil War and a source of controversy. The Irish also pointed with pride to Philip H. Sheridan, the son of John and Mary Sheridan, who had emigrated in 1830. The future Civil War hero was born near Somerset, Ohio, where the father was a canal and road worker. Bishop Hughes, perhaps the best-known Irish-American civilian, went abroad during the war for President Lincoln to urge nonintervention in Paris and to present the Union's case in England and Ireland at a critical juncture in America's foreign relations.

Less well known were such Irishmen as Captain Dominick J. Connolly, who joined the Irish Brigade as a lad of fifteen and spent a year in Libby Prison; Thomas W. Sweeny, Mexican War veteran and Civil War brigadier who achieved notoriety as a Fenian; Captain Maxwell O'Sullivan, a musician from New York who died of wounds from a fire in his tent; Captain Patrick F. Clooney, killed at Antietam; Thomas O'Neill, who recruited a company in Massachusetts and died from a wound received at Cold Harbor; Colonel Robert Nugent, a survivor of the Irish Brigade's bloody charges at Fredericksburg; Colonel Patrick O'Rorke, who saved Little Round Top at Gettysburg and was killed in the battle; St. Clair A. Mulholland, mustered out a major general of volunteers to become police chief of Philadelphia; Brigadier General Thomas Smyth of county Cork, who raised a company for the Twenty-fourth Pennsylvania Volunteers; and Colonel Richard Byrnes, killed at Cold Harbor.

Catholic chaplains, known to the soldiers as "Holy Joes," were attached to some Irish military units. Bishop Ireland as a young priest was chaplain of the Fifth Minnesota Regiment. The Jesuit, Father Nash, of Kilkenny, was chaplain of the Sixth New York Volunteer Infantry.[12] Peter Paul Cooney was with Indiana's Irish Thirty-fifth Infantry, Father Mullen with the Ninth Connecticut, and Father Thomas Quinn with the First Rhode Island. Father William Corby, son of an Irish pioneer in Michigan, left the faculty of Notre Dame to become chaplain of the New York Eighty-eighth, and Father James Dillon of the same institution was with New York's Sixty-third. Father J. F. Tracy served as chaplain at General Rosecrans' headquarters.

The record of Catholic nuns who worked as nurses on the battlefields and in the hospitals reflected additional credit upon religious orders

---

[12] See James A. Rooney, "Father Nash, S. J., Army Chaplain (1825–1895)," *The Catholic Historical Review*, II (1917), 188–94.

dedicated to the alleviation of human misery.[13] Probably the best-known was Sister Anthony (Mary O'Connell), the "Angel of the Battlefield," sometimes called America's Florence Nightingale. She came to the United States from Limerick with her parents and was educated by the Ursulines in Charlestown, Massachusetts. She became a Sister of Charity and had charge of St. John's Hospital for Invalids in Cincinnati for many years. Along with others of her community, she served as a nurse on the battlefields of the Civil War. After the war, two non-Catholic citizens of Cincinnati bought a hospital for her in recognition of her services.[14] Bridget Divers, known as "Irish Biddy," was attached as nurse and hospital stewardess to the First Michigan Cavalry, to which her husband belonged. Among the more prominent Irish surgeons in the Union army were Patrick O'Connell of the Twenty-eighth Massachusetts and Dr. Lawrence Reynolds, a graduate of the Dublin College of Surgeons, who served with the Irish Brigade.

The ineradicable black spots upon the Irish escutcheon during the war were the brutal draft riots of 1863 in New York City. The draft law was opposed in other parts of the nation and by other nationality groups, and others besides Irishmen participated in the disgraceful New York riots. The Irish, however, played such a predominant role that the result was a bitter anti-Irish reaction throughout the country.

In comparison with World War I and II, the draft law of the Civil War was clearly unfair. It provided that a draftee could escape military service by paying $300 in cash or by furnishing a substitute. The poor had good reason to complain that the law demanded "Three Hundred Dollars or Your Life." Substitutes became "a marketable commodity," and brokerage firms were established to furnish men who were willing to go to war for a price. The draft, which was contrary to American tradition, was especially unpopular with the foreign-born, who had left Europe to escape military service. To the Irish, conscription was doubly objectionable. It came almost simultaneously with emancipation, and the Irishman had no stomach for fighting for his Negro competitor in the labor market. The machinery for administering the draft, hastily improvised, proved inadequate and lent itself to manipulation for political or personal favoritism.

Opposition to the draft appeared in a number of states. There were disturbances in New England, Pennsylvania, Ohio, New Jersey, Illinois, and Wisconsin. Two marshals were attacked in Boston, hardware stores

[13] See Ellen Ryan Jolly, *Nuns of the Battlefield;* and George Barton, *Angels of the Battlefield.*

[14] *DAB;* and *The Irish World* (New York), January 1, 1898.

were robbed of knives and guns, and several persons were killed. A meeting at St. Mary's Institute on July 13, 1863, ended with cheers for Jefferson Davis.[15] In Rutland, Vermont, Irish quarry workers drove off the enrolling officers with clubs and stones. In Pottsville, Pennsylvania, armed Irish miners resisted the draft. In Troy, New York, a Negro church was torn down and a local newspaper attacked during a draft riot. Order was finally restored by the local priest and the militia from Albany. In Ozaukee County, Wisconsin, in November, 1862, Germans had threatened to lynch several Republicans; in Milwaukee, both Irish and Germans opposed conscription; and there were disturbances in parts of Indiana and in the Irish mining section around Dubuque, Iowa.[16]

Such incidents, however, were completely overshadowed by what happened in New York in July, 1863. Before the war, New York firms had many business connections with the South, and there was much sympathy for the Confederacy. At one point during the war, the mayor talked about having the city "secede." In 1863, Negroes were used as strikebreakers against longshoremen and stevedores whose wages were less than $1.50 a day. The draft was unfairly administered by Republican officials in New York City and Brooklyn,[17] and, in one respect, the draft riots represented a revolt of the poor, who did the fighting, against the "shoddy aristocracy," who did the profiteering. The New York *Herald* described the draft riots as "a popular outbreak inspired by a burning sense of wrong," and the New York *World* commented that apparently "poor men refused to be forced into a war" which was mismanaged and perverted to partisan purposes.[18] Bishop Hughes wrote his friend, the Secretary of State, that the basic cause of the riots was the attempt "to make black labor equal to white labor . . . with the difference that black labor shall have local patronage over the toil of the white man." [19]

Both Governor Horatio Seymour and Mayor Fernando Wood denounced conscription as unconstitutional. Several New York papers helped stir the Irish to fury. Everyone who was "opposed to the war for the negro . . . and in favor of the rights of the poor" was invited to a mass meeting, and the mayor used the occasion to demand an armistice and a peace conference. Of the Irish papers, the *Irish-American* and the *Metropolitan Record* were the most inflamatory. The latter, although it

[15] Lord, Sexton, and Harrington, *History of the Archdiocese of Boston*, II, 708–709; and Edith E. Ware, *Political Opinion in Massachusetts During Civil War and Reconstruction*, 129–32.

[16] Wood Gray, *The Hidden Civil War—The Story of the Copperheads*, 71.

[17] Brother Lee, *Discontent in New York City*, Chapter III.

[18] Samuel A. Pleasants, *Fernando Wood of New York*, 144–47.

[19] Brother Lee, *Discontent in New York City*, 142.

no longer assumed to speak for Bishop Hughes, carried at the masthead the words "A Catholic Family Paper." Editorially, it denounced the draft as "military despotism" and a deadly blow to popular liberties, made ugly comparisons between the administration and Russia's "fiendish rule in Poland," referred to good Americans led in chains by "a minority President," and virtually counseled insurrection. The paper pointed out that whereas it cost a white man $300 to buy exemption from the draft, in the South a Negro could not be bought for less than $2,000. When the editor finally was arrested and charged with inciting his readers to resist the draft, he was defended by Charles O'Conor and Charles Donohue and escaped conviction on a technicality.[20]

The drawings in New York City began on Saturday, July 11, 1863. Republican provost marshals were in charge, and most of the names drawn were those of poor workers, many of them Irish, who could neither pay $300 nor procure substitutes. Over the week end, the Irish sections of the city were seething with angry charges of discrimination and by Monday the steam exploded. Gangs of rioters marched to Central Park, stormed and burned the draft office, beat the superintendent of police, raided houses on Lexington Avenue, destroyed a colored orphan asylum which housed two hundred children between the ages of two and twelve, drove innocent Negroes in panic through the streets, and hanged several. Chinese, considered close enough in color to Ethiopians, also were attacked. Horsecars were held up, stores and homes pillaged, and telegraph wires cut. For three days, the city was terrorized by a brutal, frenzied mob. Estimates of the total dead fluctuated wildly from eighteen to seventy-four. Among them were some Irish and Germans.[21] Finally, the Provost Marshal announced in the newspapers that the draft was suspended, and a regiment was brought in from Meade's army at Gettysburg to restore order. On the fourth day, when the worst was over, Archbishop Hughes summoned the faithful to his home, and on the following day addressed a crowd of three thousand from his balcony. Like scores of other priests, he demanded an end to the disorder.

Archbishop Hughes' address was his last public speech. He died shortly thereafter. In August, 1862, upon his return from Europe, he had urged volunteering, but also had recommended conscription if this means was necessary to bring the war to a quick end.[22] On July 15, 1863, Hughes explained to the New York *Herald* that he had never favored

20 *Metropolitan Record* (New York), March 14, 21, April 11, 1863; August 27, 1864.

21 See David M. Barnes, *The Draft Riots in New York, July, 1863; the Metropolitan Police: Their Services during Riot Week, Their Honorable Record;* James B. Fry, *New York and the Conscription of 1863;* and Stewart Mitchell, *Horatio Seymour.*

22 *Metropolitan Record* (New York), November 1, 1862.

"coercive conscription" but had recommended that "the people of the North, who stand by the Federal government should demand conscription by their own voluntary choice and act. This would be their own system of volunteering." [23] In one of his sermons, he had urged "the people to rise and ask the government to draft them" and had said that "those who are wealthy and cannot go themselves can provide substitutes."

Hughes' address to his parishioners was a masterpiece of diplomacy. He referred to suffering and oppression in Ireland and spoke flatteringly of his Irish countrymen. He stressed the heavy loss of life and property in the riots, but carefully refrained from accusing his listeners. He pleaded for constitutional methods of redress and concluded by advising his audience to go calmly to their homes and "not to give up your principles and convictions, but keep out of the crowd in which immortal souls are launched into eternity without a moment's notice." The speech was shrewd, effective, and interspersed with references to Irish patriots and exiles and John Bull. One senses that the prelate realized he had to handle the crowd with all the skill he could muster. The comments of the New York press varied. Some were sharply critical. William Cullen Bryant's New York *Evening Post* pointed out that all Irishmen should not be condemned because of the misdeeds of the worst element among them. Many Irish had refused to join the rioters. Two of New York's Irish wards remained quiet, and their colored residents were not disturbed. In one ward, Irish porters and laborers formed a guard to beat off the mob. The police, many of whom were Irish, made a reasonably good record in trying to maintain law and order. The New York *Times* reported that one Irishman had proposed that his countrymen raise $50,-000 to rebuild the Negro orphanage which Irish vandals had destroyed.

The majority of the rioters were Irish, and there would have been even more brutality except for the intervention of the priests. Papers like the Cincinnati *Catholic Telegraph* denounced the riot and every form of resistance to the draft. The *Metropolitan Record,* whose inflammatory editorials helped bring on the riot, editorially condemned the "revolting, fiendish, cowardly, cruel" treatment of "the poor unfortunate negroes" and argued that "a superior race should disdain to vent their passions on an inferior one," especially Negroes, who were "the footballs of every party." [24] George Templeton Strong recorded in his diary that "the rab-

---

[23] See Thomas F. Meehan, "Archbishop Hughes and the Draft Riots," United States Catholic Historical Society *Historical Records and Studies,* I (January, 1900), Part II, 172; and 171–90.

[24] *Metropolitan Record* (New York), July 25, 1863.

ble was perfectly homogeneous. Every brute in the drove was pure Celtic-hod-carrier or loafer." With equal fury, he denounced "the low Irish women . . . stalwart young vixens and withered old hags . . . all cursing the 'bloody draft' and egging on their men to mischief." [25] Thomas A. Emmet agreed that the draft riots were instigated by the Irish, who "had been exasperated to a sufficient degree." He described the brutalities of the rioters in strong language and gave great credit to Archbishop Hughes for preventing more trouble.[26]

Below Mason and Dixon's line, the Irish had rallied to the defense of the South as readily as their northern brothers had to the Union cause. In both sections, the Church tried to remain aloof from the bitter internecine struggle. A number of priests privately expressed opposition to slavery, but were careful not to ally themselves with the antislavery movement. Southern Irishmen, even more than those in the North, feared the effect of emancipation on white labor.

There were nearly 85,000 Irish in the South when the war began. The majority lived in the four states of Louisiana, Missouri, Tennessee, and Virginia. Charleston, South Carolina, had about 3,300 Irish; New Orleans nearly 25,000 in 1850. The majority of southern Irish favored state rights and hated "the dirty nigger-loving Yanks." The suspension of work on levees and railroads in the lower Mississippi Valley during the war made jobless Irishmen eager to enlist. On several occasions, southern and northern Irish met face to face in combat. "Everywhere in the Confederate States," reported the *Southern Watchman* of Athens, Georgia, "they have been among the foremost to volunteer, and among the most liberal in contributing to the comfort of the brave soldiers in the field." [27] Irish blacksmiths and machinists were in great demand in the southern army, and Confederate generals spoke highly of Irish soldiers. Some preferred them as clean, spirited, fearless fighters who were loyal to their leaders and whose irrepressible sense of humor did not fail them even in moments of greatest danger.

Roberdeau Wheat's Batallion, called "The Tigers" and "The Irish Tartars," was a famous unit from Louisiana. At Fredericksburg, Georgia Irishmen defended St. Mary's Hill against Meagher's Irish from the North. The Emmet Guards and the Montgomery Guards were companies from Richmond, Virginia. The Emerald Guards of the Eighth Alabama Regiment consisted largely of Irish laborers. They wore dark green uniforms and carried a shamrock and harp emblazoned on one

---

[25] Nevins and Thomas (eds.), *Strong's Diary*, III, 335–36.
[26] Emmet, *Incidents of My Life*, 184.
[27] Quoted in E. Merton Coulter, *The Confederate States of America, 1861–1865*, 444.

side of their Confederate flag. A number of Louisiana companies were composed of Irish military organizations that had joined the Confederate army as units. There were other Irish outfits from Tennessee, and one company of Irish Confederates came from Wilmington, North Carolina. The Meagher Guards of Charleston, South Carolina, changed its name after the firing on Fort Sumter to the Emerald Light Infantry. The Fifth Confederate Regiment, commanded by General Patrick Cleburne of Arkansas and composed largely of Irish, fought gallantly at Missionary Ridge. One of John Mitchel's sons was killed at Fort Sumter, another at Gettysburg. General Joseph Finnigan defended Florida against Union attacks. David Flannery of Limerick was superintendent of telegraphs between Memphis and New Orleans. Lee's Irish orderly, Bryan, had an excellent reputation as a good forager and cook. Michael Quinn was chief engineer on the *Alabama*. It must be added that there were also Irish deserters from both Confederate and Union armies, and some were court-martialed for breaches of discipline or cowardice.

Among the distinguished southern Irish military leaders, General Patrick Cleburne, an Irish Episcopalian, was outstanding. In Ireland he had been apprenticed to a druggist. When he failed the qualifying examination, he joined the British army. In 1849, he came to the United States to resume work as a druggist, first in Cincinnati, then in Arkansas. In 1856, he was admitted to the bar. Originally a Whig, he became a Democrat during the Know-Nothing days. He was an impulsive, generous Irishman with remarkable oratorical gifts, and always spoke with an Irish accent. Though he lived in a slave state, he owned no slaves, and in 1864 he advocated arming Negroes for the Confederate army and giving them their freedom upon their discharge from service. Cleburne had a brother in each of the opposing armies. His brilliant military record made him a major general in 1862. He distinguished himself at Chickamauga and Missionary Ridge and became known as "the Stonewall Jackson of the West." He was killed, when not quite thirty-eight, at Franklin, and buried near Columbia, Tennessee.

The Confederacy, like the Union government, dispatched special envoys to Ireland to propagandize for the southern cause. Lieutenant James L. Capston and Father John Bannon, a St. Louis priest and Confederate chaplain, as well as several other native Irishmen described as "long residents of the United States," went to Ireland to stop recruiting for the Union army. Their speeches emphasized the Know-Nothing outrages and insisted that Irish Catholics could not feel at home in the northern states. A poster displayed in Cork and Limerick carried such phrases as "The Blessed Host Scattered on the Ground! Benediction Veil Made a Horse

Cover of! All the Sacred Vessels Carried Off!" and "The Priest Impris-
oned and Afterwards Exposed on an Island to Alligators and Snakes!"
Father Bannon lectured widely in Ireland, wrote under the name of
"Sacerdos," circulated handbills among parish priests to prove that
American Know-Nothings were the descendants of Cromwell, and repeated the familiar stories of the desecration of Catholic Churches in the
United States. Confederate propaganda undertook to prove that, like
Ireland, the South was fighting for self-government, and Confederate
agents quoted William Smith O'Brien, John Mitchel, John Martin, and
other Irish exiles to support their argument. Confederate broadsides also
contrasted the materialism of the North with the Christian civilization
of the South. In 1864, Bishop Lynch of Charleston was appointed by
President Davis as Confederate commissioner to the Papal States, but the
Vatican was careful to receive him only as a bishop and not as a representative of the Confederacy.[28]

[28] See Leo Francis Stock, "Catholic Participation in the Diplomacy of the Southern
Confederacy," *The Catholic Historical Review*, XVI (1930), 1–18.

CHAPTER XIV

The Fenian Fiasco

IT IS natural for nationality groups in a cosmopolitan country like the United States to follow with sentimental interest the progress of events in their fatherland and to sympathize with the aspirations of friends and relatives at home and find pleasure in their progress. The American Irish actually staged an invasion of a friendly neighbor to further the cause of Irish independence and used their adopted country as a base for military operations to carry out their plans. The Fenian invasion of Canada is the most amazing example of group activity by an immigrant element in United States history. In the words of McGee, who was an outspoken foe of the movement, the episode proved that the Irish in America were "still an alien population, camped but not settled" in America, "with foreign hopes and aspirations, unshared by the people among whom they live."

Because Ireland for centuries was both "a garrison nation" and "an underground nation,"[1] secret societies were important in Irish politics. It was not difficult to organize the Irish in the United States for the relief of their native land.

> Columbia the free is the land of my birth,
> And my paths have been all on American earth,

began a quatrain in the *Irish-American Almanac,*

> But my blood is as Irish as any can be,
> And my heart is with Erin far o'er the sea.[2]

In the United States, the Irish could give uninhibited expression to their loves and hates without fear of British courts, police, or soldiery. Whenever American issues involved England or Ireland, Irishmen could be counted upon to react and vote as "true-born sons of Ireland." They were proud of their origin. They certainly were not averse to becoming Americans; yet they were eager to remain Irish. They remained united with the homeland by what Francis Lieber called "the strong tie of bear-

[1] See P. S. O'Hegarty, *A History of Ireland Under the Union, 1801 to 1922.*
[2] Abbott, *Historical Aspects of Immigration,* 530–32.

ing one common wrong." The wellspring of Fenianism was a sentimental homesickness for the Emerald Isle. The "Young Ireland" movement of 1848 had given Eire a soul; the Fenians wanted to bring it to life again.

Fenianism in the United States burst into full flower during and immediately after the Civil War, but its plans and purposes were not new. In the 1840's, societies of "Repealers" in the eastern states had sent money to Daniel O'Connell to support his effort to secure the repeal of the union of Ireland and Great Britain in a common parliament. In 1846, when the United States and England were at odds over Oregon, Irish-Americans hoped for war with perfidious Albion. In 1854, the "Irishman's Universal Civil and Military Republican Union" was launched in New York for the liberation of Ireland and to cultivate the military art among Irishmen.[3] During the Crimean War, John Mitchel hoped he could persuade Russia to send military supplies to Ireland to create a diversion against England. The Irish-American press maintained that Russia was not unfriendly to the Catholic Church and denounced the British for recruiting Irishmen in the United States and Ireland for the Royal army. The Emmet Monument Association was directed by John O'Mahony and Michael Doheny, "men of '48" who became prominent Fenian leaders.

In August, 1855, the Massachusetts Emigrant Aid Society was organized in Boston. To avoid clerical opposition, it required no oath from its members and announced that its major objective was to aid immigrants who might wish to return to Ireland to fight for freedom. But the society denied all intention "to form a filibustering league, or raise an army of invasion, under the shadow of the stars and stripes." The society received considerable support in the Irish-American press, which published many letters, anonymous or otherwise, from enthusiastic Irishmen who were ready to take off for Erin. Organizers established branches of the organization in the larger cities. In Philadelphia, the Pennsylvania "Directory" chartered the Wolfe Tone Club, the Red Hand Club, and the Fitzgerald Club. A society in Lynn, Massachusetts, which had encountered clerical opposition boasted that "by prudence and temperance, we will gain in '55 or '56 what we lost by deceit and whisky in '98." Affiliates of these various organizations were organized by paid workers in Buffalo, Cleveland, Columbus, New Orleans, Richmond, Detroit, Sheboygan, and other cities. In Cincinnati, the Robert Emmet Club, whose members were bound by an oath and secret signs to drive the British from Ireland, was organized. Agents crossed the Atlantic to spread the movement and to

[3] *The Citizen* (New York), April 29, 1854.

co-operate with the native Irish, who presumably were drilling in woods
and hills and only awaited supplies from their American brethren to
begin a war with England. The New York *Herald* and the Boston *Trav-
eller* accused the organizers of such societies of "wringing the last cent"
from citizens of Irish birth "on the pretence of revolutionizing Ireland,"
but their leaders replied that the initiation fee was low and comparable
to other organizations.

In December, 1855, the Massachusetts Emigrant Aid Society, renamed
the American-Irish Aid Society, held a convention in New York's Astor
House which lasted three days. Delegates came from twenty-four states
and included Irish and Americans, Catholics and Protestants. The New
York and Philadelphia papers gave detailed accounts of the proceedings.
Robert Tyler, son of former President John Tyler, presided. A national
constitution and a central directory were created. The convention ended
in a "disgraceful scene," which *The Citizen* blamed on outsiders who
tried to break up the meeting. There was a bitter fight over credentials;
Michael Doheny, publisher of the rival *Honest Truth,* accused the editor
of *The Citizen* of being a British spy; and another Irish-American journalist was charged with having published an Orange paper. The convention issued addresses to the "Irish Race" and to the "Friends of Irish
Independence" in the United States, Ireland, the British colonies, and elsewhere, and offered to assist in establishing an Irish republic. At the same
time, the members promised to respect the Constitution and laws of the
United States.

Most of the New York press made light of the convention. *The Express,*
a Know-Nothing paper, described its work as a plea for Popery in Ireland. The *Tribune* observed that the delegates did nothing more than
issue "a word of good cheer." *The Daily News* was not impressed, and
the *Times* ridiculed the movement as calculated to stir the Irish to "mischievous mutiny." The *Herald* reported a rumor to the effect that a
Russian agent had promoted the Astor House assembly, and the New
York *Albion,* a British paper, commented on the turbulence of the delegates. The *London Times* devoted considerable space to "the new association formed by the unquiet Irish emigrants in the United States." [4]

In 1858, James Stephens, an Irish rebel of 1848, perfected his plans for
an Irish Republican Brotherhood, and his organization soon overshadowed all others. Stephens provided a paraphernalia of secret signs
and required an oath similar to that of the secret revolutionary societies
of the Continent, thereby incurring the hostility of most Catholic clergymen. Stephens claimed he had an Irish army of 30,000 well-drilled patri-

[4] See *The Citizen* (New York) for 1855, especially December 15, 1855.

ots, and in 1859, while he was in the United States to collect money, the American Fenian Brotherhood was born. Its spread was retarded by the Civil War, but its propaganda was circulated widely among Irish soldiers in the Union army.

The relations between Fenianism and the Roman Catholic Church were as difficult in the United States as in Ireland. Fenian leaders believed that the clergy should confine their activities to spiritual matters and let politics alone. The *Irish People* accused priests of using the pulpit and the confessional to prevent the spread of Fenianism. *The Metropolitan Record* remained skeptical of the objectives of the new organization, but the *Freeman's Journal* viewed the movement more sympathetically, although warning that it must be "in perfect accord with the Church." Father O'Flaherty, an ardent Fenian, recruited members throughout Indiana and helped make it "the banner state" of Fenianism. In Illinois, on the other hand, Bishop Duggan of Chicago was outspokenly hostile. In January, 1870, after the movement had passed its crest, it was condemned by the Holy See.[5]

During the Civil War, Fenian "circles" were organized in the army and navy. Many native Irishmen and their sons had joined the armed forces to prepare for a day of reckoning with England and welcomed the strained relations between the United States and England which developed during the war. "There is a certain party 'over the way' with whom we have an account to settle," commented the *Irish-American* of March 25, 1865. The editor advised all good Irishmen to get ready for "a dash at John Bull." At the end of the war, thousands of demobilized Irish veterans were eager to strike a blow for Ireland's independence. Anti-British feeling was running high in the United States in 1865.

The Fenian Brotherhood grew rapidly in the United States. Among its prominent leaders were John O'Mahony; P. J. Meehan of the *Irish-American;* William R. Roberts, a well-to-do dry goods merchant in New York, who became an officer in the Fenian army; the Scanlan brothers of Chicago; Henry C. McCarthy, a state senator in Illinois; P. W. Dunne of Peoria, Illinois; James Gibbons of Philadelphia; B. Doran Killian, a New York lawyer; and "Red Jim" McDermott, who had served in the Irish Papal Brigade in 1860 and who became a Fenian organizer in the United States. By the spring of 1866, the Fenians were holding national

---

[5] The account of the Fenian episode upon which I have relied heavily is William D'Arcy, *The Fenian Movement in the United States, 1858–1886.* Others of value are Clyde L. King, *The Fenian Movement* (University of Colorado Studies, VI, No. 3); and John A. Macdonald, *Troublous Days in Canada.* Also useful is John O'Leary, *Recollections of Fenians and Fenianism.* See also O'Donovan Rossa, *Rossa's Recollections, 1838 to 1898;* and John Devoy, *Recollections of an Irish Rebel.*

conventions, as well as local picnics, throughout the eastern half of the United States to stimulate interest and get financial support for their cause. In March, 1866, approximately 100,000 Fenians demonstrated in Jones' Wood in New York and raised $50,000.[6] In Cleveland, the Fenian Brotherhood began as a social club. In 1866, there were Fenian picnics in New York, Troy, Cleveland, Columbus, St. Louis, and other cities marked by passionate oratory and plenty of whiskey, which still sold at an invitingly low figure. At one of these outings, the engagement at Limerick Ridge was re-enacted. Thousands sang the "Fenian Marseillaise":

Away with speech, and brother, reach me down that rifle gun.
By her sweet voice, and hers alone, the rights of man are won.
Fling down the pen; when heroic men pine sad in dungeons lone,
'Tis bayonets bright, with good red blood, should plead before the throne.[7]

Years later, Mr. Dooley observed: "Be hivins, if Ireland could be freed be a picnic, it'd not on'y be free to-day, but an impire, begorra."

Wisconsin's Fenians assembled in convention in Milwaukee. The state had twenty Fenian circles in 1866 with over 6,000 members and an Irish Fenian regiment of 811 men commanded by Colonel John Delahnut, a veteran of the Civil War. In Illinois, Patrick W. Dunne, forebear of an Illinois governor, gave a thousand dollars to Stephens when he lectured in Peoria. The San Francisco group was led by Jeremiah Kavanagh and Thomas Mooney, who was publisher of *Mooney's California Express*. A Fenian Sisterhood made plans for an Irish Sanitary Commission to provide medicines, bandages, and nursing aid in the event of casualties in a Fenian war.

In November, 1863, in a Fenian Congress in Chicago, the delegates considered plans for the liberation of Ireland and for the promotion of military drill among Irish-Americans. For commissioned officers of the Fenian army, uniforms were approved which consisted of dark green coats, black trousers and hats, green silk sashes, and epaulets, with sunbursts, phoenixes, and shamrocks for decoration. Early in 1865, delegates numbering 348 from 273 circles met in Cincinnati and adopted resolutions to help both Ireland and the United States in a war with England. Organizers were employed at seventy-five dollars a month to enlist additional recruits. Some months later, Fenians were selling bonds to raise money to finance their project. In the center of these attractive, but worthless, pieces of paper was a figure of Erin pointing to a sword on

[6] *The Metropolitan Record and New York Vindicator* (New York), March 10, 1866.
[7] D'Arcy, *Fenian Movement*, 99, 192.

the ground, with a Union soldier kneeling in the background, ready to leave for Ireland. On the reverse side were the harp of Ireland and an Irish wolfhound, flanked by likenesses of such Irish heroes and martyrs as Robert Emmet and Wolfe Tone. The bonds promised 6 per cent interest and were redeemable six months after the recognition of Irish independence. In Peoria, Illinois, in 1864, a meeting of less than sixty men subscribed $1,500; at Quincy, Illinois, poor Irish laborers gave $505; and the Ninetieth Illinois Regiment raised a similar amount. Chicago staged a Fenian Fair to display mementoes from Ireland. The San Francisco Fenians sent a gold brick and several of silver. The dollars rolled into Fenian headquarters in New York, especially from Irish laborers and servant girls. It was not long before the national officers were charged with living in comfort and luxury from the hard-earned money of simple folk.

On October 16, 1865, a provisional government for an Irish republic modeled upon the United States was created at a convention in Philadelphia. A full complement of officials was selected, and General T. W. Sweeny, the Mexican War hero of the "armless sleeve," and a former commander of the Sixteenth United States Infantry, became secretary of war for the new republic. A sharp conflict soon developed over proper military strategy. Some favored a direct attack on Ireland; others an invasion of Canada. The New York *Times* accused the Fenian leaders of swindling the poor. Criticism was directed especially against O'Mahony, who had fitted out an executive mansion at Union Square in New York, over which he flew the Fenian flag and for which he paid an annual rent of $1,200. O'Mahony was repeatedly charged with "robbery of the poor Irish servant girls," but he died poor.

Meanwhile, in 1865, other Fenians had gone to Ireland on ships guided by Irish pilots. The Fenians of Ireland expected 100,000 rifles from the United States and 3,000 "officers from Chicago alone." [8] The British stopped the rebellion before it was really launched and suspended the habeas corpus act in February, 1866. The rebels were without plans, except to attack public barracks with pikes, and there was little co-ordination among the various districts of Ireland. The rebellion produced little except another crop of refugees and martyrs eager to sail for the United States. Many of those arrested in Dublin and elsewhere were naturalized American citizens and Civil War veterans, and their arrest precipitated new diplomatic controversies between the United States and England. Charles Francis Adams, United States minister in London, was denounced in the Irish-American press for failing to make proper pro-

8 Devoy, *Recollections*, 55 *et seq.*

tests, and Irish-American leaders demanded that Americans involved in the uprising be given free passage to the United States. By 1867, there were a sufficient number of veterans of the "Irish Republican Army" in this country to organize "The Sacred Legion of Irish Exiles."

The way now seemed clear for a full-scale invasion of Canada. Responsible officials in Washington seriously considered the possibility of a war with England, and the unsettled *Alabama* claims complicated all Anglo-American relations. Senator Chandler of Michigan talked glibly of an army of 200,000 Civil War veterans, in the event of a war with England, and suggested raising half the army in the North and half among Confederate veterans. Senator Sumner of the Foreign Relations Committee presented a heavy bill of damages against England in a speech on the *Alabama* claims and suggested the transfer of Canada to the United States as a possible settlement. Moreover, he favored the purchase of Alaska because it would put another watchful American eye on John Bull in his far-flung British-American possessions. The movement to confederate the provinces of British North America into a Dominion of Canada also aroused the suspicion of many American congressmen.

The Fenian plans for the invasion of Canada would have done credit to a great field marshal directing a major campaign. Detailed orders were issued for the mobilization and disposition of the Fenian forces, and plans were made to envelope quickly all of British North America. The center of the Fenian army was based on Buffalo, the right wing along the Vermont border, and the left wing on Chicago. "Companies" of Fenians left Boston, New York, Philadelphia, Cincinnati, Louisville, Nashville, Chicago, St. Louis, Cleveland, and other cities for their appointed rendezvous. Arms and ammunition were assembled at strategic points. In Buffalo, they were stored in a warehouse of the New York Central Railroad. Boats were ready to take the invaders across the Niagara River.

On the night between May 31 and June 1, 1866, the hosts of Fenianism crossed the Niagara under the command of John O'Neil, a daring officer in the Civil War, who, in 1864, had been a captain in the Seventeenth United States Colored Infantry. O'Neil led an army probably no larger than 800 men in an attack on the Canadian village of Fort Erie. Here the invaders threw up entrenchments and issued a bombastic proclamation to the Canadian people urging them to declare their freedom. Several minor engagements were fought before the Fenians were forced to retire to the United States. After the initial assault upon Fort Erie, the Fenian army was left virtually stranded. Three thousand men waited in Buffalo for orders to join the invasion, but the U.S.S. *Michigan* prevented supplies and reinforcements from reaching the invaders. The Canadians lost twelve dead and forty wounded; the Fenians eight dead and twenty wounded. Among those who fell into the hands of the enraged Canadian authorities were a Roman Catholic priest and an Episcopalian minister.

On June 3, the invading army retreated to the American side. A large number of the residents of Buffalo watched the spectacle as the men were picked up by the *Michigan* and the United States district marshal and his deputies. General George Meade arrived the next day and seized carloads of war supplies, and General Grant advised the arrest of "Fighting Tom" Sweeny and W. R. Roberts, high officials of the paper Irish republic. Thus ended the major operation of a campaign which Fenians hoped would bring revolution in Ireland and Canada, war with England, and recognition of an Irish republic by the United States government.

On June 7, a thousand Fenians moved on Canada from St. Albans, Vermont. The expedition was composed largely of New England Irish and proved as unsuccessful as the operations on the Niagara frontier. In 1870, another attack was made on the Vermont border. O'Neil, who was in command, planned the raid for Queen Victoria's birthday, and the New York *Times* reported that 30,000 Fenians had left the city for the invasion of Canada. Only a few hundred actually appeared, and O'Neil launched his attack with about two hundred men who retreated as soon as the shooting began. Canada had 13,000 men on the border to stop the invasion. O'Neil was arrested by a United States marshal some twenty rods from the border and sentenced to six months in jail. The last flurry of Fenian excitement occurred in 1871, when the newly formed Dominion of Canada was involved in trouble with Indians and half-breeds in what is now the province of Manitoba. Irish-Americans were accused of plotting with the western rebels, but nothing of consequence occurred.

Equally as significant as the details of this fantastic assault by Irish-Americans upon Canada was the light which the Fenian embroglio throws upon the influence of the Irish in America and the eagerness of politicians to win their votes. 1866 was a critical year in the realignment of political parties in the United States. Democrats, under a cloud because of the war, were looking for new issues and new support. Republicans were divided between conservatives and radicals on the question of reconstruction and economic and political issues. In the confused political situation, a block of votes as well regimented as the Irish was

worth winning and might prove decisive. The supporters of President
Johnson charged that Radical Republicans were former Know-Nothings
and could not be trusted by the Irish. Radical Republicans, in turn, held
Johnson and Seward, his secretary of state, responsible for the failure of
the Fenian episode.[9]

Seward waited five days after the invasion began before he issued a
proclamation of neutrality and took steps to protect the peace of the
United States–Canadian border. His delay was attributed to the fear of
losing Irish votes and a desire to use the incident to force London to
settle Anglo-American issues. Irish-American journals accused the Secretary of State of encouraging Fenianism during the Civil War to get
recruits for the Union army and then betraying the movement when
the Fenian army crossed into Canada. Johnson and his entire administration were denounced as a "dirty tool of the English Government." At a
mass meeting in Union Square, New York, "President" Roberts demanded the repeal of all American neutrality laws and regulations, and
Fenian leaders insisted that they had been encouraged to buy arms for
their invasion at United States arsenals.

Meantime, resolutions of sympathy for American Fenians and their
objectives were introduced in Congress. Nathaniel P. Banks, a former
Know-Nothing now in need of Irish votes in eastern Massachusetts,
introduced a bill in the House of Representatives for the annexation of
Canada. The President was requested to drop all prosecutions of the
Fenians in American courts for their offenses against the neutrality laws.
On order of the Attorney General, the cases were quietly dropped. The
military equipment seized by United States soldiers and marshals was
returned to its owners by order of President Johnson, on the advice of
Samuel J. Tilden. Fenians went home at government expense. The
United States appealed to Canada to release nearly a hundred Fenians
who had been captured on foreign soil and might well have been hanged,
and the American consul at Toronto employed lawyers for their defense. Twenty-six were acquitted; seven were sentenced to die, but their
penalty was commuted to twenty years in prison. In 1870, a presidential
pardon was issued to everyone involved in the Fenian invasion.

The Fenian escapade attained international proportions because of
diplomatic controversies which were the aftermath of the Civil War. It
is clear from Seward's dispatches to Charles Francis Adams that the
former used the activities of the Fenians to exert pressure on the British
Foreign Office. The Fenians were the only organization in United
States history to arm and drill in public for the invasion of a country

[9] See a poem, "The Finnigan Vote," in *Cincinnati Enquirer*, September 24, 1866.

with which the United States was at peace, and whose plans for the attack were public knowledge before the invasion began. The Cleveland *Plain Dealer* commented that the Fenians unceremoniously had knocked the Monroe Doctrine "in the head with an Irish shillelah." [10]

Fenianism disintegrated rapidly after 1870 and tapered off into other Irish nationalistic movements. Interest dwindled after the Treaty of Washington and the arbitration of the *Alabama* case removed the possibility of war with England. Factional disputes, already serious between O'Mahony and Sweeny in 1866, became more bitter, and O'Mahony was formally deposed by the Fenian Senate. The Irish-American press was bitterly divided, and Fenian meetings sometimes ended in free-for-all fights. James Stephens was disappointed by the funds he received from the United States and constantly demanded more. Stephens accused O'Mahony of extravagance, living in luxury, and wasting Fenian funds; O'Mahony sent agents to Ireland to see how Stephens was spending the money he received from America. Each faction accused the other of accepting British gold. Influential, prosperous Irish-Americans contributed relatively little to the Fenian war chest; much of the money came from Irish laborers and servant girls. The clergy, as a class, opposed the Fenian Brotherhood as a secret, oath-bound organization. D'Arcy, who has made the most thorough study of Fenianism, has concluded that the charges of serious graft and corruption were never proved and that most of the factional strife originated with sincere, impetuous Irishmen, with honest differences of opinion, who were united only by an unquenchable hatred of England.

In 1868, a crowd of 20,000 turned out in Philadelphia to honor three Fenians who had been executed in Manchester. In 1871, a number of Fenians, including Jeremiah O'Donovan Rossa and John Devoy, were released by the British and came to the United States in the ship *Cuba*. Democratic and Republican politicians vied with each other in extending a vociferous welcome to the new arrivals; Boss Tweed was grand marshal of a parade to welcome the "Cuban Five"; Tammany Hall made a generous donation and reserved a suite for them at the Astor House, which they refused. The Irish Confederation, which the exiles had come to promote, expired in 1873.

In 1867, the Clan-na-Gael, a secret society with an anti-British program more radical than that of the Fenian Brotherhood, was founded by Irish refugees. It absorbed some of the members of the earlier organization. Other American Irishmen diverted their attention to the Home Rule movement and the Irish Land League. The Fenians continued to meet

10 The *Cleveland Plain Dealer*, March 14, 1866.

in convention but attendance dwindled steadily. The convention of 1876 led to the creation of the "Skirmishing Fund," headed by O'Donovan Rossa, to provide the means for a campaign of terrorism against England. After O'Mahony's death in 1877, the group which favored violence was in complete control and made plans for new raids across the Canadian border and for a new army for the liberation of Ireland. The last convention of the Fenian Brotherhood, held in 1885, was attended by 132 delegates.

The failure of the Fenians in Ireland furnished the United States with another contingent of political refugees. Like their predecessors, they became heroes in Irish-American circles, were honored at banquets and ceremonies for many years, and had glowing obituaries in Irish-American papers when they died. They were active in many Irish societies, and a few lived long enough to join the Friends of Irish Freedom during World War I. Some had successful careers in the United States. Richard Manning was a respected lieutenant in the New York City police force, Tom Williams was secretary to Charles A. Dana of the New York *Sun*, Denis Cushman was business manager of the Boston *Pilot*, and John Boyle O'Reilly was its editor and a prominent literary figure. James J. O'Kelly was drama and art critic and reporter for the New York *Herald*, and Colonel Richard O'Sullivan Burke achieved prominence as an engineer.[11] As late as 1915, Fenian veterans of 1867 were still attending annual dinners in New York. Such occasions featured much oratory about the impending liberation of Ireland and an Anglophobia undiminished by fifty years of progress in Anglo-Irish relations.[12]

[11] For these and other names, see Devoy, *Recollections, passim.*
[12] *The Gaelic-American* (New York), March 13, 1915.

CHAPTER XV

Anglophobia and Irish Nationalism

THE Fenian movement ended in a fiasco, but Irish-Americans continued to demonstrate against the foreign enemy entrenched in the land of their fathers. Among all the immigrant groups in the United States, none has built up a folklore of fond remembrance for their native land comparable to that of the Irish, and their nostalgic memories have been bequeathed to their American-born descendants. Nothing like their St. Patrick's Day celebrations exists among other immigrant groups. Native Americans of Irish parentage are as eloquent about the wonders of Erin across the sea and their love for the "Auld Sod" as their forefathers of a century ago. The Irish have become intensely American, but for a long time, whenever Anglo-Irish relations were involved, they remained a foreign people with foreign aspirations. They insisted that they hated England for the good of the United States.

The "wrongs of Ireland" welded three generations of American Irishmen into a solid, anti-British phalanx. The Irish constituted a minority nationality block which political leaders could not afford to ignore, and American politicians quickly learned that it was profitable to gore the British lion every now and then. In the words of Shane Leslie, the Irish question has been "America's family ghost." The Britisher Goldwin Smith observed gloomily, "Nothing stands in the way of a reconciliation between the two branches of the Anglo-Saxon race except the influence of the Irish." Philip Bagenal, another English traveler in the United States, was startled by the intensity of the "romantic national sentiment" of the American Irish, including the second generation, who were "American in voice and appearance," had never set foot on Irish soil, yet continued to think of the Emerald Isle with deep affection.

British policy had pushed the Irishman westward across the ocean only to produce a new and more powerful Ireland in the free air of America. In the United States, Irishmen continued to nurse their grievances against England. "Delenda est Britannia," shouted an Irish senator from Indiana in 1846 as he demanded strong measures to solve the Oregon boundary dispute. Irish-Americans have never hesitated to use their political power in the United States to influence foreign policy for the benefit of their fatherland.[1] Edward A. Freeman, the English historian, wrote of the "mischievous element" which stood in the way of cordial Anglo-American relations during the last half of the nineteenth century and sourly concluded that "the best remedy for whatever was amiss would be if every Irishman should kill a negro and be hanged for it."[2]

A letter in the New York *Shamrock* on the eve of the War of 1812 had called upon Irish-Americans to "exult at the possibility of doing England an essential injury."[3] In 1837 and 1838, during the abortive Canadian rebellion, the American Irish had kept the border aflame with threats of invasion from the United States, and the lieutenant governor received threatening letters reading, "I am an Irishman, and the blood of Emmet and of '98 is in *soak* for every English damned murder." He was sufficiently impressed by such anonymous communications to keep Irish soldiers in British regiments away from the border, lest they fraternize with their "cousins" from the United States.[4] In 1857, Irish-American papers hailed the reports of revolt against British rule in India with unrestrained joy.[5] During the Civil War, the *Freeman's Journal* denounced the new federal income tax as "obviously a measure of finance borrowed from England."[6]

In 1860, the Prince of Wales visited New York. Colonel Michael Corcoran refused to parade with his Sixty-ninth Regiment for "the beardless youth." When he was court-martialed for his stubbornness, Corcoran was defended by Meagher for acting "lawfully as a citizen, courageously as a soldier, indignantly as an Irishman."[7] The Hibernia Greens of Philadelphia complimented the colonel for "rescuing the character of Irish-born soldiers of this Republic from dishonor and self-abasement." *The Irish News* denounced Mayor Fernando Wood, hitherto a favorite with Irish voters, for his unnecessary courtesies to this "golden calf of monarchy."[8] In 1883, the dedication of the Brooklyn Bridge was inadvertently set for Queen Victoria's birthday. Irish-Americans were promptly mobilized in mass meetings to denounce the British infamy, and the Central Labor Union threatened to dynamite the new

---

[1] Shane Leslie, *The Irish Issue in Its American Aspect*, 4, 6, 13.
[2] Edward A. Freeman, *Some Impressions of the United States* (1883), 140–41.
[3] *The Shamrock* (New York), January 18, 1812.
[4] Charles R. Sanderson (ed.), *The Arthur Papers*, II, 382, 398, 444–45.
[5] *The Irish News* (New York), August 1, September 19, 1857.
[6] Sister Kwitchen, *James Adolphus McMaster*, 122.
[7] Ahearn, *Thomas Francis Meagher*, 92.
[8] *The Irish News* (New York), September 8, 1860. Also *The Metropolitan Record* (New York), September 8, October 20, 1860.

structure.[9] Five years later, when Mayor Abram Hewitt of New York refused to review a St. Patrick's Day parade, a committee reminded him that his "vote came largely from Irishmen." The New York *World* referred to the mayor's "momentary whims and chronic prejudices," and an Irish alderman secured unanimous approval to fly the Irish flag from City Hall.[10] In later years, many Irish-Americans were convinced that the Cecil Rhodes scholarships to permit American boys to study in England were part of a British plot to reconquer America, and they were equally suspicious of Andrew Carnegie's efforts to promote international understanding, lest these too turn out to be subtle forms of aid for Britain. Occasional editorials in *The Irish World* warned that "the Episcopal Church is still loyal to England." [11]

During the Boer War, many Americans sympathized with the South African victims of British imperialism. For Irish-Americans, the war provided the last great opportunity before World War I to vent their hatred of England. Irishmen assembled in Boston, New York, and elsewhere to adopt resolutions of sympathy for "the embattled farmers of the South African republics" and to warn that the British would not hesitate to destroy the American Republic if they had the power.[12] An ambulance corps and an Irish brigade were recruited in the United States for the Boer War, and in 1900, in St. Patrick's Day parades from coast to coast, Irishmen proudly carried the Boer flag alongside the green flag of Ireland. *The Irish World* carried instructions for "persons wishing to reach the Transvaal by other than English ships." [13] Hibernian clubs of Chicago and Philadelphia collected funds for the Boers. In Chicago, when an orchestra leader ordered his players to play "God Save the Queen," the entire personnel, led by the drummer, went on strike.[14] As late as 1952, when Prime Minister Churchill was a dinner guest at the residence of Bernard Baruch, Irish-American "Minute Men" picketed the latter's home carrying signs with such slogans as "The United States has the best friends money can buy," "There will always be an England—with the hand out," and "England is called the 'mother country' because she is always expecting."

Appeals for suffering Ireland, as new economic crises developed, never failed to galvanize the Irish societies in America into action. The outpouring of sympathy and financial help for the sufferers from the "Irish

9 Gibson, *Attitudes of the New York Irish*, 375–77.
10 Nevins, *Abram S. Hewitt*, 510 *et seq.*
11 *The Irish World* (New York), October 15, 1898.
12 "A Meeting in Boston, Massachusetts," *Journal of the American Irish Historical Society*, II (1899), 119.
13 *The Irish World* (New York), January 6, 1900.
14 See *The Irish World* (New York), January 6, 13, February 24, March 24, 1900.

Famine of 1880" was amazing. Public meetings turned into wild demonstrations, and men shed copious tears as they listened to dramatic
recitals of the sufferings of the Irish nation. Private contributions from
America were estimated at five million dollars in 1881. Every Irish
leader, from O'Connell and Parnell to De Valera, has leaned heavily
for financial support on the Irish in America.

The Fenian Brotherhood had several successors. One, the Clan-na-Gael,
was founded in 1867 and survived until World War I. Its members were
concerned primarily with organizing Irish-Americans to help Ireland
and to combat British influence in the United States. They operated as
a secret organization and were under oath to promote republicanism for
Ireland. They had no faith in half-way measures like home rule. Working closely with the Irish Revolutionary Brotherhood at home, the
Clan-na-Gael favored revolution and encouraged military drill in preparation for "the day." In 1903, the *Gaelic-American,* established in New
York by John Devoy, became the organization's mouthpiece. The Clan-
na-Gael remained a fighting organization; it favored direct action and
had no faith in compromises.

By 1875, Irish leaders here and abroad were again advocating insurrection, and *The Irish World* was soliciting contributions to a "skirmishing fund." In 1878, Michael Davitt, who believed that the proper ap-
proach to Irish nationalism was through a relentless attack on the system
of landholding in Ireland, came to the United States for a lecture tour
and to confer with such Irish-American leaders as Patrick Ford of *The
Irish World,* Devoy, O'Donovan Rossa, John Boyle O'Reilly of Boston,
and other ex-Fenians and supporters of Clan-na-Gael. The son of an
Irish peasant of county Mayo, Davitt had seen his family evicted when
he was a boy of six. The father found a new home in a Lancashire cotton
town. Here the boy went to work on a twelve-hour shift, at ten years
of age, in a cotton mill. When he was hardly past eleven, he lost his
right arm in a machine. Born a Roman Catholic and taught by a
Methodist schoolmaster, he was unaffected by religious quarrels. He became the "Father of the Land League," and his activities in the "land
war" of 1879 to 1882 won him a place among the immortals of Irish
history, though he had many other achievements to his credit in later
years.[15]

Davitt lectured in a number of American cities and conferred with
many prominent Irish-Americans. On his return to Ireland, he promoted
the Irish National Land League, of which Charles Stewart Parnell,

[15] T. W. Moody, "Michael Davitt and the British Labour Movement," *Transactions of
the Royal Historical Society,* III (1953; Fifth Series), 53–76.

leader of the Irish party in Parliament, became president. The league was supported in the United States by Devoy, John Boyle O'Reilly, and other Irish-Americans who believed in a thorough agrarian revolution. In 1880, Parnell and John Dillon toured the United States to raise funds to save Irish tenant farmers from disaster in a year of famine and to unite the Irish on both sides of the Atlantic in support of a fundamental agrarian reform.

Parnell and Dillon traveled thousands of miles in the United States, made scores of speeches, and collected hundreds of dollars. Henry Ward Beecher and Wendell Phillips endorsed their efforts, and Parnell was invited to address Congress. State legislatures passed resolutions of sympathy for Ireland; ten thousand Irish heard the great Irish leader in Chicago; and in St. Paul, Bishop Ireland gave his blessing to the Land League. In Cleveland, five thousand paraded to the public auditorium to listen to an address by Parnell in January, 1880. In Des Moines, Parnell was greeted with a thirty-two gun salute, but many of his hearers were disappointed by his cold manner, thin voice, and awkwardness.[16] Many clergymen supported the Land League's campaign for funds on the assumption that its methods were nonviolent and constitutional. The Cleveland *Catholic Universe* and other Church papers were not too friendly, however, and Bishop Richard Gilmour suspected the organization was dominated by Clan-na-Gael.

The slogans of the Land League were "Down with landlordism" and "The land for the people." Davitt at first opposed the use of force. Theoretically, at least, the league was to limit its activities to passive resistance. Actually, peasants resisted evictions, refused to pay rent, sheltered those who had been evicted, kept others from taking their farms, boycotted the landlords in every possible way, and tried to defend their rights in the courts. Passive resistance degenerated into violence, beatings, and murders; cattle were maimed or killed and crops and fences destroyed as enraged peasants battled for economic security. Gladstone's sincere attempts to improve conditions in Ireland came too late and offered too little. Agricultural conditions were bad in 1880, and, on both sides of the ocean, the Irish were determined that the domination of 8,000,000 Irish by 8,000 landlords must cease.

By the summer of 1880, hundreds of branches of the Land League were functioning in the United States. Mayor Prince of Boston and John Boyle O'Reilly sent $14,000 to the Irish Land League for the relief of suffering Irishmen, and a Boston committee added $2,000 for "the agita-

16 Kenneth E. Colton, "Parnell's Mission to Iowa," *Annals of Iowa*, XXII (1940), 312–27.

tion fund." [17] In two and a half years, *The Irish World* alone collected $353,000 for the Land League. Mass meetings were held in the larger cities, and in smaller places like Corning, New York, sympathizers donated $800 for Irish relief and organized a "Fanny Parnell Branch of the Ladies' Land League." Many non-Catholics and non-Irish, such as Henry George and James Redpath, supported the movement. Thomas James Conaty, who became bishop of Los Angeles in 1903, was treasurer of the Parnell fund. In May, 1880, a convention of fifty delegates deliberated in New York under the chairmanship of Patrick A. Collins of Boston. In November, 1881, a national convention in Chicago attracted nearly 850 delegates, including a number of clergymen. The delegates considered the imminence of another rebellion in Ireland, and in two month's time, contributions totaled a quarter of a million dollars. In 1883, a convention in Philadelphia attracted a thousand delegates. The Irish-American press gave the league its enthusiastic endorsement.

Meantime, England, in 1881, again suspended habeas corpus in Ireland. Simultaneously, Gladstone's Irish land bill offered concessions to protect the tenant in the security of his tenure, establish a "fair rent," allow tenants to sell their rights under certain conditions, and create a commission to liquidate the whole system of landlordism over a period of thirty-five years. When such concessions elicited no favorable response, the English government arrested Parnell and ordered the Land League to disband. For the next two years, Ireland was in the throes of a "no rent" strike, with much disorder and crime.

The steps in the ultimate solution of Ireland's basic problem need not be chronicled here. Gladstone's Home Rule Bill of 1886, which included proposals to buy out the landlords, was defeated in Parliament. Five years later, both major parties in Great Britain recognized the necessity of creating peasant proprietors by state aid, and by 1922, when the Irish Free State was recognized by treaty, Ireland had become largely a country of peasant proprietors.[18]

In the United States, meantime, sharp divisions reappeared among the leaders of the Irish. The Clan-na-Gael, dominated by John Devoy, did not see eye to eye with more conservative Land Leaguers like O'Reilly and Collins. *The Irish World* advocated radical measures; the *Irish-American* was content to move along more conservative lines. The New England Irish generally followed Parnell's more moderate counsel; Patrick Ford and some of his New York contingent were more violent.

---

[17] *The Illustrated Celtic Monthly,* March, 1880, p. 297.
[18] For details, see Pomfret, *The Struggle for Land in Ireland.*

The most extreme were the "action men," "skirmishers" who were ready to use bullets and dynamite. Rossa's *United Irishman* demanded an eye for an eye and a tooth for a tooth and argued not only that Irish tenants should stop paying rent, a proposal approved by the Boston *Pilot* and conservatives like General W. S. Rosecrans, but that they should avenge their wrongs by blowing up English prisons and meet force with force. A number of American Irish clergy approved the "no rent policy," but Bishop McQuaid denounced "wild revolutionists," and Bishop Gilmour of Cleveland compared the rent boycott with communism.

The Phoenix Park murders of several government officials occurred in Ireland on May 6, 1882. This was an act of barbarism which hurt the whole movement and discredited the extremists in the eyes of Americans and Britishers alike. Among those arrested during the period of active "skirmishing" were a number of Irishmen who claimed American citizenship because they had declared their intentions to become citizens of the United States. Some gave false information and several had come to the United States only to get first papers which they could use if they got into trouble in Ireland.

The American State Department and James Russell Lowell, our minister to the Court of St. James, found themselves in an embarrassing position. The Irish-American press demanded that the United States defend and secure the release of anyone who claimed allegiance to this country, and denounced the government for abandoning good Irish-American patriots to British persecution. There were accounts of Union soldiers allowed "to pine in prison cells," and even Secretary of State James G. Blaine, the darling of many Irish-Americans when he ran for president in 1884, was denounced in bitter editorials which demanded his resignation. The House of Representatives called for the names of those arrested, and congressmen made numerous speeches on the crisis in Anglo-American relations for the benefit of their Irish constituents. The British government insisted that it was dealing with criminals and murderers and that nothing else was involved. Lowell in London and the State Department in Washington followed correct legal procedures. But Irishmen insisted that habeas corpus should not have been suspended and demanded that the accused have a jury trial in Ireland. When Lowell finally persuaded the British to release the prisoners, at least conditionally, and offered to send them home at the expense of the American government, many preferred martyrdom in jail. Irish-Americans collected funds to send lawyers abroad to defend the accused. Influential American Irish demanded intervention by the United States government in one of the most flagrant cases, and the House of Representatives requested the President to secure a delay of execution.[19]

Parnell, the majority of the Land Leaguers, and many Irish-Americans unequivocally repudiated the "dynamite faction." But extremists like Patrick Ford, as late as 1884, in *The Irish World,* appealed for another emergency fund to finance reprisals against Ireland's enemies. Bombs, carried in American-made valises, were occasionally picked up in British railway stations. When rents came down substantially in Ireland and farmers received a redress of grievances because of the conciliatory policy of the British government, Irishmen credited the improvement to American support. Throughout the 1880's, funds continued to flow into Ireland.[20]

In 1891, the Irish National Federation of America was organized in New York, at a meeting over which Thomas A. Emmet presided. Its purpose was to raise money for the National party in Ireland, now led by Justin McCarthy. About one hundred and fifty branches were organized in the United States to advance the cause of Irish home rule, but extremists regarded such a constitutional reform as an unworthy compromise. In 1900, *The Irish World* approved the choice of John Redmond as chairman of the Irish Parliamentary party, but the new leader almost lost his standing in America when he participated in a welcome to Queen Victoria on the latter's visit to Ireland. In 1903, the Irish National Federation of America sent $50,000 to Ireland as a campaign contribution for the election. Most of the money came from Irish-American laborers and tradespeople. The more well-to-do Irish had become lukewarm to constant appeals for money. In 1904, the United Irish League held a convention in New York which was attended by delegates from thirty-three American states and a number of representatives from Ireland. Subsequently, the latter traveled about the country and were enthusiastically welcomed by large crowds of Irish in Boston, Philadelphia, and other cities.

Simultaneously with these efforts to improve conditions in Ireland, an effort was made to revive the ancient Gaelic language. Generally, a distinctive language and literature are earmarks of a national culture. English long has been the language of Ireland, and Ireland's connections are primarily with people who speak English, whether in the British Isles or in the United States. It seems doubtful whether the revival of Gaelic will make much progress among the masses of the Irish people,

[19] For further details, see Gibson, *Attitudes of the New York Irish,* Chapter XII.
[20] See James J. Green, "American Catholics and the Irish Land League, 1879–1882," *The Catholic Historical Review,* XXXV (April, 1949), 19–42.

though it undoubtedly has its appeal to the intellectual classes. A number of ardent Irish patriots during the last century have tried hard to arouse interest in the early language and literature of Ireland. They were convinced that Ireland could not achieve her national identity, in a vast sea of 50,000,000 English and many more Americans, unless she had her own language and literature. Through the years, the most prominent leader of the Gaelic revival has been Douglas Hyde. Hyde, a Protestant from county Sligo who had studied the classics at Trinity College, was convinced that Ireland must be de-Anglicized. The Gaelic League is interested not only in reviving the ancient language of Ireland, but also in cultivating the music, customs, and history of the Irish people. It is an organization which all classes might support, whether Catholic or Protestant, Fenian, Home Ruler, or Unionist.

As early as 1857, the New York *Irish-American,* which always featured the poems and ballads of Erin, began to print a column in Gaelic. Three years later, a branch of the Ossianic Society was established in New York to co-operate with a parent organization in Dublin in publishing Gaelic manuscripts, especially historical documents, with literal translations and explanatory notes. The Phil-Celtic Society of Boston was organized in 1873. It attracted the attention of scholars in Dublin and probably had some influence upon the formation of the Society for the Preservation of the Irish Language. This, in turn, was succeeded by the Gaelic League. In 1879, a society in Brooklyn requested *The Irish World* to carry a Gaelic section as a regular feature of each issue. Before the end of the decade, groups in many American cities were studying the ancient Irish language, and several Irish-American newspapers had ordered Irish type for their Gaelic sections. It is noteworthy, however, that in most cases English translations accompanied the selections printed in Gaelic characters.[21]

In 1880, the New York Society for the Preservation of the Irish Language sponsored a concert of Gaelic songs in Irving Hall, the proceeds to be used for an Irish Literary Institute. Before the close of the century, the Ancient Order of Hibernians established a chair of Gaelic at the Catholic University of America in Washington. Thomas A. Emmet thought the Irish renaissance was so important that he began to study Gaelic, at the age of seventy-five, to set an example for others. In 1896, the Gaelic Society of Brooklyn offered free instruction in Sunday evening classes, and one of the St. Patrick's Day sermons in a New York church was delivered in Gaelic. National conventions of the Gaelic

[21] See *The Irish World and American Industrial Liberator* (New York), March 29, 1879; *The Illustrated Celtic Monthly,* September, 1879, p. 174; April, 1880, p. 309.

League became annual affairs before the end of the century; papers in Ireland wrote optimistically of the "Gaelic Revival in America"; and teachers advertised private lessons in New York papers at fifty cents an hour.[22] In 1916, the *Gaelic-American* advertised "The Gaelophone Method," guaranteed to produce Gaelic scholars with thirty-five phonograph records and printed lessons, at a charge of fifteen dollars for the course.[23]

Irish literary figures such as William Butler Yeats and Padraic Pearse emphasized the Gaelic movement during lecture tours in the United States. Gaelic festivals, known as "Feis," were arranged in a number of cities. In Boston, New York, Springfield, Massachusetts, and other cities, the "Feis" included competitive examinations in the Gaelic language and contests in dancing, essays, old Irish singing, and original stories. The New York Gaelic Society in 1904 announced its Labor Day outing as the Gaelic "Aeridheacht" and, two years later, opened a store featuring products made in Ireland. In 1952, the Cleveland Gaelic Society, a recent addition to the city's many Irish-American organizations, instituted regular Friday evening classes for those who would learn the language. In New York, in the same year, four thousand persons competed in the twentieth annual Irish "Feis" at Fordham University. The competitions included language and literature, folk dancing, and other cultural activities native to Ireland. Prominent dignitaries of the city government and the Church were in attendance.[24]

Such activities, however interesting to the intellectual, had little effect upon the mass of Irish-Americans. Gaelic was difficult to master and few had either the time or the ability to undertake the task. The experience with the Gaelic revival in Ireland has been much the same. Nevertheless, American Irish continue to give some tangible support to the Gaelic renaissance in the hope of counteracting the "denationalizing and degenerating influence known as Anglicanization." [25]

Almost every immigrant group has a historical society to record its contributions to the United States. The American Irish Historical Society, organized in Boston in 1897, has its headquarters in New York. Membership is open to anyone interested in its program, regardless of religion or party. The society was launched with the endorsement of Theodore Roosevelt, President Benjamin Andrews of Brown University, and other prominent Americans. Its basic purpose is to write "the Irish

---

[22] See *The Irish World* (New York), March 14, April 11, 1896; October 6, 1900.
[23] *The Gaelic-American* (New York), September 23, 1916.
[24] *New York Times,* June 30, 1952.
[25] *The Gaelic-American* (New York), January 30, 1915.

chapter in American history," but its indefatigable bibliographer, Michael J. O'Brien, stressed the Irish of colonial times to the neglect of later, and more important, periods. The society has been eager to deflate "the Scotch-Irish myth" and to condemn what it calls the "Anglo-Saxon Shibboleth." It is ardently patriotic and combines forces with other organizations to keep alleged British propaganda out of American history textbooks, but it has done surprisingly little with Irish-American history since the Revolution. Membership is relatively small, and financial support from well-to-do second- and third-generation Irish has been disappointing. Nevertheless, the organization has sponsored a number of publications, including a journal; it has assembled a respectable library of Irish-American history, arranged "field days" and visits to monuments and cemeteries where noted Irish lie buried, and financed prize essay contests to interest young people in the role of the Irish in United States history. Its gold medal for outstanding achievement by a citizen of Irish blood has been awarded in earlier years to Archbishop Richard J. Cushing of Boston, Cardinal Spellman, Lieutenant General Hugh A. Drum, and Judges Daniel F. Cohalan and John T. Longhran. In 1952, the medal was presented to Senator Pat McCarran of Nevada.

CHAPTER XVI

National Politics, 1865-1900

SPACE does not permit detailed discussion of the many national, state, and local campaigns since the Civil War in which the Irish vote was wooed by American political leaders who wanted its support. A volume could be devoted to local politics alone, for Irish political influence has been most effectively mobilized by city bosses and machines. The ultimate decision of many Irish-Americans at the ballot box seems to have been affected on a number of occasions by questions involving Ireland, Anglo-American relations, or the Catholic Church.

In 1868, Irishmen felt especially kindly toward Horatio Seymour, the Democratic candidate for president, because of his attitude toward conscription during the Civil War and his defense of civil liberties. Moreover, after their experiences during the war, it was safe to assume that the Irish would remain in the Democratic fold unless Republicans could discover special appeals for their support. Democrats could say little against Grant, the hero of Irish veterans, and of other Americans as well, so the party concentrated upon attacking Schuyler Colfax, his running mate, whom they charged with anti-Catholic prejudices and nativism. The Republican National Committee published a special campaign sheet for the Irish in 1868. D. O'Sullivan, editor of the Democratic *The Irish People* was induced to shift his politics to the Republican side, probably for a consideration of one thousand dollars. *The Irish Republic,* edited by David Bell and Michael Scanlan, was brought from Chicago to New York to campaign for Grant, and it was one of the few Republican papers published especially for Irish readers. Irish Republican clubs were organized in the larger cities; Republican campaign posters were printed on green paper with shamrocks and harps; and in New York eight leading Irishmen signed an appeal for Grant.[1] A few prominent Irishmen took the stump for Grant and called upon Irish veterans "to rally 'round the flag" and vote for their revered commander.

Grant won the election, and would have won it without such Irish votes as he may have been able to garner. Nevertheless, he felt it wise

[1] Gibson, *Attitudes of the New York Irish,* Chapter IX.

to continue the effort to wean the Irish away from the local Democratic machines by admitting them to a share in the political spoils which the Republican party had to distribute. Major James Haggerty was appointed consul in Glasgow, only to have the British refuse to receive him because of his earlier activities as a Fenian. General Patrick H. Jones became postmaster of New York. Michael Scanlan, orator, poet, journalist, and politician, was given an appointment in the Department of Internal Revenue. In the summer of 1869, there were enough Irish Republican officeholders to justify a convention in Chicago. The list of federal jobholders contained many Irish names, although largely in the lower ranks in customhouses and post offices.

In 1872, the fiasco of the Liberal Republican convention in Cincinnati resulted in the nomination of Horace Greeley for president. Democrats had no choice other than to accept him as their candidate also and to try to unite all the critics of Grant's first administration. Greeley, a lifelong opponent of Democrats, was a strange choice. As a teetotaler, he could hardly expect to attract Irish and German voters, for the immigrants from Ireland and Germany regarded beer and whiskey as part of their basic personal liberties. Greeley's abolitionism had offended the Irish during the war, and his flirtations with a variety of reforms during a long career of intellectual pioneering did not appeal to conservative, orthodox Irishmen. On the other hand, Greeley had a consistent record as an opponent of Know-Nothingism, and he reminded the Irish during the campaign that he had contributed $1,500 to relieve the potato famine and had always been a staunch friend of the immigrant. The Greeley campaign committee organized "Pioneer Greeley Clubs" in Irish wards of the larger cities. In New York, *The Irish World,* always strongly protectionist, supported Greeley because he favored a high tariff, and asked its readers to defeat free trade, which was sponsored by Democrats and "the English party." The *Irish-American* began the campaign by denouncing Greeley, but changed to his support before its close. A discontented segment of the Democratic party nominated Charles O'Conor of New York and John Q. Adams II of Massachusetts on a short, state rights platform, but both declined to run.[2]

Republicans represented Grant as a friend of the Irish, but could hardly deny the Know-Nothing record of his running mate, Henry Wilson of Massachusetts. The Irish were reminded that Grant had not overlooked them in the distribution of the spoils and that he had forced England to arbitrate the *Alabama* claims. In New York, Irish leaders like Charles O'Conor, James O'Brien, and Michael Crowley supported

2 Nevins and Thomas (eds.), *Strong's Diary,* IV, 434-35.

the President for a second term. Grant's military record probably was his greatest asset with his Irish comrades-in-arms.

During the campaign of 1876, Irish-Americans were relatively calm. The Democrats accused Rutherford B. Hayes of earlier flirtations with Know-Nothings, and Republicans had to assure Irishmen and Germans that Hayes was not a temperance fanatic but stopped regularly for his morning "eye-opener" in a German saloon in Cincinnati. The *Irish-American* pointed out that Hayes was not an Irishman. When the campaign ended in the famous disputed election, and the country was left without a decision until the eve of inauguration day, the Irish-American press counseled peace and wholehearted acceptance of the decision of the Electoral Commission, although many Americans believed it was flagrantly partisan.

Chester A. Arthur, Garfield's running mate in the Republican campaign of 1880, wanted it known that he was part Irish. A National Irish Republican Convention, composed largely of Irish-Americans from the Middle West, assembled in Indianapolis in July. Judge A. L. Morrison of Chicago presided. The Republican high command tried to represent the Democrats as the British free-trade party. The role of the Irish in the national campaign was not important, but the year was notable for the election of William P. Grace as Democratic mayor of New York City. Grace, a native of Queenstown, Ireland, who had arrived in New York at the age of thirty-three after adventures in many parts of the world, had become a wealthy business man with extensive investments here and abroad. He won the election with the support of Tammany and despite Republican charges that he was an enemy of public education. His administration was efficient and honest, and Grace ranks with the reform mayors of New York City.

In the unusually lively presidential campaign between Cleveland and Blaine in 1884, both parties bid high for a half-million Irish votes. The campaign was marked by unusual mudslinging, and the result finally turned on a few hundred votes in New York State. The campaign represented the greatest effort of the Republicans since the Civil War to lure the Irish from their historic Democratic allegiance and produced a group of Blaine Irish Republicans who held together for the next decade and were repeatedly recognized in the distribution of patronage.

Blaine's mother was a Catholic. A cousin, Sister Angela, referred to frequently during the campaign as a sister of the candidate, was represented as the mother superior of a convent. Blaine referred with feeling to "the ancient faith in which my mother lived and died." Moreover,

Irish voters liked a secretary of state who had been aggressive toward Great Britain. On the other hand, Cleveland, "the British candidate," advocated free trade. The Democrats retaliated by representing Blaine as a former prohibitionist and a Know-Nothing, an enemy of Catholics and the foreign-born, a renegade from his mother's Church, and a "jingo" who would plunge the nation into war.

At Irish-American rallies, prominent Irishmen sat on the platform with Blaine. Patrick Ford of *The Irish World,* an ardent protectionist, friend of labor, and inveterate hater of England, supported Blaine and referred to Cleveland as a bigoted Presbyterian. The Republican committee circulated a document attacking Cleveland for anti-Catholic sentiments, although the charges were categorically denied by the bishops of Albany and Buffalo. John Devoy's weekly *Irish Nation* shifted to Blaine in 1884 and paid heavily for the change in loss of subscribers. In Chicago, Colonel Richard O'Sullivan Burke, a Corkonian and a Fenian veteran, took the stump for Blaine. Patrick Egan, another Fenian and an active Land Leaguer who had come to the United States in 1883 to enter the milling business in Nebraska, worked for Blaine in 1884 in his capacity as president of the Irish National League of America. Joe Murray, a Union army veteran and a gang leader in New York, transferred his allegiance to the Republicans because his party had failed to properly recognize his services. John J. O'Brien, Alexander Sullivan, and Edward O'Meagher Condon, Irishmen widely known in the United States, supported the Republican candidate. Irish-American clubs took a prominent part in Republican parades.[3] In New York, huge Irish-American rallies for Blaine were held in Chickering Hall; in Boston, the Irish Land League announced that if Blaine became president of the United States, "Ireland would be free in thirty days."

The Democrats clearly were worried by the inroads made by Blaine upon their Irish supporters. Cleveland invited Patrick A. Collins, Boston's influential Irish leader, to the executive mansion in Albany to refute the anti-Catholic charges made against the Democratic candidate. Subsequently, the Democratic National Committee distributed a million copies of a speech by Collins in support of Cleveland. A letter written a month before the election by Archbishop Corrigan of New York to his brother prelate, Cardinal Gibbons of Baltimore, indicated that several prominent Democratic politicians, "some of them direct messengers from Gov. Cleveland," had waited upon both Corrigan and Gibbons to solicit their help in holding the Irish faithful to the Democratic party—

[3] David S. Muzzey, *James G. Blaine,* 203; 308-309.

an insinuation of clerical influence which Corrigan dismissed "as amusing." [4]

The election turned on New York. The famous reference of Dr. Samuel D. Burchard, Presbyterian divine, to the party of "Rum, Romanism and Rebellion" has gone down in history as an example of how dangerous alliteration can be. Blaine failed to notice the slur on Democrats and Catholics and the Democrats promptly printed handbills by the thousands and distributed them to Catholic churches and the homes of Irish voters, demanding revenge for the Republican insult to all Irishmen. The elaborate dinner in Blaine's honor at Delmonico's also may have antagonized many Irish laborers, and the weather on election day may have had some influence on the results. Cleveland carried the state by 1,077 votes, and thus became the first Democratic president to enter the White House since Buchanan.

As a practical politician, Cleveland recognized the importance of distributing political jobs among leaders of the Irish element. It was rumored that he considered Patrick Collins for a place in the cabinet. William R. Roberts, former "President" of the Irish "Republic" of the Fenians, became minister to Chile in 1885. In the Old Northwest, Patrick H. Kelly and Michael Doran, friends of James J. Hill, the railroad magnate who employed many Irish workmen, were the dispensers of Democratic patronage. Both were native Irishmen. Kelly operated a wholesale grocery in St. Paul, and Doran was a banker and commission merchant. The St. Paul *Pioneer Press* referred to the "Kelly-Doran office-broking agency," and the Minneapolis *Tribune* dubbed them "the proconsuls of the province of Minnesota." [5] In 1888, President Cleveland reviewed a parade in New York standing beside the mother of Charles Stewart Parnell, "Ireland's uncrowned king." The lady was dressed for the occasion in a green velvet dress. [6]

The reactions of the Irish to Cleveland's first term were mixed. His insistence upon a lower tariff branded him as a "British candidate." Irish leaders like Ford, Devoy, and Edward Fitzwilliam, publisher of the *Boston Sentinel,* maintained that the paramount issue was American protection versus "the British colonial system." Since most Irish-Americans were laboring men and opposed to free trade, they could not support a candidate whose renomination was welcomed by the British

---

[4] See John Tracy Ellis, "Cardinal Gibbons and New York," United States Catholic Historical Society *Historical Records and Studies*, XXXIX–XL (1952), 17.

[5] Horace S. Merrill, "Ignatius Donnelly, James J. Hill, and Cleveland Administration Patronage," *The Mississippi Valley Historical Review*, XXXIX (December, 1952), 505–18.

[6] Ellis P. Oberholtzer, *A History of the United States Since the Civil War*, V, 68.

press.[7] On the other hand, Cleveland's firm attitude toward England in the long dispute over American fishing rights in Canadian waters, and his threat to retaliate against Canada when the Chamberlain-Bayard negotiations broke down, "thrilled the Irish heart and were 'worthy of a Washington or an Emmet.'"[8] Both parties included a plank in their party platform favoring home rule for Ireland.

In 1888, Republicans continued their efforts, begun in 1884, to garner their share of the Irish vote. In Madison Square Garden, Blaine spoke for Benjamin Harrison, the Republican standard-bearer, from a platform decorated with an Irish flag inscribed "Home Rule for Ireland." All the speeches stressed that no Irishman could support a free-trade candidate without becoming "a practical ally of England." Near the close of the campaign, the Republicans provoked a dramatic crisis over the so-called Murchison letter. Actually the work of George Osgoodby of California, the letter was addressed to Sir Lionel Sackville-West, British ambassador in Washington, and carried the signature of Charles Murchison, allegedly an American citizen of English extraction, who requested advice from the ambassador on how to vote. The latter fell into the trap and advised voting for Cleveland. His letter was promptly turned over to the Republican campaign committee for circulation near the close of the campaign. Irish leaders like Collins and O'Reilly of Boston promptly informed Cleveland that Sackville-West must go, and one week after the incident was publicized, the ambassador received his passports. What effect the affair may have had cannot be accurately determined. Cleveland received a majority of the popular vote, but lost in the electoral college. Shortly after the election, Irish leaders who had supported the Republican ticket descended upon President Harrison for their political rewards. Patrick Egan, a devoted Blaine Irishman, became minister to Chile, where he had a stormy experience, and others received consular posts or other government jobs.

In 1892, the same two opponents battled again for the presidency. In contrast with the preceding two campaigns, neither party seemed greatly concerned with the Irish vote. Patrick Egan made speeches for Harrison, as was to be expected; Indianapolis had a Patrick Egan Club of about three hundred Irish who voted Republican; and Blaine made a special plea for the Irish vote in New York on the issue of protection. Devoy, who had opposed Cleveland in 1888, now asked his friends to support

---

7 See Patrick Ford, "The Irish Vote in the Pending Presidential Election," *The North American Review*, CXLVII (1888), 185–90; see also, in the same issue, John Devoy's comments on pp. 281–85.

8 Oberholtzer, *History of the United States*, V, 57.

the Democratic candidate. *The Irish World* remained anti-British, saw only evil in Cleveland's low-tariff position and his conduct of the Bering Sea arbitration, and roundly criticized virtually everything which Cleveland had done in the field of Anglo-American relations. The paper carried an editorial entitled, "Belfast for Cleveland," and publicized an alleged insult to American Irishmen by Robert B. Roosevelt, treasurer of the National Democratic Campaign Committee. By quoting favorable comments from British sources, the paper tried to give the impression that a fundamental issue of the campaign was whether England or the United States should rule the world. Cleveland won easily, despite the smear campaign of certain Irish papers. The steel strike at Homestead, Pennsylvania, which belied the argument that protection meant contented workers and a higher standard of living, may have influenced the Irish labor vote.

From the point of view of many Irish-Americans, probably the most important development of Cleveland's second administration was the President's knight errantry on behalf of Venezuela. Cleveland suddenly intervened in the long-standing boundary dispute with England and announced that, under the Monroe Doctrine, the United States was authorized to act as the moral guardian of lesser American states. Headlines in the Irish-American press revealed how eagerly many Irishmen hoped for war between England and the United States. *The Irish World* seemed pleased that a peace meeting at Cooper Union in New York was "a dismal failure." "All things considered," announced the editor in a pledge of support to the President, "Mr. Cleveland has risen superior to his former self." [9]

In 1896, McKinley and Bryan fought the "Battle of the Standards" over silver and gold. *The Irish World,* always friendly to labor, blamed both parties for the nation's financial troubles, but urged its readers to vote for the free-silver candidate.

By 1898, the controversy over money was largely forgotten. Prosperity had returned, and the Spanish-American War roused the martial spirit of America to new experiments in imperialism. Catholic papers did not welcome a war with Spain. *The Irish World* described the Spanish as a "brave" and "high-spirited people" and recalled their great service to Christendom in turning back the Moslem tide and unlocking the gates to the Western World. According to Patrick Ford, Spain was the land of saints, churchmen, and heroes, and had been forced into war by a jingo American press. In this "New England War," commented the editor of *The Irish World,* "let us fight them, yet respect them." Ford

[9] *The Irish World* (New York), December 28, 1895; January 4, 1896.

denounced "pulpit politicians" who were "doing their best to make this war a Protestant crusade." [10] When the United States extended its battle line to the Philippines, Irish-American leaders, like many other Americans, were alarmed by the sudden plunge into world politics. They protested against becoming involved in "the squabbles" of China, argued that the annexation of the Philippines "would give our government a push toward monarchy," and pointed out that if the United States needed more territory, Canada was preferable to the Far East.[11] Many Irish leaders concluded that McKinley and the Republican party were suffering from "Anglo-Saxonism," that the American people were being pushed into a dangerous policy of expansion in far distant quarters of the globe, and that the United States was about to become an ally of England in "a policy of plunder in the name of civilization and humanity."

The belief that the United States and England were on the verge of a secret alliance swept through Irish-American circles like wildfire. Protests poured into Washington, and Irish-American papers denounced the alleged plot against the independence of the United States. At a meeting of Irish in Cleveland, the national president of the Hibernians devoted his entire address to a denunciation of an Anglo-American alliance, and there were similar demonstrations in Chicago, Pittsburgh, New York, and other cities. In 1899, before the American Irish Historical Society, James Jeffrey Roche damned every Irish-American who favored an alliance with England as "unworthy of Heaven, unwelcome in Purgatory, and lonesome in Perdition." [12] One of the petitions to the United States Senate in protest against the alliance bore the signatures of such nationally known Irish-Americans as Patrick Ford; P. J. O'Connor, national president of the Ancient Order of Hibernians; Dr. T. A. Emmet; Patrick Egan; John W. Hayes, treasurer of the Knights of Labor; Judge O'Gorman of New York; and Joseph P. Ryan, secretary of the Irish Federation of America.[13]

The "new imperialism" was the major issue of the campaign of 1900. Many of America's most distinguished citizens, such as Mark Twain, Carl Schurz, Charles W. Eliot, Samuel Gompers, Jane Addams, Finley Peter Dunne, William James, and Henry Van Dyke, warned their fellow Americans not to abandon America's time-honored traditions of freedom, liberty, and isolation from world politics. Five thousand dele-

10 *Ibid.*, April 30, June 18, 1898.

11 *Ibid.*, July 9, August 27, September 24, October 1, 22, November 5, 1898.

12 James J. Roche, "The 'Scotch-Irish' and 'Anglo-Saxon' Fallacies," *Journal of the American Irish Historical Society*, II (1899), 91.

13 *The Irish World* (New York), February 5, 1898.

gates of the German North American *Turnerbund* denounced imperialism, and Irish organizations took similar action. *The Irish World* hailed Bryan's acceptance speech as a masterpiece, for it condemned imperialism, militarism, and the trusts—"all branches of one plant." An Irish gathering in Boston resolved that "free silver is less serious than free slaughter."[14] Bryan addressed 15,000 Irish at a monster demonstration of the United Irish Societies in Chicago. Patrick Egan presided over a Bryan meeting in Cooper Union, New York; Patrick Collins of Boston and John F. Finerty of Chicago made addresses. An Irish-American Union, including a number of Blaine Republicans, was organized to oppose "pro-British" militarism and imperialism, and Irish leaders directed their eloquence against McKinley and Republican imperialists.

Both Anglophobia and Catholicism were involved in the campaign. "Shall Porto Rico become America's Ireland?" queried *The Irish World*. "Imperialism is a plant of English growth," the article continued, and the fundamental issue is "Anglicanism or Americanism." The Republican party must be defeated to stop the "murdering" of Filipinos and to keep Cuba and Porto Rico from being "Protestantized." The United States government was charged with a plan to rob the Catholic Church in the Philippines by expelling the friars and confiscating their huge holdings, and it was frequently asserted that Orangemen were among President McKinley's chief advisers and supporters. Just before election day, the *Freeman's Journal* accused the President of ordering Catholic nuns out of Cuban hospitals and instituting an educational program to "paganize the schools."[15]

The major effort of Irish-Americans to free Ireland occurred during World War I and will be discussed in a later connection. Although Irish, Catholic, and Democrat are no longer synonymous terms, the Democratic-Irish alliance has continued to be formidable. The long-established tradition that the chairman of the Democratic National Committee must be an Irish Catholic has never been broken. James A. Farley, Edward J. Flynn, Frank Walker, Robert Hannegan, and J. Howard McGrath filled the post in earlier years, and Governor Adlai Stevenson's choice for the 1952 campaign followed the established pattern.

14 *Ibid.*, August 25, 1900.
15 *Ibid.*, November 3, 1900.

CHAPTER XVII

The Irish and Their Fellow Immigrants

GROUP tensions have been as marked among immigrants as among the native-born, and are as complex to analyze and as difficult to eradicate. The fact that all immigrants faced much the same problems did not assure understanding, tolerance, or co-operation. It is necessary to call attention briefly to the relations of Irish immigrants with other groups, though far more investigation of individual communities by sociologists and historians is needed before valid generalizations are possible. Economic competition, especially in unskilled labor; the clash of social customs; and quarrels over religion account for much of the friction. Membership in a common church was no guarantee of harmony among newcomers eagerly competing among themselves for economic and social status.

Irish and German immigration overlapped, a century ago, like two great waves rolling across the Atlantic. German immigrants impressed many Americans as the exact opposites of the Irish. A goodly number had money enough to finance their journey into the interior, whereas most of the Irish remained city dwellers. German immigrants were regularly pictured as patient, contented, home-loving, philosophic, phlegmatic, and stolid—hard workers who followed a trade or worked a farm, saved their money, and acquired a home where they spent the rest of their days. The Irish, in contrast, were described as temperamental, mercurial, romantic, less industrious and thrifty, and less stable. Such generalizations, to which there were many exceptions, seemed to justify the observation that the German immigration added a conservative, stabilizing force in the building of America, whereas the sudden disgorging of thousands of poor Irish on the eastern seaboard was a cause for deep concern.

Every immigration has left its human backwash in the crowded cities. New York and other large urban centers had their residue of unenterprising Germans in the 1840's and 1850's who lived in slums as bad as those which harbored the poorest Irish. Germans, Irish, and Negroes intermingled in the Five Points neighborhood of New York. German peddlers, scavengers, rag-pickers, and human derelicts differed little from the lowest Irish except in the language they spoke. New York newspapers reported many cases of petty thievery, assault, drunkenness, and rowdyism in which both Germans and Irish were involved. They also reported many rivalries between Irish and German neighbors which ended in fisticuffs.

On a number of issues, however, Germans and Irish could co-operate. In Milwaukee, they collaborated as early as 1843 in the city's political life.[1] In 1848, when the Milwaukee Germans were celebrating the outbreak of the German revolution, Irishmen joined in the demonstration and unfurled their Irish flags alongside the French, Swiss, American, and black-red-gold of the German revolution. At a "Freedom Festival," Father McLaughlin described the sorrows of Erin and the eagerness of the Irish to emulate the German revolutionists and establish a republic of Ireland.[2] In St. Louis, German military companies and singing societies marched with Irish Catholic organizations in parades to mark the progress of revolution through western Europe.[3] In later years, Irish newspapers reported the song and athletic festivals of their German fellow-immigrants and frequently commended the jovial, yet orderly, conduct of the Germans on such occasions.[4] In the 1850's, when Germans and Irish were persecuted by nativists, leading German newspapers like the *New Yorker Staatszeitung* and the *Buffalo Demokrat* collected funds for the relief of both.

During the temperance agitation of the latter half of the nineteenth century, Irish and Germans found another reason for co-operation. Both insisted that Sunday was a day of pleasure and recreation and were ready to defend the continental Sunday against the gloomy American Sabbath. "Personal liberty" to Irish and German immigrants meant, among other things, the right to drink whatever and whenever one pleased and included the open saloon on Sunday.

In 1855, in Davenport, Iowa, Germans and Irish rioted against a sheriff who had confiscated several barrels of beer, and, armed with swords, clubs, pitchforks, and shovels, marched to the local justice of the peace to protest this unwarranted invasion of their personal liberty.[5] In the same year, hundreds of Germans and Irish participated in Chicago's famous "Lager Beer Riots." Speakers at a mass meeting compared the outrage of raising the licence fee for saloons with the tyranny of the

---

[1] Still, *Milwaukee*, 81.
[2] R. H. Kloss, *Milwaukee*, 263–64.
[3] T. S. Baker, "Young Germany in America," *American Germanica*, I (1897), 73–74.
[4] *The Irish News* (New York), May 24, 1856.
[5] *Der Westbote* (Columbus, Ohio), September 21, 1855.

Stamp Act during the American Revolution. When several saloonkeepers defied the city ordinance and were brought to trial, Teutons and Celts marched on the courthouse, and the National Guard had to be called out to quell the rioting.[6] New York City experienced a similar crisis over personal liberty in 1867 when Irish and Germans mobilized to defeat or circumvent ordinances designed to close grogshops and lager beer saloons on Sunday. After the fall elections, in which their votes helped defeat "the Republican Puritan excise law," hilarious Celts and Teutons gathered in Tompkins Square to fire artillery salvos to celebrate the defeat of narrow-minded Yankees.[7] In the 1880's, when Abram Hewitt, the able reform mayor, tried once more to enforce Sunday closing, Germans and Irish joined with Italians to complain against this invasion of their rights "in a free country." [8]

Such sporadic co-operation against nativists and prohibitionists should not, however, distract attention from the many clashes that occurred between German and Irish immigrants. The early history of St. Louis, for example, was marked by brawls at amusement parks, German military balls, and outings of German societies. The Germans in St. Louis were principally concentrated in the northern and southern sections of the city. The Irish also had their own special area, and it was never safe to venture from one section into the other, especially after nightfall. Many of the residents of St. Louis preferred the Irish to the Germans. *The St. Louis American,* in 1847, contrasted the low standard of living of the Germans with that of the Irish. "Six Dutchmen can live where one Irishman would starve," commented one reporter, and an editorial in *The Crisis* deplored the disappearance of Irish "diggers and hodmen," "noble, generous-hearted," who were displaced by Germans who worked for less and were gradually getting a monopoly of city jobs.[9]

In New York, the trouble between Celt and Teuton was due largely to economic competition. In 1846, Irish laborers struck for an increase in pay from sixty-five to eighty-seven and one-half cents a day. When contractors imported Germans to work for less, a riot followed, and the Irish were defeated when the militia was called in to guard the German strikebreakers. In a number of similar incidents, in the 1840's and 1850's, "Dutchmen" were used to break strikes on the docks in the larger cities. Rioting occurred also when Irish rowdies interfered with German picnics, frequently for no apparent reason except to add excitement to an otherwise dull Sunday. German *Turner* organizations were preferred

[6] Bessie L. Pierce, *A History of Chicago*, II, 435–38.
[7] Nevins and Thomas (eds.), *Strong's Diary*, IV, 135.
[8] Nevins, *Abram S. Hewitt*, 478–79.
[9] Quoted in Walter O. Forster, *Zion on the Mississippi*, 272–73.

targets for these attacks, and since the *Turner* prided themselves on their physical prowess, they struck back. On a number of occasions, the rivalry ended in bloody street battles. In several incidents, the Germans were responsible for provoking the trouble; sometimes the fighting began when Irish loafers and rowdies drank beer and ate sausages at German picnics and then refused to pay for what they had consumed. In Wisconsin, clashes between Irish and German settlers were regular events, the Germans usually provoking the Irish on St. Patrick's Day, and the latter acting as the aggressors on German holidays.

There was much jealousy between Germans and Irish during the Civil War. Both furnished many able soldiers, but each believed the other was favored by Washington. The criticism of a New York Irish Catholic paper in 1864 was typical of the Irish attitude. It attacked Lincoln for making Carl Schurz "a general before he was fit to be a citizen" and for giving Major General Franz Sigel his pay "for doing nothing." Irishmen believed that General Kelly had been removed in western Virginia simply to create a command for Sigel,[10] and they were utterly disgusted when the rumor spread that the President was about to send his eldest son to Europe "to learn High Dutch."

In 1868, a bloody fight broke out on Ward's Island between German and Irish immigrants. The battle probably was provoked by the Germans, and the Irish fought back vigorously as they gathered around a green veil held aloft as their battle flag.[11] During the Franco-German War, Irish-American sympathy was with France. *The Irish Citizen* had no love for Prussia, and reminded its readers that France was the traditional friend of the Irish people. German newspapers explained the pro-French attitude of the New York *World, Cincinnati Enquirer, Chicago Times,* Cleveland *Plain Dealer,* and other Democratic papers on the assumption that the press could not afford to antagonize the Irish vote.[12] George Templeton Strong, greatly impressed with "New York Fenians" who were "swaggering on the side of France," feared that Irish sympathy for the French might "drive the whole German vote away from the Democratic party."[13] In 1871, the Germans of New York staged a monster victory parade, partly "to show Anglo-American and Celtic citizens the stuff of which the German immigration is made."

Many of the physical encounters between German and Irish immigrants resulted from economic rivalries or from mere rowdyism. The intellectuals in the two groups, on the other hand, quarreled over deep

10 *Metropolitan Record* (New York), February 13, March 12, 1864.
11 Costello, *Our Police Protectors,* 391–92.
12 See *Wächter am Erie* (Cleveland), July 20, 1870, and March 30, 1871.
13 Nevins and Thomas (eds.), *Strong's Diary,* IV, 298.

philosophical and religious differences. Radical Germans regarded the Irish as uncultivated, illiterate, ignorant minions of a despotic Church. German Forty-eighters referred to them as "natural enemies," not because they were Irish, but because of their "Popery." In the opinion of these anti-clerical radicals, the Irish were "nearer barbarism and brutality than civilization and humanity." Irish and German habits were utterly incompatible. One German visitor painted a bleak future for every German who would marry an Irish woman and predicted that in "ten times out of eleven" his wife would turn out to be a drunkard, a sloppy cook, a lazy housekeeper, and a common scold who would regard her husband as nothing but a "damned Dutchman." [14] Karl Heinzen advocated selective immigration to exclude "raw, uncouth" Irish Catholics.

To German liberals, Louis Kossuth, the Hungarian liberator in the Revolutions of 1848, was a symbol of freethinking Protestantism. To leading Catholics like Bishop Hughes, Orestes A. Brownson, and the editor of the *Freeman's Journal,* he was a fraud, a demagogue, and a foe of Christianity. The editor of the *National Intelligencer* agreed with Kossuth's critics and contrasted the dangers of German radicalism with "Irish conservatism, an impregnable breakwater against the assaults of an ignorant and conceited Red Republicanism." [15] Irish Catholics and the majority of the Irish-American press could find little good in the German immigration after 1848 and denounced its leaders as agnostics, infidels, atheists, "foreign anarchists," "red" republicans, organized in "barbarian clubs," and worse than Know-Nothings.

In the opinion of many Germans, Puritanism and Catholicism were twin evils which all liberals were bound to combat. As a result, there developed a German Know-Nothingism against the Irish as narrow as that of nativists against the foreign-born. The Milwaukee *Flugblätter,* Friedrich Fratny's *Volksfreund* and Hassaurek's Cincinnati *Höchwächter* could not be distinguished from the Know-Nothing sheets of the 1850's, as far as their lurid accounts of the Catholic Church and the Irish were concerned. When a liberal editor of a Cleveland German-language paper had the temerity, in 1875, to suggest that if he had to choose between Puritanism and Catholicism, "the latter is the more humane and liberal," he provoked a storm of abuse from German newspapers as important as the St. Louis *Westliche Post* and the *Buffalo Demokrat.*[16]

The nationality clash between Irish and Germans within the ranks of

[14] Karl Theodore Griessinger, "Lebende Bilder aus Amerika" (1858), in Handlin, *This Was America,* 256.

[15] *National Intelligencer,* December 10, 1851.

[16] *Wächter am Erie* (Cleveland), May 10, 1875.

the Catholic Church itself reached a crisis after 1880, although its causes were not new. As early as 1808, German Catholics in New York had requested a German priest and insisted that each nationality group was entitled to pastoral leadership by its own countrymen.[17] Irish parishioners in Pennsylvania, early in the century, had objected when the bishop sent German priests among them. In the 1880's, a vigorous and articulate minority among the German Catholics revived the controversy with their Irish fellow-religionists by demanding their own priests and their own parochial schools, to be taught in their native tongue. In German areas where there was an Irish minority, the issue became acute, although there have been parishes in which Irish and German Catholics worshipped together in harmony.

The controversy over Cahenslyism, as this particular issue is known in Church history, derived its name from Peter Paul Cahensly, a German Catholic. His father was an exporter at Le Havre, and there the son had watched hundreds of emigrants embark for the United States. He was disturbed to learn how little was done for their spiritual welfare. Cahensly became general secretary of a society for the protection of German Catholic emigrants and a member of the German Reichstag. In 1883, he visited the United States. After his return to Europe, German Catholic parishes in this country requested German parochial schools and more priests and bishops of their own nationality.

It is not necessary to follow the controversy within the Church in detail, except to say that it brought latent hostilities to the surface and developed into a German-Irish issue. The American hierarchy became divided, and German priests organized their own *Deutsch-Amerikanischer Priester Verein*. Bishop Ireland was a storm center of the quarrel. He declared war on the Germans, perhaps largely because they had condemned his school plan at Stillwater and Faribault, Minnesota. Ireland denied that American bishops desired to create an Irish Church and denounced the attempt "to harness the Church in America with the service of recently arrived immigrants from Germany." A minority of the Irish insisted their sole purpose was to force the Germans to become Americanized more rapidly. The controversy was marked with much intemperate and even abusive language. The competition for episcopal honors between Irish and German priests was in part responsible for the trouble. German leaders resented having their more cultivated parishioners "run by Irish ignoramuses." At the same time, the Germans insisted that any compromises which the Church might make with American-

[17] See United States Catholic Historical Society *Historical Records and Studies,* II, Part I (1900), 194.

izing forces could only lead to theological heresy and heavy losses in membership.

In the heat of the argument, Cahenslyism was represented by the more liberal American wing of the Church as a political plot to Teutonize the United States. Bishop Ireland was satisfied that Cahenslyism was a plot against America engineered by the *Dreibund*. The German group vehemently denied such accusations and insisted their demands constituted an honest attempt to serve their people, hold them in the Church, and resist further American inroads on Catholic doctrine. In 1892, the Pope sent a personal representative to the United States to end the battle, and Cahensly was exonerated of all ulterior, political motives. The friction between the "German party" and the "Irish party" continued in other areas for years and included a struggle for German representation at the Catholic University of America.[18]

Early in the nineteenth century, when the Irish immigration was still relatively small, the Irish had championed a kind of Cahenslyism of their own in complaining to the Holy See that French priests monopolized the American hierarchy. From Norfolk, Charleston, and Philadelphia came resentful protests against "foreigners" in control of local parishes, and the issue in some areas became entangled with the question of trusteeism as local parishes expressed a desire to control the temporal possessions of their churches. Ugly charges were dispatched to Rome to the effect that Frenchmen were intriguing to control the American Church.[19]

In the decade after the Civil War, the Irish were slowly being pushed out of the textile mills of New England by French Canadians from Quebec, and, in later years, were displaced by "southern and eastern Europeans" in the paper mills, garment trades, and other industries of this area. Irishmen contemptuously referred to the newcomers as "damn foreigners." In New England, French Canadians and Irish competed for jobs and presently for political office. They also revived the controversy in the Church whether each nationality group was entitled to its own priests. French Canadians denounced Irish influence in the Catholic Church. The Irish, on the other hand, "more American than the Americans" and with a good command of English, tried to control the newcomers from Canada by imposing Irish priests and the English language upon them. As soon as the French Canadians were numerous enough, they demanded priests who could speak their language.

[18] For Cahenslyism, see Barry, *The Catholic Church and German Americans;* and Meng, "Cahenslyism," *The Catholic Historical Review,* XXXI (January, 1946), 389–413; XXXII (October, 1946), 302–40.

[19] See O'Gorman, *History of the Roman Catholic Church,* 295–97.

New England's French Canadians became Americans politically, but for a long time remained culturally French, for it was not difficult to remain in touch with their native Quebec. Fall River, Massachusetts, and Manchester, New Hampshire, became bilingual towns. French and Irish became political rivals and contested for social position, employment, and influence in their common Church. In Fall River, some French Canadians left the Church rather than worship under Irish priests. The Irish opposed the creation of French parishes and the controversy finally was appealed to Rome. The Church eventually decided that language was an important bond in holding an immigrant group together and, in the case of the French Canadians, agreed that "qui perd sa langue perd se foi." In 1907, Bishop Guertin, American-born son of French-Canadian parents, became the first French-speaking bishop of Manchester. One of his major efforts was to secure equal status for the French and English languages in the parochial schools.[20] As late as 1898, *The Irish World* criticized the attitude of Irish-Americans in the small New England communities toward French-Canadian minorities and pleaded for more friendly relations.[21] In many New England towns to this day, French Canadians continue to vote Republican largely because the Irish are Democrats.

When southern Europeans began to arrive in the so-called "newer immigration," many Irishmen looked down upon these "foreigners" from backward countries with low standards of living. They were particularly critical of Italians, many of whom were birds of passage who had no intention of settling permanently in the United States. Cardinal O'Connell deplored the "sporadic outbursts of nationalistic feeling," as he recognized that "there was not always the most perfect harmony among all these good children of the Church, arriving here from their various fatherlands, and bringing with them their various languages, manners and customs." [22] For the Irish who were lowest in the economic scale, Italians were dangerous competitors with pick and shovel. The Italian immigrant, on the other hand, did not cherish being met at the church door by an Irish priest who knew nothing of his language, traditions, and customs. The Irish attitude toward the newcomers often was unkind; the Italian response was vigorous protest against Irish influence in the Church and politics.

In Chicago, for example, there were concentrations of more than a half-dozen large nationality groups as late as the 1930's, but Irish Catho-

20 See A. R. M. Lower, "New France in New England," *The New England Quarterly,* II (1929), 278–95; and D. M. A. Magnan, *Histoire de la Race Francaise aux Etats-Unis,* 310–33.
21 *The Irish World* (New York), February 26, 1898.
22 O'Connell, *Recollections,* 308.

lics controlled the committee structure of both political parties, although outnumbered by several nationality groups.[23] In Boston, there was bitter enmity between Irish and Italians, partly because the latter worked for lower wages. The North End, full of mementoes of the American Revolution, changed from Yankee to Irish, to Jewish, to Italian. In the 1840's, the Irish moved in and the Yankees moved out. Forty years later, the Dock Square section of Boston was predominantly Irish. After 1900, the Irish began to move out to give way to the Italians. As the Irish once complained that they were discriminated against by the Yankees, Italians now accused the Irish of treating them as inferiors. Keen economic competition led to street fights, and Irish corner gangs fought to keep their section free of Italians. In the second generation, the gangs became mixed as common interests like baseball and prize fighting improved relations between the Irish and the southern Europeans.[24] The well-to-do Irish abandoned the North End, but competition between Irish and Italian dockworkers, teamsters, and freight handlers continued for many years. The Irish huckster had to yield to the Italian pushcart man, and even the Irish cab driver was no longer sure of his monopoly. Italians voted Republican, partly because their Irish rivals were Democrats, and demanded Italian priests for their churches.[25] As late as 1927, *United America,* an Italian-American paper, attacked the Irish of South Boston and Charlestown as political gangsters and grafters, "vulgarian with the ideals of a bartender and the mentality of a ferry gate tender," whose progenitors "dug peat out of the bogs of the 'Auld Sod'" and who now indulged in "an orgy of adjective slinging." [26]

The Church provided Italian priests for Italian parishes as quickly as they became available. Realistic Irish politicians learned to address Italian political meetings in Italian to get votes for the Democratic party. In Philadelphia and New York, Irishmen became leaders in Italian wards, organized Italian political clubs, and provided jobs for Italian immigrants in the street-cleaning department. Intermarriage helped along the process of amalgamation. As Italians moved into a neighborhood in later years, they were likely to be welcomed by Irish ward committeemen. In some larger cities, political machines once dominated by Irishmen are now controlled by Italian-Americans. New York has had two Italian mayors, and Tammany Hall has had leaders with unmistakable Italian names.

In 1863, on the anniversary of the Polish Revolution, Richard O'Gor-

---

[23] Harold F. Gosnell, *Machine Politics: Chicago Model,* 45.
[24] William F. Whyte, "Race Conflicts in the North End of Boston," *The New England Quarterly,* XII (1939), 623–42.
[25] Woods (ed.), *Americans in Process, passim.*
[26] *United America,* May 7, 1922.

man, a distinguished Irish refugee of 1848, spoke in New York in a hall decorated with American, French, German, Polish, and Irish flags. In 1916, when the United Polish Societies of New York celebrated the one hundred and twenty-fifth anniversary of the Polish constitution of 1791, John Devoy of *The Gaelic-American* was among the principal speakers. Despite such evidences of fraternal feeling, the Poles have had difficulties with the Irish similar to the latter's relations with the Italians. As Polish immigration increased after the Civil War, Poles complained of Irish control of their Church. Although deeply religious, Poles did not feel at home in what they called the "Irish Catholic Church" of the United States. By 1910, there were about six hundred Polish churches in this country, and perhaps a thousand Polish priests. Protests against Irish domination and the demand for local parish control of church property finally reached such proportions that a Polish National Independent Catholic Church was organized. The seceding organization has its stronghold in Pennsylvania, a seminary in Scranton, a weekly paper known as *Straz,* and a benefit "Union" to provide insurance. The seceders insist that they are good Catholics, although they have gradually instituted a number of changes in Church practices.

In New England, a study of a typical Polish community revealed severe strains between Irish and Poles. The former were Democrats; the latter, Republicans. The Irish opposed the establishment of a separate Polish parish and resented the competition of Polish farmers who seemed to succeed on Massachusetts farms where others had failed.[27]

In recent years, there has been serious friction between Irish and Jews in several cities, such as Brooklyn and the Bronx and Dorchester, Massachusetts, and there have been numerous cases of property damage, insults, beatings, and desecration of Jewish burial grounds. Neighborhood gangs from Roxbury and South Boston Irish areas, whose members bear unmistakable Irish names, have invaded Jewish wards on a number of occasions. As late as 1944, there was considerable street fighting in Greater Boston. Such anti-Semitic demonstrations have received encouragement from organizations like the "Christian Front," which originally met in the Hibernian Hall in Roxbury, and from followers of Father Coughlin and Father Edward Lodge Curran, his eastern counterpart. Catholic writers have denounced these priests for their anti-Semitic utterances, and the Boston hierarchy has condemned anti-Semitism and ordered it stopped. Such un-American activities centered largely in the dregs of Boston's Irish community, but they provide further proof of the

[27] Edmund DeS. Brunner, *Immigrant Farmers and Their Children,* 237.

friction between minority groups over issues that originate primarily in religious prejudice and competition for economic and social status.[28]

On the Pacific Coast, the *bête noir* of the Irish, along with many other Americans, has been the Oriental, who began to appear during the Gold Rush of 1849. Originally welcomed as the "patient celestial," the Chinese were violently hated when they began to compete in the labor market with Caucasians, and the situation worsened when contract coolie labor was imported by railroad builders and mine operators. Before the end of the 1850's, the Chinese were being berated as a clannish, unassimilable element with standards of living and wages too low for any white man to meet. In the summer of 1868, when Irish laborers were building the Union Pacific and Chinese coolies the Central Pacific, the rivalry between them was encouraged by bosses who taunted the Irish with what the Chinese had accomplished. When the railroads were completed, ten thousand coolies became available for employment in California and neighboring states. The panic of 1873 brought years of deep depression, and desperate workers out of a job were largely responsible for the anti-Chinese agitation in California. The *Boston Pilot* described the Chinaman as "valueless as a citizen, valueless as a tax payer . . . a cruel, cowardly pagan," immoral, offensive, and unassimilable.[29] The *Irish World and American Industrial Vindicator* argued that the Chinese must go because all slave labor had to be eradicated from this country. It objected to the Oriental not on grounds of racial inferiority, but as a menace to the American workman.

The agitation against "John Chinaman" began with sand-lot meetings of the unemployed in 1870. From parades, mass meetings, and petitions demanding the exclusion of the Chinese, the agitation passed quickly into a more violent stage, marked by outrages against defenseless Chinese. A new nativism reared its ugly head on the Pacific Coast. It was led by foreigners, and among them, the Irish, shouting "America for Americans," were the most violent in their assaults upon the Orientals. Denis Kearney and P. H. McCarthy were the leaders of these anti-Chinese demonstrations. Their slogans were "Four dollars a day and roast beef" and "The Chinese must go."

Kearney, an Irish drayman from county Cork, had come to California in 1868. A temperate, self-educated man, he had frequently criticized his fellow Irish for their lack of ambition. He made his first speeches on the

---

[28] See Wallace Stegner, "Who Persecutes Boston?" *The Atlantic Monthly,* CLXXIV (July, 1944), 45–52.
[29] Quoted in Murphy, *Attitude of American Catholics,* 20.

Chinese issue for capital and against labor. In 1877, however, he shifted to the other side and organized his own party. The agitation became increasingly violent, and there was much loose talk about the liberal use of hemp and fire to rid America of the "yellow peril." Kearney was a good rabble-rouser, and in the fall of 1877, he became president of the Workingmen's party of California. The attack of the unemployed on the Chinese soon became an attack on capitalists and monopolists as well. Kearney was arrested for inciting the populace to riot; local ordinances were passed against the Chinese; legislators adopted resolutions denouncing the Oriental in order to hold the labor vote; and a "League of Deliverance" boycotted all Chinese products. The Workingmen's party controlled a third of the delegates elected to the California constitutional convention and forced the adoption of various discriminatory provisions, only to have them invalidated later in the courts.

By the end of the decade, prosperity had returned. Pressure upon Congress produced a new treaty with China, and in 1882, the first Chinese Exclusion Act was passed. Kearney gave up the battle for nativism, in which Irish had fought so vigorously to keep America for Americans, and transferred his allegiance to the Greenbackers, who sought salvation in the inflation of the currency.

CHAPTER XVIII

The Sociable Irish

Irishmen, as other Americans have come to know them, have a reputation for being extremely sociable. Romantics, prone to exaggeration and possessing a poetic love for their native land, the Irish unto the third and fourth generations give eloquent expression to their deep nostalgia for the Emerald Isle.

The so-called Irish temperament is a mixture of flaming ego, hot temper, stubbornness, great personal charm and warmth, and a wit that shines through adversity. An irrepressible buoyancy, a vivacious spirit, a kindliness and tolerance for the common frailties of men, and a feeling that "it is time enough to bid the devil good morning when you meet him" are character traits which Americans have associated with their Irish neighbors for more than a century. "His hand is rash, his heart is warm," ran a line in a poem in *The Shamrock* in 1815. Quick to anger and quick to forgive; frequently duped but never frightened; generous, hospitable, and loyal, "the Irish burn like chips, the English like logs." [1]

Irish love of oratory has helped Irishmen attain social success in many fields, and Irish orators are always expected to refer to their "emerald isle set in the ring of the sea." But there is something equally poetic about the everyday speech of Irishmen. The old Irish never referred to the departed without adding a pious "God rest his soul" or "heaven be his bed," nor did they let a sneeze go by without saying "God bless you." To die was "to climb the Mountain of Tears," and there was a legend in old Ireland that souls that go out to the ringing of the Angelus proceed straight to heaven. Expressions of farewell such as "God be between you and harm in all the empty places you must walk" or "God keep his arms around you" reveal the deep religious feeling that pervades all Irish social intercourse. "May the Devil fly away with the roof of a house where there's no welcome" testifies to the generous hospitality of the race, and such phrases as "in the forests where night is born" reveal their close connection with Nature. Even the lower classes, with little education, speak in similes, sometimes more forceful than eloquent. It is not

---

[1] A quotation from Henry George in *The Gaelic-American* (New York), July 1, 1922.

unusual to hear daybreak described as "the flight of night" or to encounter a reference to eternity in terms of "as long as grass grows or water runs."[2] In an Irish-American paper, a simple advertisement of a concert and recitation billed as "An Evening with Tom Moore" read, "The cup will sparkle, and the harp of Temor speak, and the collar of gold which Malachi wore will come to light, and the swords of former days will flash out as they did at Clontarf and Yellowford, in the sweet starlight of these evenings."[3]

Irish wit constitutes a large segment of American humor and is a part of American folklore. In joke books, on the vaudeville stage, and in ordinary social intercouse, the stories that begin with "Once there were two Irishmen, Pat and Mike," are legion, and so are the witty tales about Catholics, Protestants, and Jews in which Irish figure prominently. Such stories depend for success on a certain "genial gush of humor." Amid wrongs and sorrows, the Irish have not lost their capacity for laughter. Their stories reveal a vivid imagination and are usually couched in extravagant speech. Irish orators tell many stories, frequently in brogue, about their own people and give no offense. Moreover, even ordinary, untutored Irishmen have a genius for witty repartee. The Irish bartender usually had an inexhaustible fund of good Irish stories at his command. It was part of the equipment of his calling.

Several studies have been made of "Irish Bulls," a variety of humor which depends for success on blunders or on a laughable confusion of ideas expressed in absurd statements and resulting in a contradiction of meaning between one part of a sentence and the other.[4] The story of two Irishmen going on a long road on foot will serve as an illustration. When they were tired out from the journey and learned that they still had ten miles to go, one Irishman encouraged his companion, "By my shoul and St. Patrick, it is but five miles a piece."

More unusual are the stories about Irish priests, frequently related by priests themselves, which reveal the camaraderie that often existed between Irish clerics and their flocks and the good-natured fun that can be had, within reason, even at the expense of religion. Dozens of stories deal with persons in purgatory, or recently delivered from the ordeal, or with Pat, who would pay no more to get his friend cleared because he believed he could go the rest of the way by himself. A typical tale is one that might be called "sociable to the last." It tells of an old Irishman who had made his will, done his duty by the Church and charity, and had

[2] See Charles O'Neal, *The Three Wishes of Jamie McRuinn*, for other examples.
[3] *The Irish News* (New York), May 9, 1857.
[4] See Richard L. Edgeworth and Maria Edgeworth, *Essay on Irish Bulls;* and "Irish Bulls," *The Illustrated Celtic Monthly*, January, 1880, pp. 27–29.

ten pounds left. He stipulated that they be spent "with the boys" at his funeral. When his lawyer inquired whether the money should be spent while going to the funeral or coming back, the Irishman answered, "Put down tin pounds to spind goin' to the funeral, for thin I'll be wid ye." Other tales concerned Biddy Malone, who lost a certificate of character en route to the United States, and the friend who offered to provide her with another. He wrote that she "had a good character before she left the 'ould country,' but lost it on shipboard comin' over." [5] Another immigrant story told of an Irish family in America whose relatives in Ireland were not impressed by the letters they received from the United States. Eager to impress their friends and relatives, the immigrants made a trip to Washington, had their picture taken with the White House as a backdrop, and sent it home labeled "This is our summer home." In a different category belong such stories as the one about an Irishman who held a looking glass before his closed eyes so he might see how he looked when asleep; or Paddy's discussion with a friend about a severe storm in Pembroke, which ended with the comment that "we had the heaviest I ever saw, considering the size of the town."

The American vaudeville stage featured many Irish specialists and raconteurs of Irish stories. One may judge their quality by the story used many times by the Russell Brothers about Irish Maggie. When she was asked whether she had put fresh water in the goldfish bowl, she replied, "No, they ain't drunk up what I give 'em yesterday." [6] Irish-American newspapers advertised collections of Irish stories, and John Brougham's *A Basket of Chips* had a good sale in the 1850's. In later years, the popularity of Peter Finley Dunne's witty dialogues between Mr. Dooley and Mr. Henessey testified to the abiding quality of Irish humor, although the stories of the barroom and ward politics were mainly comment on current events in Irish dialect and seasoned with some homely philosophizing. By that time, the Irish had advanced far enough in social status that some of their leaders were offended by Dunne's caricatures, though they apparently had no objection to the brogue.

Before the Civil War, the Irish established many societies which indicated that a substantial minority among them were interested in cultural and intellectual progress. New York had its Irving and Moore Literary Association and the Cosmopolitan Literary Club, as well as a debating society organized for the discussion of American and Irish issues. The Thomas F. Meagher Literary Union began annual meetings in 1860,

---

[5] For this and other stories, see Walter Henry Howe, *Irish Wit and Humor.*
[6] For other Irish tales, see *The Galaxy of Comicalities,* I, *passim.*

and the Catholic Library Association of New York supported a library and reading room. The Thomas Davis Club of Washington combined sociability with the more serious purposes of a literary society.[7] Boston had a Hibernian Lyceum in the 1830's and a Hibernian Total Abstinence Lyceum in 1846. St. Mary's Reading and Library Association boasted of a circulating library of four hundred volumes and supported a night school for adults as early as 1845.[8] A Hibernian Institute in Hartford, Connecticut, in 1843, was devoted to cultural and intellectual interests. In Lowell, Massachusetts, in 1858, the Irish supported a flourishing Young Men's Catholic Library Association. The Emmet Monument Association of Boston sponsored lectures on Irish freedom in the 1850's. Irish reading rooms, Tom Moore clubs, Erina assemblies, and young men's sodalities were organized in the larger cities from coast to coast, and in far off Butte, Montana, Irish miners supported a Robert Emmet Literary Association.

The Irish also organized many benevolent and fraternal associations to pay illness and death benefits. Such organizations were especially important to immigrants whose economic status was still insecure. Frequently, as in Cleveland in 1870, Irish literary societies combined intellectual and social objectives with health insurance and death benefits. Boston had several mutual relief societies for Irish Catholics as early as the 1840's. The Irish Catholic Benevolent Union, a federation of Irish societies founded in Dayton in 1869 under the leadership of Judge Dennis Dyer, dispensed over $100,000 for charities during its first year.[9]

The Ancient Order of Hibernians was founded in 1836 and claimed to stem from a society of the fourteenth century which was "blessed by the successors of St. Patrick." The Hibernians obtained notoriety, originally of an unsavory kind, among Irish coal miners in Pennsylvania. In 1853, the society was incorporated under the laws of New York State. Although the order has done much charitable work among poor Irish immigrants, its main interest for years seemed to be in St. Patrick's Day parades. Since 1884, all Roman Catholics of Irish descent have been eligible for membership; before that time, the order was limited to native-born Irishmen. In later years, the Hibernians broadened their program to include agitation for Irish freedom, ardent support of the Church, debating and literary clubs, and the stimulation of interest in Irish history, culture, and folklore. As an insurance agency, it had paid over $300,000 by 1886 in sick benefits, burial expenses, and charities. In 1898, the Hibernians sponsored an Irish fair in Brooklyn. In 1935, its member-

---

[7] *The Irish News* (New York), April 14, 1860.

[8] Lord, Sexton, and Harrington, *History of the Archdiocese of Boston*, II, 348–49.

[9] Abell, "The Catholic Factor in Urban Welfare," *The Review of Politics*, XIV (July, 1952), 310–11.

ship was approximately a hundred thousand. In recent years, the order has encouraged the revival of Gaelic, provided scholarships for deserving students, and advocated the cause of Irish nationalism.[10] Many Irish also have been active in such organizations as the Catholic Knights of America and the Catholic Mutual Benefit Association. Moreover, Irishmen have been organized in the United States according to the counties from which they emigrated, and in the larger cities, "Sligo Men," "Mayo Men," and "County Longford Men" still gather annually for balls, outings, and other entertainment. Outdoor festivities and picnics are popular with the Irish, from May festivals of parochial schools to Irish National festivals, and games and dancing are prominent features of all such occasions. In some cases, the bar and lunch concessions are auctioned off to the highest bidder.[11]

To any list of social clubs must be added the many card clubs where Irishmen play such favorite games as euchre, and the parish organizations such as the Holy Name Society, Altar and Rosary Society, League of the Sacred Heart, Young Ladies' Sodalities, the Catholic Order of Foresters, and the Knights of Columbus. There are Irish-American athletic clubs in the major cities, and folk festivals, like Cleveland's and St. Paul's "Festival of Nations," where the Irish perform their folk music and their native dances. In Cleveland, each nationality group is represented in the city's Cultural Gardens. The Irish exhibit was dedicated in 1939, when Eamon de Valera, prime minister of Eire, was the honored guest. The garden has two heroic figures at the entrance and is laid out in the form of a Celtic cross. It contains a bed of Killarney roses planted in honor of Thomas Moore and symbolizing the Irishman's love of nature.

In high-grade choral music, the Irish have lagged behind other immigrant groups. Boston had a Gregorian Society devoted primarily to church music as early as 1836. St. Bridget's Philharmonic Society, in New York, was organized for "the study and exercise of vocal music." The society borrowed its conductor from the German *Liederkranz*.[12] Chicago has supported an Irish Choral Society for many years, and local clubs of the Friendly Sons of St. Patrick occasionally sponsor a glee club. Interest in choral singing has been so exceptional among the Irish that the Ancient Order of Hibernians in recent years has tried to promote Irish musical performances which would be comparable in quality to those of the Germans, Swiss, and Scandinavians.

Even uneducated American Irish know the story of young Robert

---

10 See John O'Dea, *History of the Ancient Order of Hibernians and Ladies' Auxiliary.*
11 *The Irish World* (New York), August 11, 1900; July 2, 1904.
12 *The Metropolitan Record* (New York), January 4, 1862.

Emmet's martyrdom on the scaffold after the insurrection of 1803, and Emmet societies have been established throughout the United States to honor his memory. In 1879, Richard O'Gorman addressed an audience in the New York Academy of Music on the occasion of the centennial of Emmet's birthday, and similar Emmet celebrations were held in Newark, Brooklyn, and other cities.[13] In 1903, the hundredth anniversary of his martyrdom was widely observed. In Columbus, Ohio, the centennial was under the auspices of the state's United Irish Societies, and forty thousand Irish proceeded to the Ohio capital. The program featured bands, a male chorus, and a quartet who sang Irish songs in Irish costume. A parade was followed by three hours of oratory, and the audience burst into wild demonstrations when the chorus sang "Come Back to Erin," "Gem of the Sea," "Wearing of the Green," "Widow Malone," and "When Erin Shall Stand Mid the Isles of the Sea." [14] During World War I, Emmet's part in the struggle for Irish independence gained new significance, and Irishmen as far away as Nome, Alaska, observed the anniversary in 1917.[15]

The Irish have been eager to participate in the observance of America's national holidays. As early as 1805, Macneven, one of the "men of '98," referred to "the important parts which the Irish bore" in the "exhibitions" of the Fourth of July.[16] In New York, in 1836, the Hibernian Universal Benevolent Society and the Hibernian Provident Society furnished two divisions for the Fourth of July parade.[17] Throughout the Know-Nothing decade, when Irishmen were excluded from Fourth of July parades, they organized their own processions, fairs, and clambakes to celebrate the day, usually ending the festivities with three cheers for the American Republic and three cheers for the independence of Ireland.[18]

No occasion, however, could equal St. Patrick's Day. It is now a deep-rooted and unique American institution. Germans have had their "German Day," United Hungarian Societies celebrate the anniversaries of Kossuth, and Italians march on Columbus Day—but there is nothing in this land of immigrants to compare with St. Patrick's Day. It is a special day of remembrance, and apparently will live among Irish-Americans, as Mary Louise Gilmore sang sixty years ago,

[13] See The Irish World (New York), March 1, 29, 1879; and The Illustrated Celtic Monthly, June, 1879, pp. 385–89.

[14] Proceedings of the Centennial Commemoration of the Martyrdom of Robert Emmet by the Irish Nationalists of Ohio (Columbus, September 20, 1903), 1–8.

[15] The Gaelic-American (New York), May 12, 1917.

[16] Emmet, Memoir of Thomas Addis and Robert Emmet, I, 394.

[17] E. Douglas Branch, Sentimental Years, 385–86.

[18] The Citizen (New York), July 21, 1855.

While in veins of Irish manhood flows one drop of Irish blood;
While in hearts of Ireland's daughters beats true Irish womanhood;
While God sends to Irish mothers babes to suckle, boys to rear;
While God sends to Irish fathers one man child thy name to bear.[19]

St. Patrick's Day was observed in Boston as early as 1737 and in New York in 1762. In the decade before the American Revolution, the New York Irish celebrated the day with "a very elegant breakfast," and when someone ridiculed them for coming to America "upon a bed of straw," they began wearing straw hats to express their resentment of the insult.[20] Washington recognized the day in his orders to the Continental army, and there were celebrations at the turn of the eighteenth century in Charleston, Savannah, Philadelphia, and Albany. In 1798, in Baltimore, Captain Stewart's Irish Brigade and Keating's Irish Grenadiers fired salutes from Federal Hill.[21] In 1811, the Juvenile Sons of Erin celebrated the day with poems, songs, and toasts at the Albany Coffee House with government officials in attendance, and on the eve of the War of 1812, there were celebrations in Washington and Fredericksburg, Virginia.[22] St. Louis had a St. Patrick's Day parade in 1820. In the early years, both Protestants and Catholics often joined in the festivities.[23] As early as the 1840's, Boston's demonstrations in honor of the saint were marked by parades and elaborate dinners. At a dinner sponsored by the Erin Fraternal Association of Brooklyn, there were fourteen regular and twenty-three volunteer toasts.[24]

Nativist hostility could not dampen the enthusiasm of Irishmen who dreamed of the day "when these plumes and banners shall be seen waving on Irish ground." The St. Patrick's Day celebration in Milwaukee in 1843 was organized by a German priest, Martin Kundig, and three thousand Catholics turned out for the occasion. In Chicago in 1855, "Dutch and Swedes" joined in the parade to demonstrate the solidarity of the foreign-born in the face of the Know-Nothing threat.[25] Before the Civil War, St. Patrick's Day celebrations were held in cities from New York to San Francisco, including smaller places like Pottsville, Pennsylvania; Keokuk, Muscatine, and Dubuque, Iowa; Madison, Wisconsin; Alton, Illinois; Augusta, Georgia; and Salem, Massachusetts. In 1857, the dinner

---

[19] The Irish World (New York), September 3, 1892.
[20] T. J. Wertenbaker, Father Knickerbocker Rebels, 14, 22.
[21] Note in Journal of the American Irish Historical Society, VII (1907), 95.
[22] See The Shamrock (New York), March 23, 30, April 6, 1811; April 4, 1812.
[23] Guilday, John England, II, 8–9.
[24] Meehan, "Pioneer Times in Brooklyn," Historical Records and Studies, II (1900), Part I, 185–86.
[25] The Citizen (New York), March 25, 1854; April 7, 1855.

in New York included among its honored guests Thomas F. Meagher, the exile of '48; John Brougham, popular Irish playwright; Charles A. Dana; editors, judges, and other dignitaries, lay and clerical.

During the Civil War, St. Patrick's Day was observed by Irish units in both the Union and Confederate armies. The Eighty-eighth New York, for example, began the day with a High Mass, in a chapel decorated with flowers and greens, and with the presentation of new vestments to their chaplain. "A Grand Irish Steeple Chase," for a purse of five hundred dollars, and athletic contests followed. Plenty of food and drink had been provided, including ten gallons of rum and twenty-two of whiskey. The evening was devoted to recitations and amateur theatricals.[26]

Officeholders and aspirants to public office found it increasingly important to attend Irish gatherings. At a dinner in Fort Wayne, Indiana, the mayor drank to the toast, "Ireland, first flower of the earth and first gem of the sea." [27] In New York, Mayor C. Goffrey Gunther reviewed the parade in 1864 holding his staff of office in one hand, and an Irish flag in the other. Six years later, Mayor Oakley Hall stood on the platform before City Hall dressed in a green coat, green kid gloves, and a green cravat. In 1880, *The Irish Record* of Peoria, Illinois, printed the St. Patrick's Day issue in green.[28]

Although the number of native Irish is much smaller today, enthusiasm for the ceremonies of the day has not lessened. In 1915, St. Patrick's Day was observed at the Panama-Pacific International Exhibition in San Francisco with a parade and High Mass, music, oratory, a banquet, and athletic games. Letters were read from John Redmond and from Joseph Tumulty, secretary to President Wilson. During World War I, Irish-Americans made special efforts to demonstrate their love of the United States and their hopes for Ireland. In 1921, one of the biggest parades in the history of St. Patrick's Day occurred in New York to protest against British outrages in Ireland and to demand recognition of an Irish republic by the American government. In Cleveland in 1953, the clergy of St. Patrick's Church were escorted to the religious services by the Shamrock Pipers Band while the chimes in the belfry played Irish music. At noon, the flags of Ireland and the United States were raised on the public square by Mayor Thomas A. Burke. In New York in the same year, the traffic lines on Fifth Avenue, which is taken over by the Irish every March 17, were painted green, the five-inch-wide strips extending for miles from Washington Square.

[26] Lonn, *Foreigners in the Union Army and Navy*, 387–88.
[27] *Metropolitan Record* (New York), April 4, 1863.
[28] Werner, *Tammany Hall*, 121.

St. Patrick's Day banquets provide a unique outlet for Irish-American oratory and for the songs of "Irish tenors" who sing the nostalgic tunes of Old Erin. Much of the oratory fairly drips with emotion and flowery phrases, but the patience of the audience seems inexhaustible, and the regular program usually is followed by "volunteer toasts." Among all St. Patrick's Day speeches, probably none ever surpassed the address of Thomas F. Meagher in 1855. He was at the height of his popularity as an Irish exile at the time and his address is a model of sentimental Irish eloquence. A paragraph extolling the love of all Irishmen for their native soil deserves quotation:

> On the girdle of faded gold there is in ancient letters the name of her— the forsaken, but not forgotten one—whose sons and daughters we this night, with love and pride, confess ourselves to be. . . . It is a festival of memory . . . on whatever spot the stars come forth and keep guard this night, the children of a little island—meet together in loving sympathy and remembrance. . . . I drink to her whose son I am proud to be, though she be poor, indeed, though we miss her crest and shield from the bright heraldry of other nations, though like her eldest sister of Zion, she has become as a widow, she that was a princess among the provinces.[29]

An occasional note of criticism has invaded these festivities so dear to Irish hearts. As early as 1854, a convention of the Irish Benevolent and Trade Societies discussed giving up their places in St. Patrick's Day parades and letting the military companies do the marching. In 1879, a South Boston Irishman protested to *The Irish World* against "the 'high fallutin' oratory of Patrick's Day spouters whose patriotism is buried in the last goblet of a Patrick's night carousal." [30] In 1917, the *Gaelic-American* expressed contempt for "the St. Patrick's Day Irishman" who gorges himself once a year, makes "maudlin speeches," and consorts with politicians whose "zeal for Ireland is a sham and a pretence." [31] Irish temperance societies have denounced the expense of St. Patrick's Day parades and banquets and urged that the money be put to better use.

There are no signs, however, that the picturesque Irish-American tradition of St. Patrick's Day is losing its appeal or that the nature of the festivities is changing in any significant way. St. Patrick's Day celebrations attract a lot of "Once-a-year Irishmen" and politicians who "drown their Shamrocks" in good liquor. But the majority of Irish-Americans, including many of the clergy, regard the day as important for the perpetuation of the cult of remembrance for the land of their origin.

29 The speech is quoted in Crimmins, *Irish-American Historical Miscellany,* 230–36.
30 *The Irish World* (New York), March 1, 1879.
31 *The Gaelic-American* (New York), December 22, 1917.

Chapter XIX

Irish-American Journalism

THERE is no language or nationality group in the United States, however small, which has not at some time maintained its own press. It is relatively easy to start an immigrant paper, but difficult to keep it alive. The fortunes of the immigrant press rise and fall with the immigrant tide. An immigrant paper is a piece of the fatherland which satisfies the reader's nostalgia for the land of his birth and preserves, for a time, the cultural heritage of his European past. Newcomers feel lonely and cling clannishly to their fellow immigrants during the early years; the immigrant press also helps its readers to find their way into the American scene. There is much going on in America—the novelty is exciting—and immigrants expect their papers to interpret the United States for them. Not until World War I was the immigrant press subject to any specific control. It was left free to perform its functions virtually as it pleased. Its most important service was to blend the cultural memories of the past with the immigrant's hopes for the future. It has been a powerful agency for Americanization, and the better it performs its task, the quicker it signs its own death warrant.

Such general observations apply to the Irish, for they were a sharply defined national and religious group a hundred years ago and, like other immigrants, had to build a new life in the United States. There was one major difference, however—the Irish-American press used the English language, and Irishmen could read many papers besides their own. Gifted Irish journalists, with no language handicap to overcome, found positions on America's leading newspapers.

Although Irish immigration did not reach a peak before the middle of the last century and some of the ablest Irish-American editors were exiles of 1848, there were a number of Irish papers in the United States before 1840. *The Shamrock,* started in New York in 1810, survived four suspensions before it finally ceased publication. *The Globe and Herald* was printed in Philadelphia in 1824, and the *Truth Teller,* often referred to as the first Catholic paper, was issued in New York from 1825 to 1855, had a circulation of 3,000 in 1833, and finally merged with the *Irish-*

American. The Irish Shield and Monthly Milesian appeared in New York in 1829 and was moved to Philadelphia, following a libel suit, where it was renamed the *Irish Shield and Literary Panorama.* Later, its owner established the *Literary and Catholic Sentinel* of Boston. *The Irish Advocate* became a rival of the New York *Truth Teller* in 1831. Charleston, South Carolina, was the home of the *Catholic Miscellany* (1822) and the *Irishman and Charleston Weekly Register,* founded in 1829 and later known as the *Irishman and Southern Democrat.* A major concern of these early Irish papers was the Irish cause. None was primarily a Church paper.

The *Irishman* of New York, a daily edited by John M. Moore, was founded as a Democratic party organ in 1835 "to protect the interest of Irishmen and foreigners of all countries and denominations."[1] The Boston *Pilot,* with cross and dove at its masthead, had a precarious existence in its early days and was saved by the heavy Irish immigration of the 1840's. In the Middle West, the pioneer paper was Detroit's *Michigan Essay and Impartial Observer,* founded by Father Gabriel Richard in 1809.[2]

Edward Gillespy and Thomas O'Connor, a "man of '98," founded *The Shamrock or Hibernian Chronicle* in New York in 1810. It was a typical Irish-American paper, ardently nationalistic for the Irish, but not specifically Roman Catholic. Funds were raised on several occasions by private subscription to prevent its early demise. The editor believed he had a mission in America to uproot "those illiberal opinions early sown by Ireland's enemies" and to introduce "the Irishman in his true character to the happy citizens of America." At the masthead of his paper was an eagle and a harp with the words, "Fostered under thy wing, we die in thy defence." The editor announced that he would take no part in local politics but would concentrate on European and national news, principally from Ireland, and strive to develop a better understanding between the Irish and their American neighbors. He advised naturalization as rapidly as possible and urged subscribers to "love and serve your country with the devotion of free men."

The weekly *Shamrock* cost three dollars a year. Later, the subscription price was raised to four dollars. Readers complained there was not enough space for news, though the paper carried little advertising. The editor had only a slight interest in local news items. He published court

---

[1] Crimmins, *Irish-American Historical Miscellany,* 215.

[2] Paul J. Foik, "Pioneer Efforts in Catholic Journalism in the United States, 1809–1840," *The Catholic Historical Review,* I (1916), 258–70. For the *Truth Teller,* see Thomas F. Meehan, "New York's First Catholic Newspaper," United States Catholic Historical Society *Historical Records and Studies,* III (1904), Part I, 115–30.

orders, the messages of the governor of New York and the President of the United States, and summaries of the proceedings of Congress. The paper covered the War of 1812 with some detail, but directed its main attention to Irish politics, music, history and biography, shipping and market reports, passenger lists of immigrant vessels, and marriage and death notices from Ireland. Its advertisements included those for books, lotteries, and "likely healthy" Negroes to be sold as slaves. *The Shamrock* suspended publication in 1816.

The Boston *Pilot,* established by Patrick Donahue in 1836, has survived to the present day. In 1838 it had 680 subscribers; by 1844 it had 7,000. Its early editorial staff included the brilliant young McGee and "Pepper Pot" George Pepper. The latter had edited papers in New York and Philadelphia before coming to Boston to berate the Pilgrims as "that atrocious and impious band of sanguinary and ignorant fanatics." Pepper left the *Pilot* in 1836 and, with Dr. John Stephen Barrett, a convert from Unitarianism to Catholicism, launched *The Emerald,* which lasted just three months.[3] In the 1840's, the *Pilot* supported O'Connell's repeal movement, published many news items about Irish life in the United States, as well as in Ireland, and was frequently referred to as the *"Vade Mecum* of the Irish emigrant." In the 1870's, the paper was in desperate financial straits. It was purchased by Archbishop Williams and has been the diocesan paper of Boston ever since. Among its later editors were James Jeffrey Roche and John Boyle O'Reilly, men of distinction in the literary field and ardent Irish nationalists.

The *Freeman's Journal* of New York was started in 1840 by James and John E. White, nephews of the Irish novelist Gerald Griffin. In 1841, it was combined with the *Catholic Register,* and in 1846, Bishop Hughes assumed control of the paper. On several occasions he raised money to keep it alive. James A. McMaster became its editor and owner in 1848, and six years later, Bishop Hughes made the paper his official organ. In 1857, however, the words "official organ of the Archbishop" disappeared from the masthead. Two years later, when McMaster and Hughes were involved in controversy, the bishop founded *The Metropolitan Record,* which John Mullaly edited from 1859 to 1873. During the Civil War, Hughes repudiated the paper's extreme anti-war attitude.

McMaster, the son of a Presbyterian preacher, had been educated for the Episcopalian ministry, but, in 1845, became a convert to Catholicism. A master of sarcasm and a keen theologian, McMaster appreciated controversy as a builder of circulation. An ultramontane Catholic, he fought for parochial schools and the temporal power of the Church. He hated

---

[3] Lord, Sexton, and Harrington, *History of the Archdiocese of Boston,* II, 335–36.

all radicals, whether abolitionists, "red" republicans like Kossuth, or socialists like Wilhelm Weitling. Though an ardent Catholic, he resented clerical pressure upon his paper. Upon his death in 1886, he was succeeded by his associate, Maurice F. Egan.

The *Freeman's Journal* remained a weekly until it expired as a casualty of World War I in 1918. In its early years, it devoted much space to foreign, national, and religious news. It catered to Irish immigrants, and had ten thousand subscribers in 1857. An extreme Anglophobe, McMaster editorialized on American, British, and Irish politics at great length. His extraordinarily long book reviews revealed great erudition. Reports on births, deaths, and crops in Ireland were intended especially for the *Journal*'s immigrant readers.[4]

The rise in Irish immigration in the 1840's and 1850's resulted in an upsurge in Irish-American journalism. Political exiles, who were men of education, believed they had a message for America and were eager to launch their own journals and use them as a sounding board for "Young Ireland." Many of their papers were short-lived, but they were well written by educated men with liberal principles. As organs of personal journalism, they indulged frequently in needless personalities, and the fact that the editors were members of the same Church in no way inhibited their zeal for invective. The Boston *Pilot* described the editorials of the New York *Irish-American* as "a compound of wind, froth, bombast, bad taste, [and] worse sense."[5] Rival publishers charged each other with bribing carriers and agents and stealing advertisers. In 1854, Meagher of *The Citizen* and McMaster of the *Freeman's Journal* used a horsewhip and a revolver in a street brawl, and both were arrested and put under bond.[6] Three years later, John Mitchel was involved in a physical encounter with the publisher of the *Knoxville Register*.[7]

Judging solely from the content of Irish-American papers, their excellent style, and the many topics which they believed would interest their subscribers—topics that included art, literature, history, the theatre, science, and the classics—there must have been many Irishmen above the level of "illiterate Paddies," for Irish-American papers had substantial circulation a century ago.

Nevertheless, it was not unusual that four papers, established by refugees in New York, failed within one year. German-language publishers had much the same experience. McGee's *Nation* clashed with the bishop, and his *American Celt* was bitterly attacked by other Irish papers and

---

4 See Sister Kwitchen, *James Alphonsus McMaster.*
5 Skelton, *Thomas D'Arcy McGee,* 168.
6 *The Citizen* (New York), July 22, 29, 1854.
7 *The Irish News* (New York), October 17, 1857.

had to be moved from place to place. *The Citizen* and *The Irish News* were the creations of John Mitchel and Thomas Francis Meagher, "men of '48." The somewhat more conservative *Irish-American* was Patrick Lynch's project. The latter avoided trouble with the bishop and claimed a circulation of thirty thousand by 1864.

The "men of '48," primarily interested in pleading Ireland's cause, stressed Irish news, spewed forth their hatred of England, and urged Irishmen to become United States citizens and, preferably, join the Democratic party. Their papers generally were sympathetic with labor and defended the immigrant against nativism. Most editors, as Catholics, were eager to uphold the faith. A few criticized the Pope as a temporal sovereign and objected to clerical influence in secular affairs. They taught respect for law and denounced the Irish for intemperance and rioting. Compared with the organs of the German Forty-eighters, Irish newspapers were far more conservative. Their editors were no "stormers of the heavens," with a panacea for all political and economic woes, and they were not tempted by the many "isms" of their day. They continued to stress the family, the home, and the church as stabilizing forces for the Irish in America.

The Citizen was founded in New York in 1854 by Mitchel and Meagher, well-educated and forceful writers who were leaders in the Irish republican movement. Their paper claimed twenty thousand subscribers in 1855. In the first issue, Mitchel announced his purpose was to revive the Irish national spirit so that Ireland could "partake in the great march of European democracy." He urged his Irish-American readers to become good citizens and "enlist under the banner of Universal Democracy," [8] and announced that his paper would be "unsectarian, broad and liberal in its views." The paper gave good coverage to foreign news, less to items from the United States, and major attention to Ireland. *The Citizen* carried excellent book reviews of Thomas Hart Benton's *Thirty Years' View* and the poems of William Cullen Bryant, literary essays, foreign correspondence, articles on science, invention, and art, and characteristically sentimental Irish poetry. It reprinted Mitchel's *Jail Journal* and carefully reported the proceedings of the American Congress.

After an auspicious beginning, the paper began to decline. At the end of the first year, Mitchel, on the plea of failing eyesight, turned *The Citizen* over to John McClenahan, a naturalized American and former editor of the *Limerick Reporter*. As a liberal and a Protestant, Mitchel had come into conflict with the clergy. He boasted that his "organ of Irish patriotism" would defy the Pope if necessary, and he attacked the

[8] January 7, 1854.

Papacy as a temporal power. He denounced the intolerance of American Catholic clergymen and their claim to a "divine right to abolish the free constitution of the United States." [9] His anticlerical heresies provoked vigorous counterattacks from the *Freeman's Journal* and the *Irish-Evangelist,* who branded Mitchel as an associate of red, radical republicans. Bishop Hughes was hostile, as he had been to McGee's earlier journalistic efforts. Mitchel became involved in American party politics and startled some of his supporters when he defended Negro slavery. Michael Doheny, dismissed from *The Citizen,* started the rival *The Honest Truth* in 1855. Mitchel retired to the South, where he issued another paper, and McClenahan continued to publish *The Citizen.*

Meagher, Mitchel's first associate, founded *The Irish News* in 1856. In form and content, it was like *The Citizen.* Its editor wrote eloquent editorials and published Irish fiction, serials on life in Ireland, and other material for the entertainment of his readers. He stressed that the paper was not only a journal of politics, but also devoted to "Literature, Art, Science and General Entertainment." In 1860, when the paper was in its ninth volume, it carried an article on George Berkeley, the philosopher, on the front page. By that time, however, Meagher had surrendered the paper to its publisher, Richard Lalor, and early in 1861, he was off to the Civil War.

Patrick Lynch described his *Irish-American,* founded in 1849, as a paper "devoted to news, literature and science" but "neutral in politics and religion." He wanted to unite "men of all creeds and ranks for political and patriotic purposes," and referred to St. Patrick's Day as "a national holiday, not merely a Roman Catholic holiday." [10] Nevertheless, the paper attacked McGee's *Nation* viciously, became involved in factional quarrels over Irish policy, and was completely out of sympathy with McGee's efforts to get the Irish out of the city slums. In 1857, the *Irish-American* began printing a column in Gaelic.

The Metropolitan Record, recognized for a time as "the official organ of the Most Reverend Archbishop of New York," was specifically directed to the Irish. It featured Irish stories, an "Irish Miscellany" from Ireland, and Irish poetry and manifested the expected amount of Anglophobia. The paper stressed foreign news affecting the Papacy and the Church and reprinted the pastoral letters of Catholic bishops. During the Civil War, *The Metropolitan Record* became a secular weekly and published more political news.

The last of these personal organs which can be specifically mentioned

[9] *The Citizen* (New York), December 30, 1854.
[10] Quoted in Skelton, *Thomas D'Arcy McGee,* 168.

here was Jeremiah O'Donovan Rossa's *United Irishman,* established after the Civil War and the Fenian fiasco. Rossa had managed a ticket agency and a hotel in the United States and edited the *Era* before starting the *United Irishman.* The latter was essentially an unreconstructed Fenian paper, the personal organ of an irreconcilable Irish republican. When Rossa died in 1915 on Staten Island, the Clan-na-Gael arranged to have the body taken to Ireland for burial, and the Irish Volunteers paraded in honor of the deceased Irish patriot.[11]

Irish-American journalism was not confined to the eastern seaboard, although New York and Boston papers had greater national influence than did the smaller journals in other parts of the country. The Irish had a paper in Milwaukee before the Germans. Known as *The Courier,* it was established in 1841 and was a Democratic party organ. Josiah A. Noonan, the publisher, also issued a semimonthly supplement known as the *Immigrant and Irish Repealer. The Catholic Citizen* of Milwaukee was the chief organ for Irish Catholics in Wisconsin. Other papers edited by Irish-Americans in the latter part of the nineteenth century in Wisconsin included the Appleton *Crescent* and the Manitowoc *Pilot.* As early as the 1860's, San Francisco had two Irish papers, the *Irish News* and the *Irish People;* in the 1880's, Minneapolis supported both a *Celtic World* and an *Irish Standard;* and St. Louis had an *American Celt. The Irish Times* was published in St. Paul.

The advertising of the immigrant press throws much light upon the customs, interests, habits, and experiences of an immigrant community. Unique features of early Irish papers were the personal notices inserted to find missing friends and relatives in the United States. "If this meets the eye of Thomas Burke or Patrick Burke, sons of one Elizabeth Burke of Dublin," read a typical announcement in *The Metropolitan Record* of September 8, 1860, they are asked to communicate with a Dublin address where "they may hear something to their advantage." *The Irish News* of March 6, 1858, reported the pathetic experience of an aged Irish woman who came from Ireland to seek her two sons, made two journeys to Wisconsin on foot, and finally was returned to Ireland at the expense of the New York Commissioners of Emigration. Typical also of the immigrant press were frequent notices by husbands about wives who had left their "bed and board."

Irish-American newspapers advertised Catholic books. In 1860, Appleton and Company announced a new $2.50 book in *The Metropolitan Record* entitled *The Path that Led a Protestant Lawyer to the Catholic Church.* Books on Irish history and novels of Irish life were popular. The

[11] Devoy, *Recollections,* 319–32.

publisher of *The Shamrock* issued *The Columbian Naval Songster,* fifty songs in honor of American naval victories in the War of 1812, which sold for fifty cents a copy. Meagher used *The Irish News* to solicit lecture engagements.

Immigrants are unusually susceptible to advertisements of patent medicines, for their health in a new land is a matter of great importance, especially when they have not yet established connections with reliable medical men. Irish papers in the 1850's carried many advertisements of books on the lungs, air passages, and tuberculosis, and for such medicines and aids as "Howe's Cough Candy," blood purifiers, trusses, "Halloway's Pills," "Ayer's Pills, for all the purposes of a family physic," "cherry pectoral" for coughs, hair restorers, and artificial teeth, drugs, and doctors, including "psychologists and electricians."

The Irish-American press carried advertisements dealing with shipping, foreign exchange, and other matters directly connected with immigration. The medium also was used by dealers in household goods and wearing apparel; brass bands eager to play for parades and balls; dealers in Irish whiskey, "sold pure at two dollars a gallon"; promoters of public entertainments, including minstrel shows; Scribner and Putnam, who advertised books from the ancient classics to modern fiction; and merchants who sold articles "desirable for family mourning." *The Citizen* of February 25, 1854, published a plea among its advertisements for money to build a new church in county Mayo, Ireland. A teacher announced the opening of an "academy" for the instruction of children and invited parents to see a specimen of his handwriting in the offices of *The Shamrock.* A woman solicited six young ladies to educate and board and announced her readiness to guide them in the "formation of their manners and the care of their morals," assisted by a gentleman "in the writing and cyphering departments." [12]

The Shamrock published rewards for the return of apprentices who had run away from their masters, and in the "help wanted" column, there were frequent requests for Irish weavers and for jobs by the unemployed. One also finds announcements of journals like *The Water Cure Journal* and *The Phrenological Journal,* and "How to Read Character, Whom to Trust," available for one dollar a year. *The Irish News* carried one of the first wood-block illustrations of a Singer sewing machine.

The Catholic press, though by no means exclusively Irish, has been an important branch of Irish-American journalism. A century ago, the cause of Ireland and the cause of the Church were virtually inseparable. In the United States, the Irish comprised a large part of the membership and

[12] *The Shamrock* (New York), March 9, April 6, 1811.

the hierarchy of the Roman Catholic Church. Boston's Cardinal O'Connell believed "a Catholic paper is as much a necessity as a church." A number of secular papers, like *The Emerald* of New York, have been published under Catholic auspices. *The Boston Leader* of the 1870's and *The Republic,* founded in 1882 and owned at one time by John F. Fitzgerald, mayor of Boston, were newspapers under Catholic management. A number of Catholic papers, moreover, have maintained a close affiliation with the Democratic party.

Bishop England's *The United States Catholic Miscellany* (1822–61) followed events in Ireland closely, especially during the battle for Catholic emancipation. *The Catholic Review,* founded in New York in 1872 by Patrick V. Hickey, had an able editorial staff including John McCarthy, Maurice F. Egan, and Margaret Sullivan. Hugh Patrick Gallagher founded the *Pittsburgh Catholic* in 1844. Cleveland's Catholic paper, known as the *Catholic Universe,* was edited in 1877 by a former officer of the Confederate army whose pro-Southern views and occasional attacks on both Germans and Irish Catholics proved a source of embarrassment for the Bishop of Cleveland. The *Catholic Standard,* established in 1853, was the first Catholic paper on the Pacific Coast. *The Irish Republican,* the *Free Lance,* and the *Irish Echo* were published in Boston. Alexander Patrick Doyle, a Paulist priest, issued the *Catholic World,* and Daniel Eldred Hudson, another priest, published the *Ave Maria* in Boston for over fifty years. Such distinguished literary figures as Bancroft, Brisbane, Parker, W. H. Channing, Margaret Fuller, and Elizabeth Peabody were among the contributors to Brownson's *Review.*[13] By 1889, America had a Catholic Press Association. A "Citizen Company" in Milwaukee owned a chain of papers in a number of cities. In 1892, the United States had 457 Catholic periodicals which were published in this country, and in 1919, the number was 313 Catholic newspapers and magazines, including those printed in foreign languages.

By 1918, the only survivors of Catholic papers founded before 1850 were the Cincinnati *Catholic Telegraph,* now known as *The Catholic Telegraph Register,* the Boston *Pilot,* and *The Pittsburgh Catholic.* The first is now the oldest Roman Catholic paper in the United States. It was the first Catholic weekly west of the Alleghenies. Founded by the first Bishop of Cincinnati and essentially a Church paper, it was concerned with all Irish matters, hostile to all things British, and a cham-

[13] For further details on the Catholic press, see Appolinaris W. Baumgartner, *Catholic Journalism;* "A Partial List of the Catholic Press in the United States," *The Catholic Historical Review,* IV (1919), 217–21; Thomas F. Meehan, "The Catholic Press," in *Catholic Builders of the Nation* (ed. C. E. McGuire), IV, 219–34; and Sister Paluszak, "The Opinion of the *Catholic Telegraph.*"

pion of Irish nationalism. The paper vigorously voiced its stand on many American issues.

Various attempts have been made to publish journals dedicated to belles-lettres and Irish lore rather than public affairs. In 1858, the *Irish Pictorial Miscellany* was established in New York. It reprinted mainly from the *Dublin Penny Journal* and carried many pictures of Irish scenes.[14] A similar paper in Boston was devoted to Irish art and literature. *The Emerald,* an illustrated literary journal established in New York in 1868 which sold for eight cents a copy, was intended as a medium for "the prolific Irish intellect" in America. Its first number carried poems, wit and humor, and an original Irish-American story called "Frank McDermody; or, Murder Will Out." The *Illustrated Celtic Monthly* was issued in 1879 under the editorship of James Haltigan for a subscription price of $2.50 a year. By the end of the next year, it had three rivals: T. F. Murphy's *The Celtic Mirror* of Augusta, Maine, Hickey's *The Illustrated American Catholic,* and a third edited by P. K. M'Cann, formerly with *The Irish World. The Illustrated Celtic Monthly* carried a variety of poems, fiction, drama, articles on Irish life, and biographical sketches of Irish celebrities. A number of Irish-American almanacs have been published in the United States at various times.

There were also Irish papers whose sole concern was Irish nationalism and fomenting revolt against English rule. Such papers flourished, especially in the years when the Fenian movement was at its peak. Michael Doheny was a frequent contributor to the Fenian *Phoenix* of New York. As late as 1873, the Fenians established the *American Gael* and the *Sunday Citizen* and an Irish National Publishing Company headed by O'Mahony. The *Irish Republic* was founded in 1867 by P. W. Dunne, Michael Scanlan, and David Bell, all of Illinois. In Philadelphia, Captain James O'Reilly, ardent Fenian and a Civil War veteran, for one year published the *Sunday Leader,* a paper devoted to "the interests of the Irish race in Ireland and America." In the 1880's, Thomas Halpin edited the nationalist *Irish Tribune* of Chicago, and Brooklyn had a paper called *Ireland's Liberator and Dynamite Monthly,* whose editorial policies were adequately revealed in the title.[15] The *Irish Standard,* a weekly founded in Minneapolis in 1885, and the official organ of the Ancient Order of Hibernians in Minnesota, was for thirty years the only Irish-American journal in that part of the country. Patrick J. Haltigan, a reading clerk in the House of Representatives, published the *National Hibernian. The Irish-American Freeman* of Chicago and the

---

[14] Ernst, *Immigrant Life,* 265.
[15] D'Arcy, *The Fenian Movement,* 406–407; also 240.

Hibernian Patriot of Natick, Massachusetts, were primarily published in the interest of the Ancient Order of Hibernians and were ardently Irish nationalist.

In recent times, *The Irish World, The Gaelic-American,* and the *Irish Echo,* published in New York, were the most influential Irish-American papers. *The World* was established by Patrick Ford in 1870 and remained under the control of the Ford family; *The Gaelic-American* was the creation of John Devoy in 1903. Both circulated widely throughout the United States and in Ireland. The *Irish Echo* today claims the largest circulation of all Irish papers in the United States.

Ford's paper, originally known by its longer title, *The Irish World and American Industrial Liberator,* retained its original format for decades, with the exception of the addition of a "woman's page." It carried many columns of Irish news about hundreds of Irish in every walk of life here and abroad. In the 1870's, it championed temperance reform and the cause of labor. It favored greenbacks and free silver; made a hero of Wendell Phillips, whom Irishmen once despised for his abolitionism and now revered as a critic of wage slavery; and advocated reforms very close to socialism. It fought machine politics, supported a liberal public-land policy, and railed against monopolists, bankers, and hard-money men who "plotted against the greenback." *The Irish World* favored the protective tariff, to preserve the American standard of living; advocated a graduated income tax; and during the Pulman strike, when Debs was the victim of a blanket injunction, believed that the law was "wrenched from its intent to work injustice." [16] As time went on, however, *The Irish World,* which had always carried the cross as part of its insignia, gave less space to labor and more to Ireland and the Church. *The Gaelic-American* was not much different in its content from *The Irish World.* It published pages of news from the Irish counties and became deeply involved in the final phases of the struggle for Irish independence during World War I.

In the days before newspaper publishers were required to file sworn statements of ownership and circulation, statistics for the number of paid subscribers were hard to get, often unreliable, and sometimes deliberately misleading. After the Civil War, specific figures were available in such annual newspaper directories as Rowell, Pettingill, and Ayer, but these too are not altogether trustworthy. Publishers either refused to report their circulation or submitted estimates which no one could verify and which were padded to impress advertisers and competitors. The circula-

16 *The Irish World* (New York), January 5, 1895.

tion of early Irish papers of the 1850's was small; readers had to be reminded that they were in arrears with their payments; and advertising produced insignificant revenue. Few editors and publishers faced the future with confidence.

By 1876, the monthly San Francisco *Irish News* had only 500 subscribers, despite the large number of Irishmen in the California metropolis. In the same year, the weekly *Irish Democrat* of New York had a circulation of 3,500, and the *Irish-American* reported 10,000, although in a paid advertisement in *Rowell's Directory*, the publisher claimed a circulation of 30,000. *The Irish World* reported 35,000 subscribers in 1876, and the weekly Boston *Pilot*, 50,167. In 1885, the *Irish Standard*, a weekly published in Minneapolis, counted 2,000 subscribers. In 1896, the Boston *Pilot* claimed 76,210, and the New York *Irish-American*, 20,000. Eight years later, the two papers reported circulations of 75,000 and 25,000, respectively. The Pittsburgh *Irish Pennsylvanian* had 4,800 subscribers in 1896. The same year, *The Irish World*, the most successful of the Irish-American papers, reported a circulation of 125,000 and advertised in Pettingill and Company's *Newspaper Directory* that it had just printed an edition of 1,650,000 copies, "believed . . . to be the largest single edition of any paper published since the invention of printing."

Many Irish editors left their mark not only upon Irish-American papers, but upon leading American dailies as well, but space permits brief mention of only five leading Irish-American journalists.

Patrick Donahue of the Boston *Pilot* was brought to Boston by his father as a lad of ten and learned the printing business here. He worked on several Boston papers, including the *Transcript*, before he established the *Pilot*. He was an ardent supporter of Father Mathew's crusade for temperance. He became a merchant and private banker and made and lost several fortunes in the United States, and at one time was known as "the richest and most influential Catholic in New England." He was a staunch Democrat and a generous contributor to the Church and Irish causes.

Patrick Ford was brought to Boston in 1842 as an orphan and was educated in the public schools. He worked on William Lloyd Garrison's paper, served as a soldier in the Civil War, and founded *The Irish World* in New York in 1870. A passionately patriotic Irishman, his paper was noted for unreasonable hatred of all things English. He helped organize the Irish Land League in the United States; favored the "no rent" campaign, and rebellion, if necessary; rejected home rule; and demanded complete independence for Ireland. He raised large sums for Irish causes and, in 1884, campaigned vigorously for Blaine.

John Savage, as a "Young Irelander," had taken part in the rising of 1848. Educated at the Dublin Art School and experienced in the ways of Irish political journalism, he came to New York in 1848 to work as a proofreader for Horace Greeley's *Tribune.* In 1854, he became literary editor of Mitchel's *Citizen.* He was an ardent Fenian and had been a member of Corcoran's Legion during the Civil War. From 1864 to 1867, he was the leading editorial writer for the New York *Times.* He wrote a tragedy, several books on Irish history, a number of campaign biographies, and many poems, among which "The Starry Flag" is the best known.

John Boyle O'Reilly was born in Drogheda and learned the newspaper business in Ireland. He served for a time in the British army, but was sentenced as a Fenian in 1863 and deported to Australia as "Convict No. 9843." In 1869, after a dramatic escape, he arrived in Philadelphia. He became a correspondent for the Boston *Pilot,* and later bought stock in the paper. A poet of considerable merit and an eloquent orator, he was a popular figure at many Irish festivities. Among his publications was a book entitled *Ethics of Boxing and Manly Sport,* published in 1888.

John Devoy's father had been active in the "Young Ireland" movement, and the son became an ardent Fenian conspirator. In 1866, he was sentenced for treason but allowed to leave for New York, where he was warmly welcomed by the Irish. He worked for several papers, including Bennett's New York *Herald,* and started his *Irish Nation* in 1881. The paper failed four years later, partly because it supported Blaine for president. Devoy was a firebrand in every Irish movement which he joined, including the Clan-na-Gael, Land League, and Sinn Fein. In 1903, he founded *The Gaelic-American,* and served as its editor until his death in 1928. During World War I he raised money for the Irish Easter Rebellion of 1916, organized the Irish in America against the League of Nations and World Court, and helped float the first bond issue for the Irish Free State in the United States. His *Recollections of an Irish Rebel* are the chronicle of an ardent, uncompromising, fierce champion of Irish freedom.[17]

The list of able Irish journalists who worked on leading American papers would be almost encyclopedic in nature, for many Irishmen had special gifts for the newspaper field. The number of well-known Irish-

[17] See James Reidy, "John Devoy," *Journal of the American Irish Historical Society,* XXVII (1928), 413–25.

American journalists includes Thomas McGuire, protégé of the elder Bowles of the *Springfield Republican;* John L. Sullivan, who probably coined the phrase, "Manifest Destiny";[18] Thomas Kinsella, editor of the *Brooklyn Eagle;* Patrick Walsh of Limerick, United States senator from Georgia and owner of the *Augusta Chronicle;* Joseph Burbridge McCullagh, who came from Dublin in a sailing vessel and was editor of the *St. Louis Globe-Democrat* at the time of his death; the colorful Bohemian, Fitz-James O'Brien of Limerick, who worked for several New York papers before the Civil War; James Jeffrey Roche, poet and journalist, author of several volumes on Irish history and literature, and a contributor to *Harpers, Century Magazine,* and the *Atlantic Monthly;* Thomas F. Murphy, who was the first editor of the first newspaper published in Alaska; John F. Finerty, founder of the *Chicago Citizen;* and David G. Croly of county Cork, who was managing editor of the New York *World* from 1862 to 1872, wrote books in the field of philosophy, and produced a campaign biography of Horatio Seymour for the Democratic party.

[18] Julius W. Pratt, "John L. Sullivan and Manifest Destiny," *New York History,* XIV (1933), 213–34.

CHAPTER XX

The Irish in the Labor Movement

IN THE 1840's, the American labor movement was still in its infancy, small in membership, unco-ordinated, and divided in strategy between those who favored the use of political methods and those who believed the strike and the boycott were the only roads to success.

Although Dublin had a labor movement in the first half of the nineteenth century, the majority of Irish immigrants upon their arrival in the United States had had little experience with labor organizations. Americans were inclined to look upon them as the "pauper labor of Europe," likely to depress American standards of living. The heavy Irish immigration probaby retarded unionization in the United States, for many Irish immigrants virtually were contract laborers when they arrived in the United States, and Irish unions were rare in the 1840's. After the Civil War, the American labor movement produced a type of Irish labor leader who was regarded as a tough, hard fighter who sometimes carried his revolver to labor meetings.

The early Irish-American press urged Irishmen to organize. The same qualities that made the Irish successful organizers and leaders in politics and the Church helped them to become successful labor leaders, and they quickly mastered the techniques of the labor movement. Probably more Irish immigrants were craftsmen than has generally been assumed, and they quickly learned a trade in the United States. The majority, however, had no choice but pick, shovel, and wheelbarrow. Employers frequently testified that the Irish were inferior in education and craftsmanship to Germans, Scandinavians, and Czechs.

Before the flood of immigration in the late 1840's, Irishmen began to drive native New Englanders, including women, out of the textile mills. Mill towns like Lowell, Massachusetts, were experiencing a change in the old benevolent, paternalistic relations between employer and employee, and labor relations began to take on the characteristics of a class struggle. In Philadelphia, another textile center in the 1840's, the early unions were largely controlled by English and Scotch weavers and Orangemen familiar with the early British labor movement. When the

Irish either refused to join their organizations or were not admitted to existing unions, serious tensions developed. Labor controversies were at least partly responsible for the bloody Kensington riots between nativist Protestants and Irish Catholics in the Philadelphia area.[1] Irish "laborer's associations," "benevolent associations," and longshoremen's and quarrymen's societies were part of the social structure of Irish immigrant communities before the Civil War and paraded as units on St. Patrick's Day and other holidays.

In 1854, nearly all the officers of the New York Tailor's Trade Association were Irish.[2] Irish bricklayers and masons were in demand, and Irishmen were entering the boot and shoe factories of Massachusetts. During a shoemaker's strike in Lynn, in 1860, they faithfully supported their union.[3] The spinners' union of Fall River was under Irish leadership in 1858 and had to meet secretly in the fields or behind the mills.[4] Seven years earlier, recent arrivals from Ireland had been hired to break a strike in a Massachusetts textile mill and were housed in a dance hall for six months.[5] In the summer of 1850, a tailor's strike in New York, characterized by the *Irish-American* as "a very unhappy and barbarous conflict," began with a walkout of the Irish. German tailors joined the demonstration and helped tear up garments and smash windows in the shops on upper Broadway. During the panic of 1857, several thousand destitute workers marched into Wall Street and past the offices of the leading newspapers, and were addressed from the steps of City Hall by "several fierce Dutch and Irish orators."

The number of Irish craftsmen in New York was surprisingly large. By 1855, practically all the shoemakers were foreigners, and one-third of them were Irish. They lived and worked in cellar shops, sometimes for Irish contractors who did not hesitate to "sweat" their own people at a rate of pay that did not exceed seven to eight dollars a week. There were many Irish barbers and waiters in New York. In the 1850's, the Irish constituted three-fourths of the foreign-born masons, plasterers, and bricklayers in the city, one-half of the carpenters, and one-third of the painters. In 1852, the *Irish-American* pointed out with pride that the Irish furnished half the machinists, shipwrights, carpenters, cabinetmakers, and other men of manual skill in New York.[6] The meetings of local Irish labor organizations were announced in the Irish-American

[1] Nolan, *The Reverend Francis Patrick Kenrick*, 307.
[2] *The Citizen* (New York), March 4, 1854.
[3] *The Irish News* (New York), April 7, 1860.
[4] George E. McNeill, *The Labor Movement*, 216.
[5] *Ibid.*, 118–20.
[6] Ernst, *Immigrant Life*, 73–79.

press. The longshoremen's societies were led by Irish labor leaders. Irishmen tried, before 1860, to organize the boiler and forge workers in the iron mills of Pittsburgh. In Boston, the Irish were interested in consumers' co-operatives and savings banks, as well as labor organizations. As early as 1846, the unskilled Irish had formed a Boston Laborer's Association, and there were other Irish workers' organizations for waiters, stonecutters, and dockworkers.[7] In 1853, an unsuccessful tailor's co-operative was converted into the Journeymen Tailor's Trade and Benevolent Association.

The American Miners' Association, founded in 1861, was the first attempt to organize the coal miners on a national scale. Among its organizers was a genial Irishman, Martin Burke. In 1866, the Ocean Steamship Firemen's Protective Association invested $3,000 in Fenian bonds, the boilermakers contributed $300, and the Longshoremen's Union Protective Association, $1,204.[8] John Siney, in whose face Terence V. Powderly once said that one "could see Christ . . . and hear a New Sermon on the Mount," organized the Irish miners of Schuylkill County, Pennsylvania, into a Workingmen's Benevolent Association. The axe-makers union was largely Irish. In 1875, J. P. McDonnell, an ex-Fenian and early Marxist, led the Irish "United Workers of America." In 1878, he organized an International Labor Union for the unskilled and, in 1883, the New York State Federation of Trades and Labor Union. He also published the Socialist *Labor Standard* in New York. On one occasion, he was sentenced to jail for calling a strikebreaker a "scab."[9] In 1887, he was instrumental in persuading the New Jersey legislature to establish Labor Day as a state holiday. On the Pacific Coast, the importance of the Irish labor group is evident from the fact that the convention which created California's Central Labor Union held its deliberations in the Irish-American Hall in San Francisco.

In general, the Irish press favored the American labor movement. Meagher's *Irish News* demanded a program of public works for the unemployed in 1857. *The Irish World* in the 1870's was read primarily by the Irish working class and had the courage to publish an article by Louis Blanc on the evils of the competitive system.[10] During the epidemic of strikes in 1877, the Irish press, though opposed to violence and the European "commune," expressed strong sympathy for the strikers. The Boston *Pilot,* more conservative than *The Irish World* on

---

[7] Handlin, *Boston's Immigrants,* 163–64.
[8] D'Arcy, *The Fenian Movement,* 126.
[9] Commons, *et al., History of Labour in the United States,* II, 222.
[10] April 5, 1879.

labor matters, exposed the conditions under which the Irish were forced to work in the coal mines—the "murderous neglect" of ventilation, the "rancid provisions" sold at company stores, and the needless explosions in mines owned by men who had "neither the conscience of Christian nor of Pagan." [11] During the 1880's, the *Pilot* commented favorably on the Knights of Labor and carried considerable labor news. At a time when many Americans were ranting about the Haymarket riots and welcoming the execution of the Chicago anarchists, the *Pilot* commented, "Of their moral guilt there is no doubt. Of their personal responsibility for the awful Haymarket tragedy there is less certainty." [12] With unabated hostility to the Negro, the *Pilot* advocated segregation in the labor movement and resented the presence of colored delegates at labor conventions. Organized labor generally supported a "Free Ireland," and as late as World War I, the Chicago Federation of Labor joined in "tag days" for Ireland.[13]

The attitude of the Catholic clergy cannot be so clearly defined. For decades after the Irish immigration reached its peak, both Protestant and Catholic churches had no specific program of social action. Some prominent Catholics, including Irish labor leaders like Terence Vincent Powderly, have asserted that the clergy did not enter the fight for social justice until the victory was practically won.

As Irish workers became prominent in labor organizations, their point of view began to be reflected in the attitude of their Church. The hierarchy not only became increasingly aware of the worker's thinking, but realized the necessity of keeping labor unions within proper bounds to prevent the development of secret societies. The line between reform and radicalism always is difficult to draw, and the Catholic press, as well as the leaders of the Church, were divided on labor matters. A struggle between the advocates of a vigorous "social gospel" and those who wanted to confine the activities of the Church to a more traditional sphere occurred in the Catholic Church, as well as among Protestants and Jews. In the end, Rome adopted friendly attitudes toward labor groups, as the encyclicals of Leo XIII and Pius XI show.

Meantime, labor papers and labor leaders on numerous occasions flayed organized religion for its failure to lead in the labor field. In 1879, Terence V. Powderly, the Irish Catholic leader of the Knights of Labor, charged that the president of the Philadelphia and Reading Railroad

[11] May 24, 1862.

[12] Quoted in Henry J. Browne, *The Catholic Church and the Knights of Labor*, 306.

[13] See *The Gaelic-American*, December 9, 1916; and Samuel Gompers, *Seventy Years of Life and Labor*, II, 31–33.

had insured his company against strikes by guaranteeing to the clergy that no workman would ever be discharged if he absented himself from work on the Church's holy days. On another occasion, Powderly referred in bitter terms to an unholy alliance between priests and Pinkerton detectives.[14] John Siney believed that the clergy had blocked his efforts to work among the miners in the 1870's. In Ohio, at commencement exercises at St. Xavier College in 1872, Archbishop John B. Purcell of Cincinnati attacked the demand for an eight-hour day and reforms which seemed to envisage a "division of property" by saying that "every loafer and drunkard" would want "a new subdivision every Saturday night."[15] Archbishop Ireland approved of President Cleveland's intervention in the Chicago railroad strike with federal troops.

There also were many members of the clergy who were favorable to labor's program. Father Cornelius O'Leary, for example, supported the Knights of Labor, and it was rumored that the Missouri Pacific Railroad protested against his activities to the Archbishop of St. Louis and offered to pay off a church debt if the troublesome priest were removed. It was not reassuring to the friends of labor to discover that he actually lost his parish and had to wait until the archbishop's retirement eight years later before he got another assignment.[16] Another sincere champion of labor was Father John Augustine Ryan, a big, blunt Irishman from Minnesota who took holy orders after having been a single taxer and a Populist. Richard T. Ely wrote the introduction for his book, *A Living Wage.* On the basis of Leo XIII's *Rerum novarum,* Father Ryan advocated social insurance, a minimum wage, slum clearance, and a more equitable distribution of the national wealth.

As the New York draft riots damaged the standing of the Irish throughout the country during the Civil War, so the "Molly Maguires," the first large-scale Irish labor agitation, gave Irish workmen and labor leaders a reputation for disorder and violence which it took decades to dispel. The Molly Maguires were not a labor union, in the strict sense of the term, but rather a clandestine organization which emerged from the failure to organize and recognize responsible unions in the Pennsylvania anthracite coal fields. Labor operated in secret in this area because it was afraid to act in the open. Labor conditions were substandard, and the constant supply of new immigrants kept wages down. In 1848, a miner earned $1.48 a day, and an ordinary laborer, eighty-three

---

[14] Browne, *The Church and Knights of Labor,* 46, 53; also Harry J. Carman, Henry David, and Paul N. Guthrie (eds.), *The Path I Trod, The Autobiography of Terence V. Powderly,* Chapter XXVII; and Powderly, *Thirty Years of Labor.*

[15] Browne, *The Church and Knights of Labor,* 24.

[16] *Ibid.,* 158–59.

cents. In a busy season, a miner might earn as much as thirty dollars a month, but there were long periods of idleness when he earned nothing at all. He lived in company houses, had to deal at company stores, was paid in company scrip, and it was not unusual to get a "bobtail check" at the end of the month showing that the worker actually owed his employer. Though the bosses usually were English, Welsh, or Scotch, the majority of the miners were Irish.

From such conditions the militant Molly Maguires drew their support. Employers fought labor by infiltrating their organizations with spies and detectives. One need not conclude, as a recent writer has done, that the Mollies were merely a labor organization led by men innocent of all wrongdoing and convicted on charges trumped up by capitalists.[17] Although the connection between Hibernians and Mollies was denied, many Irish belonged to the Ancient Order of Hibernians, which at that time was a very different organization than it is now. Intolerable economic conditions motivated secret societies and terrorists who were described throughout the country as "a gang of Irishmen." They terrorized the area for years, committing outrages, mayhem, arson, and murder and intimidating voters at the polls. Irishmen had learned to despise the law in their battles with landlords, and many did not find it difficult to continue to practice old methods in a new location. The New York *Tribune* maintained that the Molly Maguires originally were decent people, interested in legitimate political and social objectives, and attributed the violence to conditions in the coal fields where a miner "eats his salt pork, sleeps like pigs."

The details of the terror need not be recounted here. The leading characters in the drama were Irishmen. James McParlan, the Pinkerton agent who wormed his way into the organization and on whose testimony the leaders were imprisoned or executed, was a red-headed Irish Catholic from Ireland who came to Chicago in 1867 and worked as a teamster, deckhand, lumberman, coachman, policeman, and saloon-keeper before joining the Pinkerton detectives in 1872. McParlan was a jovial Irishman, a good singer, a nimble dancer, and a pugilist who easily won the confidence of the Hibernians with his tall tales while he was being paid twelve dollars a week and expenses for his work as a labor spy. The leading prosecutor of the Molly Maguires was Franklin B. Gowan, born in Philadelphia in 1836 as the son of immigrant Irish parents. A hard-headed lawyer, railroad executive, and mine operator, and a bitter foe of labor organizations, he had few scruples about the methods used in breaking up labor movements. He imported Irishmen

---

[17] Anthony Bimba, *The Molly Maguires*, *passim.*

under contract, to keep wages down, and hired spies and detectives for his mines. He was on friendly terms with the Bishop of Philadelphia, and frequently cited clerical approval for his fight against the "Mollies." [18] Thomas Ainge Devyr, another Irishman with a fine record as a champion of liberal causes in England and Ireland, carried on a vigorous newspaper campaign in defense of the Irish miners and described the sentencing of the Molly Maguires as "judicial murder." [19] There is some evidence of a deliberate frame-up to convict some of the Mollies, and McParlan's later, highly questionable career does not help to buttress his reputation for reliability. The heavy preponderance of Irish names in this unsavory episode in American labor relations damaged the reputation of Irish labor groups in the minds of many Americans for many years.[20]

The Noble Order of the Knights of Labor, the first significant attempt to build a great national army of labor, was organized in Philadelphia in 1869. It was founded on the assumption that, with the exception of doctors, lawyers, bankers, and liquor dealers, all who worked for a living had common interests and should join forces in improving working standards. The Knights were a mixed body of skilled and unskilled laborers bound together by an oath and a ritual, partly secret, and patterned on Masonic lines. They functioned through local assemblies, a general convention of delegates, and a Grand Master Workman at the top of the organization. The leaders of the movement believed secrecy was imperative if their efforts were to be successful. From a slow beginning, the order grew rapidly in the 1870's and reached its peak of about 800,000 members in 1886. Its program was moderate and stressed the co-operative movement rather than socialism. In its ranks were thousands of Irish workers, and in some districts, the Knights were almost exclusively Catholic.

In 1879, Terence V. Powderly was chosen Grand Master Workman, and he continued in that position until 1893. Powderly was the son of Irish Catholics and a practicing Catholic himself. His father, after his arrest in Ireland for an altercation with a landlord, came to the United States in 1827, worked for a farmer in New York State, and then moved to Carbondale, Pennsylvania. He remained an ardent Irish nationalist. The son learned the machinist's trade, worked as a brakeman on a railroad, joined the machinist's and blacksmith's union, lost his job in the panic of 1873, and as a devoted union man soon found his

[18] Browne, *The Church and Knights of Labor,* 22.
[19] Henry Christman, *Tin Horns and Calico, passim.*
[20] See J. Walter Coleman, *The Molly Maguire Riots.*

name on the employers' blacklists. Powderly was elected mayor of Scranton for three terms and, following his career as a labor leader, became a good Republican. He campaigned for McKinley in 1896 and was rewarded with several jobs in the Bureau of Immigration and Naturalization. He was essentially conservative in labor matters, favored co-operatives and profit-sharing, was an ardent temperance reformer, and opposed strikes because of their wastefulness and violence.

Of special interest in the history of the Knights of Labor is the controversy between this organization and the clergy over the matter of secrecy. Thousands of Irish laborers were devoted to Powderly and his organization. *The Irish World* described the Grand Master Workman as a man of character and principle, and the Boston *Pilot* endorsed both him and his organization. Bishop Richard Gilmour of Cleveland and several fellow bishops looked favorably upon Powderly's leadership and were deeply concerned about the "ominous risings of the poor for bread and butter." To a large section of the clergy, however, the Knights were suspect as a secret society, with single-tax, communist, and even anarchist leanings, and Powderly was charged with being both a Mason and a Molly Maguire. Efforts were made to have the Vatican condemn the organization. The Grand Master Workman insisted that neither he nor his members were tainted with radicalism, and he explained the nature of the organization's secret ritual to Cardinal Gibbons. Powderly was not averse to abandoning secrecy if this would end the opposition of the Church. For his diplomatic tactics and his cordial relations with the cardinal, Powderly was denounced by the American Protective Association and by labor leaders who believed he was too obsequious to Rome. Cardinal Gibbons, vigorously supported by Bishop Ireland, induced the Vatican to issue a *tolerari possunt,* and thus prevented a formal condemnation of the Knights in the United States. Powderly secured exceptions to the oath which protected loyal Catholics in the confessional and in their private consultations with priests, and finally the order abandoned its secret features altogether. Cardinal Gibbons had revealed his usual talents as a conciliator. He understood that it would be unwise and impolitic for the Church to denounce a labor organization which included so many Irish and Catholics. Furthermore, he was eager to refute the charge that his Church was "Un-American" and had ceased being the friend of the common man.[21]

A somewhat similar controversy arose in the 1880's over Henry

---

21 Browne, *The Church and Knights of Labor;* also Henry J. Browne, "Terence V. Powderly and Church Labor Difficulties of the Early 1880's," *The Catholic Historical Review,* XXXII (1946), 1–27.

George's single-tax reform. Archbishop Corrigan condemned the proposal in 1886 as anti-Christian and an attack on private property. When George ran for mayor of New York, a letter from the vicar-general was circulated to the effect that the Roman Catholic clergy would "deeply regret the election of Mr. George to any position of influence."[22] Dr. Edward McGlynn, a lovable Irish priest with genuine sympathy for labor and the miseries of the underprivileged, had the temerity to challenge his archbishop by campaigning for George. He was promptly separated from his pastoral duties and ordered to Rome to make his submission. McGlynn's parents were Irish immigrants from Donegal. When his father died, McGlynn was ten years old and the widow was left with ten other children. Young Edward attended public schools until he was thirteen, and then Bishop Hughes gave him the opportunity to prepare for the priesthood. A sensitive friend of the poor and a zealous reformer, McGlynn regarded Henry George's *Progress and Poverty* as a penetrating analysis of the defects of American society. He accepted the single tax to "make room at the Father's table for all his children." McGlynn also was an ardent Land Leaguer and the organizer of the Anti-Poverty Society in 1887.

The controversy over McGlynn's status in the Church continued for five years. When he was removed from his parish, it was reported that 25,000 Irish wage earners paraded in protest. When he refused to go to Rome, pleading ill health and a misunderstanding of instructions, he was excommunicated. For five years, the priest spoke every Sunday afternoon for the single tax and promoted his Anti-Poverty Society. Cardinal Gibbons was successful in his efforts to keep *Progress and Poverty* off the Prohibitory Index for two years. The Bishop of Cleveland opposed public condemnation of the book lest it "look as if the Church sided with capital and against labor."[23] In 1889, however, the book was declared "deserving of condemnation," although the enforcement of the decree was to be kept *sub secreto,* probably because of its possible effect upon Irish workers. Cardinal Gibbons defended McGlynn's right to advocate social reform, even under the banner of Henry George. Maurice F. Egan supported the priest in an editorial in the *Freeman's Journal* entitled *"Fiat justicia."* The New York *Catholic Herald* was strongly pro-McGlynn. *The Irish World* took a similar position until clerical opposition became too determined. Father Thomas Ducey, an Irish-born priest whom Powderly had personally conducted through a mine, defended McGlynn. After five years, McGlynn was reinstated in

---

[22] Commons, *et al., History of Labour,* II, 451–57.
[23] Hynes, *Diocese of Cleveland,* 183.

his parish duties. Four professors of the Catholic University of America examined a statement of his opinions and testified that they were not heretical, and *The Irish World,* on December 31, 1892, carried an editorial to express delight that so staunch a friend of labor and the Irish cause had at last been exonerated.[24] Incidents of this kind probably were not without effect upon the gradual development by the Holy See of a standard pattern of Catholic social thought.

After the close of the Civil War, Irish, German, and Welsh coal miners in Pennsylvania were complaining of "newer" immigrants who took "bread from the lips of decent, law-abiding Americans." In the 1870's, Irishmen repeatedly voiced their protests against the importation of "foreign labor" and "durrty furruners" into this grand and glorious country.[25] In 1875, serious riots resulted when a Pennsylvania mine operator brought in Italians armed with breechloaders, and there were other occasions when Irishmen showed their antagonism toward Poles, Hungarians, Swedes, and Negroes.[26] In 1879, French-Canadian "knobstick" spinners were brought to Fall River, Massachusetts, to break a textile strike, with unfortunate results. In 1882, in Frostburg, Maryland, Irish workers, led by a man who claimed to have studied for the priesthood, attacked "Box-car Hunkies" who were brought in as strikebreakers.[27] During the anthracite coal strike of 1902, when a miner's average yearly pay was no more than $450 to $500, German miners protested that the Irish monopolized the union offices, favored their own people in the distribution of strike funds, and exploited their positions in the union for personal gain.[28]

One need only thumb through a book like Samuel Gompers' *Seventy Years of Life and Labor* to be impressed with the many names of Irishmen who have been prominent in the development of the modern American labor movement. One encounters Duffy, Hennessy, McGuire, Dunn, Farley, Fitzgerald, McDonnell, Keegan, McBryde, McSweeny, O'Connell, O'Connor, Sullivan, Tobin, and many others. Ignatius Donnelly, a genial, portly Irishman, born of Irish parents in Philadelphia, achieved fame among the Populists. Michael J. O'Leary, a native of Cork, was

[24] See Browne, *The Church and Knights of Labor,* 250, 268, 305, 336; M. F. Egan, *Recollections of a Happy Life,* 132–34; *DAB;* and Sylvester L. Malone, *Dr. Edward McGlynn.*

[25] Edward A. Steiner, *On the Trail of the Immigrant,* 75; and *From Alien to Citizen,* 139.

[26] McNeill, *The Labor Movement,* 259–60.

[27] Richard Lowitt (ed.), "Frostburg 1882: German Strikers vs. German Strikebreakers," in *28th Report of the Society for the History of the Germans in Maryland* (1953), 72–79.

[28] *Report of the Anthracite Coal Strike of May–October 1902* (Washington, 1903), 177–80.

secretary of the Telegrapher's Mutual Benefit Association in 1897. J. P. McDonnell, an ardent Fenian, organized the workers of the textile industry. Jeremiah Tierney, Meagher's comrade in the Civil War, was the first national secretary of the United Hatters' Union of North America.[29] Alexander M. Kenaday, a second-generation Irishman, was president of the San Francisco Trades Assembly in 1863, and lobbied for the eight-hour day before the California legislature.[30] Henry J. Skeffington organized the Brussels carpet weavers of Philadelphia in 1864. John Siney was president of the Miner's National Association in 1873. Joseph Wilkinson was one of the founders of the Amalgamated Trade and Labor Union of New York. Frank Roney of Belfast, a former Fenian, became president of the moulders' union of Omaha. John Golden, perennial president of the United Textile workers of America, which was organized in 1901, was a Lancashire Irishman, and most of his lieutenants were British or Irish. Denis Kearney began his labor activity in the Drayman and Teamster's Union. The executive board for the United States of the First Socialist International had two Irish members.

Hugh Frayne was an organizer for both the Knights of Labor and the American Federation of Labor, and helped establish the Actors' Equity Association. Tom Mooney achieved international notoriety from a miscarriage of justice in California. Mary Harris Jones—"Mother Jones" —was a Corkonian whose father was a railroad worker. She was educated in a convent school, married an iron moulder in 1861, and was left a widow with four children six years later. She lost her few possessions in the Chicago fire. She became a propagandist for the Knights of Labor and an agent for the Socialist *Appeal to Reason,* spending her later years working for the United Mine Workers and speaking at strikers' meetings. At ninety-three, she was still active in a West Virginia coal strike. She was buried in a United Mine Workers' cemetery in Illinois with the rites of the Catholic Church.[31]

Peter J. McGuire is remembered as the "father of Labor Day." He was the son of Irish immigrants and grew up in New York's East Side slums. The young wood joiner became a greenbacker and a socialist, organized the Brotherhood of Carpenters and Joiners, and served as its secretary for a quarter of a century. He was also one of the founders of the American Federation of Labor and served as its secretary and a member of its executive committee. He proposed a "Labor Day" at a

---

29 *The Gaelic-American* (New York), August 12, 1916.
30 Commons, *et al., History of Labour,* II, 147.
31 *DAB.*

meeting of the federation in New York, and workmen began to observe the day in 1882. A dozen years later, Congress made it a national holiday.

The Irish labor leader still is a familiar figure on the labor scene. The New York Rapid Transit System and the Transport Workers Union (C.I.O.) are largely in the hands of Irish Catholics. Michael Quill, the leader of the latter union, has not lost his Irish brogue. Edward F. McGrady was president of the Boston Central Labor Union in 1917. In an industrial city like Cleveland, Irish names continue to be prominent in labor ranks. In 1952, James C. Quinn was executive of the Cleveland Industrial Union Council; William Finnigan, executive secretary of the Cleveland Federation of Labor, and Patrick J. O'Malley, regional director for the C.I.O. Auto Workers' Union. Maurice J. Tobin, secretary of labor in the Truman cabinet, was the son of an Irish carpenter who settled on "Cork Hill" in Roxbury. Tobin has the distinction of having been one of Boston's youngest mayors, and was governor of Massachusetts at forty-three. Daniel J. Tobin, Irish-born wagon driver who came to Massachusetts as a boy of fifteen, was the leader of the teamsters' union and a power in the Democratic party for many years. It is also true that Irish names have not been missing from the list of labor racketeers who use their unions for personal profit, and the International Longshoreman's Association was suspended by the American Federation of Labor in 1953 because of alleged collusion between dockworkers and New York gangsters.

Chapter XXI

Business and the Professions

In MARY ANTIN's PHRASE, the biography of many self-made Americans "smells of the steerage." From ditchdigger to merchant, lawyer, banker, or doctor in two or three generations, and sometimes in one, is the record of many Irish-Americans who helped build America. The *Dictionary of American Biography* contains many Irish names, both Catholic and Protestant, and five volumes of the *Catholic Builders of the Nation* provides additional names of successful American Irishmen from all walks of life.[1] Although some Irishmen have failed to rise in the economic and social scale, the majority belong to the great American middle class whose achievements are seldom recorded, and an appreciable number have risen to positions of genuine distinction.

Many Irishmen who began their careers in the United States as bosses of Irish section gangs became contractors, business men, and bankers. Irishmen have been especially prominent in the building trades, and ambitious Irish bricklayers and masons quickly aspired to becoming the bosses of Irish crews who built roads, canals, sewers, and gas lines. Thomas Costigan, a Philadelphia Irishman from county Tipperary, became a railroad contractor. John B. McDonald arrived in New York with his father in 1847, and the elder McDonald rose quickly from day laborer to contractor, alderman, and loyal Tammany brave. The son got his first job because of his father's political connections, learned how to build railroads and tunnels, and constructed stretches of the Illinois Central, the Baltimore and Ohio, and a New York subway. When he was buried after a funeral from St. Patrick's Cathedral in 1911, all power was shut off on the subways for two minutes in his honor. John Daniel Crimmins not only built skyscrapers, but wrote Irish-American history as well. Born of Irish parents in New York City, the boy began work with his father's construction firm. During his long career as a capitalist and contractor, he erected over four hundred buildings, built miles of streets, viaducts, and gas lines, paved Broadway, laid much of the elevated-railway mileage, and did the tunneling for underground

[1] C. E. McGuire (ed.), *Catholic Builders of the Nation.*

electric wires. An ardent Democrat, Catholic, and Irish nationalist, he is remembered by historians of immigration for his useful *Irish-American Miscellany* (1905) and his two volumes on *St. Patrick's Day—Its Celebration in New York and Other American Places, 1737–1845* (1902).[2] Daniel Foley of county Kerry, who came to the United States at the age of seventeen, moved from railroad laborer to foreman, roadmaster, and head of a construction company. Michael J. Mahony, active in the Clan-na-Gael for nearly half a century, was a well-known New York builder and contractor. Lawrence O'Brien of Tipperary, Civil War veteran and Fenian, was a mason contractor in New Haven. William Charles Kinsella, second-generation New York Irishman, built sewers, waterworks, and reservoirs and argued for the feasibility of a bridge across the East River to Brooklyn.[3]

Business attracted many Irishmen. John F. Sweeney, a draper's apprentice in Ireland, was the owner of a department store in Buffalo.[4] George Allen entered the millinery and silk goods business in Philadelphia after the Civil War and became a director of the Atlantic City National Bank. John Dignon, who arrived in 1856, was a wholesale grocer in New York, and Michael J. Dohan, a wholesaler of tobacco. Thomas Gray, a colonel in the Civil War from Kaskaskia, Illinois, worked in lead mines, operated steamboats, and was successful in the lumber and steel business. Michael W. Norton, who came to Massachusetts with his father in 1887, launched a livery business with one horse and wagon, and eventually owned taxicab companies in several eastern cities.[5] Thomas B. Fitzgerald as a boy earned two dollars a week. He eventually became a partner in one of Boston's largest wholesale dry goods houses.

Dennis Coghlin died in 1900 as one of the highly respected citizens of Toledo, Ohio. He had come to America as a boy of sixteen with his father, Timothy Coghlin, who had found a temporary job in a stone quarry in Montreal before crossing the St. Lawrence into the United States. Father and son joined the westward movement as members of a construction gang on the Erie and Kalamazoo Railroad. Young Dennis' first job in Toledo was grading the city streets. During a long and extraordinarily successful business career, he dealt in furs, dry goods, boots and shoes, and hardware, published a newspaper, and finally settled in

2 Edward J. McGuire, "A Memoir of John D. Crimmins," *Journal of the American Irish Historical Society*, XVII (1918), 9–25.

3 Herbert D. A. Donovan, "William C. Kinsella," *Journal of the American Irish Historical Society*, XXI (1922), 146–53; also Mrs. Charles F. Oswald, "Captain Lawrence O'Brien, 1842–1923," *Journal of the American Irish Historical Society*, XXIII (1924), 133–43.

4 See note in *Journal of the American Irish Historical Society*, XII (1912–13), 359–60.

5 See note in *Journal of the American Irish Historical Society*, XXVI (1927), 361.

the brewing business. He invested heavily in real estate, owned stock in nearly every bank in Toledo, and when he died at eighty, the *Toledo Blade* called him the only multimillionaire in the city.

Perhaps the most successful Irish-American business tycoons were William R. Grace, Alexander T. Stewart, and James Butler. Grace's first job in America was in a New York restaurant. From that humble beginning, he rose to become the builder of W. R. Grace and Co. and the founder of the Grace Steamship line. He supplied the material for Peru's railroads and virtually took over the national debt of that country in return for enormous concessions, developed business relations with most of Latin America, and exploited its mineral resources. In 1880, the "Pirate of Peru," as he was known in some quarters, became the first Catholic mayor of New York with the help of "Honest John" Kelly of Tammany. He left millions when he died, and among other benefactions, founded Grace Institute to train girls in stenography, home economics, and dressmaking. Stewart, "the lucky Irishman," in less than twenty years after leaving Ireland became the proprietor of the finest store in the world of his time and the owner of vast real estate in New York. Butler came to the United States at twenty, virtually penniless. He worked on farms and in hotels, saved two thousand dollars, and entered the grocery business. He was the founder of the James Butler Grocery Company, the first great chain-store system in the United States.

Irishmen have been equally successful in banking. Edward O'Neill, who came from Kilkenny in 1837, was a bank president in Milwaukee and mayor of that city in 1863. Eugene Kelly, whose father was ruined by the Irish rebellion of 1798, entered the dry goods business in New York and San Francisco, invested in banks, railroads, shipping and other activities, and became a multimillionaire. William Wilson Corcoran, son of Baltimore Irish parents, started as a dry goods merchant, became a banker and broker in Washington, and built the Corcoran Gallery of Art in the national capital. He gave generously to many causes and institutions and financed the removal of the body of John Howard Payne, composer of "Home, Sweet Home," [6] from Africa to the United States.

Patrick Qualey, who began life with pick and shovel in the coal mines of Illinois, became a wealthy banker and cattleman in Wyoming. Andrew Carney, who came to Boston in 1816, manufactured men's clothes and retired thirty years later as one of the wealthiest citizens of Massachusetts. James Phelan of county Queen's started as a grocery

[6] Lord, Sexton, and Harrington, *History of the Archdiocese of Boston*, III, 403.

clerk in New York, became a banker and builder in San Francisco, and left an estate estimated at $7,500,000. John Flannery, whose family was ruined by the famine and the rebellion of 1848, was a successful cotton broker in Georgia and president of the Cotton Exchange. Joseph Tagert of county Tyrone was president of the Farmers and Mechanics Bank of Philadelphia for forty years. Bernard Rafferty, born in 1812 in New York of Irish parents and apprenticed to a sheet-iron worker in Philadelphia at sixteen, organized the Mechanics' Insurance Company in 1854 and established and managed thirty-five building and loan associations with a total capital of $15,000,000. Samuel Sloan, a New York Irish boy, lost his father when he was fourteen. In 1867, he was president of the Delaware, Lackawanna and Western Railroad. Richard C. Kerens, a mule driver in the Civil War, got a mail contract after the war from the Pony Express, became a railroad builder with headquarters in St. Louis, and owned mines and lumber in West Virginia. From 1884 to 1900, he was Republican National Committeeman from Missouri and a generous contributor to the party's campaign funds.

Mining seems to have had a special appeal for adventurous Irishmen. In and around Butte, Montana, Irishmen furnished most of the labor in the copper fields and developed a sizable Irish-American community. A few struck it rich. Marcus Daly, for example, played an important role in developing the Anaconda Silver Mine and the Anaconda Copper Mining Company, with its many subsidiaries, during the latter part of the last century. Daly made millions and fought bitterly for control of his enterprises. Dennis Sullivan, another prosperous miner, became a banker and cattle breeder in Wyoming. John W. MacKay, who came to the United States in 1840 and was apprenticed to a shipbuilder, became a prospector in California and Nevada and led the party which uncovered the Comstock silver lode. A millionaire almost overnight, he invested in many businesses and, in 1886, organized the Postal Telegraph Company. William Shoney O'Brien, who clerked in a New York store and ran a saloon in San Francisco during the Gold Rush, struck it rich in "Big Bonanza" in Nevada. Dennis Sheedy, one of twelve children, mined in Montana, freighted in Utah, bought cattle in Texas, was a banker in Denver, and became president of the Globe Smelting and Refining Company and the founder of Globeville, Colorado.[7]

Edward Creighton, pioneer builder of telegraph lines in the Middle West, and Edward L. Doheny, the oil magnate, were American-born children of Irish parents. Martin Maloney, whose parents fled to Penn-

---

[7] For these sketches, see *DAB*. For successful Irish capitalists in California, see Hugh Quigley, *The Irish Race in California*, Chapters XXI and XXII.

sylvania during the famine of 1848, advanced from clerking in a grocery to the plumbing and gas lighting business, and invented a gasoline burner for street lamps. In 1882, he helped organize the United Gas and Improvement Company of Philadelphia. Particularly generous with his charities, he built a home for the aged in Scranton and a chemistry laboratory for the Catholic University of America, and was made a papal chamberlain.

A number of Irish-Americans distinguished themselves in the history of American inventions. Humphrey O'Sullivan originated the rubber heel. John Robert Gregg, from Rockcorry, Ireland, perfected the Gregg system of shorthand. John Good, whom his widowed mother brought from Ireland to New York, became a ropemaker and a machinist, owned several plants in the United States and England for the manufacture of cord, and held over a hundred patents related to spinning and ropemaking. Michael Hicks, a native of county Meath, invented the "Hurricane lamp" for railroaders. Patrick Bernard Delaney, who was educated in Hartford, Connecticut's parochial schools, obtained some one hundred and fifty patents for electricity, the telegraph, cables, and submarine detection and won the medal of the Franklin Institute.

W J McGee, who stubbornly defended his right to use his initials without punctuation, was well known in the fields of anthropology, geography, and conservation. His father came from Ireland and worked in the lead mines of Galena, Illinois, before turning to farming. McGee was born in Iowa in 1853. His wife, a schoolteacher from Kentucky, taught him to write. Among other things, W J read through Webster's unabridged dictionary several times. McGee made a geological and topographical survey of Iowa, became chairman of the editorial board of the *National Geographic* and editor of the *American Anthropologist,* and until 1903 was the chief ethnologist for the United States Bureau of Ethnology. He worked closely with Gifford Pinchot in the field of conservation and is credited with having written Theodore Roosevelt's message of 1903 urging the creation of a national forest reserve in the Appalachians. McGee also was primarily responsible for the plans for the Inland Waterways Commission and served as secretary of the National Conservation Commission.[8]

James J. Wood of county Cork became a mechanical engineer, patented an arc-light dynamo in 1880, and took out over two hundred additional patents in the electrical field. Michael Cudahy of county Kilkenny went to work in the meat-packing business in Milwaukee as a boy of fourteen,

[8] Whitney R. Cross, "W J McGee and the Idea of Conservation," *The Historian,* XV (1952–53), 148–62.

became head of the Cudahy Packing Company, and developed the process for the summer curing of meats under refrigeration. John Philip Holland, educated in a Christian Brothers' school in Limerick, came to America in 1873. He built the first successful submarine in the United States. Fenians, hoping for a quick way to sink the British navy, financed his first experiments with underwater craft. Michael Maurice O'Shaughnessy, a Dublin-trained engineer, was city engineer for San Francisco from 1912 to 1932, and built the water works to bring water to the city from Yosemite National Park. James O'Farrel, another engineer from Dublin who settled in California in 1843, was the surveyor who laid out much of San Francisco.

If the Irish have not been especially outstanding in the field of science and invention, they took eagerly to law and brought to the legal profession the same genial character traits that made them so successful in other fields of public relations. Irish immigrants had no language barrier to overcome on their way to admittance to the American bar. A century ago, one simply "read law" and had relatively few educational requirements to meet. Many Irish immigrants prepared for a law career while temporarily employed at other tasks. Lawyers trained in Ireland and admitted to practice in the United States advertised in the Irish-American press as specialists in Irish jurisprudence in cases involving inheritances and titles to real estate, which often were of special importance to recently arrived immigrants.

John Cunneen, whose family was ruined by the Irish famine, came to the United States as a boy of fourteen with forty dollars of borrowed money. He worked as a farm laborer, a machinist, and a carpenter before he completed his legal studies. He practiced successfully in Buffalo and, in 1903, became attorney general of New York State.[9] Matt O'Doherty was a prominent lawyer of Louisville. His first job in the United States was pushing a truck in a freight depot. Patrick E. C. Lally, who arrived penniless as a boy of eighteen, worked in a grocery in Chicago while studying law. Martin Jerome Keogh, of Wexford, a lawyer and judge in New York, entered the profession by way of reporting for the New York *Herald*. Patrick Henry Byrne came to New York with his mother in 1849 and was a marble cutter and traveling salesman before he became a lawyer. Patrick J. McCarthy, an orphan whose parents died in quarantine in Boston in 1850, was the ward of a Catholic society of Boston. He became a protégé of Charles Eliot Norton of Harvard and was admitted to Harvard Law School in 1876.[10]

9 McGuire (ed.), *The Democratic Party of New York*, II, 426–28.

10 T. Z. Lee, "Hon. Patrick J. McCarthy," *Journal of the American Irish Historical Society*, XX (1921), 97–100.

There is hardly an American city without its quota of distinguished Irish-American members of the bar. Many have specialized in criminal law. During the last half of the nineteenth century, Dennis Dougherty was one of Philadelphia's outstanding lawyers, politicians, and silver-tongued orators. James T. Brady and Charles O'Conor were giants of the New York bar. Both were the sons of Irish immigrants. O'Conor's father was one of the "men of '98," and the son began his career in America as an apprentice to a lamp-black manufacturer at the age of twelve. At twenty, he was a lawyer. He practiced for half a century and was one of the highest-priced attorneys in New York. It was O'Conor who said, "In worn out, king-ridden Europe, men must stay where they are born. But in America, a man is accounted a failure, and certainly ought to be, who has not risen above his father's station in life." [11] Despite his unusual success, he continued to feel that being an Irish Catholic was "a most serious political, social and professional disadvantage." [12] Richard O'Gorman, a prominent corporation lawyer in New York, was a popular Irish-American orator. Among Boston's Irish lawyers, Patrick A. Collins, Charles F. Connelly, counsel for the Roman Catholic Church, and Thomas Gargan were outstanding, and Gargan became speaker of the Massachusetts legislature. Dr. W. J. O. Sullivan, who came to the United States as a young man of twenty-five and studied law and medicine at Yale, became a well-known medico-legal expert in the field of criminology.[13]

With their training in law and their skill as politicians, many Irish lawyers found the road to judgeships fairly easy. Thomas Burke, son of New York Irish immigrants, practiced law for fifty years in Seattle, defended the Chinese during the riots of 1886, and was a probate judge. John Belton O'Neall, son of an Irish grocer and saloonkeeper, became chief justice of the South Carolina Supreme Court in 1859. James Vincent Coffey, a San Francisco judge, published *Coffey's Probate Reports* in six volumes, from 1894 to 1916. John Erskine, educated in Ireland, was appointed to a federal judgeship by President Johnson. Charles Patrick Daly, second-generation New York Irish, was an able legal scholar who served on the common pleas bench for forty-two years. Timothy David Hurley, a Chicago judge, pioneered in juvenile court work and edited *The Juvenile Court Record*. John W. Goff, an ardent Fenian from county Wexford and a New York judge, was active in exposing political corruption in the late 1890's. Constantine Joseph Smyth, who worked as a

[11] Quoted in Eric F. Goldman, *Rendezvous With Destiny,* 9.

[12] J. C. Walsh, "Charles O'Conor," *Journal of the American Irish Historical Society,* XXVII (1928), 285–313; and *DAB.*

[13] *The Gaelic-American* (New York), January 29, 1921.

railroad laborer in Nebraska before he was admitted to the bar, was appointed chief justice of the Court of Appeals for the District of Columbia by President Wilson in 1917.[14]

Irishmen have been less prominent in medicine, but as early as the 1850's, Irish physicians in New York formed their own medical organization, probably because, as foreigners, they were not admitted to the societies and hospitals of native American doctors. The name of Thomas Addis Emmet was outstanding among Irish-American doctors. His grandfather was a refugee of 1798, and his father a member of Jefferson's faculty at the University of Virginia. Emmet was a well-known surgeon and gynecologist who published many medical articles, as well as a volume on *The Principles and Practise of Gynecology* in 1879. He collected American prints, was an active Irish nationalist, and wrote two volumes on *Ireland under English Rule*. As a convert to Catholicism after the Civil War, he was especially honored by the Pope.

John Benjamin Murphy, an Irish farm boy from Wisconsin, became a distinguished abdominal surgeon. He made substantial contributions to his specialty, held professorships in several medical schools, and was president of the American Medical Association in 1910. The Murphy Hospital of Chicago perpetuates his name. Dr. Joseph O'Dwyer, American-born son of Irish immigrants, was the first to use intubation of the larynx in diptheria cases.[15] Patrick Sarsfield Donnellan of Limerick was associate editor of the Philadelphia *Medical Times* and a contributor to the famous London *Lancet*.

A number of Irish physicians made reputations in the literary field. Robert Dwyer Joyce of Boston wrote ballads about the Emerald Isle. John O'Kane Murray of Brooklyn and Chicago published *A Popular History of the Catholic Church in the United States* in 1876. Denis Mulcahy, a Newark, New Jersey, physician, had been a journalist in Dublin.[16] Edmund Bailey O'Callaghan is honored by historians for his two-volume *History of New Netherland* and his multivolumed documentary history of colonial and early New York. A native of Mallow, Ireland, he had been trained in Europe for a medical career. After the Canadian rebellion of 1837, in which he was deeply involved, he escaped to Albany to begin his notable work of calendaring and editing historical manuscripts.

[14] See *DAB*; Arthur F. Mullen, "Judge Constantine Joseph Smyth," *Journal of the American Irish Historical Society*, XXIV (1925), 246–48, 274–78; Alexander Pope, "Chief Justice Timothy D. Hurley," *Journal of the American Irish Historical Society*, XXV (1926), 307–14.
[15] *Catholic Encyclopedia*, VIII, 143.
[16] O'Leary, *Recollections of Fenians and Fenianism*, I, 114.

The Irish, a highly imaginative people, are also well represented in the field of art, from the craft of sign painters to artists of reputation with studios in the larger art centers of the United States. In the early nineteenth century, the United States had a number of itinerant Irish portrait painters eagerly soliciting commissions. Charles C. Ingham, a Dublin painter and a founder of New York's Academy of Design, made his living before the Civil War by painting the belles of New York society. George Peter Alexander Healy, son of an Irish sea captain, painted "Webster Replying to Hayne" for Fanueil Hall and "Franklin Urging the Claims of the American Colonies upon Louis XVI." [17] Peter Duggan did portraits in crayon and occasionally in oil and taught at the New York Academy. James O'Malley, son of a shopkeeper and farmer in county Mayo, did a portrait of Bishop Hughes in 1853. William J. Hennessy from Kilkenny was best known as a book illustrator, although he also did oils and watercolors. James Hamilton did the illustrations for a life of John Paul Jones, Coleridge's *Ancient Mariner,* and other books. John Nevins of Dublin was one of the first illustrators for *Harper's Weekly.* Thomas Hovenden, an Irish orphan, came to America during the Civil War and studied art in New York and Paris. His "The Last Moments of John Brown" hangs in the Metropolitan Museum of New York. John Kane was a well-known Irish-American painter of landscapes who had been a miner in Galway and a steel worker in Pennsylvania. As an eccentric house painter, he loved to dangle on sky-hooks from tall buildings. Near the end of his life, he began to send his paintings to art exhibits. When he died of tuberculosis in 1934, his paintings were on exhibit in several museums of modern art. Patrick Moran and his four sons were a notable family of artists. One son concentrated on marines; another was an animal painter. Jeremiah O'Rourke, trained in design in Ireland, became a well-known architect in the United States. Louis Henri Sullivan, one of the greatest of American architects, had a wandering Irish musician and dancing teacher for a father.

Laurent Thompson, a native of county Queen's, was a sculptor of distinction. John Donaghue, born in Chicago of immigrant parents, is best known for his "Boxer," which he did for an exhibition in Boston in 1881 as a tribute to his hero, John L. Sullivan, the noted Irish heavyweight champion. Martin Millmore of county Sligo made busts of prominent Bostonians, as well as many monuments, including the Soldier and Sailors Monument on the Boston Common, which set a pattern of doubtful artistic merit for other local Civil War memorials throughout

[17] Lord, Sexton, and Harrington, *History of the Archdiocese of Boston,* II, 343-44.

the land. Charles Mulligan, who came to the United States at seventeen and worked as a stonecutter in Illinois, became a protégé of the sculptor Lorado Taft. Denis B. Sheehan taught at Yale and made sun dials and equestrian statues. Both the French and the Irish claim Augustus Saint-Gaudens, the greatest sculptor of them all. His father was a French shoemaker; his mother, Mary McGuinness, the daughter of a plaster-mill employee in Dublin. The family moved to Boston six months after the future sculptor was born, and then on to New York, where the father made shoes and the son was apprenticed to a cameo-cutter.[18]

There have been many Irish musicians and bandmasters, but Patrick Gilmore and Victor Herbert outrank all others in their contributions to American music. Gilmore was born near Dublin. He was intended for the priesthood but turned to band music instead. He came to the United States at nineteen, and a week after his arrival in Boston was the leader of a band. During the Civil War, he recruited and trained army bands and, after the war, gave concerts in Boston, New York, and other cities. He was known as the greatest bandmaster of his time, both at home and abroad. Combining showmanship with musical ability, he directed such gigantic musical festivals as the National Peace Jubilee in Boston in 1869 and the World Peace Jubilee of 1872, with mammoth bands and "tornado choruses," the firing of cannon, the ringing of church bells, and fifty firemen beating out the "Anvil Chorus" on fifty anvils. Gilmore composed many dance pieces, marches, and songs, and wrote the words for "When Johnny Comes Marching Home." He was an intimate friend of Patrick Ford of *The Irish World* and gave frequent concerts for the benefit of the Land League and other Irish causes.[19]

Victor Herbert was the greater musician, and his compositions will live long after Gilmore has been forgotten. Herbert was born in Dublin. His mother was the daughter of the Irish novelist Samuel Lover, who also wrote Irish songs. Herbert received his musical education in Germany and Austria and married the prima donna of the Vienna Opera. He began his career in the United States as a cellist with symphony orchestras and then became a conductor. He composed an amazing number of musical pieces, from songs to grand opera, and for piano, bands, and orchestras. He wrote the scores for several of Ziegfeld's Follies, as well as incidental music for movies, but he is best known for his light operas. Herbert belonged to many Irish-American societies

---

[18] For these and other Irish artists, see *DAB; The Irish World* (New York), February 9, 1895; William Dunlap, *The Arts of Design in the United States;* and Walter G. Strickland, *A Dictionary of Irish Artists.*

[19] *DAB* and *The Irish World* (New York), September 3, October 1, 1892.

and was completely identified with the cause of Ireland. He was president of the Friendly Sons of St. Patrick and of the Friends of Irish Freedom. He attended St. Patrick's Day banquets to direct the orchestra in Irish airs. He composed his "Irish Rhapsody" for a *Feis Ceoil* of the Gaelic Society of New York, and during World War I, when Irish-Americans were pressing hard for Irish independence, Herbert completed a romantic opera, *Hearts of Erin,* which opened in Cleveland on January 1, 1917. The piece had its setting in the Irish insurrection of 1798.

Finally, brief mention must be made of the activity of the Irish in the field of American education. In colonial days and later, the itinerant Irish schoolmaster was a well-known figure, and the number of Irish teachers multiplied rapidly with the expansion in Irish immigration after the War of 1812. Many early Irish schoolmasters were exiles who had taught school in their homeland. In the United States, they scattered over the country from the Atlantic seaboard to the Mississippi Valley. Perhaps the majority were Protestant Irishmen, but some were Roman Catholics who advertised their profession and their schools in early Catholic papers like *The Truth Teller.* Some flogged their pupils more than they taught them, kept a bottle in their desk, and failed to appear on Blue Monday.

Apparently teachers were employed without much investigation of either their moral character, their knowledge, or their skill as pedagogues. Their pay was wretched—teachers often had to accept grain in lieu of money—they were "boarded around," and were expected to supplement their salaries by menial labor. Some remained for the entire school term of two or three months; other "vagrant foreign masters," as Governor John Wentworth of New Hampshire called them, disappeared to parts unknown in the middle of the term. Some were indentured servants who were sold as "excellent teachers." Almost any craftsman brought a higher price. Nevertheless, a number of these miserably treated and wretchedly underpaid Irish schoolmasters made a contribution in a time when education was at a low level. Some tutored famous Americans such as Roger B. Taney, who described one of his early tutors as "an Irishman, a ripe scholar and an amiable and accomplished man." [20] The names of most of the early Irish pedagogues have

[20] For details, see Purcell, "Schools and Early Irish Teachers in New Hampshire," *The Catholic Educational Review,* XXXII (1934), 608–10; Purcell, "Education and Irish Teachers in Colonial Maryland," *The Catholic Educational Review,* XXXII (1934), 133–143; Purcell, "Education and Irish Schoolmasters in Maryland's National Period," *The Catholic Educational Review,* XXXII (1934), 198–207; Purcell, "Irish Cultural Contribution to Early New York," *The Catholic Educational Review,* XXXV (1937), 449–60, XXXVI

been forgotten, and in many cases, their students were not eager to keep their memory green. In later years, the Irish found opportunities to teach in the rapidly growing parochial schools, but a much larger number have been devoted and able teachers in the public schools.

A few Irish names deserve special mention in the history of American education. Bernard Kearney, who came from Dublin in 1822, taught school in America for sixty years. He was an expert penman and established one of the first institutes for penmanship, bookkeeping, and stenography.[21] Cornelius Mahoney who was blind and taught vocal and instrumental music in New York, invented a system of piano instruction similar to Braille.[22] Edward Roth, who emigrated in 1847, founded the Broad Street Academy, a Catholic boys' school in Philadelphia, and published several textbooks. John Oliver's Hibernian Free School was established in Baltimore specifically for Irish-American children. The Fenian John O'Donovan taught classics in St. Louis. Cornelius Conway Felton, who was born in Newbury, Massachusetts, of Irish parents in 1807, taught Greek literature at Harvard.

Irish nuns have played an important role in convent schools and colleges scattered throughout the country, and some proved to be educators of unusual ability and administrative talent. Sister Julia (1827–1901), among others, earned a place in the *Dictionary of American Biography*. Her father, a farmer in county Donegal, was a railroad contractor in the United States and left ten children when he died in 1838. Sister Julia was educated by nuns and became a teacher, a mother superior, and a builder of Catholic schools. The latter included an institution for free Negroes, a school in Rittenhouse Square in Philadelphia, and an orphanage in California. She also was largely responsible for the building of Trinity College for women, at the gates of the Catholic University of America, a project which many leaders of the Church opposed.

Thomas Hunter, an Anglican "Young Irelander" and rebel from Belfast, came to New York in 1850. Here he distinguished himself as an educational pioneer and reformer. He opposed corporal punishment, favored tenure rights for teachers and a better teacher-training program, edited several texts, advocated adult education, and pleaded for greater educational opportunities for women. In 1914, Hunter College, one of

(1938), 28–42; Purcell, "Rhode Island's Early Schools and Irish Teachers," *The Catholic Educational Review*, 402–15; and Michael J. O'Brien, "Early Irish Schoolmasters in New England," *The Catholic Historical Review*, III (1918), 52–71.

21 W. H. Mahony, "The Irish Element in Newark, N. J.," *Journal of the American Irish Historical Society*, XXI (1922), 131–45.

22 Herbert D. A. Donovan, "Cornelius Mahoney," *Journal of the American Irish Historical Society*, XXI (1922), 154–56.

New York's four city colleges, was named in his honor. Charles McCarthy, though not a member of any school system, distinguished himself by pioneering in another field which also was highly educational. He was born in Brockton, Massachusetts, the son of Irish immigrants, and as a youngster, ran off to sea. He worked on docks and in factories, was a stage carpenter in a Bowery theatre, and a football star at Brown. He finished his graduate work at the University of Wisconsin and became an able historian and political scientist. He is remembered primarily for the Legislative Reference Bureau which he founded at Madison, Wisconsin, to help legislators draft bills in a scientific manner. Through the bureau, McCarthy influenced much of the progressive legislation in the years when Wisconsin was a unique laboratory for political experimentation, and in due time, other states, as well as the federal government, copied McCarthy's "bill factory."

Irishmen have been prominent in the administration of many parochial school systems and Catholic institutions of higher learning in America. Such universities as Fordham, Notre Dame, and Holy Cross have been predominantly Irish in faculty and student body. Thomas Galberry, whose family came to Philadelphia from Ireland in 1836, became rector of Villanova in 1872 and later served as bishop of Hartford. Maurice F. Egan, a prominent Irish-American journalist, was professor of English at Notre Dame and at the Catholic University of America. Brother Philip (John Eagen), who worked as a "breaker" boy in the coal mines at the age of ten, was president of St. Thomas College in Scranton in 1919. Brother Azarias, from Tipperary, was president of Rock Hill College in Maryland. Bishop Denis Joseph O'Connell, a native of county Cork, became the third rector of the Catholic University of America in 1903. Thomas O'Gorman, a second-generation Irishman from Boston, was a professor of Church history and wrote the volume on the Roman Catholics for the *American Church History Series*. Peter Guilday, son of Irish parents who settled in Pennsylvania, was a prolific scholar in the field of history who directed the Catholic Historical Association in its early days and edited *The Catholic Historical Review*.[23]

[23] John Tracy Ellis, "Peter Guilday," *The Catholic Historical Review*, XXXIII (1947), 257–68.

CHAPTER XXII

In Song and Story

Every Irish youngster grows up on fairy tales and the saga of his beloved Ireland. He learns them from his mother's lips and at his mother's knee. Ireland is a land of miracles and pilgrimages to holy places where religion and poetry blend. It is a land where people have lived close to a Nature that is both cruel and kind, where they love the sea and the hills, and where they observe customs and superstitions that go far back to pagan times. It is a land of bonfires on the hills, rollicking fairs, fights, and wakes; a land of romance, gayety, and melancholy. It is a land where people are proud of their own kind and cherish the ballads of the ancient bards and tales that are centuries old. Whenever Irishmen meet, they sing the old songs, and, wherever they are, they bequeath to their children and their children's children the folklore of their island home.

The Irish who came to America more than a century ago cherished the songs and the dances of their native land. But, like every great folk movement, Irish immigration also produced its own literature. Irish music, Irish poetry, and Irish stories are popular with Americans who have never seen Ireland and who readily accept the Irish-American stereotype which such portrayals of the Irish represent. The Irish immigration furnished a new field for American novelists, and sentimental Irish songs, "made in America," became a profitable source of income for the tunesmiths of Tin Pan Alley.

Irishmen love the "merry dance," "the ring of the piper's tune," and the Irish fiddler, who is necessary to every social occasion. Irish dances became popular in America and were used even in the programs of blackface minstrels. The music and steps were so unique that the dance became known as the "Irish jig." It remained the favorite of Irish dancers, but the reel, the hornpipe, and the country dance also were popular. In the old Five Points and Greenwich Village districts of New York, Irish square dances were popular before 1850 and were performed to such tunes as "The Priest of the Parish," and "The Irish Washerwoman." To this day, prizes are offered at Irish-American picnics for jigging, eight-hand reels, and other Irish dances. As long as a century ago, the Irish-

American press introduced Americans to such old sentimental favorites as the "Rose of Tralee." [1]

Most songs about Irish immigrants are songs of farewell to their loved, lost island and songs of hope for a bright future across the sea. The familiar "The Wearing of the Green" closes with the lines,

> I've heard whispers of a country that lies far beyond
> the sea,
> Where rich and poor stand equal in the light of
> freedom's day. [2]

And in the "Lament of the Irish Emigrant" we learn of a land where

> They say there's bread and work for all,
> And the sun shines always there. [3]

Irishmen never forgot the relief ships that brought food from the United States in the dark days of famine. "Erin, Repeal and Liberty," recounted the persecution and suffering under English rule and expressed the Irishman's gratitude to the United States in the stanza,

> But there's a bright land where the sun goes to bed,
> That talked sweet relief in her beef, meat and bread,
> And the stars of Columbia ne'er glistened so braw,
> As when wet wid her tears for poor Erin go bragh. [4]

"The Irish Girl's Lament" recalled melancholy days when famine drove Irishmen on "red hot" packets from "Erin's flowery vale" across the "Western Ocean" to "Columbia's shore." [5] Carl Sandburg found songs of the Irish famine which had penetrated the corn belt of the Middle West shortly after the middle of the last century, and Irish tunes like "Erin's Green Shore" and "Erin's Lovely Home" are part of the folksong treasures of the Ozarks. [6]

In 1840, Joseph Le Fanu wrote the famous ballad about "Shamus O'Brien," in which the hero of 1798 cheated the scaffold with the connivance of a priest who loosened the rope as he said his last prayers over the doomed man. The original version of the ballad contained no reference to America, but so traditional was the connection between Irish refugees and the harbor of hope in the United States that when Samuel

[1] For Irish music, see P. W. Joyce, *Old Irish Folk Music and Songs.*
[2] *Wehman's Irish Song Book,* 90; also 25.
[3] *The Song Book for the Million,* Part III, 183–84.
[4] *Ibid.,* 5–7.
[5] See William M. Doerflinger, *Shantymen and Shantyboys,* 317–19; and other examples in Mary O. Eddy, *Ballads and Songs from Ohio,* 319.
[6] Carl Sandburg, *The American Song Bag,* 36–43; and Vance Randolph, *Ozark Folksongs,* I, 75–76, 356–57; III, 236–37; 474.

Lover in 1846 recited "Shamus O'Brien" on a lecture tour in this country, he added lines that brought the hero to America:

> He has mounted his horse, an' soon he will be,
> In America, darlint, the land of the free.

The poem made such an appeal to exiled Irishmen who heard him recite it that Lover has been mistakenly credited with authorship of the entire ballad.[7]

Irishmen recounted many of their American experiences in song. "Paddy on the Canal" told the story of an Irishman who liked his work and loved a boss who dispensed good whiskey and "was father now unto us all."[8] In 1855, the New York *Citizen* published a poem dedicated to "The Poor Irish Maid" who toils and saves to bring her family to America.[9] There also was a song entitled "No Irish Need Apply."[10] Boston's Denis A. McCarthy, who wrote "Sweet is Tipperary in the Spring," also published "The Land Where Hate Must Die," a plea for an American patriotism in which there would be no room for nativism and bigotry. The song "Billy O'Rourke" recounted the perils of the Atlantic crossing,[11] and "Tim Flaherty," copyrighted in 1876, told the story of a light-hearted Irish lad of eighteen and his unhappy experience with an immigrant runner.[12] "I Left Ireland and Mother Because We Were Poor" closed with a reference to "a neat little cot on America's shore" to which the happy immigrant promised to bring his family.[13] Songs like "Maggie Murphy's Home" were strictly American creations, developed from the folklore of the New York tenements.

Songs of success were popular, although through many of them there ran a note of homesickness.

> I've left Ballymornack a long way behind me
> To better my fortune, I've crossed the big sea,

recounted a stanza of "Nora McShane," but the poem continued with

> But I'm sadly alone, not a creature to mind me,
> And faith, I'm as wretched as wretched can be.

The writer sighed for his Nora, the beautiful hills and the "Emerald plain," and fresh Irish buttermilk.[14]

[7] See S. M. Ellis, *William Collins Le Fanu and Others*, 151.
[8] *Song Book for the Million*, Part III, 81–83.
[9] *The Citizen* (New York), November 10, 1855.
[10] *Wehman's Irish Song Book*, 51.
[11] Eddy, *Ballads and Songs*, 311.
[12] Philip D. Jordan and Lillian Kessler, *Songs of Yesterday*, 203–204.
[13] *Wehman's Irish Song Book*, 63.
[14] *Song Book for the Million*, Part III, 135–36.

There was real pathos in the song about "Pat Malloy," an Irishman who could not overcome his nostalgia for Ireland:

> From Ireland to America
> Across the seas I roam,
> And every shilling that I got,
> Ah, sure, I sent it home.
> Me mother couldn't write, but, ah,
> There came from Father Boyce:
> "Oh, heaven bless you, Pat!" says she—
> I hear me mother's voice.[15]

Irish songs enjoyed their greatest vogue in America in the period from 1860 to 1900. By that time, Irish laborers had risen far enough on the social ladder so that George M. Cohan could sing in "Harrigan":

> Proud of all the Irish blood that's in me,
> Divil a man can say a word agin me.

Nevertheless, as one song had it, to live in "me bran' brownstone manshin in Fifth Av'noo over th' way/The Cathedral round Th' corner, an' the Lord Archbishop to tay," still left the Irishman sighing for "Shanahan's Ould Shebeen." [16] "Has Anybody Here Seen Kelly?"—one of the last of the Irish songs which enjoyed national popularity—told the story of a Michael Kelly of Cork who lost his sweetheart in the crowds of New York City. When the lady sang the song during a St. Patrick's Day parade, "five hundred Kellys" stepped out of the ranks to claim her as their own.[17]

The devotion of Irish immigrants and their offspring to the island of their origin was responsible for scores of patriotic songs dedicated to Ireland's struggle for freedom. "The Manchester Martyrs," "Home Rule for Ireland," "My Emmet's No More," and "Oh, Breathe Not His Name" were typical of this category of immigrant-song literature. One may judge their content by the opening lines of "God Save Ireland":

> High upon the gallows tree,
> Swung the noble-hearted three
> By the vengeful tyrant stricken in their bloom . . . .[18]

The melodies of many of these songs have long been forgotten, and one may conclude that they were recited more often than they were sung.

In 1866, John Daly, a music dealer in New York, published a collection of "Fenian War Echoes." It contained "The Fenian Girl's Song," "Step

15 *Wehman's Irish Song Book,* 109–10.
16 Mark Sullivan, *Our Times,* III, 396–97.
17 *Ibid.,* 349–50.
18 *Wehman's Irish Song Book,* 28; also 16, 31–33, 88.

Together," "Green above the Red," "The Irish Marseillaise," "The Wild Irish Boy," and "Father Drinks No More." The latter was described by the publisher as "a suitable ballad for temperance societies."[19] The song, "Poor Pat Must Emigrate," recounted the hardship of life in Ireland and ended with "If ever again I see this land, I hope it will be with a Fenian band."[20] World War I provided additional songs of this nature. One collection, "The Martyrs of Ireland," sold for twenty-five cents a copy in 1916. In 1917, the popular Irish tenor Thomas Egan sang "I Had a Dream that Ireland Was Free among the Nations of the Earth" in Carnegie Hall. Other favorites of World War I were "When Ireland is a Nation Once Again," "My Irish Home Sweet Home," and " 'Tis only a Sprig of Shamrock."[21]

Songs like "Sprig of Shillelah," "Donnybrook Fair," and "The History of Paddy Denny's Wife and His Pig" stressed the Irishman's love for fighting and drinking. Their humor was based largely upon the Celt's presumably irresistible love of whiskey. "Tim Finnigan's Wake" recounted the tale of a wild Irish wake which ended in a fight and the corpse's jumping from his bed when a gallon of whiskey was accidentally splattered over him.[22] "The Night Before Larry Was Stretched" reveals the sardonic humor of the Irish on even the grimmest occasions.[23] "Barney Brallaghan's Wedding" described the genial Father Murphy, whose behavior at the nuptial festivities fell somewhat short of the decorum expected of clergymen.

Dozens of Irish songs represent the Irish as good-natured, roistering, and brawling individuals who "get drunk, meet their friend, and for love knock him down." An old song, "St. Patrick Was a Gentleman," brought by the Irish to America, explained that

> Saint Patrick taught the happy knack of drinking
> of the whiskey,
> 'Twas he that brewed the best o' malt, and under-
> stood distilling,
> For his mother kept a sheeban shop, in the town
> of Inniskillen.[24]

Such collections of Irish comic songs as *The Barney Williams Songster* and *Collin's Irish Songster* sold well in the United States as early as the 1840's.

19 *Metropolitan Record* (New York), March 30, July 21, 1866.
20 *Wehman's Irish Song Book*, 13. For others, see *Song Book for the Million*, Part III, 12–13, 220–21; and *Hyland's Mammoth Hibernian Songster*.
21 *The Gaelic-American* (New York), September 9, 1916; April 5, 1917.
22 *Wehman's Irish Song Book*, 55.
23 *Song Book for the Million*, Part III, 166–68.
24 *The Universal Songster, or Museum of Mirth*, I, 10.

Songs of love and longing outnumbered all other categories. This is the kind of Irish music which continues to come from Tin Pan Alley, and much of it is written by Jewish song writers who have mastered the standard technique. Many Irish songs of love, courtship, and marriage are known to millions of Americans. "Killarney," "Come Back to Erin," "Moonlight on Killarney," "My Irish Molly O'," "The River Shannon," "Sweet Rosy O'Grady," and "I'll Take You Home Again, Kathleen" are part of America's treasure house of song. Some were written by composers who never saw Ireland and in whose veins there was not a drop of Irish blood. "Kathleen Mavoureen," for example, was the creation of a young Englishman, Frederick N. Crouch, who came to the United States in 1849 and fought in the Confederate army.[25] John McCormack, the greatest of the Irish tenors in the opinion of thousands of American concertgoers, for years featured "Mother Machree," a song of universal reverence for motherhood. It was written by Ernest R. Ball, a Cleveland composer who also wrote "When Irish Eyes are Smiling," which Chauncey Olcott made popular. Olcott made "My Wild Irish Rose" an American classic in 1899. American-born, but of Irish ancestry, he was billed as "America's Foremost Irish Actor." Actually, he began his stage career as a blackface minstrel and, before he turned to Irish melodies, specialized in such favorites as "When the Robins Meet Again." Olcott became the star of Irish "musicial dramas." He wrote many Irish plays and songs and had a loyal Irish following who loved the sentimental, Celtic charm of his performances. He was the last great exponent of an age of Irish-Americanism which is rapidly passing.[26]

The words and music of the songs of the sentimental Irish-American era followed a common pattern. They dealt with what the immigrant had left behind and what he missed so sorely—the song of the thrush in the hazel glen at twilight, the dark, mysterious woods, the cattle grazing on meadows of luscious green, the clear water of Ireland's many crystal streams, the Irish dawn and the eternal miracle of the dying day, the hillsides, "touched with gold"—in short, an unqualifiedly beautiful Erin, still unredeemed.

> Erin! the tear and the smile in thine eyes,
> Blend like the rainbow that hangs in the skies
> Shining through sorrow's stream,
> Sadd'ning through pleasures beam.
> Thy suns, with doubtful gleam,
> Weep while they rise.[27]

[25] *The Irish World* (New York), August 29, 1896.
[26] *DAB; The Irish World* (New York), March 7, 1896; *The Gaelic-American* (New York), February 24, 1917.
[27] *Song Book for the Million*, Part III, 178.

A prose "Irish literature" also has been developed in the United States, some of it from the pen of immigrants, much of it by others who exploited the characteristics of the Irish immigration for their literary purposes. The number of Irishmen who read and bought books in the first two decades of the immigration could not have been large. *The Irish News,* in an editorial on July 26, 1856, devoted to "Irish Literature in America," complained that fully two-thirds of the purchasers of books on Ireland or by Irish writers, here or abroad, were Americans. Judging from the advertisements in the Irish-American press of the 1850's, the market in America was not impressive. *Bits of Blarney,* a collection of legends and stories about Ireland and eccentric Irishmen, sold for one dollar.[28] Mary Anne Sadlier wrote Catholic stories for the rising Irish-American generation. They were without literary merit, but have some sociological importance for the emigrant life which they try to portray. Her *The Blakes and the Flanagans* (1855) stressed the danger to Irish Catholics from public and Protestant schools.[29] By 1860, leading Catholic bookstores in the larger cities inported books on Irish themes, but their main stock in trade continued to be religious books and devotional literature. The sale of books in the field of history and literature did not develop materially until the American-born sons and daughters of Irish immigrants had enough leisure and money to indulge their interest in the land of their fathers.

The Irish intellectuals of 1848 worked hard to stimulate their countrymen, and native Americans as well, to read books on Irish history and civilization. Unfortunately, illiteracy among the first generation was high, and much good literature was rejected because of its English and Protestant origin. As late as the 1880's, Maurice F. Egan regretted that "a large proportion of the books of fiction printed by Catholic publishers were rather anaemic. . . . Many of the books were written for the Irish immigrant of the first generation who had but recently arrived." This distinguished Irish Catholic scholar believed that the tastes of those who had arrived before 1840 were higher than the tastes of those who came after the famine years and that "the newcomers were unwilling to read anything except what concerned itself with the history of Ireland or with the history of the Church." Apparently if a publisher wanted to make money, he concentrated on "the lives of deceased bishops" or "the lives of St. Patrick and St. Brigid," and even such volumes had to be gilded and profusely illustrated in order to attract buyers.[30] In later years, the

---

28 *The Citizen* (New York), September 15, 1855.

29 See a review in *The Citizen* (New York), September 22, 1855; also C. E. McGuire (ed.), *Catholic Builders of the Nation,* IV, 190–91.

30 Egan, *Recollections,* 144; also Thomas F. Meehan, "Catholic Literary New York, 1800–1840," *The Catholic Historical Review,* IV (1919), 399–414.

books of outstanding prelates like Spalding and Gibbons, who were men of learning, enjoyed great popularity, especially in Catholic circles. Gibbons' *Faith of Our Fathers* is said to have sold over two million copies.

Any anthology of Irish-American poetry might well begin with the poems which appeared in *The Shamrock,* the first important Irish-American paper. The output continued unabated in the Irish press through the nineteenth century. For the most part, the poetic effusions of romantic Irishmen were little more than sentimental rhyming, though they revealed the poetry inherent in the soul of every Irishman. Richard Henry Wilde, distinguished student of law and literary historian who lived in the United States from 1789 to 1847, wrote many sonnets and other poems, but only "My life is like a summer rose" is still remembered, perhaps because Sidney Lanier set it to music. McGee was a prolific rhymer. Bishop Hughes wrote "To the Home of My Fathers" and "Green Isle of the Sea." [31] Joseph Brenan, an Irish newspaperman in New Orleans, left two volumes of poetry entitled "Brenan in Ireland" and "Brenan in America" when he died in 1857. The famous lines in Conklin's nomination speech in 1880 for Grant, who "comes from Appomattox and its famous apple tree," were taken from a stanza of Charles Graham Halpine's "A Bumper to Grant." Halpine was an Irish journalist who wrote under the pseudonym of "Miles O'Reilly." [32] The Confederate chaplain Father Abram Ryan wrote "The Conquered Banner" and "The Sword of Robert E. Lee." John Savage wrote "The Muster of the North," and Michael Scanlan, "Sister Stella, the Angel of the Hospital Ward." [33]

No less a person than Oliver Wendell Holmes regarded John Boyle O'Reilly as a poet of great ability. O'Reilly published several volumes, including *Songs from the Southern Seas* (1873), *Songs, Legends and Ballads* (1878), *The Statues in the Block* (1881), and *In Bohemia* (1886), and wrote fresh lines for almost any Irish-American gathering which solicited his talent. Joseph I. C. Clarke, ex-Fenian, journalist, and Irish-American playwright, was best known for his poem "The Fighting Race" (the Kellys and Burkes and Sheas), which he wrote to commemorate the many Irish names in the *Maine* disaster of 1898. Thomas Walsh, born in Brooklyn of Irish parents, published several volumes of verse, as well as translations of Spanish poetry. As late as 1914, *The Gaelic-American* advertised a new volume of poems for one dollar entitled *Ballads of Rebellion.*[34]

[31] Henry A. Brann, *John Hughes,* 142–43.

[32] *New York Times,* October 26, 1952.

[33] See also, Reverend William J. M'Clure, "Irish-American Poetry," *The Illustrated Celtic Monthly,* July, 1880, pp. 8–10; and D. J. O'Donoghue, *The Geographical Distribution of Irish Ability,* 12, 69, 141, 220.

[34] September 5, 1914.

Since 1900, much American fiction has appeared which has the present-day Irishman as its theme. In 1815, Hugh Henry Brackenridge's satirical *Modern Chivalry* had introduced the Irish character to American literature in his portrayal of the strange episodes in the career of Captain John Farrago and his Irish servant Teague O'Ragan, "a real Paddy," fresh from the Irish bogs, totally illiterate, but supremely confident. *Gerald French's Friends* (New York, 1889), by G. H. Jessup, dealt with the Irish of California in the 1870's and contained many stories about Irish character, including such tales as "The Rise and Fall of the 'Irish Aigle,'" a nationalist paper dedicated to the overthrow of English rule.[35] In the 1890's, American readers were interested in Alvan F. Sanborn's *Moody's Lodging House* (Boston, 1895) and *Meg McIntyre's Raffle and Other Stories* (Boston, 1896) for their tales of Irish boardinghouse characters in Boston; and in Edward W. Townsend's *Chimmie Fadden* (New York, 1895) and James W. Sullivan's *Tenement Tales of New York* (New York, 1895) for much the same reasons. Edgar Fawcett's *The Evil That Men Do* (New York, 1889) is a realistic story of the Flynns and Bridget Costigan of the tenements. The scene of one of Brander Mathews' *Vignettes of Manhattan* (New York, 1894) was located in an Irish slum.

In the present century, Irish themes and Irish-American fiction have become more popular. Theodore Dreiser, who admired the Irish as "a vigorous and wilful if degraded, pitiful and strange" people, portrayed them in *The Titan,* and has many Irish minor characters in his novels. Upton Sinclair's Mary Burke in *King Coal* (New York, 1917) was portrayed as a class-conscious strike leader with the romantic nature of a modern Irish Joan of Arc. Jim Tully's *Shanty Irish* (New York, 1928) was to some degree autobiographical. The author was the son of a drunken Irish ditchdigger and a country schoolteacher and was reared in an orphanage. He was a hobo, a pugilist, and a salesman before he turned to writing. The story of *Shanty Irish* begins with the Great Famine and is a tale of Irish immigrants, ditchdiggers, house servants, boardinghouse keepers, and the like, who "live by ignorance and die by faith." The book abounds in references to fairies, ghosts, witches, and wakes, revealing the Irish gift for words and a nature so poetic that it can describe a rainbow as resulting from the sun's shining on the tears of angels.

The output of Irish-American novels has increased materially since 1940. That year marked the appearance of Margaret Marchand's *Pilgrims on the Earth,* a moving story of an Irish laundress, hard and inflexibly

---

[35] Elwood P. Lawrence, "The Immigrant in American Fiction, 1890–1920" (Ph.D. dissertation, Western Reserve University, 1943).

religious, who worked for immigrants employed in a tin mine while bringing up a bastard grandchild whose father was an Orangeman. The novel deals with Catholic Ribbonmen, Orange meetings, and demonstrations, "stiff old Irish creeds," and the personal tragedies arising therefrom. It features a fight on the green on the anniversary of the Battle of the Boyne, with Orangemen shouting, "Ten thousand micks get soaked with bricks, at the battle of Boyne Water." The characters are fighting, shooting Irishmen, exhibiting life in all its rawness, and other Irishmen as simple and lovable as the wild ones are intolerant and brutal.

Thomas Sugrue's *Such Is the Kingdom* (New York, 1940) is a story of Irish and other immigrants in the rubber factory of an industrial town. It reveals the ever-present concern about religion and is a typical Irish mélange of firemen's balls, fairs, yarns about fairies told by old men to the children, drinking sprees, fights, baseball, politics, theology and wakes, and detailed descriptions of the Catholic Church.

The scene of John Henry Reese's *Sheehan's Mill* (New York, 1943) is Nebraska, about 1900, and the leading character is a wild Irishman who fights, loves horses, wants to be his own boss, but never quite succeeds. There is little plot. The book is devoted primarily to episodes in the life of an Irishman whom the author adores for his many warm human traits, although he spends far too much time in Pat Corrigan's saloon. The action in Clyde F. Murphy's *The Glittering Hill* (New York, 1944) is located in the Irish community of Butte, Montana, during boom times, when Irish laborers dug in the mines and Irish tycoons battled for control of the Anaconda country. John Dunphy's *John Fury* (New York, 1946) opens with an Irish wedding and traces the steady degradation of the leading character, a hard-working, simple Irish laborer whose life is an unbroken tragedy. The scene is laid in the Irish section of Philadelphia. With the exception of several incidents dealing with the Church, the story might be that of almost any poor ignorant laborer.

Mary Deasy's *The Hour of Spring* (Boston, 1948) follows the fortunes of an Irish family from 1870 to 1928 and deals with the inevitable conflicts between three generations. Mary Doyle Curran's *The Parish and the Hill* (Boston, 1948) is a nostalgic, partly humorous and partly tragic record of the memories of a childhood spent in Boston's Irish Parish and Money Hole Hill. It is a tale of shanties, red brick tenements, clay pipes, Irish laborers in the mills, and the psychological conflicts which arise when immigrants move up the social scale to become "lace curtain" Irish. Charles O'Neal's *The Three Wishes of Jamie McRuin* (New York, 1949) is a fantasy about fairies, miracles, legends, and the supernatural centering around a boy who wanted to go to America. The book won a prize for its emphasis upon Christian virtues, but is relatively unimportant as a portrayal of Irish immigrant life in the United States.

Roger B. Dooley's *Days Beyond Recall* (Milwaukee, 1949) is a Catholic author's portrayal of the Irish of Buffalo from the canal era to the present, the class distinctions among the Irish themselves, and the friction that arises with other nationality groups. Howard Breslin's *Let Go of Yesterday* (New York, 1950) is a story of an Irish-American family in Manhattan. There also is a growing literature dealing with the friction between Jews, Catholics, and Protestants, youthful gangs of "Micks" who battle with "Jew boys," and the problems of mixed communities where there is economic, religious, and social conflict.[36]

Stephen Crane's *George's Mother* (1896), a picture of Rum Alley and a poolroom environment, and his *Maggie: A Girl of the Streets* (1893) foreshadowed the stark realism of James T. Farrell's *Studs Lonigan* trilogy (New York, 1935). In many respects, the Farrell volumes are the most important in this list of sociological novels, though their stark realism has made them the center of controversy and, on occasion, the special object of censors who regard parts of the story as pornographic. Farrell deals with the Chicago Irish of the 1920's and 1930's of the "drug-store cowboy" type who hang around the poolrooms with little purpose in life except excitement and the indulgence of their baser passions. There is little about the earnest young Irish who rise from the slums and the saloons of their fathers to become successful in business or the professions. Farrell is concerned primarily with those who could not overcome their dreary environment and slowly sank into moral and physical ruin. His gripping, unforgettable trilogy is full of rough scenes and rough words; it is often uncomplimentary to the Church, to say the least; it is concerned with sex, profanity, sports, Irish hatred of Jews and Negroes, the low levels of poolroom society, the effects of the depression, and other problems, which are presented with stark realism and a coarseness often gross and even repellent.

These examples of recent novels about Irish America must suffice. Most of the stories weave into their plot the role of the Church and Irish nationalism in the life of the immigrant and his American-born descendants. Almost all contain detailed descriptions of the ritual of the Roman Catholic Church and the customs and institutions, such as fairs and wakes, peculiar to the Irish people. Many follow a standard pattern of content and stress the bizarre and the unusual to hold the reader's inter-

---

[36] See, for example, Samuel Ornitz, *Bride of the Sabbath*.

est. Nevertheless, they are sociological documents and, although uneven in value, must not be overlooked by historians who would understand the experiences of one of America's most important immigrant groups and their distinctive social and religious background. Such books are important in recent American literature as documents of value to the social historian.

CHAPTER XXIII

The Stage Irishman

IN THE long history of the American theater, the immigrant has provided dramatic entertainment and comic relief for American theatergoers.[1] From the characters portrayed in vaudeville acts or full-length plays, certain immigrant stereotypes have emerged. As early as 1850, at the peak of German and Irish immigration, the American theater was exploiting the peculiar and the ludicrous in the lives of the newcomers for public entertainment, and the average American was likely to accept the characterizations he saw on the stage as authentic. The Irishman, "as an insistent figure" on the American stage, was a popular character until the end of the century.

The Irish themselves have a love for acting, and amateur theatricals are nurtured in the many clubs and societies in which Irish-Americans find an outlet for their gregariousness. However, Irish immigrants had neither the time, the resources, nor the interest to develop an Irish theater in America comparable to the high standards of performance of the German theater.

Notices of Irish concerts and readings appeared in *The Shamrock* as early as 1811. In 1850, the Murdock Dramatic Association of New York, an amateur Irish theatrical group, sponsored its third annual ball. Teresa Esmond gave readings in the 1850's from Tom Moore and other Irish poets, and Dion Boucicault occasionally read an original play. In New York in 1855, an Irish comedian, assisted by a harpist, featured Irish stories and anecdotes, and a Mrs. Alexander Gibbs performed at the Appolo Rooms on Broadway with songs, stories, Irish legends, and "Dioramic views of 'Ould' Ireland" for an admission charge of twenty-five cents.[2]

Irish characters could be seen on the American stage as early as 1767, and they appeared in at least a score of American plays before 1828.

---

[1] Carl Wittke, "The Immigrant Theme on the American Stage," *The Mississippi Valley Historical Review*, XXXIX (1952), 211–32.

[2] See *The Citizen* (New York), October 6, 1855; also September 22, October 27, 1855; and January 7, November 11, 1854; *The Irish News* (New York), April 25, 1857, and February 6, 1858.

Tyrone Power, a famous portrayer of Irish characters on the English stage, made three tours of the United States in the 1830's and won popular favor with romantic comedies which had their scene in Ireland and included a number of Irish songs and dances. In 1837, Power appeared in *O'Flannigan and the Fairies, or a Midsummer Night's Dream, not Shakespeare's,* a musical fairy story built around Irish superstitions and love of whiskey. In the 1840's, Irish plays dealt with patriotic themes and Ireland's struggle for freedom. By the 1850's, a distinct Irish stereotype had evolved, the scene of Irish plays was America, and the dialogue contrasted Irish with Yankee traits.

Irish farce comedies with Irish scenes and singing and dancing were extremely popular. The stock Irish play generally portrayed a virtuous peasant girl and a high-minded Irish patriot, dressed in knee breeches and speaking with a brogue, and almost always in trouble with the law because of his illicit whiskey still. The villains were dukes and landlords, constables and soldiers, and needless to add, fists and shillelaghs figured prominently in the action. The stage Irishman was a bizarre figure, preposterously dressed for comic effect. In Pilgrim's *Shandy Maguire,* the English police were portrayed as "spindle-legged, down-looking, cabbage-faced, big-mouthed, long-nosed, dirty peelers." The Irish hero, on the other hand, was a gay blade, rough with the police, but charming and seductive with Irish colleens. Theatergoers in the 1850's preferred a simple plot, and Irish plays were as popular as the American minstrel show which flourished during the same period. Irish plays exaggerated the absurdities of Irish character and used such Irish words as shillelagh, colleen, begorra, smithereens, and Erin go bragh, which promptly found their way into the American language.

As one reads the old plays of the 1850's, they hardly seem funny, and many of the jokes are pointless by modern standards. Apparently, comedy effects depended on the actor, his dialect, his gestures, and his appearance rather than on the lines of the play. The extreme poverty of the Irish was frequently so exaggerated that it became unpleasant to observe on the stage. Irish-Americans gradually became bored with the same standard characters of landlord, bailiff, redcoats, and unprincipled informer.

The American urban Irishman almost always was costumed in ragged, dirty clothes; he was imprudent and pugnacious—an eloquent braggard and a master with the shillelagh—and the nemesis of "dirty peelers." This was the stereotype of a century ago whose Irish "bulls" became a part of American folk humor.

Few Irish plays had literary or dramatic merit, and most have long since been forgotten. Dion Boucicault and John Brougham in their day were regarded as leading dramatists and perhaps deserve a place in the history of the American theater. Boucicault, who came to New York in 1853, achieved success primarily by his delineation of Irish characters and toured the country for many years. Though he helped himself generously to the work of others, Boucicault generally improved what he borrowed. His plays pleaded the cause of the Irish nation and attempted to prove to the world "that England lies when she brands Ireland as a nation of whiskey-drinking, fight-loving vagabonds." [3] Irish journalists and some American critics thought he "raised the stage Irishman from the whiskey still and peat fire to regions of chivalry and poetry." [4]

Boucicault wrote many Irish plays. His *The Poor of New York* (1857) was based on *Les Pauvres de Paris* and was later reissued as *The Poor of Liverpool* and *The Poor of London*. It was concerned with the suffering in New York during the panic of 1857, but contained little that was specifically Irish. His *The Colleen Bawn* (1860), on the other hand, dealt entirely with Irish gentlefolk. It had more than three thousand performances. *The Shaughraun* (1874), full of Irish bonhomie, was an authentic portrayal of the "Irish type." Boucicault's total output as a playwright was 124 plays, but by the end of his career, audiences no longer were thrilled by the melodramatic effects in which he specialized.

John Brougham spent fifty years on the stage and wrote about seventy-five plays, all of them forgotten. He made his debut at the Park Theatre in New York in 1842, and his reputation was built largely upon his portrayal of Irish characters. Brougham's *The Irish Emigrant,* for example, dealt with the more bizarre features of Irish life in a delineation of "Milesian eccentricities" and "the peculiar idiosyncracies of Hibernian character." [5] Brougham wrote dozens of similar plays in which he himself played the role of the funny Irishman. His *The Irish Yankee; or the Birthday of Freedom,* first presented in the St. Charles Theatre of New Orleans, was full of stilted patriotic discourse.

The mass production of Irish farces and melodrama proved profitable for playwrights like James Pilgrim, Samuel D. Johnson, Boucicault, and Brougham. Leading actors like John Drew and Barney Williams carried their plays from coast to coast, and specialists in Irish comedy skits like W. J. Florence and Mr. and Mr. F. S. Chanfrau played to packed houses from New York to San Francisco before the Civil War.

Robert Emmet, the Martyr of Irish Liberty was one of Pilgrim's most popular plays. Another was *Shandy Maguire, or The Bould Boy of the*

---

[3] *The Illustrated Celtic Monthly* (1879), 375.
[4] *DAB.*
[5] *Porter's Spirit of the Times,* June 13, 1857, p. 240.

Mountain, presented in Philadelphia in 1851. It dramatized oppression in
Northern Ireland, and among its characters were the familiar revenue
man, the heartless landlord who wanted to tear down the widow's cottage, and the squire's worthless son, who lusted for the miller's daughter.
Tyrone Power wrote *Born to Good Luck, or, The Irishman's Fortune*
and *Paddy Carey, or, The Boy of Cloghan.* Barney Williams and his wife
starred in *Ireland and America, or Life in Both Countries.* The action
raced along from a fair in Ireland to the Battery and Five Points area of
New York,[6] with a cast that included a British army officer in pursuit
of an Irish girl. *A Day in New York* was advertised as a new, local
drama in New York in 1857. The opening scene was laid in Castle Garden. Among its immigrant characters were an Irish father and his beautiful daughter Mary, who had been spirited away to a "den of iniquity"
in the Bowery by an immigrant runner. The action shuttled back and
forth between Broadway and the Bowery before virtue was finally rewarded and sin properly punished.[7]

The pattern of this "most favorite class of modern dramatic entertainment" was much the same. It consisted of practical jokes, rough comedy,
absurd caricatures, melodramatic effects, and simple, romantic plots generously interspersed with lilting popular tunes, jigs, and reels. Nevertheless, a brief description of the plots of several additional Irish immigrant
plays will illustrate their importance as material for American social history.

Brougham's *The Irish Emigrant,* which dealt with a truckman and a
hungry, ragged Irish immigrant who found $5,000 but was too honest to
keep the money, required two whole acts to unfold this simple story. In
Brian O'Linn, a farce especially written for Barney Williams, the hero
was presented in dark brown breeches, gray stockings, a frieze coat, and
red vest. The cast included a priest, a British army officer, and women
in Irish peasant dress. As the curtain rose, the audience saw Williams in
his mother's humble cottage, singing an Irish love song and trimming
his trusty shillelagh. The dialogue abounded in Irish blarney and witti-
cisms, and the plot stumbled along through absurd, tumultuous scenes
while the hero fought with the police and made love to his Sheelah. The
action was utterly preposterous, but the play was a great success.

Irish Assurance and Yankee Modesty was a comedy concerned with
Pat, "the devil after the girls," and his amorous pursuit of a "tigress
Yankee girl." *Ireland and America,* another of Barney Williams' special
vehicles, opened with an Irish fair and a chorus singing

[6] George C. D. Odell, *Annals of the New York Stage,* VI, 121.
[7] *Porter's Spirit of the Times,* December 5, 1857, p. 224.

The flowers of all Europe
Are the pretty girls of Paddy's land.

The villains were excisemen in search of the Irishman's "mountain dew," and redcoats, whose captain was intent upon seducing the hero's sweetheart. Finnegan, the hero, who had been "kidnapped" for military service while under the influence of liquor, escaped to America, "the home of the stranger." Here three years of honest toil made him a prosperous Irish-American. In the last act he returned to New York, where he encountered his ancient enemy, the British captain, who had become an immigrant runner after his dishonorable discharge from the army. Peggy, the heroine, and her mother were in his power, under lock and key in an immigrant boardinghouse. The hero, dressed once more in the clothes he had worn as an immigrant, discovered their hiding place in time to save the heroine from being divested of both her money and her virtue. The play closed with a wild fight, during which the hero cracked heads with his shillelagh, and the girl rushed into her lover's arms.

Brougham's *The Irish-Yankee, or the Birthday of Freedom* stressed the patriotic note. The cast of characters included George Washington, costumed as he is painted in Leutze's *Washington Crossing the Delaware,* Lord Howe, Israel Putnam, and an Irishman, O'Donahoo, who was dressed for contrast in pantaloons, buff vest, and canvas jacket and had a name with "a real good potato flavor." O'Donahoo was the bearer of a secret letter for the commander in chief. Before the play ended, the audience had seen the Boston Tea Party, a tableau of Bunker Hill, and had listened to "The Star Spangled Banner." As the curtain fell,

The soldier, tired of war's alarms,
Beat a retreat to beauty's arms.

William Kelly's *The Harp Without a Crown, or Mountcashel's Fair Daughter* (New York, 1867) opened with the defeat of the Irish at the Battle of the Boyne and chronicled the continuing struggle for Irish freedom and the Catholic faith. It featured marching, flags, and hairbreadth escapes; the lines were full of "acushlas" and "ashtore machrees"; and the play ended with the dying hero's kissing the green flag of Ireland.

Harrigan and Hart, two of the most successful delineators of Irish character, made an important contribution to the American stage. No less a critic than William Dean Howells thought that Harrigan and Hart were unsurpassed in the fidelity and refined perception of their portrayals of immigrant types, and that their sociological and psychological studies constituted true American art.[8]

Harrigan and Hart started in vaudeville. Harrigan began writing sketches of a half hour in length and gradually expanded them into full-length plays. During the decade of the 1870's, Harrigan composed about eighty such sketches, most of them devoted to "the pageant of American immigration." They included not only humorous, good-natured characterizations of the Irish, but Negro, German, Italian, and Chinese types as well. Much of the success of the Harrigan and Hart productions depended on the contrast of honest, impulsive, irascible, and sometimes intemperate, but always generous, Irishmen with types of other nationalities.

Edward Harrigan was born in New York in 1845 and worked in Sacramento, California, as a caulker before going on the stage. He met his partner, Tony Hart (Anthony Cannon), while the latter was playing in a variety theater in Chicago, and formed a partnership which lasted for several decades. Harrigan wrote the songs, dialogues, and plots for the "Mulligan Series" in which he chronicled the adventures of Dan Mulligan and the Mulligan Guards. A Harrigan and Hart first night was an event in New York. Irish military organizations took whole blocks of seats, led the applause, and listened eagerly for songs which would become popular favorites.

"The Mulligan Series" were good-natured, realistic portrayals of New York Irish. Dan, the leading male character, was a veteran of the Civil War. His wife, Cordelia, originally a frugal, prudent, simple Irish woman, developed into a social climber. In *Cordelia's Aspirations,* her rise and fall and her return to the old grocery and boardinghouse and to her Dan, for whom she had a motherly affection, were wittily and touchingly described. In *Squatter Sovereignty* (1882), Harrigan played the part of a Shantytown astronomer and Hart the role of the Widow Dunn. The play satirized the battle for prestige between two clans in New York's social structure. Other plays were built around the rivalry of Dan Mulligan and Gustav Lochmüller, the German butcher who was Dan's competitor and the foil for his Irish wit. *The Mulligan Guard* burlesqued the outings, target practice, and riots of the old volunteer militia companies. *The Mulligan Ball,* which ran for a hundred nights in New York, described the complications which arose when a Mulligan fell in love with the daughter of a Lochmüller. *Reilly and the 400* was Harri-

---

[8] William Dean Howells, in *Harper's New Monthly Magazine,* LXXIII (July, 1886), 316; and LXXIX (July, 1889), 315–16; and *Harper's Weekly,* XL (October 10, 1896), 997–98.

gan's last great success. It opened in his own theater in 1890, with Harrigan playing the part of an Irish pawnbroker, and Annie Yeamans, the society leader.

Harrigan's humor was clean and good-natured. His plots are not without significance in the history of the American melting pot. His characters included street cleaners, contractors, grocers, butchers, shyster lawyers, policemen, politicians, truckers, and washerwomen. The scenes shifted from dives, shantytowns, the water front, the clothing stores of Jews, the German *Turnverein,* and corner groceries, to picnics and barber shops. Few of the plays were published. They were intended for the stage, not the library. They depended heavily for their success upon the songs, written by Harrigan's father-in-law, David Braham, which the nation whistled and sang from 1870 to the end of the century.

Among the songs made popular by Harrigan and Hart were such former favorites as "The Pitcher of Beer," "Remember, Boy, You're Irish," "The Babies in Our Block," "Give an Honest Irish Boy a Chance," "Why Paddy's Always Poor," "The Last of the Hogan's," "Johnny Reilly's Always Dry," "The Gallant 69th," and "The Land of the Shamrock." [9] The song hit of *Reilly and the 400* was "Maggie Murphy's Home":

> There's an organ in the parlor, to give the house a tone
> And you're welcome every evening at Maggie Murphy's home.

Another favorite told the story of

> Murphy's tenement, in the First Ward near the dock,
> Where Ireland's represented by the Babies on our Block.

The catchy "Danny By My Side," from *The Last of the Hogans,* was written in 1891 and was a favorite of the late Jimmie Walker, mayor of New York. Al Smith sang it in 1933 at the celebration of the fiftieth anniversary of the Brooklyn Bridge.

Plays about Irish-American characters and themes continued to be written to the end of the nineteenth century. Many conformed to the old pattern, but none achieved the popularity of the Harrigan and Hart series. Irish plays began to decline in merit and popularity by the end of the 1880's. By 1900, Irish characters seldom appeared on the American stage in rags as they had done a half century before, but Irish singers and comedians continued to be popular until well into the twentieth century.

Pat and Kate Rooney played in *Pat's Wardrobe,* Chauncey Olcott in *Mavoureen,* Murray and Mack in *Finnegan's 400,* and Barry and Fay in

[9] Isaac Goldberg, *Tin Pan Alley,* 83.

Irish Aristocracy.[10] *On the Bowery* was rewritten to introduce Steve Brodie's notorious leap from the Brooklyn Bridge, and one of the settings showed the interior of Brodie's saloon. In 1896, *The Irish World* announced a new romantic play, *On Erin's Shore*, "a picture of Ireland framed in smiles and tears." [11] J. Hartley Manners, born in London of Irish parents, wrote *Peg O' My Heart* for Laurette Taylor. Eugene O'Neill's *A Moon for the Misbegotten*, a sordid tale of Irish characters who supplanted the original Connecticut Yankees in the 1920's, had a heroine who was the daughter of a shiftless farmer and bootlegger. Irish characters have appeared in a few modern American comedies, written since 1920, although little of the comic effect depended upon national traits. *Abie's Irish Rose* was an exception. It reverted to some of the techniques of earlier years and was designed to preach tolerance in the days of the Ku Klux Klan, when attacks on Irish and Jews were notorious. It is doubtful whether a play of this kind would have been a success in any other country or have had much meaning for any people other than Americans. Several of Philip Barry's plays, such as *Without Love* (1943) and *Joyous Season* (1934), deal with Irish characters and have occasional flashes of humor about the "lace curtain" Irish. George F. Kaufman and Moss Hart's *Merrily We Roll Along* used a little "shanty Irish" atmosphere as a setting for one of the social climbers in the play.[12]

Countless vaudeville actors have made a living as Irish comedians. Their makeup exaggerated Irish physical characteristics and often consisted of red wigs, red noses, green whiskers, or little beards known as "gaulways" or "Galway Sluggers." Such performers became particularly distasteful to Irish-Americans of the second and third generations, although their "misrepresentations" were popular with many theatergoers in the 1870's and 1880's. Their acts usually included a song-and-dance routine. In the 1880's, for example, a vaudeville team known as the "Four Shamrocks" did an act on ladders and a scaffold; they tossed bricks at each other and fell into a mortar box, but finished with a song and dance. Pat Rooney from Cork, the first in three generations of famous American song-and-dance men, appeared for his act in the 1880's in a cutaway coat, tight sleeves, fancy waistcoat, checked pants, battered plug hat, and the traditional Irish whiskers.[13] Rooney originated the popular "Pretty Peggy," and one of his songs, "Is that Mr. Riley," contained the lines,

10 Harlow, *Old Bowery Days*, 456–60.

11 *The Irish World* (New York), April 25, 1896.

12 For these items on American comedy since 1923, I am indebted to a former student of Western Reserve University, Miss Barbara Joseph.

13 Fred J. Beaman, *Pearls from Past Programs*, 24–27.

I'd have nothing but Irishmen on the police
Patrick's day would be the Fourth of July.
I'd get me a thousand infernal machines
To teach the Chinese how to die.

The present Pat Rooney, still a nimble song-and-dance man at seventy-six, is known throughout the entertainment world for his singing and dancing of "Rosie O'Grady."

Kelly and Ryan, as coal heavers, did their song-and-dance act with scoop shovels, and Bradford and Delaney sang a song about "The Irish Knights of Labor." The Russell Brothers were famous in vaudeville as "The Irish Servant Girls." Maggie Cline, another old-timer, sang

> T'row him down, McClosky
> Was to be the battle cry—
> T'row him down, McClosky
> You can lick him if you try.

John and Harry Kernell were a team of Irish "sidewalk" comedians specializing in Pat and Mike stories.[14]

Acts and songs of the vaudeville era, or reasonable facsimiles, have survived into the present age of radio and television. Walter Scanlan, a young American tenor, was featured in the 1920's in *Irish Eyes,* a comedy of youth which took place in Galway and New York. Eugene Patrick McNulty, known to cameras and microphones as Dennis Day, received the annual actor's award of the Ancient Order of Hibernians, a statuette of Ireland's patron saint, which is always presented on St. Patrick's Day. Morton Downey sings Irish songs in Irish brogue on television, and Barry Fitzgerald appears occasionally in Irish plays. Eddie Cantor, a Jewish actor who began as a blackface performer, saluted the Irish with a special program over the network of the National Broadcasting Company, and some radio stations carry regular Irish-American programs.

A list of Irish actors who won fame on the American stage would begin with John Drew and Barney Williams (Bernard Flaherty). Drew, a native of Dublin whose father settled in Buffalo, began his career as an actor at the Bowery Theatre at the age of eighteen. He was the father of one of America's most noted stage families. Born in Cork and reared in the Bowery, where he had observed the old Irish "fire laddies," Williams was regarded as without an equal in the presentation of "the genuine Paddy, the true Irish peasant." William J. Florence

14 See Douglas Gilbert, *American Vaudeville, Its Life and Times;* Edward B. Marks, *They All Sang from Tony Pastor to Rudy Vallee,* 278–98; and Joe Laurie, Jr., *From the Honky-Tonks to the Palace.*

and his wife, Malvina Pray, patterned their acts on Williams' characterizations. John Collins, a contemporary of Drew with an excellent singing voice, specialized in Irish character parts. Baltimore's favorite was Dominick Murray. John T. Kelly, who began as a clog dancer, became a star on Broadway in Irish vaudeville acts and musical comedies.

There also were Irish-American actors who became famous on the American stage and never played an Irish part. Matilda Agnes Heron, a native of Londonderry who settled in Philadelphia, was one of the early favorites in *Camille*. Peter C. A. Daly, born in Brooklyn of Irish parents, played in Shaw's *Candida* at least 150 times, and did much to create the Shaw vogue in the United States. Blanche Walsh, born on New York's lower East Side, where her father, "Fatty" Walsh, was a saloonkeeper and a Tammany henchman, began her stage career at fifteen in Boucicault's *London Assurance*. In 1895, she was Nat Goodwin's leading lady. James O'Neill from Kilkenny began playing the leading role in *Monte Christo* in 1882, and played it the rest of his life—a total of over 6,000 times. His son was the distinguished American playwright Eugene O'Neill. William Florence Owen of Limerick played such comic parts as Toby Belch, Falstaff, and Touchstone. William Niblo, an Irish immigrant, sold turtle soup and salmon as an apprentice to a coffeehouse proprietor in New York before he went into the amusement field in 1828. He became the owner of Niblo's Garden, in which many great stars made their debut.[15]

As the Irish became Americanized, they deeply resented the caricatures of their people which they saw on the stage. Every immigrant group, after residing in the United States for a generation or two, is eager to "clean up the caricature" and stop the racial comedy which makes fun of their people. As early as 1850, Irishmen complained that their people were represented on the stage with "gorilla-shaped face," dirty clothes, brimless hat, short-stemmed pipe, shillelagh, and boorish manners. For a time, the stage Irishman and a drunkard were practically synonymous.[16] The Boston *Pilot* in 1860 repudiated "the stage Irishman." Four years later, *The Metropolitan Record* denounced most "Irish Drama" as trash, full of "coarseness, vulgarity, sensation and an impossible peasantry," "always vulgar and seldom witty," and demanded that it be driven from the stage.[17] The writer admitted, however, that any criticism of

---

[15] *DAB;* Philip D. Jordan, *Singin' Yankees,* 67.

[16] Emmet, *Incidents of My Life,* 131; and P. H. Morris (ed.), *A Memoir of the Very Reverend Theobald Mathew,* Chapters XIII and XIV.

[17] *The Pilot* (Boston), October 6, 1860; *The Metropolitan Record* (New York), May 14, 1864.

"the shillelagh drama" provoked an "out-pouring of wrath on the unfortunate critics."[18]

By 1900, the Irish were ready to attack the problem in earnest. One of the special projects of the Ancient Order of Hibernians was to rid the United States of the "infamous stage Irishman." The Hibernians threatened to boycott theater managers and booking agencies. In 1904, the order announced that its campaign had been successful. Therefore, it directed its attention to magazines and newspapers which featured unfriendly and inaccurate cartoons and caricatures of the Irish.[19] When the local lodge in Baltimore gave a "Hibernian Entertainment" with Negro farce and minstrelsy, it was promptly censured in *The Irish World* for such "improper selections."[20] The editor insisted that "The Stage Irishman Must Go," for he had always been a "repulsive idiot," a compound of ignorance and stupidity, without a gleam of the wit and pathos that were genuinely Irish.[21]

Nevertheless, "Gus" Hill, whom Irish-Americans hated, was still making money in 1900 and later with his *McFadden's Flats*. In 1904, at a performance in the Opera House in Wilkes-Barre, an Irishman leaped from his seat when a servant girl in *The Fatal Wedding* drank a bottle of wine on the stage. He insisted the scene was an insult to Irish womanhood.[22] In 1912, the Ancient Order of Hibernians denounced the plays of Synge, Yeats, and "other so-called Irish dramatists" when they were presented in this country by a company from the Abbey Theatre of Dublin. In some places, the plays could be given only under police protection because of the protests of local divisions of the order.[23] One of their most violent attacks was on the charming *Playboy of the Western World*, which Hibernians considered indecent and full of slurs on the Church. At the same time, several theater companies were organized in the United States to present Irish plays, develop an "Irish Theatre of America," and sponsor performances which would stress such features of true "Irish life" as peasants sitting before turf fires, singing the old Irish songs, and recounting the familiar tales of Erin.

The Irish stereotype has virtually disappeared from the American stage. The theatrical tastes of American audiences have changed materially, and Irish immigration has long since ceased to be a topic of interest or concern.

18 *The Metropolitan Record and New York Vindicator* (New York), January 21, 1865. See also Handlin, *This Was America*, 381–82.

19 O'Dea, *Ancient Order of Hibernians*, III, 1286.

20 *The Irish World* (New York), January 30, 1904; also July 9, 1904.

21 *Ibid.*, September 3, 1904.

22 *Ibid.*, December 3, 1904.

23 O'Dea, *Ancient Order of Hibernians*, III, 1470–71.

CHAPTER XXIV

The Field of Sport

THE Irish are fond of sports, from fishing to horse racing to baseball, and they have excelled in all its branches. When their efforts to introduce such native games as hurling and Gaelic football failed, they took what they found in their new home and made it their own.

As early as 1833, the New York Irish organized the East River Fishing Club and, the next year, held a "Jackson fishing party" with a "celebrated Irish piper" to provide the entertainment.[1] Irish athletic associations developed later in the century, and still are enthusiastically supported by many Irish-Americans. Roger F. Scannell, an Irish immigrant who came to Boston in 1864 and took part in the Fenian raid at St. Albans, became the first president of the American-Irish Athletic Association. Michael Cosgrove, commissioner of docks in New York and a Tammany leader, was one of its organizers. James Edward Sullivan, an all-round athlete whose father bossed an Irish construction gang for the New York Central Railroad, helped found the Amateur Athletic Union of the United States. Almost every sizable Irish community in the United States still sponsors an annual "Irish Sports and Field Day." The Irish Athletic Association of Greater New York has its annual field day at Celtic Park on Long Island and sponsors indoor meets in Madison Square Garden, where Irish athletes compete for prizes, especially in track events. The outdoor festivals of the Irish generally end with football, hurling, and a baseball game.

Hurling, a major Irish game, is somewhat like field hockey, except that the players catch the ball on the side of their stick, balance it, and run with it down the playing field. Under no conditions may a player use his hands, either to pick up the ball from the ground, hurl it, or run with it. The ball is of rubber, about ten inches in circumference, and weighs about four ounces. The stick is about three feet long, with a four-inch blade at the widest point. The ball must be hurled off the stick. There is a goal post with a crossbar at each end of the field, which is 140 yards by 80 yards in dimension. A ball successfully hurled between the

---

[1] Ernst, *Immigrant Life,* 127.

posts and under the crossbar counts three points; one hurled over the bar counts only one. As in hockey, a goal tender stands guard with blade up-raised to ward off the opponents' shots. Everything about the game is regulated except the weight of the stick. The strenuous game requires tremendous physical stamina. Irishmen love it; to an outsider, the game appears to be plain carnage.[2]

In January, 1858, an Irish Hurling Club of New York played Hoboken in a football and hurling match. After the teams had made five goals in hurling, they had enough strength left to play "several matches of foot-ball." [3] On St. Patrick's Day of the same year, there was another hurling match in Hoboken, behind the Elysian Fields, where early baseball teams used to play. The two hurling teams, with twelve men on a side, played nearly two hours without registering a goal. After a twenty-minute res-pite, they went at it again and played another two and a half hours without a score. The Irish News described the game as one for heroes only! [4] Although hurling never became an American sport, the Irish continue to play it. In 1953, the Rochester All-Stars met the Chicago All-Stars, champions of 1951, for the Midwestern hurling title, during a week end of fun and sport sponsored by the Gaelic League of Cleveland. Hurling teams are organized in leagues, and at the end of each season, all-star players selected from the various geographical areas play in semi-finals and finals for the championship of the United States.[5]

Gaelic football, as played in Ireland and cultivated by Irish athletic clubs in the United States, is something like soccer. There are fifteen players to a side. Throwing or running with the ball is prohibited. The ball may be dribbled, as in basketball, kicked along the ground or in the air, or punched with the fist. Kicking or punching the ball over the crossbar counts one point, getting it into a small net behind the goal posts counts three points. The game consists of two thirty-minute halves. Like hurling, it makes strenuous demands on the players, and because punching with the fist is an approved method of propelling the ball, the game is frequently marked with gory incidents. The Irish support Gaelic football teams in a number of cities, and the stars of the game engage regularly in championship matches on Irish-American field days and picnics.

The younger generation has found an outlet for its love of sports in college and professional football. Many Catholic schools like Notre

2 See Parker Cummings, *Dictionary of Sports.*
3 *The Irish News* (New York), January 2, 1858,
4 *Ibid.*, March 27, 1858.
5 Cleveland *Plain Dealer,* July 3, 1953.

Dame, Fordham, and Boston College, which are attended largely by Irish-Americans, have emphasized "big-time" football. The number of Irish names on football rosters from Harvard to California is impressive, and Irish coaches have been among the most successful in the game. While the rosters of modern football teams now contain so many names from the newer immigration that they read like a roll call of the United Nations, the team from Notre Dame still is known as "The Fighting Irish."

Michael Phelan, an enthusiastic Irish nationalist, was America's first billiard champion. In 1851, he visited Ireland and England, ostensibly to demonstrate his skill with cue and billiard balls, but actually to establish contact with Irish revolutionaries. In 1858, Phelan won $10,000 in a billiard match in San Francisco, and the next year, he became national champion in a match in Detroit which carried a purse of $15,000. Early in 1860, Phelan made an exhibition tour of the South. With his son-in-law, Hugh W. Collender, he began manufacturing billiard tables. The new firm advertised "Phelan's Improved Billiard Tables and Combination Cushions" and published *The Billiard Cue,* a journal devoted to the game. Phelan owned "Phelan's Magnificent Billiard Rooms" in New York at Broadway and Tenth Street.[6]

The preponderance of Irish in the manly art of self-defense has been so great that it is unnecessary to dwell at length on the success of the Irish in the prize ring. The stamina of the early fighters, before state boxing commissions tried to refine the sport, is amazing. In 1842, a prize fight in Westchester County, New York, in which Young Sullivan was one of the boxers, went 120 rounds, and ended with the death of Sullivan's opponent, not from a blow, but from sheer exhaustion and suffocation.[7] In 1856, Barney Ford and James Laverty fought in Rhode Island for a purse of $500. When Laverty lost the decision because of a foul, the crowd divided into two groups, pulled out knives and revolvers, and prolonged the argument in a free-for-all fight.[8] In 1860, Anglo-American relations reached a new crisis over the Sayers-Heanan fight in London. Tom Sayers, an English bricklayer who had fought many battles, including one of forty-four rounds, was regarded as the British champion. He was matched for a world-championship fight with John C. Heanan, an Irishman from the United States. Michael Phelan, the billiard champion, was chairman of a committee to raise money for the Irish-American challenger. The referee awarded the decision to Sayers on the ground

[6] *The Irish News* (New York), January 9, 1858; May 5, July 28, August 11, 1860.
[7] Nevins and Thomas (eds.), *Strong's Diary,* I, 185–86.
[8] *The Irish News* (New York), July 19, 1858.

that Heanan had fouled the Englishman. Actually, Heanan knocked his opponent down twenty times without going down once himself. The Irish-American press made good use of the incident to portray the character and untrustworthiness of the Britishers, and *The Irish News* suggested that Americans reciprocate for such shabby British treatment of distinguished Americans when the Prince of Wales arrived for his American tour.[9]

John Morrissey, who learned to fight as an immigrant runner in New York, became a world's heavyweight champion, a race-track operator, and a United States congressman. "Gentleman Jim" Corbett, one of ten children of an Irish livery-stable owner in San Francisco, began boxing at eighteen, attracted national attention by his six-round bout with Jack Kilrain in New Orleans in 1890, and went on to become the world's heavyweight champion. In 1891, Corbett fought sixty-one rounds with the Negro, Peter Jackson, whom John L. Sullivan had refused to meet. In 1892, Corbett defeated Sullivan for a purse of $45,000. He went on to knock out Bob Fitzsimmons in 1897, but had to yield the championship to Jim Jeffries in a fight in 1900 which went twenty-three rounds. After his retirement from the ring, Corbett turned to vaudeville and radio.

Billy Conn, the Pittsburgh Irishman, lasted thirteen rounds in his fight with Joe Louis in 1941. Mike McTigue, "Bold Michael" from county Clare, fought in the light-heavyweight class for twenty-one years. On St. Patrick's Day, 1923, he won the title in a twenty-round bout in Dublin with Battling Siki, the Senegalese from French West Africa who had recently knocked out the Frenchman, Georges Carpentier, in Paris.

However long the list of Irish pugilists, the name of the immortal John L. Sullivan leads all the rest. John Lawrence Sullivan was a Bostonian. His father was a fiery little man from Tralee; his mother was a powerful woman. After grammar school, John became a plumber's assistant and a tinsmith, and a member of William Muldoon's variety troupe. In his first fight in Boston, when Sullivan was nineteen, he knocked his opponent into the orchestra pit with the first blow. Thereupon he challenged all comers, and agreed to pay twenty-five dollars to anyone who could knock him out. In the days when pugilists still fought with bare knuckles, "The Boston Strong Boy"—weight 180 pounds, height five feet ten and a half inches—became the idol of the Boston Irish. In 1882, he knocked out Paddy Ryan, the national heavyweight champion. In 1889, Sullivan fought Jack Kilrain seventy-five rounds with bare knuckles. Three years later, he lost the championship to Corbett. Unfortunately, the giant of the prize ring spent too much time in sa-

9 *The Irish News* (New York), May 5, 19, 1860.

loons, and he had to sell his diamond-studded, ten-thousand-dollar championship belt to pay off his creditors. In his later years, Sullivan traveled with shows and vaudeville troupes, operated saloons in New York and Boston, and became a temperance lecturer in 1905. Reform came too late. "The Boston Strong Boy" died poor.[10]

By 1905, the Ancient Order of Hibernians, convinced that it had driven "the stage Irishman" from the American theater, turned its attention to the prize ring. The Hibernians, in convention assembled, noted "with growing alarm the nefarious custom of criminals, pugilists, and the abandoned and submerged tenth of society adopting Irish names, both Christian and surnames," and resolved to fight a practice which injured the Irishman's reputation in the United States even more than the caricatures of the stage.[11] The Irish had become so prominent in the world of pugilism that many boxers, without a drop of Irish blood, took Irish names to advance their careers. In Boston's North End, for example, where young Italian pugilists had a hard battle for recognition because both fans and promoters were largely Irish, Italians fought under such names as Little Jack Dempsey, Sammy Fuller, and Mickey Landis. It was not until the 1930's that they entered the ring under their own Italian names.[12]

Although the Irish have been neither as interested nor as successful in wrestling as in boxing, William Muldoon deserves special mention. He was born in New York State, the son of Patrick Muldoon and Maria Donohue. At eighteen, he began to earn a living as a "bouncer" in dance halls and eating places in New York. Thereafter, he worked as a laborer, longshoreman, and cab driver on New York's East Side. He became a policeman in 1876 and organized the Police Athletic Association. He won national fame as a wrestler and, on one occasion, wrestled Clarence Whistler for eight hours without a decision. Muldoon took a troupe of American wrestlers to Japan, and when he retired from the police force in 1900, operated a saloon in New York and became a trainer of pugilists and wrestlers. On an estate in Westchester County, the ex-policeman opened a training and health center for tired businessmen. Here he put the tycoons of Wall Street through their paces, kept them on a strict diet, forbade all alcoholic drinks, and invented "the medicine ball" for his aristocratic clientele. In 1921, "The Iron Duke" was appointed chairman of the Boxing Commission of New York.

---

10 For these sketches, see *DAB*.

11 O'Dea, *The Ancient Order of Hibernians*, III, 1363, 1372.

12 Whyte, "Race Conflicts in the North End of Boston," *The New England Quarterly*, XII (1939), 623–42.

Irish athletes have been particularly successful in track. Thomas Conneff held the mile record for twenty years, and Arthur Duffey of Georgetown was one of the first sprinters to run the hundred yards in less than ten seconds. In 1895, Thomas Burke won the quarter-mile in an international meet in New York between American and English athletes; Michael Sweeney won the high jump; and James Mitchel the hammer throw. Burke went on to two Olympic championships. John Flanagan, Matt McGrath, and Pat Ryan at various times held the record in the hammer throw.[13] Martin Sheridan, a latecomer from Ireland, in 1897 became a New York policeman and was a star for the Irish-American Athletic Club. A great, all-round athlete, he established a dozen world's records in track and won the discus throw at the Olympic Games in Athens.[14] Michael Charles Murphy, a Massachusetts Irishman and an excellent sprinter, became a famous coach and athletic trainer for Yale and Pennsylvania. In 1908 and 1912, he coached the American Olympic teams. He is credited with inventing the crouching start for sprinters. The Irish-American Athletic Club has sent many champions to the Olympic Games, including Pat McDonald, Simon Gillis, and Johnny Hayes. It has also sponsored others, like Hans Kohlemainen, who wore the colors of the famous club but were anything but Irish.

Walking has become almost a lost art, but in earlier times, the professional pedestrian played a minor role in the world of sport. In 1860, *The Wheeling Union* reported that Tom Buckley, the "Limerick Boy," walked one hundred hours with a cane and without sleep under a tent on a plank forty feet long.[15] Of higher caliber were the pedestrian feats of Daniel O'Leary, immigrant from county Cork, who laid claim to the world championship among pedestrians. In 1874, he walked one hundred miles in twenty-three hours and seventeen minutes; the next year, he covered five hundred miles in three hours less than six days. In 1879, O'Leary was matched with the Englishman Charles Bowell and walked night and day for six days in Gilmore's Garden in New York, winning the championship belt.[16] O'Leary set many records for distances and time, and in his eighties, still could do six miles an hour.

The Irish adopted the national pastime of baseball with greater immediate success than any other immigrant group. Only in later years have the sons of the newer immigration challenged the Irishman's pre-

---

[13] C. E. McGuire (ed.), *Catholic Builders of the Nation*, III, 312, 314; *The Irish World* (New York), August 13, 1904.

[14] *The Gaelic-American* (New York), April 6, 1918.

[15] *The Irish News* (New York), June 23, 1860.

[16] *The Irish World* (New York), March 8, 29, 1879.

ponderance in the national game. The reputation of Irish ballplayers was so great that others frequently took Irish names to help them in their baseball careers. Leopold Christopher Hoernschemeyer of Cincinnati, for example, played in the National League as Lee Magee in the second decade of the present century. Several catchers whose names are of southern or eastern European origin have taken the name "Mickey" in emulation of "Mickey" Cochrane, one of the greatest catchers in the history of the game. The All-Time Register of Players and Managers in Hy Turkin and S. C. Thompson's *The Official Encyclopedia of Baseball* (New York, 1951) abounds with Irish names. Some were first-generation immigrants; the majority were American-born of Irish immigrant parents. Every baseball fan knows Ernest L. Thayer's "Casey at the Bat" and Grantland Rice's "Casey's Revenge."

In a region as remote as Iowa, the Irish helped establish the game before the Civil War. A box score for a six-game series between Dubuque and Davenport in 1878 indicates that almost all the players had Irish names. Charles Comiskey on that occasion caught for Dubuque. Ten years later, when the Des Moines Colts wanted to bolster their pitching staff, they brought in Bill Fagan, an old, hard-drinking Irish pitcher, from New York and paid him $225 a month.[17] Peter J. ("Smiling") Daniels, a native of Ireland, was a big-league pitcher in the 1890's. Edward C. Duffy, born in Ireland in 1844, played shortstop for Chicago in 1871. Ferguson Malone, another native Irishman, caught and played first base for the old Athletics in the 1870's. Anthony Mullane of Cork pitched and played the infield a decade later. John Joseph ("Dirty") Doyle was a National League infielder in the 1890's. Jimmy Archer, who caught for Pittsburgh and Chicago in the first two decades of this century, was a native of Dublin. As late as 1952, of the thirty-four men on the roster of the Cleveland Indians, representing eighteen nationalities, the Irish led with fourteen.

Michael J. Kelly ("King Kelly") was the son of an Irish immigrant papermaker in Troy, New York. "King" played with several minor teams and was with the Cincinnati Reds when "Pop" Anson brought him to Chicago, where he remained from 1879 to 1887. A big, convivial, hard-to-manage Irishman, and a great umpire-baiter, Kelly did equally well as a catcher, outfielder, or shortstop, and led the league in batting in 1886. When he was sold to Boston in 1887, he was known as the "Ten Thousand Dollar Beauty," but his real claim to baseball immortality

17 W.P.A. Writers' Project, "Baseball, the Story of Iowa's Early Innings," *Annals of Iowa*, XXII (1939–41), 625–54.

rests upon his feats as a base runner, celebrated in the popular song, "Slide, Kelly, Slide." In 1888, Kelly published *Play Ball: Stories of the Diamond*. He died in 1894. He was appearing in a Boston theater at the time, with the London Gaiety Girls, in the role of "Casey at the Bat." Legend has it that when he fell off a stretcher during his last illness, he remarked with the Irish humor that never failed him, "This is my last slide." [18]

John Joseph ("Muggsy") McGraw came from Truxton, New Jersey, and was the eldest in an Irish family of nine. What little education he had he received at St. Bonaventure College after he had begun his baseball career. He was a slight, little man whose aggressiveness made up for his lack of avoirdupois. McGraw played the infield for the Baltimore Orioles before he began managing the New York Giants in 1902 at the age of twenty-nine. "The Little Napoleon," a rough disciplinarian and a real master of the game, won ten National League pennants. It was he who converted Christy Mathewson from a first baseman to a pitcher. "The Old Roman," Charles A. Comiskey, was the son of an Irish immigrant who came to the United States with his family in the bleak year of 1848. The father became a politician in the Irish ward of Chicago, and here Charles was born. The boy was apprenticed to a plumber, but in 1875, at seventeen, he began to play third base for Milwaukee. During his long career as an active player, he also pitched and played first base. He helped Ban Johnson organize the American League and was the owner of the Chicago White Sox until his death in 1931.

The list of big-league managers contains such familiar Irish names as Pat Moran, Hugh Jennings, Joe McCarthy—the stocky Irishman from Buffalo who won pennants for the Yankees—"Connie" Mack, Joe Cronin, Steve O'Neill, and many others. In Baseball's Hall of Fame in Cooperstown, New York, there are plaques for George ("Mickey") Cochrane, one of the game's greatest catchers; "Iron Man" Joseph Jerome McGinnity, the pitcher; James H. O'Rourke ("Orator Jim"), one of baseball's early heroes, who played behind the plate and in the outfield in twenty-one major league seasons until he was past fifty; Hugh Duffy, brilliant outfielder who batted .438 in 1894; "King Kelly," who stole eighty-four bases for Boston in 1887; Cornelius McGillicuddy, great catcher, manager of the Philadelphia Athletics, and the game's "Grand Old Man"; Ed Delahanty, one of the game's greatest sluggers; and Roger Patrick Bresnahan, "the Duke of Tralee," battery mate of the

[18] *DAB.*

great Mathewson and a manager in the National League. There have also been famous Irishmen in the ranks of the "men in blue" who rule the game.

America has had several Irish baseball clans, but there is none to surpass the Delahanty tribe of Cleveland. The six sons born to James Delahanty and Bridget Croke, Irish immigrants, all left their mark in the annals of the national game. Five of the boys played in the major leagues; the sixth might have done so, and already had been drafted by Brooklyn, when he was hit by a pitched ball which ended his career. Big Ed Delahanty, the eldest of the tribe, once hit four home runs in one game, and was the only player who won the batting championship in both the National and American League. He batted .408 for Philadelphia in 1889 and .376 for Washington in 1902.

With the Irishman's great love for sports and his unusual talents for journalism, it is not surprising that many sports writers have been of Irish origin. John Kiernan of New York is without a peer. Thomas Aloysius Dorgan, the son of Irish immigrants from the San Francisco tenements "south of the slot," began working for the San Francisco *Bulletin* at the age of fourteen. He became a cartoonist for William Randolph Hearst, an authority on boxing, and a highly respected referee. From 1900 to 1920, he reported all major prize fights. As a cartoonist, he developed several comic strips, and he is credited with inventing such popular sayings as "23, skidoo," "Yes, we have no bananas," "the first hundred years are the hardest," "applesauce," and "as busy as a one-armed paper hanger with the hives." [19]

James Parnell Dawson, boxing editor of the New York *Times* and a baseball writer, was the son of Irish immigrants. He left parochial school when his father died, and his formal education ended with the seventh grade. Dawson was a colorful figure in the world of sports writers and was with the *Times* for forty-four years. Peter Finley Dunne ("Mr. Dooley"), another notable sports reporter, helped develop a unique journalistic technique for sports writers. Along with others, he enriched the "American Language" with that incomparable argot of professional ballplayers which no European can understand without a glossary. Eugene McGillicuddy (Gene Mack) was a sports cartoonist for the *Boston Globe* for more than thirty-five years. A semipro ballplayer in his younger days, he is remembered primarily as a cartoonist of sports events. His sketches of Babe Ruth and Lou Gehrig hang in Baseball's Hall of Fame in Cooperstown.

[19] *Ibid.*

CHAPTER XXV

World War I

THE outbreak of World War I in the summer of 1914 came as a thunderclap from a cloudless sky. In a nation like the United States, which is a composite of many nationalities, a European war always creates special emotional crises. Immigrants and the descendants of immigrants have natural sympathies for the country of their origin and believe they have a right to express their views on the nature of the international crisis as long as the United States is not actually at war. As the cold draft of a European war blows over the molten mass of the American melting pot, the normal fusion process is retarded, and some of the elements seem to crystalize out again.[1]

World War I raised especially acute problems for Americans of German extraction, and to an only somewhat lesser degree, for those Americans who were of Irish origin. The loyalty of neither group had ever been questioned. But now even the most harmless activities of German-Americans were regarded by excited patriots as a Pan-German plot to win the United States for the Kaiser. The German element, on the other hand, primarily through a vigorous German-language press, embarked upon a public campaign to counteract the effect of British propaganda in America and to maintain the neutrality of the United States. What others described as "pro-German," they considered mere "fair play," legitimate counterpropaganda, and a policy of "putting America first."[2]

The views of many Irish-American leaders were almost identical with those of their German fellow-citizens, but for different reasons. Not instinctive love for Germany, but an all-consuming Anglophobia accounted for the "pro-German" attitude of the Irish-American press and many prominent Irish-Americans. Although home rule for Ireland was approved by the British Parliament, the problem of unification with Ulster remained unsolved in 1914. John Redmond, leader of the Irish party in Parliament, agreed to a postponement of the issue and offered

---

[1] Walter V. Woehkle, "Confessions of a Hyphenate," *Century*, XCIII (1916), 930.
[2] For details, see Carl Wittke, *German-Americans and the World War*.

Irish support for the war with the Central Powers. A substantial number of American Irish, once satisfied with home rule, now demanded complete independence for their native land, and apparently expected either a German victory or pressure from the United States to bring it about. British propaganda in the United States made little impression upon Irish-Americans, who were inclined to accept the German interpretation of the causes and objectives of the war. England remained "perfidious Albion."

Irish-Americans were by no means unanimous about what was best for Ireland. Direct actionists distrusted political methods, and advocates of an Irish republic could not be satisfied with home rule or dominion status in the British Empire. In 1892, *The Irish World* had denounced Irish nationalists who talked of bloodshed, and apparently was ready to accept a solution of the Irish question which would have included imperial supremacy in military and foreign affairs, a royal veto, and special guarantees to the Protestant minority.[3] In 1914, *The Irish World* still supported Redmond, home rule, and parliamentary procedures. Devoy's *Gaelic-American,* on the other hand, was convinced that England would never voluntarily surrender control of Ireland. The Ancient Order of Hibernians favored complete independence, and the Clan-na-Gael, in convention at Atlantic City, denounced Redmond for promising aid to England in her hour of distress. Eventually *The Irish World* came around to the position of *The Gaelic-American* and broke with Redmond. The Ancient Order of Hibernians were sharply divided on the proper policy to follow toward England. Differences of opinion among Irish groups in New York, Chicago, and other cities became so acute that considerable rowdyism marked some of their meetings; funds were solicited for conflicting objectives; and charges were made that much of the money failed to reach its proper destination. Personal rivalries and the ambitions of certain leaders who sought prestige among the Irish-American group greatly aggravated their differences of opinion.

A *rapprochement* between Irish and German-Americans began to take form about 1898, when the press and the spokesmen of both groups believed a secret alliance with England was imminent. An "Irish National Alliance" had been organized in 1895, ostensibly to cultivate the study of Irish history and literature and to work for the independence of Ireland. Four years later, the National German-American Alliance was born. Both organizations insisted their objectives were "America

---

[3] *The Irish World* (New York), July 9, October 1, 1892; also August 29, 1896; May 28, 1898.

first," and both were opposed to entanglements with foreign nations unless they should prove of positive benefit to their native land.

The Irish World and other Irish-American papers stressed the dangers of an Anglo-American secret alliance and insisted that London had begun a campaign of lies long before the war to create anti-German sentiment in the United States. Whitelaw Reid and Lyman Abbott were accused of being British propagandists.[4] A mass meeting of Poles and Germans in Chicago protested against the secret "Anglo-American Alliance," and Irish-American demonstrations throughout the United States demanded that America resist all foreign entanglements. The Irish-American press commended the Germans for their opposition to a pro-British foreign policy which would make America the tail of the British kite, and Irish societies sent petitions of protest to Washington. German-Americans signed Irish petitions, and respected Irish leaders like Patrick Ford, Mayor James A. McGuire of Syracuse, national President P. J. O'Connor of the Hibernians, Judge James A. O'Gorman of New York, Thomas A. Emmet, and Patrick Egan reciprocated by adding their names to German petitions. *The Irish World* reprinted from the Chicago *Illinois Staatszeitung* in the original German and in translation.[5] President Wilson's request in 1913 for the repeal of the exemption from tolls in the Panama Canal for American vessels engaged in coastwise trade stimulated a flood of telegrams from Irish and German societies demanding an "American as against a British interpretation of the Hay-Pauncefote Treaty." The incident helped create an impression in Irish and German minds of a President who was at heart a Britisher masquerading in American colors. Irish- and German-Americans also combined their forces in opposing prohibition, women's suffrage, and a literacy test for immigration.

While focusing attention upon the activities of leading Irish and German organizations in America during Wold War I, it must be emphasized that many Irish- and German-Americans belonged to no organizations of a political character. The silent majority was not necessarily in agreement with the professional German- or Irish-American leaders. The German-American Alliance, for example, never enrolled more than a small segment of the German element in the United States. There is no evidence of a Pan-German plot to "Teutonize" the United States.

As early as 1907, a conference of the national officers of the German

---

[4] *Ibid.,* July 23, August 6, 1898.
[5] *Ibid.,* March 5, May 28, June 4, 1898.

Alliance and the Ancient Order of Hibernians had agreed that it would be "for the good of this Republic" to combine forces against foreign entanglements, further restrictions on immigration, and new inroads upon "personal liberty." The Hibernians approved the agreement in 1908 as a "master stroke in Irish affairs" and claimed that German- and Irish-Americans together constituted 57 per cent of the American people. The Hibernians officially sanctioned the display of the Irish flag on German holidays.[6] By 1914, the Clan-na-Gael, the American Truth Society, and several smaller Irish societies virtually were parties to the pact of the German and Irish leaders, and in some localities, Irish-German Leagues and Boards of Mutual Conference implemented the agreement to co-operate.[7]

There also were Irish-Americans who believed that their countrymen were playing the game of German propagandists in the United States. Patrick Egan opposed the German-Irish entente, and conventions of the Hibernians revealed sharp differences of opinion. Many Irish were outraged by Germany's "rape of Belgium"; many Irish-American financiers and industrialists were pro-Ally; and the historic relations between France and Ireland were a factor of some importance in Irish-American circles. Nevertheless, when Mayor Curley of Boston early in the war supported Great Britain against the Central Powers, *The Gaelic-American* damned him as "a yellow dog" and "a contemptible cur" who had "foresworn the country of his parents and become an Anglo-Saxon." [8]

When Austria declared war against Serbia, John Devoy hailed the empire of the Habsburgs as "Ireland's Ally," [9] and organizations of Irish nationalists throughout the United States actively sympathized with the Central Powers and wished them success. At a picnic in Celtic Park in New York, the Irish Volunteers resolved that England was "the real fomenter and instigator of this war." Irishmen complained about the way the war was being reported in "the subsidized and corrupt papers" of the "Anglo-American press." German and Irish societies met in joint assembly; a committee of the Clan-na-Gael conferred with the German Ambassador at the German Club in New York, and may have discussed ways and means to foment a revolution in Ireland. Jeremiah O'Leary, Timothy S. Hogan of Ohio, Robert E. Burke of Illinois, and other prominent Irish were suddenly popular with German-American audiences, and Dr. C. J. Hexamer, president of the German-American

---

[6] O'Dea, *Ancient Order of Hibernians,* III, 1387–88.
[7] See Clifton J. Child, *The German-Americans in Politics, 1914–1917.*
[8] August 1, 1914.
[9] *The Gaelic-American* (New York), August 1, 1914.

Alliance, and Dr. Julius Hoffmann of Baltimore addressed several Irish groups.[10] The German and Austro-Hungarian bazaars which were held in many cities to raise money for German and Austrian wounded and orphaned almost always featured at least one "Irish Night."

A comparison of such Irish papers as *The Gaelic-American* and *The Irish World* with the German-language press indicates how closely they followed a common propaganda line. They were agreed that Germany was fighting a purely defensive war for the freedom of the seas; that German culture was threatened by Russian barbarism; and that the war was viciously misrepresented in the pro-British press of the United States. Irish papers called attention to the fact that German scholars were among the few who genuinely appreciated the ancient Irish culture. *The Gaelic-American* reported that the Kaiser carried a four-leaf shamrock, given him by his grandfather, as a good-luck charm.[11] The Irish press reprinted from the German press and recommended George Sylvester Viereck's *The Fatherland* to their readers. A gigantic demonstration at Madison Square Garden in 1915 resulted in the formation of a German-Irish organization known as "The Friends of Peace." In San Francisco and elsewhere, Irish units marched proudly in German-American parades. Viereck, Bernhard Ridder of the *New Yorker Staatszeitung,* and F. F. Schrader were prominent members of O'Leary's American Truth Society.

German propagandists exploited the liaison between Germans and Irish; Professor Kuno Meyer was dispatched to lecture in the United States on "The Golden Age of Irish Civilization, and Its Influence on Germany"; and the German Information Service in New York had a news service for the Irish press in which James K. McGuire was especially active.[12] German-American business houses, the Germania Life Insurance Company, and the *New Yorker Staatszeitung* paid for advertisements in the Irish press. *The Gaelic-American* carried an article in 1916 to show that nearly two-thirds of the German Empire was Catholic. A leading British propagandist, in a report to his superiors in London, urged sending over "some authoritative loyal Irish members [of Parliament] preferably a Catholic . . . to silence the Irish-American party which exude poison from every pore." John Redmond, Horace Plunkett, and other "loyal Irishmen" furnished interviews and articles in support of Great Britain for the American press. After the Easter Rebellion of

10 *Ibid.*, August 22, 29, December 12, 1914.
11 *Ibid.*, October 3, 1914.
12 Robert E. Park, *The Immigrant Press and Its Control*, 427–28.

1916, when Irish emotions were at white heat, British propaganda head-quarters circulated a book entitled *The Irish at the Front* with an introduction by Redmond.[13]

The controversy over America's rights as a neutral raged on from 1914 to 1917 and involved many questions of international law and practice. Although all belligerents violated international law when it was to their interest to do so, British violations involved American property rights, and Germany's submarine warfare resulted in the loss of American lives.

Many Irish-Americans were convinced from the outset that Woodrow Wilson would not dispense even-handed justice in the battle over the neutral rights of America. By 1915, his sins against "impartial neutrality" were many. They involved, in Irish eyes, such questions as contraband, blockade, the freedom of the United States mails, and the sale of Allied bonds to the American public. Overshadowing all others, however, was the shipment of vast quantities of war material to the Allies by private American manufacturers who were making America's great industrial potential available to the British side. Although the administration explained that the procedure was entirely legal and that Germany was as free to come and buy as any other power, German- and Irish-Americans remained unconvinced.

The Wilson administration was accused of trying to make the United States a "vassal state" of England. Many Germans and Irish demanded an embargo on the munitions traffic and an end to the sale of British and French war bonds to American investors. They seriously doubted the Belgian atrocity tales, branded what they called the Northcliffe press in America a "dirty English rag," and refused to find anything to criticize in the machinations of German agents in the United States. The feud between Irish- and German-American papers with the New York *World,* the New York *Tribune,* Villard's New York *Evening Post,* the *Providence Journal,* and other metropolitan dailies became furious. Comfort and support could be found only in the Hearst press.

The sinking of the *Lusitania* in 1915 by a German submarine, resulting in the loss of many American lives, was justified on the ground that the British passenger vessel was a "floating arsenal." The Irish press promptly demanded a law to keep Americans from traveling on the ships of belligerents. When William Jennings Bryan resigned as secretary of state because he feared President Wilson's vigorous protests to Germany might lead to war, the former "Billy Sunday humbugger" and "grape-juice clown" "of pro-British sympathies" became an Irish and German

---

[13] H. C. Peterson, *Propaganda for War,* 241–42.

hero. Mass meetings to protest Wilson's unneutral neutrality were staged in Baltimore, New York, Philadelphia, New Orleans, Minneapolis, Chicago, Denver, Seattle, and in other cities from coast to coast. Jeremiah O'Leary spoke in New York's Carnegie Hall. In March, 1916, a convention of "the Irish Race in America" assembled, nearly 2,300 strong, in Hotel Astor to reassert Ireland's claim to nationhood and to demand that the United States keep out of war. The delegates admonished the government not to curtail the effectiveness of German submarines "by unwarranted action." [14] Victor Herbert opened the convention; Justice John W. Goff, Judge Daniel F. Cohalan, and John Devoy were among the speakers; and the list of permanent officers included other prominent Irishmen and a number of Catholic clergymen. The Boston *Pilot* approved of the convention. The Catholic *America,* edited by Richard Henry Tierney, who was both a priest and a journalist, opposed American entry into the war. *The Gaelic-American,* as late as the spring of 1917, hailed the dozen senators who blocked the President's request for "armed neutrality" as "Twelve Brave Men who stood for the preservation of American Liberty." [15] Some Catholic papers were pro-Ally, however; a number of prominent Irish-Americans refused to accept the pro-German position without reservations; and leaders of the Clan-na-Gael admitted that the "moneyed" Irish had little interest in their propaganda.

Meantime, there were new manifestations of Irish Anglophobia. Devoy believed a half-million American Irish were ready to fight for Germany, provided transportation to Europe could be arranged. At Irish picnics and social occasions, resolutions were adopted to speed the defeat of England. John McCormack, the popular Irish tenor, was condemned for sending cigarettes to British soldiers, and even Cardinal Gibbons did not escape censure because of his friendliness toward Redmond and his participation in various international movements. British defeats were headlined in the pro-German Irish-American press. In New York State, Irishmen protested when a legislative manual printed the Magna Charta ahead of the Declaration of Independence. The singing of the popular war song "Tipperary" was shouted down as a "dirty London doggerel" intended to ridicule the Irish.[16]

The war stimulated a revival of interest in all things Irish. *The Irish Voice* of Chicago, *The Irish Review* of Los Angeles, and other weeklies were launched to further "Irish national needs." Dr. Patrick McCartan,

14 *The Gaelic-American* (New York), February 12, March 11, April 1, 1916.
15 *Ibid.,* March 10, 1917.
16 See *The Gaelic-American* (New York), May 8, 1915; April 1, 1916.

"ambassador" for Ireland's provisional government, started *The Irish Press* in Philadelphia in 1918. *Bull,* a satirical weekly whose contents may be judged from the title, was Jeremiah O'Leary's organ and featured "original caricatures" and "pointed criticism." *The Gaelic-American* enlarged its format and increased its advertising. However, when the United States entered the war in 1917, the paper lost ground rapidly because of its extreme views and could be kept alive only by donations from friends.

A moving-picture theater in New York devoted 5,000 feet of film to "Ireland a Nation"; a two-act propaganda play, *John Bull on Trial,* was presented in 1915 in the Yorkville Casino; and *The Gaelic-American* sold Irish flags and pictures of Irish martyrs. In Philadelphia, two priests wrote a play entitled *Ireland's Easter,* which dealt with the Easter Rebellion of 1916. A similar play by Father P. A. Sharkey was presented in Brooklyn. Lecturers arrived from Ireland to discourse on Irish history and poetry and were welcomed by Irish audiences from New York to Butte, Montana. There also was a revival of interest in Irish music. The Bobbs-Merrill Company prepared a book on the Irish orators who had figured in Ireland's fight for freedom. Claude G. Bowers was its editor, Cardinal Gibbons wrote a foreword, and the volume was enthusiastically endorsed by *The Irish News,* the New York *Catholic News,* Mayor Curley of Boston, Viereck, Senator Thomas J. Walsh of Montana, and Champ Clark of Missouri.[17]

The Easter Rebellion of 1916 produced a new group of martyrs and galvanized the American Irish into action. Sir Roger Casement—Ulsterman, Protestant, poet, religious mystic, and former British consul in Africa—was the leader of this new Irish rising. A sincere champion of the underprivileged, and respected for his exposure of conditions in the Belgian Congo, Casement belatedly had turned his attention to the Irish cause. In 1913, he joined the Gaelic League and Wolfe Tone became his idol. Casement was in New York during the summer of 1914 raising money for the Irish Volunteers, who were to resist the Ulster Volunteers who opposed the inclusion of the Northern counties in home rule for Ireland. While here, Casement conferred with Bourke Cochran, Devoy, and other Irish leaders, wrote an anti-British propaganda article for *The Gaelic-American,* and talked with the German ambassador in New York.

Confident that the Central Powers would win, the Clan-na-Gael paid Casement's expenses for a trip to Germany, where he made a treaty between himself and Germany and apparently discussed plans for an

Irish uprising during Easter week of 1916. Devoy always contended that Sir Roger went to Ireland to stop a hopeless insurrection and to avert bloodshed. Whatever the details of his mysterious mission may have been, he was immediately arrested by the British when he came ashore in Ireland. Some Irish-Americans believed that the American government had forwarded the information which led to the failure of his plans. The time schedule for the insurrection went wrong; when a British cruiser appeared, the Germans sank the supply ship which was to furnish the rebels with arms; there was a week of bloody fighting in Dublin, but order was soon restored.

Irish-Americans disagreed in their appraisal of the incident and on the question whether Casement had accepted German gold. It is certain that the date of the rising had been sent to New York in code, that Devoy and the Clan-na-Gael were involved, that Devoy was a liaison man with Von Papen of the German embassy, and that the Clan had sent substantial sums to Dublin just before Easter week.[18] When Casement and fifteen others were executed without civil trials, Irish-Americans, along with many other Americans, were shocked by Britain's stupidity in creating additional Irish martyrs. Funds were raised to relieve the hundreds still held in jail. Masses for the martyrs were celebrated in the churches, and Boston had a public meeting to honor "Ireland's Holy Dead." In New York, Bourke Cochran, Bainbridge Colby, Victor Herbert, and Father Duffy, chaplain of the Sixty-ninth Regiment, addressed a similar gathering. Other demonstrations against "the Butchery of Irish Patriots" occurred in Chicago and elsewhere. The sedate New York *Times* agreed that the executions were "incredibly stupid"; Senator Borah condemned them on the floor of the Senate; and Cardinals Gibbons, Farley, and O'Connell appealed for the relief of the victims of Ireland's bloody Easter week.

The issues raised by the war were projected into the campaign of 1916 as soon as Woodrow Wilson announced his intention to seek a second term. For many German- and Irish-American voters, the President's policy toward the belligerents was the major issue of the campaign. To the long Irish and German indictment of the Democratic administration, the President himself added the charge of "hyphenism."

As early as May, 1914, President Wilson, at the dedication of a monument to John Barry, the Irish-American naval commander, had made pointed remarks about the patriotism of the foreign-born. He had referred to Barry as an Irishman whose "heart crossed the Atlantic with him," and had spoken sharply about Americans who "need hyphens in

18 See Devoy, *Recollections*, 397–484.

their names, because only part of them has come over." The historian
for the Hibernians, as well as other Irishmen, immediately resented "the
unnecessary injection by President Wilson of references to the 'hyphen.'"[19] As the controversies developed over American neutrality, both
Wilson and Theodore Roosevelt repeated the slurs on "hyphenated
Americans"—obviously meaning the Irish and Germans. Both groups
regarded such statements as defamation of their loyalty. The issue added
unusual bitterness to the campaign of 1916 and produced sharp racial
cleavages within the United States. *The Gaelic-American* denounced
priests and recreant Knights of Columbus for condoning such "Know-
Nothing" attacks on "hyphenated Americans."[20]

The maneuvering for the vote of the foreign-born in 1916 was in-
tricate and on various levels of party activity. Charles Evans Hughes, the
Republican candidate, apparently met in secret with O'Leary, who
demanded promises favorable to the Irish. Hughes admitted having
attended such a meeting, but said he was unaware of whom and what
O'Leary represented. O'Leary, as president of the pro-German American
Truth Society, sent Wilson an insulting telegram accusing him of becoming a dictator and bowing the knee to England. Wilson, who hated
O'Leary, Cohalan, and Devoy, replied that he wanted no support from
the disloyal. *The Gaelic-American* accused the President of branding
legitimate criticism as disloyalty, of betraying Irish patriots to the British, and reviving Know-Nothingism in the United States. Devoy, on
the other hand, considered the Republican candidate as neither pro-
English nor an "anti-Irish bigot," and therefore devoted to impartial
neutrality. "The Irish are with us," said a prominent official of the
German-American Alliance of Chicago, "especially since the revolt in
Dublin and the Sinn Fein Executions."[21]

Wilson was re-elected in an extremely close race. He carried such
strong German centers as Milwaukee and St. Louis, but in several
eastern cities which had large groups of Irish, the Democratic vote fell
off markedly. Hughes polled his greatest vote in some areas where the
"hyphenates" were weakest. It appears that the latter exercised less
influence than expected, and that they probably divided their votes, as
in earlier elections, between the two major parties and rejected the advice
of their most vociferous leaders. It is conceivable that the alleged dangers
of hyphenism caused enough of the electorate to vote for Wilson to

[19] O'Dea, *Ancient Order of Hibernians,* 1483–86.
[20] *The Gaelic-American* (New York), October 23, 1915.
[21] Child, *The German-Americans,* 132.

offset the defection of the "hyphenates." In addition, the Democratic slogan, "He Kept Us Out of War," was undoubtedly very effective west of the Alleghenies.

Early in 1917, Germany resumed unrestricted submarine warfare. That decision, along with several irritating incidents, led the President to break off diplomatic relations and, after a brief period of "armed neutrality," to ask for a declaration of war.

To the last possible moment, German and Irish organizations continued to bombard Congress with petitions against war. The decision, however, went against them. After a relatively short period of emotional readjustment, Irish and Germans closed ranks to support a common cause. The purchase of war bonds and the conscription of their sons gave almost every American family a direct stake in the war. Contrary to earlier, gloomy predictions, the hyphen dissolved in the heat of war. Government officials from the President down testified repeatedly to the loyalty of the foreign-born.

As far as the Irish were concerned, the war did not, however, imply taking England to their bosom. Extremists continued to attack the British and to rejoice in the reports of British defeats. At the same time, they insisted they were completely loyal to the United States and simply were putting "America first." "Irish citizens are loyal," editorialized *The Gaelic-American* on April 7, 1917. Nevertheless, the editor contended that the war was not popular and had been declared by a Congress "browbeaten" by "an autocratic President" who was swayed by British propaganda. Irishmen were advised to insist upon their rights as free Americans to criticize the administration. Irish-American societies warned of entanglements with England and denounced the Espionage Act as a revival of "the infamous alien and sedition laws" of Adams' administration. But *The Brooklyn Tablet* reminded its Irish readers that they were Americans first of all, not "simply Irishmen in America," and that therefore they were obligated not only to fight Germany, but also to give aid to America's allies.

The famous Sixty-ninth New York, under "Wild Bill" Donovan, was one of the first American units to go to the European front. The Irish proved to be the same excellent fighters that they were in earlier wars. The Catholic Church actively supported the war, provided chaplains for the armed forces, and did welfare work among soldiers and sailors. On the first anniversary of America's entry into the war, Irish in many cities called attention to their patriotic record and pledged loyalty to the United States. They also direced attention to the fact that, in their opinion, President Wilson's formula of self-determination applied to Ireland.

A small minority of Irish-Americans got into serious trouble during the war, primarily because they refused to accept England as an ally. O'Leary and others who were prominent in the American Truth Society and the Friends of Irish Freedom continued their anti-British tirades from soapboxes on the street corners of New York. American patriots accused the New York police of shielding the rabble-rousers instead of arresting them for treason. Elihu Root, Theodore Roosevelt, and John Purroy Mitchel, grandson of the rebel of 1848, specifically accused Cohalan, Devoy, and O'Leary of disloyalty. Roosevelt wanted American Sinn Feiners interned. Patriotic societies kept watch over "soap box seditionists." When the activities of the extremists finally were broken up by the police, the action was denounced as a violation of free speech. In the New York mayoralty campaign of 1917, many Irish voters refused to support Mitchel and voted either for the Democratic candidate or for Morris Hillquit, the Socialist.

Although proclaiming its loyalty to the United States, *The Gaelic-American* attacked the British throughout 1917. It referred to England as a foe of democracy and welcomed Russia's collapse in 1917 as a forecast of the defeat of the Allied powers. The editor denounced Irish-American "Anglomaniacs" who, in turn, labeled him a "professional Irishman" who could not speak for the Irish in America. Charges that certain Irish-American papers and societies received money from German sources were frequently made, but vehemently denied.

Issues of *The Gaelic-American, The Irish World,* and *The Freeman's Journal* were barred from the mails or held in the post offices pending investigation of their contents. In September, 1918, *The Gaelic-American* lost its second-class privileges, and the paper had to be sold at newsstands or shipped by express. Devoy attributed his troubles to what his critics considered "abuse of England," but what he believed was only honest criticism. He insisted that, since the United States entered the war, he had never criticized the war measures of the government. O'Leary's *Bull* was suppressed, and its editor, now at odds with the Friends of Irish Freedom and other Irish organizations, was indicted under the Espionage Act. After many months, the case ended in a mistrial in the court of Judge Learned Hand. *The Freeman's Journal* suspended publication on July 4, 1918. Its last editorials dealt with such subjects as "The Freedom of the Press on Trial" and "A Blow at Personal Liberty." In San Francisco, the editor of the *Leader* was convicted for helping German officials get out of the United States. *The Irish Press* of Philadelphia, founded to espouse an Irish republic, was suppressed after several months of publication.[22]

Incidents of this kind affected the reputation of Irish-Americans as a class. They resented reflections upon their patriotism and were particularly irritated when secret-service men attended the meetings of Irish organizations. The Ancient Order of Hibernians, in national convention, called upon the government to stamp out treason and sedition, "which is being openly conducted under the guise of Irish patriotism," but resented the fact that the conduct of a few extremists was putting "the loyalty of the Irish race . . . on trial before a tribunal of American public opinion."

When the war ended in November, 1918, most Americans hoped that the animosities of the war years would be quickly forgotten. For the Irish, here and in their native island, the peace conference had special importance. The question uppermost in their minds was what would President Wilson do for Ireland.

22 See *The Gaelic-American* (New York), January 26, February 2, 23, 1918; September 22, 1917; and Patrick McCartan, *With De Valera in America,* 39.

CHAPTER XXVI

The State of Eire

THE Easter Week Rebellion of 1916, regarded by some as a sublime act of patriotic devotion, and by others as criminal folly, made it impossible to put the Home Rule Act of September, 1914, into effect after the close of hostilities, although Prime Minister Lloyd George in 1916 had announced his readiness to stand by the original legislation. In 1917, Sinn Fein renewed its agitation, both in Ireland and in the United States, for an independent Ireland. It had been a life-long ambition of Eamon de Valera, a former resident of New York, to make Ireland a Gaelic Catholic state of equal status with all other nations in the family of nations. He was a volunteer in the Easter Rebellion, was elected to Parliament as a Sinn Feiner, and, in 1917, became president of the Sinn Fein party. Redmond's death in 1918 weakened the moderates and played into the hands of the extremists. In 1917, Lloyd George's request for an Irish convention to settle the Irish question was repudiated by the Sinn Feiners. Ulster remained the greatest obstacle in the way of any plan for the unification of Ireland.

In the Irish elections of 1918, the Sinn Fein party won seventy-three seats in the British Parliament. The successful candidates refused to go to London, however, and promptly created a parliament of their own known as the Dail Eireann. When the Dail proclaimed an Irish republic in January, 1919, prayers of thanksgiving were offered in many American Catholic churches, but the British countered by arresting the Sinn Fein leaders, including De Valera. Early in 1919, the latter escaped to the United States to begin another campaign for Irish-American political and financial support and to raise six million dollars for the Irish republic.

Ireland, meantime, was the scene of violent guerilla warfare. Irish republicans raided military and police barracks, government post offices and revenue offices, murdered policemen, shot people from ambush, and by intimidation, assassination, and the destruction of property, tried to prove that only Sinn Fein could bring peace to the island. With two groups claiming legal authority in Ireland, England fought back to restore order. "Black and Tans," recruited with the blessing of the British government, fought with Sinn Feiners, and the island was racked from end to end with civil war. Irish leaders publicized the "Black and Tan" outrages to undermine whatever was left of England's reputation among the Irish in America. By 1920, Irish-American papers were full of atrocity tales about the British in Ireland which resembled the gruesome reports from Belgium during the war.

The Sinn Feiners who had been arrested went on a hunger strike, and Terence MacSwiney, mayor of Cork, died from the effects in October, 1920. His widow was brought to the United States to tell the story of her martyred husband to Irish-American audiences from coast to coast. Longshoremen in New York struck against British shippers; Irishmen picketed British consular offices; Irish-American societies appealed for financial support for the latest victims of British oppression; and Oswald Garrison Villard of *The Nation* organized a committee of a hundred prominent Americans of all parties and creeds to investigate the terror in Ireland. "Is bayonet rule in Ireland what our boys died for in the World War?" queried *The Gaelic-American*.[1] American Irish demanded a solution of the Irish question by the peace conference of Versailles on the principle of self-determination proclaimed by President Wilson as one of the criteria for a just and lasting peace.

By this time, most Irish-Americans regarded home rule as a thing of the past and supported complete independence for Ireland. Nevertheless, leaders like Devoy and Cohalan, the latter more discreet than during the early war years, seemed uncertain of what was best for Ireland. In December, 1918, Cardinal O'Connell of Boston spoke in Madison Square Garden. The Garden was decorated with the green, white, and orange tricolor of the Irish republic, and the Catholic prelate addressed a huge crowd of "Irish Republicans" and demanded justice for Ireland as a "test of sincerity" for the Allied powers. Early the next year, Cardinal Gibbons and twenty-eight bishops attended an Irish Race Convention in Philadelphia which endorsed independence and promised substantial financial support. The delegates argued all night over a resolution to get the Irish question before the peace conference, and on this occasion, Judge Cohalan sided with the moderates. The legislature of Massachusetts declared for independence, and in 1921, the Illinois legislature recognized the Irish republic. Cardinal O'Connell, in a number of public addresses, continued to advocate an independent Ireland.

Robert Lansing, President Wilson's secretary of state, had called attention to the dangers inherent in the new principle of self-determina-

---

[1] *The Gaelic-American* (New York), August 14, 1920.

tion. Irishmen here and abroad insisted, however, that it applied specifically to Ireland. They were not disturbed by the argument that England and the United States had been allies in the war, and therefore the American government could not dictate the solution of a purely internal problem of the British Empire. In the congressional elections of 1918, Irish-American leaders supported congressmen who favored the President's plans for the reconstruction of Europe. Most Irish-Americans, and even such extremist organs as *The Gaelic-American,* at this point were willing to leave the settlement of the Irish question to the American President. Senator Phelan of California presented a petition to the President demanding self-determination for Ireland. It carried the signatures of many clergymen. Mass meetings in leading American cities demanded the liberation of Ireland. Congresswoman Jeanette Rankin of Montana introduced a resolution for Irish independence in the lower house of Congress, and in 1919, the question was argued before the Foreign Relations Committee of the United States Senate. Sinn Feiners in Ireland quoted extensively from the speeches of President Wilson.[2]

Woodrow Wilson's antagonism toward certain Irish-American leaders had become a matter of public knowledge. It was traceable largely to what the President regarded as their disloyal attitude during the war. The accused vehemently denied that they had been anything but 100 per cent American. Before leaving for Paris, Wilson refused to meet with a committee to discuss the Irish question as long as Judge Cohalan was a member. The rift between the President and the Cohalan majority in the Friends of Irish Fredoom undoubtedly played a part in the campaign of 1920.

Frank P. Walsh of Kansas City, able attorney and friend of labor; Edward F. Dunne, ex-governor of Illinois, whose grandfather was a Fenian; and Michael J. Ryan, a Philadelphia lawyer and banker, went to the Paris conference as the unofficial spokesmen of the Irish-Americans. The delegation proved embarrassing to President Wilson, and the speeches which they made in Ireland were still more so. Relations between the President and the representatives of the Irish vote in the United States became strained, and Wilson did not hesitate to show his irritation. He may have tried to persuade Lloyd George, the British prime minister, to grant the American committee an audience and to permit De Valera to present the case for Ireland to the peace conference. In any event, Wilson's efforts were completely unsuccessful, and the President

---

[2] For an excellent, detailed discussion for these years, see Nelson M. Blake, "The United States and the Irish Revolution, 1914–1922" (Ph.D. dissertation, Clark University, 1936), especially Chapter IX.

finally had to inform the petitioners that the procedures of the peace conference made it impossible to grant their request. Wilson became increasingly resentful of the political pressure group which he thought was disrupting his peace program, and Lloyd George was more stubborn than ever in his attitude toward the Irish. Many Irish-Americans concluded that Wilson was pro-British and anti-Irish, ready to fight for self-determination for Poland but not for Ireland.[3]

In June, 1919, De Valera arrived in New York as a stowaway and began a tour of the United States to sell bonds for the Irish republic. He was welcomed by governors, mayors, and other public figures. He usually began his addresses with a few sentences in Gaelic, but turned quickly to English so that his Irish sympathizers could follow him. The Clan-na-Gael, *The Irish World, The Gaelic-American,* and many other Irish-American papers and organizations supported the bond drive. The Friends of Irish Freedom advanced a hundred thousand dollars from a "Victory Fund," originally collected to fight British propaganda in the United States, to meet the expenses of the bond drive. Sentimental Irish-Americans bought paper, exchangeable for Gold Bonds of the Irish republic, at 5 per cent interest, when Ireland would be independent. Although a minority denounced the transaction as a swindle, the bonds were endorsed by Governor Alfred E. Smith of New York, Archbishop Hayes, and other clerical and lay Irish leaders. Eventually, about five million dollars were raised in America for the Irish cause.

It is interesting to observe that even in these last stages of the battle for Irish freedom, factional strife among Irish-Americans could not be avoided. Devoy of *The Gaelic-American,* who was enthusiastic for De Valera and Sinn Fein in 1917, began to suspect the Irish leader as a compromiser. *The Irish World* continued to regard him as a dependable statesman. Before the close of 1920, *The Gaelic-American* accused De Valera of ignoring the Friends of Irish Freedom and trying to form his own organization. The next year, a "splinter" organization was campaigning for members, and there were bitter rows between the competing factions in New York, Cleveland, and elsewhere which sometimes ended in police court. The Irish-American press from coast to coast reported the controversy *ad nauseam. The Irish World, The Irish Press,* and the Newark *Monitor* attacked Devoy as a "wrecker" and "a pest to the Irish cause." *The Gaelic-American* replied that *The Irish World* had "hounded Parnell into the grave and escorted Redmond into the British recruiting camp." [4] De Valera insisted there should be no finan-

---

3 See also Joseph P. Tumulty, *Woodrow Wilson as I Know Him,* Chapter XXXIX.
4 *The Gaelic-American* (New York), July 31, November 6, 1920.

cial "drives" save his own; O'Leary, who supported De Valera, attacked the Clan-na-Gael, to which he once belonged, and described Cohalan as an "altar-whacking Judge" who considered himself the leader of the Irish in America and could brook no rival.

By 1920, the League of Nations was an issue in American politics. The more vocal Irish-American leaders were certain that the League was an instrument to increase the influence of the British Empire in international affairs and another product of the machinations of British propagandists in the United States. To Judge Cohalan, isolation meant independence, and he and others went to Washington to oppose both the League and the World Court. Senators William E. Borah and James M. Reed were favorites of the Irish because they favored "America first," and they were frequently invited to address Irish audiences. Cohalan described Article X of the League Covenant as "a League to Preserve the British Empire."

The Friends of Irish Freedom spent thousands of dollars to prevent ratification of the Covenant of the League of Nations. Costly advertisements in leading American papers prove that Irish propaganda against the League was well financed. Devoy opposed all postwar international agreements, including treaties for disarmament, because he believed they were to England's advantage. "Stand up for America" remained the battle cry of *The Gaelic-American*.[5] The National Council of the Friends of Irish Freedom demanded that England withdraw from North America, that Canada become independent, and that the British West Indies be ceded to the United States in payment of the British war debt.[6] In the spring of 1920, Irish women picketed the British embassy in Washington. They were arrested by a policeman named Robert Emmet Doyle and defended by Frank P. Walsh.

The campaign of 1920, by Woodrow Wilson's own choice, was a solemn referendum on the peace settlement, including the League of Nations. Cohalan, sometimes called "the peerless leader of 20,000,000 of the Irish Race in America," went to the Republican convention in Chicago to oppose the League and to get the party to endorse independence for Ireland. His personal choice for president was Senator Hiram Johnson of California. The Irish staged an impressive parade in Chicago, with bands, banners, and fires, and listened to speeches in the Auditorium Theatre by De Valera, Walsh, and Robert Mors Lovett, a Chicago University professor whose life has been devoted to championing the causes of minorities. Despite the huge demonstration, the Republican

5 *Ibid.,* July 3, 10, August 20, 1920.
6 *Ibid.,* March 5, 1921.

platform remained silent about Ireland. De Valera blamed Cohalan, and Cohalan blamed De Valera for the defeat. Each maintained separate headquarters in Chicago. The Friends of Irish Freedom urged De Valera to return to Ireland, but he refused to go, and in November, 1920, launched his own American Association for the Recognition of the Irish Republic. His organization made heavy inroads on the older societies, and De Valera was promptly accused of misappropriating money from bond sales to finance his own propaganda.

The Gaelic-American, the San Francisco Leader, and other Irish papers urged the election of isolationist and anti-League senators in 1920. To Devoy, Wilsonism was "more dangerous to Irish independence than even Lloyd Georgeism." The Gaelic-American opposed Al Smith for governor of New York because he favored a League of Nations.[7] The Irish World urged its readers to vote for either the Socialist or the Farmer-Labor candidate, but The Gaelic-American objected to wasting votes on third parties and advised voting for Warren G. Harding to save the United States from European entanglements.

Governor James M. Cox of Ohio, the Democratic candidate, tried to hold the Irish vote. Irish leaders readily admitted that he was greatly superior in ability to his Republican opponent, but refused to support him because of his identification with Woodrow Wilson and the League of Nations. When Bourke Cochran spoke for Cox in Tammany Hall, the popular Irish orator was badly heckled. The defeat of Cox was overwhelming. Other factors contributed to the result, but the Irish vote was important in large cities like New York, Boston, and Chicago. Harding carried New York City by over 434,000 votes, but Al Smith carried the city as the Democratic candidate for governor. The vote for Harding in Irish districts was astonishingly large.[8] The Gaelic-American claimed full credit for the outcome for the Irish. Governor Cox himself believed that he was opposed by "a militantly anti-Wilson Catholic oligarchy" and that "the professional Irish," enraged because Wilson had not included the independence of Ireland in the peace treaty, "mustered enough to be effective." [9]

In 1920, the British government offered the Irish a fourth edition of home rule, proposing two Parliaments and two executive councils—one for Northern Ireland and the other for the rest of the country. Irish nationalists rejected "partition"; the Sinn Feiners demanded a republic; and civil war continued in Ireland, with murders and outrages of every

7 Ibid., October 23, 30, 1920.
8 Ibid., November 13, 1920.
9 James M. Cox, Journey Through My Years, 273–74.

kind. On December 6, 1921, a "treaty" for Ireland was signed which created the Irish Free State, giving it dominion status on the Canadian model. Ulster elected to remain out of the new Free State. De Valera, whose representatives had been a party to the treaty, resigned his seat, and his republican army continued the guerilla warfare. In the United States, even Devoy and *The Gaelic-American* became disgusted with the turn of events, and blamed De Valera for continuing a "civil war over a quibble." [10] In 1932, after nearly a decade of government by the more moderate Irish party, De Valera achieved the presidency of the executive council. The next year, he abolished judicial appeals to the British Privy Council and the oath to the Crown, which he regarded as the final steps in establishing the complete independence of Ireland. The centuries-old struggle was ended. Ireland still was disunited, and an uneasy peace between Ulster and Eire was established after considerable difficulty. The boundaries were defined, and a customs barrier between the two areas established.

The battle with England is over. De Valera has proceeded with his plans to make Ireland a Gaelic Catholic nation. Her internal affairs and her economic relations with Great Britain remain serious problems. Not all the fruits of independence have been sweet. The cost of government has risen steadily; population remains stationary; and emigration still goes on. In times of unemployment, Irishmen still turn to England for jobs; and the movement to make Gaelic the national tongue has met with little success among the masses. As Nicolas Mansergh has put it, "In 1921, the romance of Irish independence was over, its history had begun." [11] "The heroic age was over" and "prose had succeeded to poetry."

The Irish question in America has faded into the background, and even "professional Irishmen" find it difficult to arouse the old Anglophobia among Irish-Americans. England no longer can be charged with deliberate oppression, for the destinies of the Emerald Isle now are in Irish hands. The Irish in America and the Irish in Ireland have begun to grow apart; yet Ireland could learn much from the United States about the workings of democracy.[12] The only evidence of a survival of Anglophobia in the United States is an occasional attack by Irish societies, aided by Daughters and Sons of the American Revolution, the American Legion, the German Steuben Society, and other patriotic organizations, upon American history textbooks which they believe "de-

[10] *The Gaelic-American* (New York), April 22, June 24, 1922.

[11] Nicholas Mansergh, *Ireland in the Age of Reform and Revolution,* 229.

[12] See Francis Hackett, "Love of Ireland," *Journal of the American Irish Historical Society,* XXIX (1930–31), 117–20.

nationalize" red-blooded Americanism in the interest of British propaganda. In 1922, the Knights of Columbus offered prizes for original research in American history, "to interpret and perpetuate the American impulse, the impulse of the patriots who founded and . . . preserved the Republic." What was wanted was "propaganda-proof" history, "stripped of all manner of European and Asiatic coloring." [13]

Americans no longer think of the Irish when they speak of the Americanization of the foreign-born. The Irish quickly developed a real sense of belonging to the United States. Their constant preoccupation with the causes of their native land may have been partly responsible for the fact that they developed no distinct Irish culture in the United States or any consistent program of "Irishism." Even when they wanted to fight England, they insisted that it was for the best interests of the United States.

The Irishman of a century ago has practically ceased to exist. "Paddy" long ago turned over his pick and shovel to French Canadians, Italians, Serbs, and Poles. He moved up in the economic and social scale to become a factory worker, tradesman, clerk, bookkeeper, salesman, journalist, lawyer, priest, business man, and employer. Bridget left the kitchen to become a factory girl, saleslady, secretary, schoolteacher, or business woman. Neither her dress nor her manner any longer identifies her as Irish. The Murphys are becoming Murfies; the O'Briens, Bryants; and the Delaneys, Delanos. Bridget changes her name to Belle; Mary and Mollie to Marie and Mae. The beautiful Irish Kathleen has become Kathryn. Irish reels and jigs have been forced to yield to American jazz.

Like every other immigration, Irish immigration has had both its brighter and darker sides. At times the contrast has been sharp indeed. A century ago, there were many Americans who believed that Irish clannishness endangered the normal Americanization process. Fifty years later, the same critics commented ruefully that whereas their offspring were using the libraries primarily to read novels, the sons and daughters of Irish stock were reading history, biography, and law. Like other immigrants, the Irish have been forced to yield to the fusion processes of the American melting pot, and there is little danger that the amalgam will be affected again by events in England or the Emerald Isle.

There are American Irish who have never escaped from the slums and whose mode of life is little different from that of their immigrant forefathers. The majority, however, have attained middle-class respectability. In the main, Orestes A. Brownson's prophecy of a century ago has come

[13] See Bessie L. Pierce, *Public Opinion and the Teaching of History in the United States*, 225–39; also *The Irish World* (New York), October 1, 1892; March 26, 1898; January 13, 1900; *The Gaelic-American* (New York), September 3, 10, 1921.

true: "Out of these narrow lanes, blind courts, dirty streets, damp cellars, and suffocating garrets, will come forth some of the noblest sons of our country, whom she will delight to own and honor." [14]

[14] *The Pilot* (Boston), July 1, 1854.

List of Works Cited in the Text

GENERAL AND SPECIAL WORKS

Abbott, Edith. *Historical Aspects of the Immigration Problem.* Chicago, 1926.

Adams, W. F. *Ireland and Irish Emigration to the New World from 1815 to the Famine.* New Haven, 1932.

Ahearn, Robert G. *Thomas Francis Meagher, An Irish Revolutionary in America.* Boulder, Colorado, 1949.

Ander, O. F. *T. N. Hasselquist.* Rock Island, Illinois, 1931.

Asbury, Herbert. *The Gangs of New York.* New York, 1929.

Bannan, Teresa. *Pioneer Irish of Onondaga.* New York, 1911.

Barnes, David M. *The Draft Riots in New York, July, 1863; the Metropolitan Police: Their Services during Riot Week, Their Honorable Record.* New York, 1863.

Barry, Colman J. *The Catholic Church and German Americans.* Milwaukee, 1953.

Barton, George. *Angels of the Battlefield.* Philadelphia, 1898.

Baumgartner, Appolinaris W. *Catholic Journalism.* New York, 1931.

Beaman, Fred J. *Pearls from Past Programs.* Boston, 1931.

Benton, Elbert Jay. *Cultural Story of an American City* (Cleveland). Cleveland, 1946.

Billington, Ray A. *The Protestant Crusade, 1800–1860.* New York, 1938.

Bimba, Anthony. *The Molly Maguires.* New York, 1932.

Bland, Sister Joan. *Hibernian Crusade, the Story of the Catholic Total Abstinence Union of America.* Washington, 1951.

Blied, Benjamin J. *Catholics and the Civil War.* Milwaukee, 1945.

Branch, E. Douglas. *Sentimental Years.* New York, 1934.

Brann, Henry A. *John Hughes.* New York, 1892.

Browne, Henry J. *The Catholic Church and the Knights of Labor.* Washington, 1949.

Brunner, Edmund DeS. *Immigrant Farmers and Their Children.* Garden City, 1929.

Buck, James S. *Pioneer History of Milwaukee.* Milwaukee, 1876.

Burns, J. A. *The Growth and Development of the Catholic School System in the United States.* New York, 1912.

Busey, Samuel C. *Immigration: Its Evils and Consequences.* New York, 1856.

Byrne, Stephan. *Irish Emigration to the United States.* New York, 1873.

Campbell, John H. *History of the Friendly Sons of St. Patrick and of the Hibernian Society for the Relief of Emigrants from Ireland.* Philadelphia, 1892.

Carman, Harry J., Henry David, and Paul N. Guthrie (eds.). *The Path I Trod, The Autobiography of Terence V. Powderly.* New York, 1940.

Catholic Builders of the Nation (ed. Constantine E. McGuire). 5 vols. Boston, 1923.

Catholic Encyclopedia. 15 vols. New York, 1907.

Cavanagh, Michael. *Memoirs of General T. F. Meagher.* Worcester, Massachusetts, 1892.

Child, Clifton J. *The German-Americans in Politics, 1914–1917.* Madison, 1939.

Christman, Henry. *Tin Horns and Calico.* New York, 1945.

Clark, George F. *History of the Temperance Reform in Massachusetts, 1813–1883.* Boston, 1888.

Cole, Arthur C. *The Era of the Civil War, 1848–70.* Chicago, 1922.

Cole, Arthur H. *The American Wool Manufacture.* 2 vols. Cambridge, 1926.

Coleman, Charles H. *The Election of 1868.* New York, 1933.

Coleman, J. Walter. *The Molly Maguire Riots.* Richmond, 1936.

Commons, John R., *et al. History of Labour in the United States.* 4 vols. New York, 1918.

Conyngham, D. P. *The Irish Brigade and Its Campaigns.* Boston, 1869.

Costello, Augustine E. *Our Firemen: A History of the New York Fire Departments.* New York, 1887.

——. *Our Police Protectors, History of the New York Police.* New York, 1884.

Coulter, E. Merton. *The Confederate States of America, 1861–1865.* Baton Rouge, 1950.

Cox, James M. *Journey Through My Years.* New York, 1946.

Crimmins, John D. *Irish-American Historical Miscellany.* New York, 1905.

Cullen, James B. *The Story of the Irish in Boston.* Boston, 1890.

Cummings, Parker. *Dictionary of Sports.* New York, 1949.

Curti, Merle. *The Growth of American Thought.* New York, 1943.

Daniel O'Connell and the Committee of the Irish Repeal Association of Cincinnati. Cincinnati, 1863.

D'Arcy, William D. *The Fenian Movement in the United States, 1858–1886.* Washington, 1947.

Darling, Arthur B. *Political Changes in Massachusetts, 1824–1848.* New Haven, 1925.

Davenport, John I. *The Election Frauds of New York City and Their Prevention.* New York, 1881.

Davie, Maurice R. *World Immigration.* New York, 1936.

Davis, Philip (ed.). *Immigration and Americanization.* New York, 1920.

Devoy, John. *Recollections of an Irish Rebel.* New York, 1929.

Dictionary of American Biography (ed. Allen Johnson and Dumas Malone). 20 vols. New York, 1928–44.

Doerflinger, William M. *Shantymen and Shantyboys.* New York, 1951.

Dondore, Dorothy A. *The Prairie and the Making of Middle America: Four Centuries of Description.* Cedar Rapids, 1926.

Dunlap, William. *The Arts of Design in the United States.* Boston, 1918.

Eddy, Mary O. *Ballads and Songs from Ohio.* New York, 1939.

Edgeworth, Richard L., and Maria Edgeworth. *Essay on Irish Bulls.* London, 1803.

Egan, M. F. *Recollections of a Happy Life.* New York, 1926.

Ellis, John Tracy. *The Life of James Cardinal Gibbons.* 2 vols. Milwaukee, 1952.

Ellis, S. M. *William Collins Le Fanu and Others.* London, 1931.

Emmet, Thomas Addis. *Incidents of My Life.* New York, 1911.

――. *Memoir of Thomas Addis and Robert Emmet.* 2 vols. New York, 1915.

Ernst, Robert. *Immigrant Life in New York City, 1825–1863.* New York, 1949.

Fare, George. *The Catholic Church in Detroit, 1701–1888.* Detroit, 1951.

Field, Henry M. *The Irish Confederates and the Rebellion of 1798.* New York, 1855.

Fish, Carl Russell. *The Rise of the Common Man.* New York, 1927.

Fite, E. D. *Social and Industrial Conditions in the North During the Civil War.* New York, 1910.

Fitton, James. *Sketches of the Establishment of the Church in New England.* Boston, 1872.

Flick, Alexander (ed.). *History of the State of New York.* 10 vols. New York, 1933–37.

Forster, Walter O. *Zion on the Mississippi.* St. Louis, 1953.

Freeman, Edward A. *Some Impressions of the United States.* New York, 1883.

Fry, James B. *New York and the Conscription of 1863.* New York, 1885.

Garraghan, Gilbert J. *The Catholic Church in Chicago, 1673–1871.* Chicago, 1921.

Gates, Paul W. *The Illinois Central Railroad and Its Colonization Work.* Cambridge, 1934.

Gibson, Florence E. *The Attitudes of the New York Irish Toward State and National Affairs, 1848–1892.* New York, 1951.

Gilbert, Douglas. *American Vaudeville, Its Life and Times.* New York, 1940.

Goldberg, Isaac. *Tin Pan Alley.* New York, 1930.

Goldman, Eric F. *Rendezvous With Destiny.* New York, 1953.

Goldmark, Josephine. *Pilgrims of '48.* New Haven, 1930.

Gompers, Samuel. *Seventy Years of Life and Labor.* 2 vols. New York, 1925.

Gosnell, Harold F. *Machine Politics: Chicago Model.* Chicago, 1937.

Gray, Wood. *The Hidden Civil War—The Story of the Copperheads.* New York, 1942.

Guilday, Peter. *The Life and Times of John England.* 2 vols. New York, 1927.

Guillet, Edwin C. *The Great Migration.* New York, 1937.

Gunn, Thomas B. *The Physiology of New York Boarding Houses.* New York, 1857.

Hackett, James D. *Bishops of the United States of Irish Birth or Descent.* New York, 1936.

Hale, Edward Everett. *Letters on Irish Emigration.* Boston, 1852.

Handlin, Oscar. *Boston's Immigrants, 1790–1865—a Study in Acculturation.* Cambridge, 1941.

―― (ed.). *This Was America.* Cambridge, 1949.

Hansen, Marcus L. *The Immigrant in American History.* Cambridge, 1940.

――. *The Atlantic Migration, 1607–1860.* Cambridge, 1940.

Harlow, Alvin F. *Old Bowery Days.* New York, 1931.

Hayes, Richard. *Ireland and Irishmen in the French Revolution*. London, 1932.

Hecker, Isaac. *The Church and the Age*. New York, 1887.

Henthorne, Sister Mary Evangela. *The Career of the Right Reverend John Lancaster Spalding, 1879–1892*. Urbana, Illinois, 1932.

Holbrook, Stewart H. *The Story of American Railroads*. New York, 1947.

Howe, Walter Henry. *Irish Wit and Humor*. Philadelphia, 1898.

Howlett, W. J. *Life of Right Reverend Joseph P. Machebeuf*. Pueblo, Colorado, 1908.

Hyland's Mammoth Hibernian Songster. Chicago, 1901.

Hynes, Michael J. *History of the Diocese of Cleveland*. Cleveland, 1953.

Jolly, Ellen Ryan. *Nuns of the Battlefield*. Providence, 1930.

Jordan, Philip D. *Singin' Yankees*. Minneapolis, 1946.

——. *The National Road*. Indianapolis, 1948.

——, and Lillian Kessler. *Songs of Yesterday*. New York, 1941.

Joyce, P. W. *Old Irish Folk Music and Songs*. Dublin, 1909.

Kahoe, Lawrence. *The Complete Works of the Most Reverend John Hughes*. 2 vols. New York, 1864.

Kelly, Sister Mary Gilbert. *Catholic Immigrant Colonization Projects in the United States, 1815–1860*. New York, 1939.

Kenngott, George F. *The Record of a City*. New York, 1912.

Kernan, J. Frank. *Reminiscences of the Old Fire Laddies and Volunteer Fire Departments of New York and Brooklyn*. New York, 1885.

King, Clyde L. *The Fenian Movement* (University of Colorado Studies, XL, No. 3). Boulder, 1909.

Kirkfleet, Cornelius J. *The History of the Parishes of the Diocese of Rockford, Illinois*. Chicago, 1924.

Kloss, R. H. *Milwaukee*. Milwaukee, 1871.

Kofoed, Jack. *Brandy for Heroes*. New York, 1938.

Laurie, Joe, Jr. *From the Honky-Tonks to the Palace*. New York, 1953.

Lee, Brother Basil Leo. *Discontent in New York City, 1861–1865*. Washington, 1943.

Leslie, Shane. *The Irish Issue in Its American Aspect*. New York, 1917.

Lonn, Ella. *Foreigners in the Confederacy*. Chapel Hill, 1940.

——. *Foreigners in the Union Army and Navy*. Baton Rouge, 1951.

Lord, Robert H., John E. Sexton, and Edward T. Harrington. *History of the Archdiocese of Boston, 1604 to 1943*. 3 vols. New York, 1944.

McCartan, Patrick. *With De Valera in America*. New York, 1932.

Macdonald, John A. *Troublous Days in Canada*. Toronto, 1910.

McDonald, Sister M. Justille. *History of the Irish in Wisconsin in the Nineteenth Century*. Washington, 1954.

McGee, Thomas D'Arcy. *A History of Irish Settlers in North America*. Boston, 1852.

McGuire, James K. (ed.). *The Democratic Party in the State of New York*. 3 vols. New York, 1905.

McLaughlin, J. Fairfax. *The Life and Times of John Kelley, Tribune of the People*. New York, 1885.

McMaster, J. B. *History of the People of the United States*. 8 vols. New York, 1914.

McNamara, Robert F. *A Century of Grace, History of St. Mary's Parish, Corning, New York*. Corning, 1948.

McNeill, George E. *The Labor Movement*. Boston, 1887.

Madden, Richard R. *The United Irishmen, Their Lives and Times*. 7 vols. London, 1860.

Magnan, D. M. A. *Histoire de la Race Francaise aux Etats-Unis*. Paris, 1912.

Maguire, John Francis. *The Irish in America*. New York, 1868.

Malone, Sylvester L. *Dr. Edward McGlynn*. New York, 1918.

Mansergh, Nicholas. *Ireland in the Age of Reform and Revolution*. London, 1940.

Marks, Edward B. *They All Sang, from Tony Pastor to Rudy Vallee*. New York, 1934.

Martineau, Harriet. *Society in America*. 3 vols. London, 1930.

Maynard, Theodore. *The Story of American Catholicism*. New York, 1941.

Mearns, David C. *The Lincoln Papers*. 2 vols. New York, 1948.

Meehan, Thomas F. "The Catholic Press," in *Catholic Builders of the Nation* (ed. C. E. McGuire; *q.v.*), IV.

Miller, John C. *Crisis in Freedom, the Alien and Sedition Acts*. Boston, 1951.

———. *Triumph of Freedom, 1775–1783*. Boston, 1948.

Mitchell, Stewart. *Horatio Seymour*. Cambridge, 1938.

Mooney, Thomas. *Nine Years in America*. Dublin, 1850.

Morris, P. H. (ed.). *A Memoir of the Very Reverend Theobald Mathew*. New York, 1841.

Morse, Edward Lind (ed.). *Samuel F. B. Morse; His Letters and Journals*. 2 vols. Boston, 1914.

Moynihan, James H. *The Life of Archbishop John Ireland*. New York, 1953.

Muzzey, David S. *James G. Blaine*. New York, 1934.

Myers, Gustavus. *History of Bigotry in the United States*. New York, 1943.

———. *The History of Tammany Hall*. New York, 1901.

Nevins, Allan. *Abram S. Hewitt*. New York, 1935.

———, and Milton H. Thomas (eds.). *The Diary of George Templeton Strong*. 4 vols. New York, 1952.

Nichols, Thomas L. *Forty Years of American Life*. 2 vols. London, 1864.

Nolan, Hugh J. *The Most Reverend Francis Patrick Kenrick, Third Bishop of Philadelphia, 1830–1851*. Philadelphia, 1948.

Oberholtzer, Ellis P. *A History of the United States Since the Civil War*. 5 vols. New York, 1937.

Oberste, William H. *Texas Irish Empresarios and Their Colonies*. Austin, 1953.

O'Connell, William Cardinal. *Recollections of Seventy Years*. Boston, 1934.

O'Dea, John. *History of the Ancient Order of Hibernians and Ladies' Auxiliary*. 3 vols. Philadelphia, 1923.

Odell, George C. D. *Annals of the New York Stage*. 14 vols. New York, 1927–45.

O'Donoghue, D. J. *The Geographical Distribution of Irish Ability*. London, 1906.

O'Donovan, Jeremiah. *A Brief Account of the Author's Interview with his Countrymen*. Pittsburgh, 1864.

O'Gorman, Thomas. *A History of the Roman Catholic Church in the United States*. New York, 1895.

O'Hegarty, P. S. *A History of Ireland Under the Union, 1801 to 1922*. London, 1952.

O'Leary, John. *Recollections of Fenians and Fenianism*. 2 vols. London, 1896.

O'Neal, Charles. *The Three Wishes of Jamie McRuinn*. New York, 1949.

Ornitz, Samuel. *Bride of the Sabbath*. New York, 1951.

Overdyke, W. D. *The Know-Nothing Party in the South*. Baton Rouge, 1950.

Paré, George. *The Catholic Church in Detroit*. Detroit, 1951.

Park, Robert E. *The Immigrant Press and Its Control*. New York, 1922.

Peel, Roy V. *The Political Clubs of New York City*. New York, 1935.

Peterson, H. C. *Propaganda for War*. Norman, 1939.

Phelan, Josephine. *The Ardent Exile, the Life and Times of D'Arcy McGee*. Toronto, 1951.

Phisterer, Frederick. *New York in the War of the Rebellion, 1861 to 1865*. 6 vols. Albany, 1912.

Pierce, Bessie L. *A History of Chicago*. New York, 1940.

———. *Public Opinion and the Teaching of History in the United States*. New York, 1926.

———. "The Fabric of Chicago's Early Society," in *Essays in Honor of William E. Dodd*. Chicago, 1935.

Pleasants, Samuel A. *Fernando Wood of New York*. New York, 1948.

Pomfret, John E. *The Struggle for Land in Ireland, 1800–1923*. Princeton, 1930.

Powderly, Terence V. *Thirty Years of Labor*. Columbus, 1890.

Proceedings of the Centennial Commemoration of the Martyrdom of Robert Emmet by the Irish Nationalists of Ohio. Columbus, 1903.

Purcell, Richard J. "Immigration from the Canal Era to the Civil War," in Alexander Flick (ed.), *History of the State of New York* (*q.v.*), VII.

Quigley, Hugh. *The Irish Race in California*. San Francisco, 1878.

Randolph, Vance. *Ozark Folksongs*. 3 vols. Columbia, 1946.

Report of the Anthracite Coal Strike of May–October 1902. Washington, 1903.

Rice, Madelein Hooke, *American Catholic Opinion in the Slavery Controversy*. New York, 1944.

Riis, Jacob A. *The Battle with the Slum*. New York, 1912.

Roberts, Edward F. *Ireland in America*. New York, 1931.

Roemer, Theodore. *The Catholic Church in the United States*. St. Louis, 1950.

Rose, William G. *Cleveland, the Making of a City*. Cleveland, 1950.

Rossa, O'Donovan. *Rossa's Recollections, 1838 to 1898*. New York, 1898.

Sandburg, Carl. *The American Song Bag*. New York, 1927.

Sanderlin, Walter S. *The Great National Project, a History of the Chesapeake and Ohio Canal* (Johns Hopkins Studies in History and Political Science, LXIV, No. 1). Baltimore, 1946.

Sanderson, Charles R. (ed.). *The Arthur Papers*. 2 vols. Toronto, 1947.

Savage, John. *'98 and '48, the Modern Revolutionary History and Literature of Ireland*. New York, 1856.

Scanlan, Michael J. "Catholic Charitable and Social Work in the United States," in *Catholic Builders of the Nation* (ed. C. E. McGuire; *q.v.*), II.

Schafer, Joseph. *Social History of American Agriculture*. New York, 1936.

Schlesinger, Arthur M. *Political and Social Growth of the American People, 1865–1940.* New York, 1941.
———. *The Rise of the City, 1878–1898.* New York, 1933.
Schlesinger, Arthur M., Jr. *Orestes A. Brownson.* Boston, 1939.
Schmeckebier, Lawrence F. *History of the Know-Nothing Party in Maryland* (Johns Hopkins Studies in History and Political Science, XVII). Baltimore, 1899.
Scisco, Louis D. *Political Nativism in New York State* (Columbia University Studies, XIII, No. 2). New York, 1901.
Shaughnessy, Gerald. *Has the Immigrant Kept Faith?* New York, 1925.
Shea, J. G. *History of the Catholic Church in the United States.* 4 vols. New York, 1892.
Shryock, Richard H. *Georgia and the Union in 1850.* Durham, 1926.
Skelton, Isabel. *The Life of Thomas D'Arcy McGee.* Gardenvale, N. Y., 1925.
Smith, Samuel B. *The Flight of Popery from Rome to the West.* New York, 1836.
Smith, Sherman M. *The Relations of the State to Religious Education.* Syracuse, 1926.
Spalding, J. L. *The Religious Mission of the Irish People and Catholic Colonization.* New York, 1880.
Steiner, Edward A. *From Alien to Citizen.* New York, 1914.
———. *On the Trail of the Immigrant.* New York, 1906.
Still, Bayrd. *Milwaukee, the History of a City.* Madison, 1948.
Stoddard, Lothrop. *Master of Manhattan, The Life of Richard Croker.* New York, 1931.
Strickland, Walter G. *A Dictionary of Irish Artists.* Dublin, 1913.
Sullivan, Mark. *Our Times.* 6 vols. New York, 1930.
Sweeney, Helen M. *The Golden Milestone, 1846–1896.* New York, 1896.
The Song Book for the Million. Philadelphia, 184?
The Universal Songster, or Museum of Mirth. 3 vols. London, 1826.
Trollope, Frances. *Domestic Manners of the Americans* (ed. Donald Smalley). New York, 1949.
Tryon, Warren S. *A Mirror for Americans.* 3 vols. Chicago, 1952.
Tumulty, Joseph P. *Woodrow Wilson as I Know Him.* New York, 1921.
Walsh, Louis J. *John Mitchel.* London, 1934.
Ward, George W. *The Early Development of the Chesapeake and Ohio Canal Project* (Johns Hopkins Studies in History and Political Science, XVII, Nos. 9–11). Baltimore, 1899.
Ware, Edith E. *Political Opinion in Massachusetts During Civil War and Reconstruction.* New York, 1916.
Ware, Norman. *The Industrial Worker, 1840–1860.* Boston, 1924.
Warfel, Henry R., Ralph H. Gabriel, and Stanley T. Williams (eds.). *The American Mind.* New York, 1937.
Wehman's Irish Song Book. New York, 1887.
Werner, M. R. *Tammany Hall.* New York, 1928.
Wertenbaker, T. J. *Father Knickerbocker Rebels.* New York, 1948.
Whitridge, Arnold. *Men in Crisis.* New York, 1949.
Wittke, Carl. *Against the Current, the Life of Karl Heinzen.* Chicago, 1945.
———. *German-Americans and the World War.* Columbus, 1936.

———. *Refugees of Revolution, the German Forty-eighters in America*. Philadelphia, 1952.
———. *We Who Built America, the Saga of the Immigrant*. New York, 1939.
Woods, Robert A. (ed.). *Americans in Process, a Settlement Survey North and West Ends, Boston*. Boston, 1902.
——— (ed.). *The City Wilderness, a Settlement Study*. Boston, 1898.
Zwierlein, Frederick J. *The Life and Letters of Bishop McQuaid*. 3 vols. Louvain, 1925.

ARTICLES

Abell, Aaron I. "The Catholic Factor in Urban Welfare: The Early Period, 1850–1880," *The Review of Politics*, XIV (July, 1952), 289–324.
"A Friendly Mission—John Candler's Letters from America, 1853–1854," *Indiana Historical Society Publications*, XVI (1951), No. 1.
Baker, T. S. "America as a Political Utopia of Young Germany," *Americana Germanica*, I (1897), 62–102.
Bean, William G. "Puritan Versus Celt, 1850–1860," *The New England Quarterly*, VII (1934), 70–89.
Bennett, William H. "Some Pre-Civil War Irish Militiamen of Brooklyn, New York," *Journal of the American Irish Historical Society*, XXI (1922), 172–80.
Billington, Ray A. "Maria Monk and Her Influence," *The Catholic Historical Review*, XXII (1936–37), 283–93.
Bocock, John P. "The Irish Conquest of Our Cities," *Forum*, XVII (1894), 186–95.
Boyle, Watson. "John Boyle, United Irishman, and His Descendants," *Journal of the American Irish Historical Society*, XVIII (1919), 224–32.
Browne, Henry J. "Archbishop Hughes and Western Colonization," *The Catholic Historical Review*, XXXVI (1950), 257–85.
——— (ed.). "A Memoir of Archbishop Hughes, 1838–1858," United States Catholic Historical Society *Historical Records and Studies*, XXXIX–XL (1952), 129–90.
———. "Terence V. Powderly and Church Labor Difficulties of the Early 1880's," *The Catholic Historical Review*, XXXII (1946), 1–27.
Carman, Harry J., and Reinhard H. Luthin. "Some Aspects of the Know-Nothing Movement Reconsidered," *The South Atlantic Quarterly*, XXXIX (April, 1940), 213–34.
Colton, Kenneth E. "Parnell's Mission to Iowa," *Annals of Iowa*, XXII (1940), 312–27.
Corrigan, Michael A. "Register of the Clergy Laboring in the Archdiocese of New York from Early Missionary Times to 1855," United States Catholic Historical Society *Historical Records and Studies*, II (1900), Part I, 36–81; Part II, 227–67.
Corrigon, O. B. "Chronology of the Catholic Hierarchy of the United States," *The Catholic Historical Review*, I (1916), 367–89; II (1917), 131–45, 283–301.
Cosgrove, John I. "The Hibernian Society of Charleston, South Carolina," *Journal of the American Irish Historical Society*, XXV (1926), 150–58.
Cross, Whitney R. "W J McGee and the Idea of Conservation," *The Historian*, XV (1952–53), 148–62.

Desmond, H. J. "A Century of Irish Immigration," *The American Catholic Quarterly Review*, XXV (1900), 518-30.

———. "Early Irish Settlers in Milwaukee," *The Wisconsin Magazine of History*, XIII (1929-30), 365-75; also in *Journal of the American Irish Historical Society*, XXIX (1930-31), 103-11.

Dolin, Mary C. "American Irish Women 'Firsts,'" *Journal of the American Irish Historical Society*, XXIV (1925), 215-21.

Donovan, Herbert D. A. "William C. Kinsella," *Journal of the American Irish Historical Society*, XXI (1922), 146-53.

———. "Cornelius Mahoney," *Journal of the American Irish Historical Society*, XXI (1922), 154-56.

Ellis, John Tracy. "Cardinal Gibbons and New York," United States Catholic Historical Society *Historical Records and Studies*, XXXIX-XL (1952), 5-32.

———. "Peter Guilday," *The Catholic Historical Review*, XXXIII (1947), 257-68.

Ernst, Robert. "The One and Only Mike Walsh," *The New York Historical Society Quarterly*, XXXVI (January, 1952), 43-65.

Foik, Paul J. "Pioneer Efforts in Catholic Journalism in the United States, 1809-1840," *The Catholic Historical Review*, I (1916), 258-70.

Ford, Patrick. "The Irish Vote in the Pending Presidential Election," *The North American Review*, CXLVII (1888), 185-90.

Gladden, Washington. "The Anti-Catholic Crusade," *The Century Magazine*, XLVII (1893-94), 789-95.

Green, James J. "American Catholics and the Irish Land League, 1879-1882," *The Catholic Historical Review*, XXXV (1949), 19-42.

Guilday, Peter. "The Church in the United States, 1870-1920," *The Catholic Historical Review*, VI (1921), 533-47.

Gwynn, Denis. "The Rising of 1848," *Studies—An Irish Quarterly Review of Letters, Philosophy and Science*, XXXVII (1948), 7-17.

Hackett, Francis. "Love of Ireland," *Journal of the American Irish Historical Society*, XXIX (1930-31), 117-20.

Hansen, Marcus L. "The Second Colonization of New England," *The New England Quarterly*, II (1929), 539-60.

Higham, John. "The Mind of a Nativist: Henry F. Bowers and the A. P. A.," *American Quarterly*, IV (Spring, 1952), 16-24.

Hogan, Peter E. "Americanism and the Catholic University of America," *The Catholic Historical Review*, XXXIII (1947), 164-77.

Ireland, John. "The Catholic Church and the Saloon," *The North American Review*, October, 1894, 498-505.

"Irish Bulls," *The Illustrated Celtic Monthly*, January, 1880.

Lee, T. Z. "The Hon. Patrick J. McCarthy," *Journal of the American Irish Historical Society*, XX (1921), 97-100.

Linehan, John C. "The Irish Pioneers of Texas," *Journal of the American Irish Historical Society*, II (1899), 124-26.

Lower, A. R. M. "New France in New England," *The New England Quarterly*, II (1929), 278-95.

Lowitt, Richard (ed.). "Frostburg 1882: German Strikers vs. German Strikebreakers," *28th Report of the Society for the History of the Germans in Maryland* (1953).

McAvoy, Thomas T. "The Catholic Minority in the United States, 1789–1821," United States Catholic Historical Society *Historical Records and Studies,* XXXIX–XL (1952), 33–50.

——. "The Formation of the Catholic Minority in the United States, 1820–1860," *The Review of Politics,* X (1948), 13–34.

M'Clure, Reverend William J. "Irish-American Poetry," *The Illustrated Celtic Monthly,* July, 1880, pp. 8–10.

McCormack, Margaret J. "I Met with Napper Tandy," *Journal of the American Irish Historical Society,* XXIX (1930–31), 132–40.

McGuire, Edward J. "A Memoir of John D. Crimmins," *Journal of the American Irish Historical Society,* XVII (1918), 9–25.

McNamara, Robert F. "Trusteeism in the Atlantic States, 1785–1863," *The Catholic Historical Review,* XXX (1944), 135–54.

Meehan, Thomas F. "Archbishop Hughes and the Draft Riots," United States Catholic Historical Society *Historical Records and Studies,* I (1900), 171–90.

——. "Catholic Literary New York, 1800–1840," *The Catholic Historical Review,* IV (1919), 399–414.

——. "New York's First Catholic Newspaper," United States Catholic Historical Society *Historical Records and Studies,* III (1904), 115–30.

——. "Pioneer Times in Brooklyn," United States Catholic Historical Society *Historical Records and Studies,* II (1900), 172–91.

Meng, John J. "Cahenslyism: The First Stage, 1883–1891," *The Catholic Historical Review,* XXXI (January, 1946), 389–413.

——. "Cahenslyism: The Second Chapter," *The Catholic Historical Review,* XXXII (October, 1946), 302–40.

Merrill, Horace S. "Ignatius Donnelly, James J. Hill, and Cleveland Administration Patronage," *The Mississippi Valley Historical Review,* XXXIX (December, 1952), 505–18.

Moody, T. W. "Michael Davitt and the British Labour Movement," *Transactions of the Royal Historical Society,* III (1953; Fifth Series), 53–76.

Morehouse, Frances. "The Irish Migration of the 'Forties,'" *American Historical Review,* XXXIII (1927–28), No. 3, pp. 579–92.

Mullen, Arthur F. "Judge Constantine Joseph Smyth," *Journal of the American Irish Historical Society,* XXIV (1925), 246–48; 274–78.

O'Brien, Michael J. "Early Irish Schoolmasters in New England," *The Catholic Historical Review,* III (1918), 52–71.

O'Donnell, John Hugh. "The Catholic Church in Northern Indiana, 1830–1857," *The Catholic Historical Review,* XXV (1941), 135–45.

O'Grady, John. "Irish Colonization in the United States," *Studies—An Irish Quarterly Review of Letters, Philosophy and Science,* XIX (1930), 387–407.

Oswald, Mrs. Charles F. "Captain Lawrence O'Brien, 1842–1923," *Journal of the American Irish Historical Society,* XXIII (1924), 133–43.

Pope, Alexander. "Chief Justice Timothy D. Hurley," *Journal of the American Irish Historical Society,* XXV (1926), 307–14.

Pratt, Julius W. "John L. Sullivan and Manifest Destiny," *New York History,* XIV (1933), 213–34.

Purcell, Richard J. "Education and Irish Schoolmasters in Maryland's National Period," *The Catholic Educational Review,* XXXII (1934), 198–207.

————. "Education and Irish Teachers in Colonial Maryland," *The Catholic Educational Review*, XXXII (1934), 133–43.

————. "Irish Cultural Contribution to Early New York," *The Catholic Educational Review*, XXXV (1937), 449–60; XXXVI (1938), 28–42.

————. "Rhode Island's Early Schools and Irish Teachers," *The Catholic Educational Review*, XXXII (1934), 402–15.

————. "Schools and Early Irish Teachers in New Hampshire," *The Catholic Educational Review*, XXXII (1934), 608–10.

————. "The Irish Emigrant Society of New York," *Studies—An Irish Quarterly Review of Letters, Philosophy and Science*, XXVII (1938), 583–98.

————. "The New York Commissioners of Immigration and Irish Immigrants," *Studies—An Irish Quarterly Review of Letters, Philosophy and Science*, XXXVII (1948), 29–41.

Quinlan, Richard J. "Growth and Development of Catholic Education in the Archdiocese of Boston," *The Catholic Historical Review*, XXII (1937), 27–41.

Reidy, James. "John Devoy," *Journal of the American Irish Historical Society*, XXVII (1928), 413–25.

Risch, Erna. "Immigrant Aid Societies before 1820," *Pennsylvania Magazine of History and Biography*, LX (1936), 15–33.

Roche, James J. "The 'Scotch-Irish' and 'Anglo-Saxon' Fallacies," *Journal of the American Irish Historical Society*, II (1899), 89–92.

Rooney, James A. "Father Nash, S.J., Army Chaplain (1825–1895)," *The Catholic Historical Review*, II (1917), 188–94.

Smith, Alice E. "The Sweetman Irish Colony," *Minnesota History*, IX (1928), 331–46.

Solomon, Barbara M. "Background of Immigration Restriction," *The New England Quarterly*, XXV (March, 1952), 45–59.

Stegner, Wallace. "Who Persecutes Boston?" *The Atlantic Monthly*, CLXXIV (July, 1944), 45–52.

Stock, Leo Francis. "Catholic Participation in the Diplomacy of the Southern Confederacy," *The Catholic Historical Review*, XVI (1930), 1–18.

Tissot, Reverend Father. "A Year with the Army of the Potomac," United States Catholic Historical Society *Historical Records and Studies*, III (1908), Part I, 42–87.

Tucker, Gilbert. "The Famine Immigration to Canada, 1847," *American Historical Review*, XXXVI (1930–31), No. 3, pp. 533–49.

Walsh, J. C. "Charles O'Conor," *Journal of the American Irish Historical Society*, XXVII (1928), 285–313.

Whipple, James B. "Municipal Government in an Average City, Cleveland, 1876–1900," *The Ohio Archaeological and Historical Quarterly*, LXII (1953), 1–24.

Whyte, William F. "Race Conflicts in the North End of Boston," *The New England Quarterly*, XII (1939), 623–42.

Wittke, Carl. "The Immigrant Theme on the American Stage," *The Mississippi Valley Historical Review*, XXXIX (1952), 211–32.

Woehkle, Walter V. "Confessions of a Hyphenate," *Century*, XCIII (1916), 930–34.

W.P.A. Writers' Project, "Baseball, the Story of Iowa's Early Innings," *Annals of Iowa*, XXII (1939–41), 625–54.

Zwierlein, Frederick J. "Catholic Beginnings in the Diocese of Rochester," *The Catholic Historical Review,* I (1916), 282–98.

Unpublished Theses and Dissertations

Bartha, Stephen J. "A History of Immigrant Groups in Toledo." Unpublished Master's thesis, Ohio State University, 1945.

Blake, Nelson M. "The United States and the Irish Revolution, 1914–1922." Unpublished Ph.D. dissertation, Clark University, 1936.

Canisius, Sister Mary. "James A. McMaster: Pioneer Catholic Journalist." Unpublished Master's thesis, Catholic University of America, 1935.

Carey, Sister Mary Helen. "The Irish Element in Iowa Up to 1865." Unpublished Master's thesis, Catholic University of America, 1944.

Fitzpatrick, Franklin E. "Irish Immigration into New York from 1865 to 1880." Unpublished Master's thesis, Catholic University of America, 1948.

Hickey, Mathew E. "Irish Catholics in Washington up to 1860." Unpublished Master's thesis, Catholic University of America, 1933.

Kwitchen, Sister Mary Augustine. "James Alphonsus McMaster, a Study in American Thought." Unpublished Master's thesis, Catholic University of America, 1949.

Lawrence, Elwood P. "The Immigrant in American Fiction, 1890–1920." Unpublished Ph.D. dissertation, Western Reserve University, 1943.

Murphy, John C. "Attitudes of American Catholics toward the Immigrant and the Negro." Unpublished Master's thesis, Catholic University of America, 1940.

Paluszak, Sister Mary Cecilia. "The Opinion of the *Catholic Telegraph* on Contemporary Affairs and Politics." Unpublished Master's thesis, Catholic University of America, 1940.

Quirk, Robert D. "The Irish Element in New Hampshire to 1865." Unpublished Master's thesis, Catholic University of America, 1936.

Walsh, Sister Mary E. "The Irish in Rhode Island from 1800 to 1865." Unpublished Master's thesis, Catholic University of America, 1937.

Index